SEXUAL LABOR IN THE ATHENIAN COURTS

SEXUAL LABOR IN THE ATHENIAN COURTS

ALLISON GLAZEBROOK

UNIVERSITY OF TEXAS PRESS
Austin

This book has been supported by an endowment dedicated to classics and the ancient world and funded by the Areté Foundation; the Gladys Krieble Delmas Foundation; the Dougherty Foundation; the James R. Dougherty, Jr. Foundation; the Rachael and Ben Vaughan Foundation; and the National Endowment for the Humanities.

Copyright © 2021 by the University of Texas Press
All rights reserved
Printed in the United States of America
First edition, 2021

Requests for permission to reproduce material from this work should be sent to:
Permissions
University of Texas Press
P.O. Box 7819
Austin, TX 78713–7819
utpress.utexas.edu/rp-form

♾ The paper used in this book meets the minimum requirements of
ANSI/NISO Z39.48–1992 (R1997) (Permanence of Paper).

Library of Congress Cataloging-in-Publication Data

Names: Glazebrook, Allison, author.
Title: Sexual labor in the Athenian courts / Allison Glazebrook.
Description: First edition. | Austin : University of Texas Press, 2021. | Includes
bibliographical references and index.
Identifiers: LCCN 2021003513 (print) | LCCN 2021003514 (ebook)
ISBN 978-1-4773-2440-0 (hardcover)
ISBN 978-1-4773-2441-7 (library ebook)
ISBN 978-1-4773-2442-4 (non-library ebook)
Subjects: LCSH: Prostitution—Greece—Athens—History—To 1500. |
Prostitution—Social aspects—Greece—Athens—History—To 1500. |
Speeches, addresses, etc., Greek—Greece—Athens. | Athens (Greece)—Social
life and customs—History—To 1500. | Greece—Civilization—To 146 B.C. |
Athens (Greece)—Civilization—History—To 1500.
Classification: LCC HQ113.G54 2021 (print) |
LCC HQ113 (ebook) | DDC 306.7409495/12—dc23
LC record available at https://lccn.loc.gov/2021003513
LC ebook record available at https://lccn.loc.gov/2021003514

doi:10.7560/324400

For DCS

CONTENTS

LIST OF FIGURES ix

A NOTE TO THE READER xi

ACKNOWLEDGMENTS xv

INTRODUCTION 1

1. UNDER THE INFLUENCE 21

2. IN THE *OIKOS* 43

3. PART OF THE FAMILY 63

4. SAME-SEX DESIRE 95

5. CITIZEN SEX SLAVES 117

CONCLUSION 151

NOTES 163

BIBLIOGRAPHY 199

GENERAL INDEX 221

INDEX LOCORUM 237

LIST OF FIGURES

FIGURE 1. *Map of the Agora in the fourth century BCE*   12

FIGURE 2.1. *Family Tree I: Euktemon*   45

FIGURE 2.2. *Family Tree II: Kallippe*   46

FIGURE 2.3. *Family Tree III: Alke*   47

FIGURE 2.4. *Map of Peiraieus and Athens in the fourth century BCE*   50

FIGURE 3.1. *Red-figure cup by the Brygos Painter, 490–480 BCE*   70

FIGURE 3.2. *Map of Neaira's travels and client base*   77

FIGURE 5.1. *Spatial Networks for Timarchos, I*   128

FIGURE 5.2. *Spatial Networks for Timarchos, II*   130

FIGURE 5.3. *Map of the Pnyx and vicinity in the fourth century BCE*   133

A NOTE TO THE READER

I have transliterated Greek terms and names on a Hellenizing orthographical principle instead of Latinizing them, except in the case of well-known persons such as Socrates or Thucydides, whose names are more familiar to a wide audience in their Latinized form. There is variation among scholars on how to transliterate certain Greek letters: for the letter chi, I have used *ch* rather than *kh*.

Abbreviations of authors' names and their texts follow the *Oxford Classical Dictionary* (4th edition, edited by Simon Hornblower, Antony Spawforth, and Esther Eidinow [Oxford, England: Oxford University Press, 2012]), with the exception of Latinized titles. In such cases, an English translation is given instead, as in Ar. *Wasps*.

All speeches referred to in the text are identified by the author's name in abbreviated form (as per below) and speech number in the standard corpus, except the speeches of Hypereides, for which there is no universally acknowledged numbering system. I list here the main speeches appearing in the body of the text with their titles:

Aischin. 1   Aischines, *Against Timarchos*

[Dem.] 59   pseudo-Demosthenes, *Against Neaira*

[Dem.] 48   pseudo-Demosthenes, *Against Olympiodoros*

Hyp. *Ath.*   Hypereides, *Against Athenogenes*

Isai. 3   Isaios, *On the Estate of Pyrrhos*

Isai. 6   Isaios, *On the Estate of Philoktemon*

Lys. 3   Lysias, *Against Simon*

Lys. 4   Lysias, *Concerning an Intentional Wounding*

A NOTE TO THE READER

Modern editions of these speeches are listed under the name of the editor and included in the bibliography.

The original Greek text does not accompany my translations, but I include in transliterated form the Greek terms and phrases important to the discussion.

ABBREVIATED TITLES

APF   *Athenian Propertied Families.* See Davies 1971 in the bibliography.

Dilts   *Scholia Demosthenica.* Edited by M. R. Dilts. 2 vols. Leipzig, Germany: B. G. Teubner, 1983, 1986.

IG I²   *Inscriptiones Graecae.* Volume 1, *Inscriptiones Atticae Euclidis anno anteriores.* 2nd edition. Edited by Friedrich Hiller von Gaertringen. Berlin, Germany: Georg Reimer and Walter de Gruyter, 1924.

IG I³   *Inscriptiones Graecae.* Volume 1, *Inscriptiones Atticae Euclidis anno anteriores.* 3rd edition. Edited by David Lewis. Berlin, Germany: Georg Reimer and Walter de Gruyter, 1981.

IG II²   *Inscriptiones Graecae.* Volumes 2 and 3, *Inscriptiones Atticae Euclidis anno posteriores.* 2nd edition. Edited by J. Kirchner. Berlin, Germany: Georg Reimer and Walter de Gruyter, 1913–1940.

Jensen   *Hyperidis orationes sex cum ceterarum fragmentis.* Edited by C. Jensen. Leipzig, Germany: B. G. Teubner, 1917.

K   *Comicorum Atticorum Fragmenta.* Edited by T. Kock. 3 vols. Leipzig, Germany: B. G. Teubner, 1880–1888.

LGPN II   *Lexicon of Greek Personal Names.* Volume 2, *Attica.* Edited by M. J. Osborne and S. G. Byrne. Oxford, England: Clarendon Press, 1994.

LSJ   *A Greek-English Lexicon.* Compiled by H. G. Liddell and R. Scott; revised by H. S. Jones. 9th edition. Oxford, England: Clarendon Press, 1940. [Revised supplement 1996.]

Montanari	*The Brill Dictionary of Ancient Greek.* Edited by F. Montanari; English edition by Madeleine Goh and Chad Schroeder. Leiden, The Netherlands: Brill, 2015.
PA	*Prosopographia Attica.* Compiled by J. Kirchner. Berlin, Germany: Georg Reimer and Walter de Gruyter, 1901–1903. [Reprint: 1966.]
PAA	*Persons of Ancient Athens.* 22 vols. Compiled by J. S. Traill. Toronto, ON: Athenians, 1994–2016.
PCG	*Poetae Comici Graeci.* Edited by R. Kassel and C. Austin. 10 vols. Berlin, Germany: Walter de Gruyter, 1983–.
SM	*Pindari carmina cum fragmentis.* Part 2, *Fragmenta, indices.* Edited by Bruno Snell and Herwig Maehler. 4th edition. Leipzig: B. G. Teubner, 1975.

ACKNOWLEDGMENTS

THIS PROJECT ORIGINALLY began as a social and cultural history of sexual labor in Classical Athens. But as I delved deeper into the topic I realized that in order to do a history of sexual labor I first had to unravel the complex discourse around the sex trade in the Attic orators. Rather than the who, what, where, and how much, I became interested in the intersections between sexual labor and Athenian society more broadly. The project has taken me back to some texts first examined during the writing of my dissertation: Isaios 6 and pseudo-Demosthenes 59. Twenty years on, these texts read quite differently and engage me with new questions. Still, I would be remiss if I did not acknowledge my debt to Susan G. Cole, who guided me through my first readings of these two texts. Her work ethic, curiosity, and inquisitive mind helped shape me into the academic I am today.

While preparing the manuscript I have been able to present material from all chapters except chapter 3 and have depended on audience feedback to keep the project moving forward. Drafts of chapters were presented in the Department of Classics Research Seminar at Brock University; at the annual meetings of the Classical Association of Canada (2015, 2016, 2017, 2018), Society for Classical Studies (2019), Fédération internationale des associations des études classiques (2019), Classical Association of the Middle West and South (2017), International Society for the History of Rhetoric (2017), and the Classical Association of Canada West (2015); as well as at Feminism and Classics (2016) and the annual symposium of the Humanities Research Institute, Brock University (2014). I am particularly grateful to Ben Akrigg and Judy Fletcher for the opportunity to present parts of this project to the Midwestern History and Theory Colloquium (2015, 2018), to Kelly Olson for the invitation to the University of Western Ontario (2016), to Rosalia Hatzilambrou for an invitation to the University of Athens (2018), to Zoe Delibasis of the Embassy of Canada in Greece at Athens for organizing a second talk at the University of Athens (2019), to

ACKNOWLEDGMENTS

Noreen Humble for the opportunity to undertake the Western Tour of the Classical Association of Canada (2019), and to Naomi Campa for the invitation to the University of Texas, Austin (2021). In each case the lively audience helped me fine-tune and push my arguments further. I am especially grateful for feedback and questions from Matthew Christ, Lesley Dean-Jones, Judy Fletcher, Michael Gagarin, Mark Golden, Rosalia Hatzilambrou, Thomas Hubbard, Lisa Hughes, Mark Joyal, Naomi Campa, Konstantinos Kapparis, Hilary Lehman, C. W. Marshall, David Mirhady, Charles Stocking, and Katharine von Stackelberg.

I have been able to reread some of these texts with graduate students and to present some of my ideas to students in research seminars on the Athenian lawcourts and ancient slavery. I am particularly grateful for the stimulating conversations in those classes and want to thank Keegan Bruce, Rick Castle, Vanessa Cimino, Emma Fotino, Aleks Mirosavljevic, and Simone Mollard in particular. I thank the graduate students in the Department of Classics at the University at Buffalo for their invitation to present material from chapters 1 and 4 (2019) and to the Brock University Archaeological Society for the opportunity to present material from chapter 5 at their annual symposium (2018). Thanks are owed to Esther Knegt for her work as a research assistant for chapter 5.

I am also grateful to Dave Sharpe and Jeremy Trevett for reading the manuscript in full, to Victoria Wohl for offering feedback in the early stages of the project on chapters 2 and 5, and to Christina Vester for her comments on material in chapter 1. Thanks are also owed to Joseph Roisman and the anonymous reader, the reviewers for the press. The final text has benefited greatly from their expertise and insights. All remaining errors and weaknesses are invariably my own.

I have been fortunate in the financial support I have received. An insight grant from the Social Sciences and Humanities Research Council of Canada allowed me to travel to present my work as it progressed and to spend precious sabbatical time in Athens at the Blegen Library of the American School of Classical Studies at Athens. It also allowed me to hire a research assistant with the right technical expertise to help with the research for chapter 5 and to commission drawings by Tina Ross. Teaching release paid for by the Humanities Institute at Brock University provided the time in the fall of 2020 to complete my final revisions of the manuscript. Funds from the Vice President Research, Brock University, made it possible to hire an indexer to compile the index. I acknowledge this support with gratitude.

During my sabbatical in 2016 I was able to complete first drafts of chapters 1 and 4 at the Blegen Library, and I am very grateful to the staff at that library for generosity with their time. I am also thankful to the staff at the library at Brock University, who helped me obtain some publications despite the restrictions of COVID-19 so that I could finish my revisions on time.

I am grateful to Jim Burr at the University of Texas Press for his guidance through the process of publication and his patience as the project met with unanticipated delays. I'd also like to express my thanks here to other members of the Press: Robert Kimzey, Demi Marshall, Sarah McGavick, and freelance copy editor Paul Psoinos, all of whom played a part in guiding the project through to publication and release.

A special debt is owed to my partner, Dave Sharpe, for his love, patience, and indulgence during the project. Without his day-to-day support, the manuscript might never have made it to completion. To him I dedicate this book.

INTRODUCTION

ATTIC ORATORY INCLUDES numerous accounts of sexual labor with vivid portraits of individual sex laborers. For these reasons, oratory is an important source for reconstructing the practices, legalities, and complex attitudes surrounding paid sexual labor in Classical Athens.[1] Oratory provides evidence of male and female sex laborers, the private ownership of "sex slaves," Athenian brothels, sex traffickers (the majority of whom appear to have been female), the cost of sex, the use of contracts between sex laborers and clients, manumission practices for those so enslaved, and even clients sharing a sex laborer as either joint owners or through a contract for exclusive use. Yet oratory also presents a picture of sex laborers very different from what appears in other genres, such as New Comedy and philosophy (specifically Xenophon and Plato). The witty, wealthy, free, and independent *hetaira* does not feature in the orators' depictions.[2] Instead, portrayals of sex laborers, like Alke and Neaira, stress their past enslaved status and frequently present them as dangerous transgressors who threaten social stability. A quick comparison between Theodote and Neaira illustrates this point well.

In Xenophon's *Memorabilia*, Socrates and his disciples visit the *oikos* of Theodote, renowned for her physical beauty. Although no specific label is applied to Theodote, she is described as the sort willing to join with whomever can persuade her. The Greek verb employed, *suneinai* (join with), commonly signifies a sexual connection. After admiring her beauty for some time, Socrates takes note of her clothing and her surroundings. She stands out for her expensive attire and comfortable surroundings, as well as her beauty, and this leads Socrates to begin questioning her (*Mem.* 3.11.4):

> And Socrates, seeing that she was expensively and richly adorned, that her mother was also in fine dress and well looked after, that the many female attendants were both attractive and in no way neglected, and that

in addition the house was nicely furnished, said, "Tell me, Theodote, do you own land?"

When she responds in the negative, he continues to interrogate her about her property, her profession, and how she acquires her "friends." Theodote is notably reserved in her responses throughout. When she denies any artifice in making and keeping her friends, Socrates offers her advice on how to increase her success (even hinting at the use of magic). At the end of their conversation, in an interesting reversal, she is eager to become Socrates' client and promises to visit him. Theodote is a likable character in this dialogue for her feigned innocence and her refusal to discuss her profession and its craft in detail even though Socrates hints at trickery and deception. The exchange is entertaining, since it reverses the roles of the sex laborer and client. Xenophon presents an intelligent businesswoman whom men flock to and who engages in suggestive and witty conversation with her clients, but who is careful about whom she associates with. It is not money that buys her but persuasion. What will persuade her, however, is never made crystal clear. Her clients are *philoi*, suggesting a continued reciprocity and thus putting a positive spin on Theodote, her exchanges, and her activities.

In Apollodoros' pseudo-Demosthenic lawcourt speech *Against Neaira*, Neaira too appears richly adorned with expensive clothes and jewelry, but her representation is very different from Theodote's. Owned by a female sex trafficker, she was a child sex laborer in Corinth. Apollodoros expresses shock at the early age at which she began her trade. Given that Athenian girls typically married between the ages of twelve and fourteen, Apollodoros' comment suggests that Neaira was even younger than this. She soon became the property of two wealthy young men who paid the expensive sum of three thousand drachmas for her. Once they tired of her, they allowed her to buy her freedom, but she could do so only with the help of past clients. Despite gaining her freedom, however, she had little independence. She traveled to Athens with Phrynion, who contributed the largest amount toward her freedom, but he treated her so badly that she fled to Megara. There she was unable to sustain her lifestyle and wished to return to Athens but was afraid to do so. She eventually returned to Athens with another Athenian, Stephanos, who agreed to act as her protector. And she needed one. Upon her arrival, Phrynion tried to claim that she was his runaway slave, but Stephanos asserted her freedom. With arbitration, Phrynion had to accept her freed status, but Neaira was required to spend half her time with him (and half with Stephanos). Apollodoros' aim, however, was not to excite sympathy in his audience with this narrative. Although he refers to her as a *hetaira* (sexual companion), the fact that she worked for money is repeated throughout his speech. He also refers to her as a *pornē* (woman for sale; sex slave), a less glamorous term related to *pernanai* (sell as a slave), and describes her as shamelessly dragged through the mud by Phrynion (*aselgōs proupēlakizeto hupo tou Phruniōnos*, [Dem.] 59.35). She plies her trade everywhere and is not choosy in her customers but available to anyone so long as a client has money. She is also arrogant and impious. Apollodoros sums her up in a climactic moment of his speech as follows ([Dem.] 59.107–108):

> Will you allow her who has openly sold herself for sex so shamefully and recklessly in all of Greece, who has insulted the city and committed sacrilege against the gods, to be acquitted? She whom neither parents bequeathed Athenian status to nor the people made a citizen? For where has she herself not worked with her body, or whither has she not gone to earn her daily pay? Has she not traveled the entire Peloponnese, Thessaly, and Magnesia with Simos of Larisa and Eurydamnos son of Medeios, in Chios, and most of Ionia with Sotados of Crete? Was she not hired out by Nikarete, when she was still owned by that woman? What do you think she does, who is under the influence of others and follows him who pays her? Does she not cater to all the desires of those who use her?

Unlike Theodote, Neaira seems to have little choice or control over where her activities take her. She follows clients. They do not come to her. She plies her trade throughout the entire Greek world, performing whatever acts a paying client desires. The fact that Apollodoros delivered his text in a court of law in which Neaira was on trial for being illegally married to Stephanos explains his negative portrayal, but her characterization likely builds on attitudes and anxieties about sex laborers already in play; otherwise it would not be helpful to Apollodoros' arguments.

ATTIC ORATORY

Oratory straddles the line between history and literature, but frequently its historical value is privileged over its literary merits. Social, economic, and legal historians, for example, have traditionally favored these speeches over other genres in their research. More recently, cultural historians interested in Athenian mentalité have also relied on forensic oratory.[3] But there has not been enough attention on the speeches of forensic oratory as texts in their own right.[4] They regularly include detailed narratives with elaborate plots and engaging characters.[5] They entertained their audiences and remain popular today for their vividness and complex scenarios. As researchers we commonly prefer to pillage the speeches for specific tidbits rather than consider their plot devices and character portrayals as we might a dramatic text, for example.[6] By organizing each chapter around a specific speech I can explore its complexity while still drawing out its historical and cultural significance. Since each speech chosen centers on sex laborers and sexual labor, their careful examination reveals the complex relationship between sexual labor and Athenian society. Although sexual labor was an accepted practice and commonly engaged in without penalty or disparagement, like pederasty it was at times a troubling practice. Sex laborers became loci for a diverse set of anxieties concerning social legitimacy that not only threatened such legitimacy but also acted as antitheses that in fact defined legitimacy and in turn proscribed social behaviors.

It is important to bear in mind that the orators were trained speakers well versed in rhetorical techniques despite their assertions otherwise. Claims to character and exploiting emotions of fear, anger, pity, and so on—what Aristotle labels *ēthos* and *pathos*, respectively—as well as the narrative and argument (*logos*) are more persuasive to their audiences than straight facts.[7] But it is because of the emphasis on these artful proofs that we gain familiarity with the tensions underlying the practice of sexual labor and the complex attitudes toward sex laborers in Classical Athens. Although the orators rely on intricate narratives and arguments to persuade their audiences of specific viewpoints, they exploit and test common perceptions. Their speeches still require some factual basis and reliability if they are to be convincing to the majority. The trick is in recognizing what issues they exaggerate and push the boundaries of, as it is at these points that the orators reveal anxieties already in place despite exploiting these tensions further. They present a public discourse for a broad cross section of Athenian society, and as such they are a good source for popular views, social realities, and behavioral codes of conduct:[8] I am interested in how speakers manipulate these attitudes and practices in their discourses around sexual labor to cement and problematize social and civic boundaries. By looking at some key speeches in full I can complicate the history of sex laborers and their labor and move beyond a discussion of *hetairai* and *pornai*.

INTRODUCTION

LOOKING AT SEXUAL LABOR

As Simon Goldhill (2015) has argued, there is no easy way to approach the study of sexual labor in Classical Athens. It intersects with ideas about desire but also gender, sexuality, the body, the household, and citizenship itself. Just as scholars now recognize the diversity of the sexual labor market and the experiences of individuals working within that market, the sources represent a diversity of attitudes toward sexual labor and sex laborers that depends very much on context. Different writers and genres (Old and New Comedy, philosophical and historical texts) emphasize particular attitudes (as noted above), but so do social institutions and social contexts such as symposia, brothels, streets, households, and lawcourts. We encounter multiple constructions of sexual labor and sex laborers. Although we can identify underlying stereotypes to some extent, different writers and contexts manipulate these stereotypes differently. In oratory, we generally encounter a negative view of sex laborers, but how they interact with others in these texts and connect with society differs, and the difference reveals the complexity and diversity not only of sexual labor itself but also the complex attitudes, ambiguities, and anxieties that surrounded sexual labor in Classical Athens. In Old Comedy, for example, sexual labor focuses on the symposium and also the brothel, whereas oratory is more interested in the sex laborer in relation to the family, citizenship, and the city itself. Both problematize the issue of desire through sexual labor. It is the complex cultural constructions of sex laborers and their labor that this study aims to unravel in the chapters that follow.

My previous work has focused on stereotypes of sex laborers in various media, including forensic oratory.[9] I have been interested in the sex laborer as a type and its manipulation in different contexts. My prior research has also examined the place of sexual labor in the urban landscape, outside the symposium, as well as the material reality of women working in the sex trade.[10] This book builds on that work to consider how the sex laborer of Classical Athens was problematized in relation to gender, the body, sexuality, the family, urban space, and the polis while enlarging my scope to include male alongside female sexual labor. My intention is not to provide a social history of sexual labor within these pages. It's not possible given my focus on oratory alone. Two publications offer detailed analyses of the economic, legal, and social aspects of ancient Greek sexual labor: Edward Cohen (2015) focuses on the economics of sexual labor, and Konstantinos Kapparis (2018) offers a comprehensive study of sexual labor in ancient Greece. Both focus on Greek sex laborers of the Classical period and primarily female sexual labor as opposed to male. Kapparis includes some discussion of Archaic Greece and the periods (Hellenistic and Roman) following the Classical. He also provides a helpful overview of all court trials involving sex laborers.

In other important studies, Kate Gilhuly, Leslie Kurke, and James Davidson consider the discursive use of the sex laborer, but largely at the expense of female material reality.[11] These authors suggest the *hetaira*'s representation is significant for male subjectivity and important for ideological negotiations between elite and non-elite in particular within the context of emerging middling and democratic values. Kurke, for example, argues that the *hetaira* is a creation of the Archaic symposium. At elite symposia, the *hetaira* represented aristocratic values grounded in social relations in opposition to the rise of commerce and commercial wealth, represented by the *pornē*. She was a companion and not a commodity. Such an identity, however, was not stable: Kurke argues that elite symposiasts also (and even simultaneously) differentiated themselves from the *hetaira* figure in their midst by reconfiguring her as a *pornē*. Both identities might appear in a single recited poem or as images on a drinking vessel. Such tactics differentiated these elites from their contemporaries and kept their elitism intact.[12] The *hetaira*'s creation responded to the socioeconomic changes sweeping across Archaic Greece. Kurke's work engages with James Davidson's idea that the *hetaira* is modeled on elite ideals of gift exchange, with the *pornē* based on commodity exchange; but whereas Davidson concentrates on economic exchanges, Kurke's work centers on the political significance of such an image. In both cases, however, the focus is on the importance of the *hetaira* figure to male subjectivity. But when we consider the representation of the sex laborer in these trials, in speeches delivered in a court of law, distinctions between the *hetaira* and the *pornē* are not so significant. Instead, the important distinction is of the female sex laborer versus female kin. As such, female identity and even subjectivity emerge as concerns for male citizens as well. The speeches reveal the social constraints surrounding women but also the significance of women to the family and polis, and thus citizenship, as well as the importance of maintaining distinctions between women. At the same time, the portraits of sex laborers mark such associations as troubling. It is such points of tension that the orators exploit and develop for their audiences.

The speeches also provide rich examples of male sex laborers: although scenarios and portraits of male and female sex laborers in Greek oratory differ, they also connect in significant ways. Scholarship on male sexual labor is not as ready and available as it is for female sexual labor. Nick Fisher provides a useful overview of male sexual labor in his commentary *Aeschines: Against Timarchos* (2001), but his comments are scattered throughout and thus not an accessible account for the nonspecialist.[13] Konstantinos Kapparis also discusses male sexual labor, largely from the legal perspective, in his book on prostitution in ancient Greece.[14] Edward Cohen looks at it from the standpoint of economics.[15] Much of the scholarly discussion focuses on the physical acts of male sex laborers, particularly their submission to anal intercourse.[16] According to David Halperin, working as a sex laborer was a liability for a male citizen, since it required being penetrated and, in effect, relinquishing control of his *phallos*: that is, his citizen privilege to penetrate other bodies (male, female, free, enslaved, noncitizen, or foreign).[17] James Davidson, however, has rightly questioned the view that the Athenians were anxious about male penetration and sought to legislate such behaviors in the case of Athenian citizens.[18] In his book on male homosexuality (2007), he argues instead that the concern with male sexual labor was largely a fourth-century phenomenon centered on payment and how such a mercenary practice affected an individual's trustworthiness and integrity, especially in the public sphere in the context of democracy. It was concerned not with sexual acts more generally but with what he terms being "gay for pay" and identifies as the "*charis* crisis."[19] What interests me about the transactions between male sex laborers and their clients is the slippage between pederasty and sexual labor that orators exploit in their speeches.

GENDER, PLACE, AND MOBILITY

I include speeches focusing on male sexual labor and female sexual labor side by side, making it possible to think about how gender affected presentations of sex laborers and attitudes toward sexual labor more generally. Gender has remained an important analytical tool for the study of the ancient world since the early 1990s, after Joan Wallach Scott advocated for gender as a prime category of analysis in all areas of history.[20] In addition to social roles and status, gender also intersects with concerns about the body, including its sexuality and appetites.[21] When we consider sexual labor through the lens of gender, the orators' narratives connect with larger sociocultural concerns and expose Athenian anxieties associated with the body and legitimacy. Along with James Davidson's work on appetites, Joseph Roisman's work on masculinity in the Attic orators has been central to my discussions of sexual labor in relation to ideals of manhood.[22] Both authors highlight a complex view of masculinity as centered around self-control and its display. I also rely on Josine Blok's recent discussion of the importance of descent and participation in ritual to citizenship identity. In her definition men and women were equally considered citizens and heirs to the city of Athens, even though their specific roles were segregated, and this understanding of citizenship is crucial to the orators' incorporation of sex laborers' participation in cult in their narratives.[23] Similarities between the representations of male and female sex laborers are to be expected, but the differences are significant to broader conceptions of masculinity and femininity in Classical Athens and how the ancients constructed these identities. Male and female sex laborers both transgress gender norms, but they do so in very different ways.

I also add a spatial dimension to my consideration of the sex laborer in these speeches. Place as an idea dependent on material, personal, historical, mythical, and communal associations has had a significant impact on the study of ancient literature, history, and archaeology.[24] Paul Millett recognized the importance of a sense of place to Athenian public discourse and showed how thinking about the topographical details in oratory was a useful interpretive lens for understanding the rhetorical effect of the orators on their audiences.[25] The details are not simply for reconstructing events and locating offenses, but they also color the narratives and arguments. More recently, M. P. de Bakker has shown how orators employ place in the production of character.[26] James Davidson has also pointed out the gendered conception of space in the Athenian polis.[27] I have found all three works helpful in thinking about sexual labor and sex laborers in oratory. The orators are specific in where they position sex laborers in their narratives and vivid in their descriptions. They develop complex topographies depending on the audience's knowledge of the city as well as their associations with these spaces. The locations themselves are suggestive of attitudes, but they are also effective means of repositioning sex laborers' relationships with household and polis as troubling. In some cases, the association with place actually alienates the sex laborer, despite paid sexual labor being an accepted practice in Classical Athens—what Tim Cresswell refers to as "anachorism."[28] According to Cresswell, the normative expectations of who belongs where mark certain bodies as transgressive and out of place, producing outsiders. The orators exploit ideas of place just like they exploit ideas about gender and sexuality in their characterizations of sex laborers.

In recent years mobility, the concept that types of movement within and between spaces have social significance and are imbued with ideology, has

INTRODUCTION

begun to influence the field of Classics.[29] It includes all types of motion, from global flows, to transport-aided, to simple bodily movements, and looks at how movements interconnect and relate to space. Like gender, mobility expresses a power dynamic that enables some and restricts others.[30] It depends on immobility for its acquisition of meaning. Ariadne Konstantinou's recent discussion of female mobility in Greek myth offers a dynamic way of thinking about femininity in the ancient world. With the "mobility turn" focused on the present and on individual experience, Konstantinou challenges us to find ways to think about mobility in the ancient world.[31] The mobility of sex laborers is of prime importance as an analytical tool to this study. Orators use a gendered mobility to develop uneasy portraits of female sex laborers and suggest an ideal for Athenian women. Direction of movement is particularly important, regardless of gender. Male sex laborers are disconcerting because their actions move out of public view, whereas Athenian males normally conduct relations in public, at gymnasia and symposia. In the case of sex laborers, spatial mobility also relates to social mobility. The movement of female sex laborers between the brothel and the *oikos* mirrors their ability to transgress status boundaries.

SITTING IN COURT

The speeches examined here were delivered in a court of law.[32] The Athenian courts were significantly different from modern lawcourts, the main difference being that no judges presided over trials. Cases of homicide or wounding with intent, as well as arson and poisoning, were overseen and judged by the Council of the Areopagus. Members of this council also likely oversaw the court at the Palladion for trials of unintentional homicide as well as the killing of metics, foreigners, and enslaved people, and at the Delphinion for trials in which the defendant claimed a justifiable homicide. In all three courts, litigants and witnesses swore special oaths (*diōmosiai*) and were somewhat limited as to what could be presented in their arguments.[33] Citizen juries, numbering anywhere from 201 to 5,001, decided all other cases, from assault to inheritance, in the popular courts (known as *hē Hēliaia* or *ta dikastēria*).[34] As was the case for the Assembly, only male citizens were eligible to participate as jurors, but in this case only citizens thirty years old and older could serve.

By the fourth century BCE jurors in the popular courts were paid three obols, the equivalent of a day's pay for an unskilled laborer working on building projects on the Akropolis (409–407 BCE).[35] Such pay facilitated

9

the participation of a cross section of Athenian citizens as *dikastai* (jurors; judges).[36] Each juror was chosen by lot from a group of 6,000 citizens selected annually. The selection process guaranteed equitable representation, with six hundred potential jurymen chosen from each of the ten tribes, and kept the juries free from manipulation. Before serving, jurors also had to swear an oath to abide by the laws and decrees of the Assembly (*Ekklēsia*) and Council (*Boulē*), to act in accordance with what seemed most just, and to remain impartial (Dem. 24.149–151).[37] All trials were decided in a single day. Punishments included fines, confiscation of property, loss of citizen rights, exile, death, or even a combination, but not internment. Although there was no formal process of appeal, an unsuccessful litigant could charge the opponent's witnesses, who swore to the accuracy of their testimony, with false witnessing to initiate a new trial or could bring forward a new charge against the opponent.

State prosecutions in Classical Athens were rare.[38] Private citizens initiated most trials, even those of interest to the state, such as a *graphē* (public trial).[39] Only the injured party could bring forward a *dikē* (private suit). Any male citizen, referred to as *ho boulomenos* (the one wishing), could launch a *graphē*. In both types of trials litigants were responsible for collecting evidence, determining laws violated, deciding on charges, and garnering witnesses. As the first step, both parties appeared before a magistrate who reviewed the case. The magistrate then posted a public notice of a trial (including a statement of charge, the penalty, a sworn denial, and the date, time, and location) on the railings enclosing the statues of the Eponymous Heroes of Athens (Dem. 21.103, 45.8).[40] The information was for the litigants, and the public notice meant that the general public knew the details of all upcoming trials. Litigants, in addition to collecting their own evidence (including witnesses), were required to represent themselves, but they could arrange to have a close relative or friend speak for them. Trials did include witnesses, but by the early fourth century BCE they were no longer cross-examined, instead simply affirming the facts contained in a statement prepared by the litigant.

The involvement of women and enslaved persons in the legal system was limited. They had no part in juries; nor could they initiate legal proceedings.[41] Instead, the *kurioi* (guardians; heads of households) of citizen women and enslaved household members brought forward their suits and acted as litigants on their behalf (Isai. 3.2–3; Dem. 43.9). Their *kurioi* were also responsible for addressing any charges brought against them (Antiph. 1; Dem. 57.8). Another limitation of the legal system was that neither women nor the enslaved could act as witnesses, but orators might informally incorporate their testimony as part of a narrative (Lys. 32.11–18). They could also include as evidence pretrial oaths sworn by free women (Dem. 39.3; [Dem.] 40.10–11) and statements extracted from enslaved members of society through torture.[42] Despite such restrictions, women might occasionally be present in court. A defendant would sometimes bring along his mother, wife, or children to a trial to evoke jurors' pity and win their support for an acquittal. It was thus indirectly that women and enslaved persons participated in trials. Otherwise, the court was very much a gendered space, just like the Athenian Assembly.

The Athenians considered the nonprofessionalism of the lawcourts one of its strengths, but although such legal experts as judges and lawyers did not exist, an Athenian could hire a logographer to craft his speech for him. In the case of the speeches under investigation here, two were written by the actual speakers (Aischin. 1; [Dem.] 59), and three were produced by professional speechwriters (Lys. 3, 4; Isai. 6). Unfortunately, the outcomes of these cases are unknown. The legal system did not produce a summary of trials. Our only evidence is the published speech of the logographer, and in the majority of cases only one side of the lawsuit survives.[43] Sometimes, however, these speeches refer to outcomes of earlier trials. Demosthenes, for example, tells us that Aischines won his suit against Timarchos (Dem. 19.257, 284–286). Inscriptions also hint at the success of a litigant or the lack of it. It is possible that Chairestratos, the litigant of Isaios 6, lost his inheritance claim based on a later dedicatory inscription by a Chairestratos son of Phanostratos, of the deme of Kephisia (*IG* II² 2825.11). Had he won, he presumably would have been the son of Philoktemon, not still "of Phanostratos."[44]

Homicide and wounding trials of the Areopagus, Palladion, and Delphinion took place in the open air on the slopes of the *Areios Pagos* ("Areopagus": Hill of Ares) or the Akropolis. The popular courts likely had four courts in the fourth century BCE (410–340 BCE).[45] The exact locations of these, aside from the Stoa Poikilē, are uncertain, but they likely corresponded to a series of structures under the Hellenistic Stoa of Attalos (labeled A, B, C, D).[46] The Odeion of Perikles, the Theater of Dionysos, or even the Pnyx could have served for very large juries.[47] (See fig. 5.3.) Early courts were likely no more than large open areas, but roofed colonnades eventually defined the areas in the Agora. The courts still remained visually and aurally accessible to the public, since orators mention audiences of bystanders (including foreigners and even metics).[48] Today it is difficult to experience the Classical Agora, given the Hellenistic, Roman, and Byzantine remains that fill much of the area, but the Panathenaic Way, a major artery

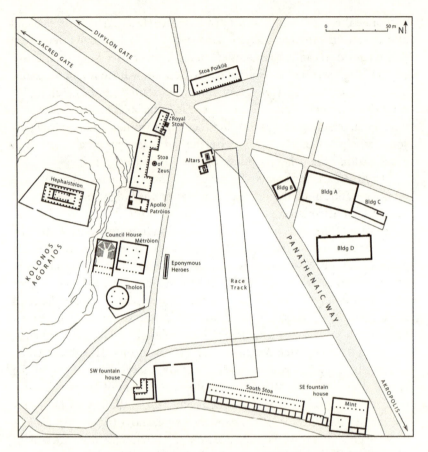

FIGURE 1. *Map of the Agora in the fourth century BCE. Drawing by Tina Ross, based on R. C. Anderson in Boegehold 1995: 258 fig. 2.*

cutting through the Agora, passed directly by the courts, Buildings A, B, C, and D, and the Stoa Poikilē (fig. 1). Their location in high traffic areas meant that passersby might easily stop and listen. The central region of the Agora was an open space, with only trees and market stalls, allowing for clear sight lines from one end of the Agora to the other.[49] It would have been possible to notice a crowd gathering outside the courts even if at a distance, and this group likely attracted other curious onlookers. Their presence made for lively trials, since the bystanders and jurists heckled the speakers, probably with whistling, hissing, and shouting to demonstrate their disapproval. They could also express approval with hand clapping.[50] Such responses meant the speakers and speechwriters might aim to engage and entertain this audience so as to garner their support and approval or their disdain for the opponent in an attempt to influence the actual dikasts (Dem. 18.318–319).[51] Philokleon in Aristophanes' *Wasps* notes speakers' use of stories, fables, and jokes to amuse him (Ar. *Wasps* 566–567).[52] Although Aischines suggests that the Council of the Areopagus provided judges more rational than the jurists of the popular courts (Aischin. 1.92), Edith Hall argues that a defendant likely based his decision to withdraw from Athens after the first speech, a right unique to this court, on the reaction of the spectators (Antiph. 5.13; Dem. 23.69).[53]

Similarities between dramatic performances and forensic oratory likely encouraged the view that speakers in the courts should cater to the crowds. Not only do they share practical procedures, both being judged and voted on; they also center on conflicts between two or more individuals.[54] Aristotle, furthermore, comments in his *Rhetoric* that just as with an actor's delivery of his speech, the orator's performance of his speech was more important and persuasive than its content.[55] Edith Hall, in discussing the trial of Phryne, who in the manner of Helen may have exposed her breasts to the court in a case of impiety, comments: "Whatever the truth of these pleasurable anecdotes, they do at least confirm that such spectacular and titillating tactics were not beyond the imagination of the ancient courtgoer."[56] Such parallels suggest that orators attempted to engage their audiences using techniques drawn from dramatic performances, and that audiences in turn, whether sitting in the courts or in the theater, expected to be entertained in similar ways. That expectation is perhaps one reason why we have such rich character portraits in oratory.

SEX LABORERS IN CONTEXT

Although this book focuses on oratory, comedy is an important backdrop for these speeches in terms both of literary precedents and of social attitudes.[57] The interplay between comedy and oratory is evident from the speeches themselves, which sometimes refer to recent comic performances. Aischines, for example, reminds his audience of a comedic chorus that alluded to Timarchos (1.157). Such references suggest that they expected their audiences to be familiar with the latest comic plays.[58] The exchange, in fact, worked both ways: Timokles and Philemon wrote plays entitled *Neaira* likely after Apollodoros delivered his speech against her in court. There is also a reference to Neaira in Philetairos' *Kunagis*.[59] These examples suggest an affinity between stage performances and the courts in the fourth century BCE and demonstrate that neither the comic poets nor the orators had qualms about exploiting the other genre if it would serve their purposes with their audience. My primary interest in this study, however, is the influence of comedy on oratory.[60]

Sex laborers of all varieties (brothel workers, sex traffickers, streetwalkers, trafficked women, independent sexual companions) appear in the comic corpus. The earliest references equate sex laborers to food, something to be consumed, and thus present them as passive objects used by others for their sexual gratification and then quickly disposed of. They are likened to objects meeting a need as opposed to a person performing a service.[61] A good example of this is the market scene in Aristophanes' *Acharnians* in which Dikaiopolis barters with a Megarian merchant (729–835; cf. 880–896, 960–961, 1198–1201). The Megarian has disguised his daughters as *choiroi* (young piglets: 739) and tries to sell them to Dikaiopolis (729–835). The Megarian comments that with some fattening up, they will be excellent on the spit and a fitting sacrifice to Aphrodite (791–796). The exchange plays on the double meaning of *choiroi*: piglets and female genitals.[62] The references to being on the spit and to Aphrodite indicate the daughters are being trafficked for Dikaiopolis' sexual pleasure. Other innuendos suggest their availability for oral and vaginal sex.[63] The association of sex laborers with enjoyment and pleasure renders these figures a regular feature of comic revelry and celebration (*Peace* 337–345, 439–440). The Megarian piglets are only available for purchase because of the success of Dikaiopolis' personal peace agreement with the rest of Greece. In addition to *Acharnians*, many surviving plays indicate a happy resolution and the reestablishment of social stability at their conclusion by the presence of such party women (Ar. *Ach.* 1198–1234; *Knights* 1389–1408; *Lys.* 1114–1178).[64]

Sex laborers also highlight the excess and greed of other characters. In Aristophanes' *Knights*, for example, they represent Kleon's corruption (765; cf. *Wasps* 34–36, 1015–1035; *Peace* 648–660).[65] Negative stereotypes of sex laborers as lusty (*Thesm.* 339–346; *Clouds* 53–55), greedy (*Wealth* 244), bibulous (Pherekrates' *Korianno* 67, 69, 70K), mercenary (*Wealth* 149–156, 502–506), and generally deceptive (*Eccl.* 689–709, 718–724, 1159–1162; *Frogs* 1325–1328) also abound. A discourse of blame occasionally attaches to sex laborers, whom the poets denounce for men's woes, like war, and censure for their impiety (Ar. *Ach.* 529–537). Named women associated with the sex industry (Aspasia, Kyrene, Salabaccho, and Kynna) are normally arsenals against well-known politicians and not attacked simply for their own sake.[66] Old Comedy presents an image of sex laborers at best as easily accessible pleasures to be consumed and enjoyed, a sign of good times, and at worst as lacking in self-control, untrustworthy, and a self-indulgent extravagance for the purchaser of their services. The mentions are largely pejorative. Only brief reference is made to male sex laborers (*Knights* 1242; *Wealth* 153–159).

The speeches examined in these pages are roughly contemporary with what some scholars label "Middle Comedy" (390–320 BCE), roughly the period between Aristophanes (representing Old Comedy) and Menander (representing New Comedy), but for which we have no extant plays.[67] While the same uses and stereotypes in Old Comedy persist, there are also some interesting changes and innovations.[68] The sex laborer is now likened to an enchantress who bewitches and dominates men (Anaxilas' *Kalypso* 11K, *Kirke* 12–13K).[69] Related to this image is the emphasis on the sex laborer's use of cosmetics and other adornment as a form of deception and entrapment (Alexis Fr. 103 *PCG*). At the same time, the availability of sexual labor is accepted as necessary for the stability of Athenian democracy (Xenarchos Fr. 4 *PCG*). Historical sex laborers themselves become the object of derision and lampooning. It is also during this period that they develop as characters with personalities and speaking roles, and become part of the playwright's plot development (Alexis' *Agonis/Hippiskos* 1–3K, Euboulos' *Kampylion* 43K, Hipparchos' *Thais* 3K).[70] At the same time, the plays of Middle Comedy anticipate Menander with the occasional positive portrayal of such women as good or even beneficial to others. Their methods of deception get used to entice and entrap men, especially young ones, who are considered vulnerable to their advances. In contrast, male sex laborers do not appear on stage.

The stereotypes of Old and Middle Comedy appear in the portrayals of sex laborers in oratory, although in a somewhat subdued manner.[71] They are still self-absorbed and untrustworthy. As in comedy, orators use associations with sex laborers to critique others. For example, Aischines claims Timarchos was enslaved to flute girls and *hetairai* to demonstrate his inability to exert any self-control over his appetites (Aischin. 1.42, 75, 115). Young men continue to be particularly susceptible to such women, who are blamed for their ruin (Isai. 3.17). Opponents are accused of selling themselves for sex (Dem. 22.21–24; And. 1.100). With the increasing popularity of the sex laborer as a character, it is likely no coincidence that the extensive portraits and attacks on sex laborers in forensic oratory appear at this time. Their extended narratives may reflect some of the plots of such comedy.[72] The fragmentary material from Middle Comedy does not allow detailed comparisons, but the prevalence of this character type in these plays suggests that jurors and bystanders would be familiar with the type and be entertained by its representations in oratory. Orators, in turn, could rely on

OVERVIEW OF THE CHAPTERS

familiarity with the character type to influence their audiences' view of sex laborers in their speeches.

Sexual Labor in the Athenian Courts describes the complex relations between sexual labor and Athenian institutions, social values, gender ideologies, and practices. The chapters analyze in detail five key speeches involving male and female sex laborers: Aischines 1, *Against Timarchos*; pseudo-Demosthenes 59, *Against Neaira*; Isaios 6, *On the Estate of Philoktemon*; Lysias 3, *Against Simon*; and Lysias 4, *Concerning a Case of Intentional Wounding*. Up-to-date commentaries are available for most of the speeches under consideration, and I have relied greatly on them for textual considerations as well as for context: Stephen Todd on Lysias 3 and Lysias 4 (2007); Nick Fisher on Aischines 1 (2001); Konstantinos Kapparis on pseudo-Demosthenes 59 (1999). The one exception is Isaios 6, for which the commentary by Wyse (1904) is still the best source. A new commentary on Isaios by Brenda Griffith-Williams (2013) does not include Isaios 6, covering *Orations* 7–10 only. These are also the best sources to consult for further information on the background of these speeches and previous scholarship. Each chapter engages with a variety of themes—the body and sexuality (chapters 1, 3, 4, 5), the *oikos* (chapters 2, 3), the polis (chapters 2, 3, 5), and dangerous women (chapters 1, 2, 3)—and considers these topics in relation to characterizations, social networks, physical spaces of the household and city, Athenian sexualities, and Athenian concepts of gender.

The first chapter covers Lysias 4, a dispute over a female sex laborer. While the narrative section of Lysias 4 does not survive, the argument and proof sections clearly lay out the cause of the quarrel that resulted in a physical altercation between the speaker and his opponent. In this case, two unnamed men appear to have pooled their money together to purchase or free a female sex slave (also unnamed). The men shared access to the woman, but the arrangement fell apart when one of the partners began to treat the woman as his own. Characterization plays a significant role, and the focus of this chapter is how relations to sex laborers amplify the characters of the speakers and their opponents, particularly in terms of their relationship to desire. This chapter centers on the use of *duserōs*. It also considers the female sex laborer of Lysias 4 as a precursor to the more elaborate portraits of Alke (Isai. 6) and Neaira ([Dem.] 59) and the social anxiety concerning the influence and mobility of such women. This speech is often included in discussions of sexual labor and there are two dedicated studies of it: an article by Dimos Spatharas (2006), the first individual treatment of the speech, and a chapter by C. W. Marshall (2021), who offers a new reconstruction of the events behind the speech.

Isaios 6 is the subject of chapter 2. Brenda Griffith-Williams offers an overview of the speech's narrative and delivery with some discussion of its comic influences, but otherwise this speech has received surprisingly little scholarly attention, despite its colorful portrait of Alke.[73] It is part of a dispute over the rightful heir to the estate of Euktemon, which consisted of considerable wealth and property. Drawing on an ideal of the Athenian family as nuclear, the speaker of Isaios 6 focuses on what constitutes the *genos* of Euktemon. He constructs genealogies both for a legitimate family and for an illicit one, obfuscating what appears to be a complex family history including a divorce, remarriage, and half-siblings. In an alternative version of the sons' origins, the speaker identifies Alke, a former brothel worker, as the mother. The focus of this chapter is the use of space and the speaker's construction of a topography within the speech that highlights Alke's transgressions but also problematizes the flow of persons to and from the inner space of the *oikos* to the external polis. The ease with which Alke moves through the city and transgresses the physical and social spaces of the household, polis, and *astu* plays into societal apprehension about the place of enslaved persons, non-Athenians, and even women within the family and the polis, since Alke's role as a female sex laborer associates her with all three groups. Although the speaker's main interest is her effect on his friend's household, he uses his narrative about Alke to strengthen the connection between the *oikos* and polis, *genos* and *dēmos*, and thereby exposes the fragility of these institutions to outsiders.

Chapter 3 focuses on the trial of Neaira in pseudo-Demosthenes 59, the best-known and best-studied woman and sex laborer in Classical Athens. Although the speech appears in the corpus of Demosthenes, most scholars accept it as the work of Apollodoros, who also largely delivers it. Even though Neaira features in the title, the trial is a public suit (*graphē xeniōs*) against Stephanos for treating an alien as a legitimate wife and thus as *astē* (citizen woman). Neaira is primarily a pawn in a personal dispute, but the risks for her are still great. As with Aischines 1 (chapter 5), the intent of this speech is political. The trial likely aimed at removing Stephanos from public life as a supporter of Philip. Kate Gilhuly, Jess Miner, and Cynthia Patterson have done important work on this speech. Debra Hamel's publication examines the life of Neaira in depth and focuses on reconstructing a factual account of Neaira's life.[74] My previous work on this speech focuses on the characterizations of Neaira and Phano, but here I focus on the issue of female citizenship in relation to important social institutions and rituals.[75] Although Athenian women did not participate in the political Assembly, they were active in the religious life of the polis. Josine Blok has argued that a share in religious ritual was an important indicator and privilege of citizenship for both men and women.[76] In addition to Athenian women's role in the determination of citizenship, the chapter considers the significance of Athenian women as performers of ritual in the polis. Although the obligations of citizenship differed based on gender, Athenian women were citizens as much as men were. Neaira's (and Phano's) participation in Athenian ritual is another example of her usurpation of status that renders her so threatening to the polis.

Chapter 4 examines Lysias 3, in which the speaker defends himself against a charge of intentional wounding brought forward by Simon in a dispute over the affections of the male sex laborer Theodotos. Like Lysias 4, this speech appears in snippets in larger studies on law, status, and sexuality, but it has not been given the detailed scholarly attention it deserves or considered in full in conjunction with Aischines 1, a speech more often studied for male sexuality.[77] Although there is some dispute concerning the identity of Theodotos as enslaved in the sex trade, I explore how the speaker purposefully obscures status and the nature of the relationship in discussing his own relations with Theodotos. It appears, however, that Theodotos was hired by Simon under contract as a male companion, but he became exclusive to the speaker before his contract with Simon had expired. This speech is unique in that the speaker is in a relationship with a sex laborer at the time of the trial and thus discusses his own relationship with such a figure. The chapter focuses on the use and meaning of *epithumia* (desire) in the speech and the body of the sex laborer as a locus for different types of desire. It also explores key moments in the speech that amplify the distinction between sexual labor and pederasty. In the process, it outlines anxiety about desire in relation to masculinity and its effect on citizens.

Like Apollodoros' speech *Against Neaira*, Aischines 1, *Against Timarchos*, the topic of chapter 5, is a public suit (in this case a *dokimasia tōn rhētorōn*, "scrutiny of public speakers"), brought against Timarchos to prevent him from addressing the Assembly or bringing forward a public suit himself. It represents a political trial, since Aischines hopes to prevent Timarchos from bringing forward his charge of misconduct against Aischines on an embassy to Philip II. The chapter considers Aischines' use of sexual labor to discredit and convict Timarchos. This speech has been central to the study of sexuality in ancient Greece and the focus of important studies on same-sex relations at Athens. Sir Kenneth Dover developed his penetration model of sexual relations in large part based on Aischines 1. David Halperin developed this model further as a privilege of male citizenship.[78] I move away from discussions of sexual penetration, and thus the actual performance of purchased sex, to look instead at the physical body and its appetites in relation to sexual labor and a new kind of citizenship. Given this focus, James Davidson's discussion of the Athenian relationship to pleasure and Giulia Sissa's discussion of male sexuality in this speech have been very helpful.[79] The chapter builds on the work of Susan Lape to explore the different uses of *sōma* (body) and *bdeluria* (degeneracy) as well as *hubris* (abuse) and its cognates in the speech.[80] It also considers the markers separating the pederastic relationship from sexual labor, including in the use of space.

By considering all five speeches in depth in a single monograph I can examine complex attitudes and social tensions in a key arena of Athenian society. Although not the subjects of individual chapters, other speeches that incorporate passages on sex laborers provide an important context for the discussion of these speeches, including Isaios 3, *On the Estate of Pyrrhos*; pseudo-Demosthenes 48, *Against Olympiodoros*; and Hypereides' *Against Athenogenes*. By focusing on a single genre and context, I explore how the orators constructed identities using sexual labor and magnified the anxieties surrounding an accepted but at times troubling practice. Such a close examination sheds light on Athenian values and concerns, especially in relation to sex and gender more generally. The discourse on sex laborers is in fact a discourse on Athenian society, its values, and its institutions.

A NOTE ON TERMINOLOGY

In recent years there has been much discussion on the most appropriate terminology for discussing the sexual economy in the ancient world.[81] An ancient term like *hetaira* remains obscure and imbued with nostalgia both within and outside the field of Classics, and so I only use it when ancient authors do.[82] Many English terms carry connotations both positive ("courtesan") and negative ("whore") not always present in the original contexts. Instead, the terms "sex worker" and "sex work," coined by the sex worker and activist Carol Leigh in the 1970s, are increasingly used in reference to the ancient world.[83] But although these terms are devoid of the social stigma associated with terms like "prostitute" and "whore," they also mislead and misappropriate the original intention behind this terminology.

19

Sex workers today are a mobilizing group asserting choice, agency, and the right to choose their work as a profession with the same rights as other workers to safe working conditions. "Sex work" highlights purchased sex as a legitimate form of labor in a free-market economy. When we use this same terminology for the ancient world, we dilute the fact of enslavement as a crucial element of the ancient sexual market. We also undermine the significance of "sex work" as a revisionist term in the modern context by associating it with ancient slavery and exploitation. Although even today, on the global scale, sex trafficking is linked to sexual slavery, mobilized sex workers condemn forced sexual labor. Activist sex workers also dispute the claim that sexual labor must always be exploitive. They focus on choice and the right to choose sex work as a profession. Such agency rarely existed in the context of ancient sexual labor and it is difficult to recognize individual consent in the sources.

As the reader will have already noted, I favor the terms "sexual labor" and "sex laborer" as more appropriate to the ancient context. This choice may appear broad to some, since it can encompass entertainment like exotic performers at the symposium, and unpaid labor like domestic sexual labor between enslaved and free members of a household. I use the terms here for commercial and transactional sex only, sex that required a form of payment to proceed. The terms disassociate the practice from stigma and, conversely, nostalgia, but they do not obscure the dependence of the ancient sex trade on an enslaved labor force and elide differences between ancient and modern practices. They are also broad enough to allow for the diversity of transactional sex that existed in the ancient world. *Hetaira, pornē, pornos*, and their derivatives appear where used by the ancient author. I offer the translation "sexual companion" for *hetaira* to highlight the euphemistic use of the word but not necessarily a specific status as a sex laborer (Plut. *Sol.* 15.3). *Pornē* and *pornos* are more difficult to translate. They derive from the Greek verb *pernanai*, "sell," frequently used in the ancient sources to describe the selling and purchase of slaves. The *pornē* and *pornos* are thus literally individuals enslaved for sex. The terms are used indiscriminately in oratory as a form of denigration regardless of status.[84] A popular translation is "whore." But since that term today often indicates a moral lapse, as in an "immoral woman," that is not always present in the original texts, I prefer "sex slave" in order to highlight the slavish connotations of the term as well as commodification as the slight.[85]

———— ONE ————

UNDER THE INFLUENCE

LYSIAS 4, *Concerning an Intentional Wounding*, centers on a home invasion in which the speaker's opponent was attacked with a potsherd in a dispute over an enslaved sex laborer. Fights over sex laborers appear to have been a common feature of Athenian urban life. The orators mention violent brawls over sex laborers as a commonplace in their speeches. They occur both in the streets and at symposia. Fights over *hetairai* appear just as common as fights arising out of drunkenness, gaming, or personal insults.[1] In some cases, quarrels over sex laborers led to formal arbitration to establish ownership or the juridical status of a sex laborer ([Dem.] 59.45–47). Jealousy, strong emotions, and legal rights surrounding access to a sex laborer were behind these conflicts and more formal disputes. The fact that groups of men might share ownership or jointly finance the freedom of a sex laborer made such disputes inevitable.[2] Lysias 4 is rare in that it focuses on these clashes in a legal setting. In this trial the speaker defends himself in a *graphē* or *dikē traumatos ek pronoias* against the accusation that he physically attacked his opponent in a long-standing dispute over a sex laborer.[3] In this chapter I explore Lysias' use of desire for a female sex laborer to amplify and test the character of the disputants against core masculine values. I also examine Lysias' portrayal of the disputed woman and consider her portrayal in the larger context of fourth-century BCE oratory and comedy more generally.

AUTHENTICITY

The speech of Lysias 4 appears incomplete, since only the proof section and epilogue are extant.[4] No names appear in the speech or title, and so the defendant, prosecutor, and even the enslaved sex laborer remain unknown today.[5] The fragment makes no reference to contemporary events, and thus the date of the speech and its delivery are also unknown.[6] It is part of an ongoing disagreement over a sex laborer that eventually led to a violent confrontation between the two men. One of the men sought justice in the Athenian courts, where he accused the other of forcibly entering his home and physically attacking him with a pot or potsherd in an attempt to kill him and abduct the woman (4.5). He brought his rival before the court of the Council of the Areopagus with a charge of *trauma ek pronoias* (intention to do physical harm). The surviving speech presents the arguments of the defendant. The assault and resulting trial had many features in common with Lysias 3: the attack was the result of a personal dispute over a sex laborer, it occurred on the opponent's property, and the weapon involved was also an *ostrakon* (a pot or broken fragment of a pot). The rhetorical strategies of the two speeches are also similar: both speeches misleadingly treat *ek pronoias* as premeditation, dispute the location of the altercation, and focus on the opponent's infatuation with a sex laborer to distract the judges.[7] They include references to *diōmosia* (the oath), *antidosis* (a challenge to an exchange of property), and *basanos* (evidentiary torture of enslaved persons) in their arguments. The parallels with Lysias 3 combined with the lack of personal details and the absence of an introduction and narrative have led some commentators to suggest that Lysias 4 is simply an exercise in argument modeled on Lysias 3 and not an extant speech from an actual court case.[8]

Although the speeches do have many resemblances, their differences support Lysias 4 as an independent text delivered at an actual trial rather than a rhetorical exercise. In addition to the differing sexes of the sex laborers (male versus female), the speaker of Lysias 3 never had an agreement to share the sex laborer with his rival, whereas the speaker of Lysias 4 did. At the time of trial, the defendant is still involved with Theodotos. In Lysias 4, the sex laborer is involved with the speaker's opponent only. A dissatisfied client is now the defendant, and yet his allegations against his rival are somewhat more subdued than those of the defendant in Lysias 3, in which accusations of *hubris* against Simon, for example, are common. In contrast to Theodotos, who has little character development or blame in the dispute in Lysias 3, the unnamed sex laborer in Lysias 4 emerges as a dangerous personality skilled in the manipulation of her clients.[9] The references to her as *pornē* (sex slave) are intentionally disparaging, whereas the speaker of Lysias 3 elides Theodotos' status as enslaved. Even the references to broken pots and torture are not so similar on closer inspection. Although the weapon in each case is said to be a potsherd, in Lysias 3 the prosecutor accuses the speaker of having brought the sherd with him, whereas the prosecutor of Lysias 4 only claims he was struck by a potsherd. While both speakers refer to *basanos*, the refusal of the opponent to provide the enslaved sex laborer for such torture is a substantial element of the argument in Lysias 4, whereas *basanos* was never a formal challenge in Lysias 3. Given these differences, I agree with Stephen Todd that Lysias 4, like Lysias 3, was most likely written for and delivered at a genuine trial, and that it was originally a complete speech with an introduction and narrative.[10]

THE DISPUTE AND CHARGE

Although the introduction and narrative sections of Lysias 4 are missing and the various players remain nameless, details of the disputants and the case can be reconstructed from the remaining *pistis* (proof section) and *epilogos* (conclusion).[11] Both men are of the liturgical class. We know this because one of the disputants requested an *antidosis* (exchange of property) of the other when he was approached about performing a liturgy (4.1).[12] The sex laborer is possibly of freed status, since the speaker's opponent claimed she was *eleuthera* (free: 4.12, 14).[13] Although her current status is uncertain, it is clear that she was at one time an enslaved sex laborer. The two men had pooled their resources to purchase or free her (4.10, 12, 16). Although the men agreed to share the woman, she may have begun living with one of the men in his home. As a result, the other partner to the agreement demanded repayment of his contribution, but the man refused to comply. A fight over the woman broke out at this man's home. He claimed that he was seriously injured in the head with a potsherd and sought justice in court with a charge of *trauma ek pronoias*. What remains is the defense speech from the trial.

Trials for *trauma ek pronoias* appeared before the court of the Council of the Areopagus, and given that court's association with murder trials, Christopher Carey and Stephen Todd argue that this charge may be equivalent to one of attempted murder.[14] David Phillips concludes further that *pronoia* in intentional wounding trials had the same force as in trials for intentional killing, which were the specific type of murder cases overseen by this same court: it indicated "an intent to act, not (necessarily) an attempt to kill."[15] Both types of trial began with special oaths sworn by the accuser (Lys. 3.1, 10.11).[16] Its close association with a *dikē phonou* suggests other similarities. Murder trials in this court included three preliminary hearings with two opportunities at trial for the defense to speak against the charge before the vote was taken. Stephen Todd reasonably infers that the court of judges likely followed these same procedures in judging cases of intentional wounding.[17] The penalty on conviction in a charge of *trauma ek pronoias* was certainly very serious: exile and confiscation of property for the guilty party (Lys. 3.38, 41).

A conviction on a charge of *trauma ek pronoias* required proof of a weapon, but not necessarily of premeditation.[18] The use of the weapon demonstrated an intention to cause serious physical injury (*trauma*), especially in cases where the actual injury was a head wound.[19] Although the weapon could be a knife, and thus an instrument manufactured to do harm, it could also be a random object, like a rock or ceramic pot, acquired in the heat of the moment. It was thus distinct from a mere physical brawl, for which an individual could bring a private suit, like a *dikē aikeias*, for assault and battery ([Dem.] 47.40). The opponent's claim that the speaker struck him with an *ostrakon* is thus crucial to the opponent's argument.

BROKEN PROMISES

A quarrel centering on the status of the woman and the nature of her arrangement with the speaker and his opponent led to the fight. The two men may have purchased her together and shared her companionship. Sex laborers could be expensive, and jointly owning an enslaved one would not be considered an unusual setup. The speech against Neaira (chapter 4) includes this very same scenario. While Neaira was still enslaved, two young men purchased her from a female sex trafficker and proceeded to keep her as their personal sex slave. They continued with this arrangement until they married, whereupon they allowed Neaira to buy her freedom ([Dem.] 59.29–30). The speaker appears to argue for a similar arrangement in Lysias 4 when he claims that they agreed to share the woman (4.1) and, later, that he had contributed half the money to purchase her (4.10). If the speaker was telling the truth, they could both legally claim ownership of her. Under such circumstances the speaker had reason to be angry if his opponent now excluded him from the arrangement and refused to recognize their joint ownership. The speaker provides no evidence of any contract or witnesses to the arrangement, however, and as Stephen Todd observes, he never offers proof of any payment.[20] His only corroboration would be the woman, whom he challenged his opponent to hand over for questioning (4.12, 14).[21]

The opponent, in contrast, seems to have claimed that the woman was now free and not enslaved (4.12, 14), as the speaker would have his audience believe, and denied she was ever their common property (4.1, 10). If the opponent was telling the truth, the two men may have pooled resources to purchase her freedom from her owner. Under such circumstances, the men would not gain control over her person, and she would have been free to choose whom she preferred.[22] The example of Neaira in pseudo-Demosthenes 59 is again helpful. In the narrative, the speaker, Apollodoros, argues that Phrynion was the primary contributor in the purchase of Neaira's freedom, but Neaira herself and other former clients also contributed funds ([Dem.] 59.31–32). Upon being freed, Neaira traveled with Phrynion from Corinth to Athens, apparently by choice, where she remained with him as his personal sexual companion. After some time, however, dissatisfied with her situation, Neaira left Phrynion and traveled to Megara, where she again worked as a sex laborer. There she met another Athenian, Stephanos, and eventually returned to Athens with him as her protector ([Dem.] 59.35–37). When Phrynion found out about her return, he immediately claimed she was still enslaved—in this case as his slave—but Stephanos supported her status as freed. The matter was settled through arbitration, with the arbitrators ruling in Neaira's favor ([Dem.] 59.40, 45–47). The fact that the opponent in Lysias 4 refused to provide recompense to the speaker suggests the money was paid to her owner in a *prasis ep' eleutheriai* (purchase for the purpose of freedom).[23] The opponent felt no obligation to reimburse him, since what was purchased was not the woman herself, but her freedom.

THE TRIAL

At trial, the accuser maintained the speaker was his personal enemy. The two had been in conflict before over an *antidosis* (exchange of property: 4.1), and he used this fact as a demonstration of their long-standing animosity. He argued that on the night in question the defendant came to his home with the intent to kill him and abduct the woman (4.5). In this version of events, the accused violently entered another's home, making the brawl much more serious than if the altercation had happened in a random encounter on the street.[24] He then proceeded to attack the opponent with an *ostrakon*. An *ostrakon* could be either an entire pot or a sherd. An attacker might smash someone with the pot or break the pot and use it more like a sharp weapon as someone might a broken bottle today.[25] In either case the attacker could do considerable harm to his victim.

In his defense speech, the speaker makes no attempt to deny that they got into a physical fight or that his opponent got hurt, but he claims that he never entered the home by force and that he certainly had no intent to kill his opponent (4.7, 12, 18).[26] He admits to going to the opponent's house (4.15), but in his own version of events he came with wine and was seeking boys (and flute girls, 4.7). Rather than in search of the woman specifically, he was looking for a good time. The vocabulary evokes the symposium and suggests the speaker came to his opponent's house hoping to join in a drinking party. Stephen Todd suggests that he entered his opponent's home in the course of a *kōmos* (drunken revelry), which normally occurred after a symposium and often included drunken fights over flute girls, but in the current speech the emphasis is on coming to the opponent's house *met' oinou* (with wine) and suggests a more convivial motivation.[27] The speaker alludes more than once to the fact that he was invited to explain his presence at the opponent's home: "we went because we had been sent for [*metapemphthentes ēlthomen*]" (4.11, 15).

The speaker claims that he did not strike the first blow and thus start the fight, and he indicates to the judges that the woman knows which of them is telling the truth about such discrepancies (4.15). He acknowledges that his opponent received a black eye (4.9), but he avoids terminology that suggests any weaponry and instead refers to punching and striking with bare fists (*paiomenos*, 4.6; *epataxa*, 4.11; *eplēgēn ē epataxa*, 4.15) when describing the actual incident.[28] He argues that he himself acted in self-defense and that his opponent exaggerated his injuries by being carried about in a litter after the altercation.[29] In this telling, the opponent lacks composure and has come forward with what may be a spurious charge (4.14).

He also positions himself as the wronged party in the dispute by claiming that he shared the woman in common with the opponent and that he equally contributed to her cost (4.1, 10, 16) but that the opponent was no longer honoring the arrangement.[30] Despite these circumstances, he stresses that he has always reacted calmly and reasonably, keeping his head: "For my part, I have been easygoing [*eukolōs eichon*] from the start and remain so now" (4.9). He is overcome neither by desire for the woman nor by anger at his opponent. Instead, like any reasonable person, he wants to be bought out of the deal and have his money restored (4.9).

Another strategy is the characterization of his opponent as out of control with drink, as inflamed with desire, as quick to fight, and as overcome with a perverse love (4.8) and an insanity (*barudaimonia*, 4.9). These descriptors come at the listener all at once and relate to the opponent's desire for a *pornē anthrōpos* (4.9). In 4.19 she is emphatically a *pornē kai doulē anthrōpos* (sex slave and enslaved nobody).[31] Her status as sex laborer, enslaved, and merely *anthrōpos* (person; woman) are equally highlighted throughout the speech as identities to be disdained, but these identities also undermine the masculinity and credibility of the opponent who is overcome with desire for her.

LOVE-CRAZED

An important contrast between the two opponents is desire, which functions as a marker of difference in this speech more generally. It distinguishes the opponent not only from the speaker but also from all members of society. After a discussion of his relationship with the opponent (4.1–4) and a summation of the accusations versus his own version of events (4.5–7), the speaker blames the dispute on his opponent's desire for the woman and his resulting volatility (4.8):

> But this man, in contrast to other men [*enantiōs tois allois*], is love-crazed [*duserōs*] and wants both outcomes: to not have to pay back the money but also to keep the woman [*anthrōpon*]. And so, inflamed [*parōxummenos*] by the woman [*hupo tēs anthrōpou*], he is very quick to fight [*oxucheir*] and gets out of control with drink [*paroinos*], making it necessary to defend oneself.

The passage does not dispute paying for sex and becoming involved with a sex laborer or even deny that strong emotions may develop between such individuals, but it does position the opponent's response to sexual desire as different from what was normally expected, describing him as feeling *enantiōs* (in a contrary way) to other people. The adverb constructs his opponent's relationship with the woman as abnormal and justifies the speaker's use of *duserōs* immediately following. This term presents him as out of his mind with desire for the woman and suggests that his intensity of feeling is affecting his behavior and other relationships more broadly by rendering him prone to violence.[32] Stephen Todd translates it "lovesick" here, and the Loeb edition offers "lovesickness," but the Greek word is more intense than these terms, which typically refer to the despondency of an unrequited love.[33] The prefix *dus-* suggests "bad" or "difficult," a love perverse or mad, and signals that *erōs* (desire) has overcome the opponent's capacity for self-control and even reason. I have settled on the translation "love-crazed" to capture its nuance here.

Lysias' use of *duserōs* is unique in oratory and rare in other genres until at least the second century CE. It would have caught the attention of his audience. Of Classical authors, it appears twice in Thucydides, but in a single context: when the general Nikias attempts to dissuade the Athenians from embarking on the Sicilian Expedition in 415 BCE (6.13, 24). Its use marks their desire as irrational, setting their sights on the spoils of Sicily in the absence of any conflict and starting a new war far away, given the volatile peace accomplished in the Peloponnesian War at home. Victoria Wohl interprets it, moreover, as a "morbid passion" and an "erotic disease" that drives imperial Athens to its own destruction.[34] It is the worst kind of *erōs*. In other Classical authors it also connotes a desire that overwhelms and subverts a person's reason. It represents a negative condition (Eur. *Hipp.* 193; Xen. *Oec.* 12.13). Likewise, in Lysias' speech, *duserōs* suggests an extreme state. It identifies the opponent as someone who is so unable to control his emotions that he becomes irrational and impossible for any reasonable person to contend with. In this sense, his *erōs* is a mental illness.[35]

In this same passage the speaker describes the opponent as quick with his fists (*oxucheir*) and a violent drunk (*paroinos*). Each term connotes intemperate behavior. *Oxucheir*, another rare term in oratory, is further intensified by the adverb *lian* (exceedingly, very). *Paroinos* highlights the nature of the speaker's opponent as out of control with drink. It does not simply describe being drunk (*methuōn*) but indicates an excessive use of alcohol that can lead to extreme violence.[36] These terms' use as general descriptors, detached from a specific event, identify excessive fighting and drinking as regular features of the opponent's character. Both states, being prone to fights and to drunken violence, are a direct result of his perverse passion for the enslaved sex laborer, who is the root cause of his negative behavior. Joseph Roisman suggests that since alcohol and sex are often paired together, Athenians viewed behavior under the influence of either of them similarly, as a touchstone for the inner self and a true reflection of an individual's masculinity and worthiness as a citizen.[37]

Barudaimonia also highlights the opponent's psychological state and, like *duserōs*, is equally difficult to translate (4.9 and quoted below). The force of *barus* (heavy, oppressive) in combination with *daimōn* (spirit, fate) suggests "ill-fatedness," but given the context it must be stronger, "a state of possession," "insanity."[38] In describing an inappropriate passion, Aischines refers to *daimoniōs espoudakōs* (wretchedly devoted) with *daimōn* again suggesting some sort of spirit behind an intense desire (Aischin. 1.41).[39] Likewise, the *daimōn* at the core of *barudaimonia* evokes the opponent's disturbed mental state. It also alludes to the woman who just two lines earlier is presented as behind the speaker's absurd passion (see 4.8 quoted above). She becomes the *daimōn* inflaming his desire. In the context of *duserōs*, *parōxummenos* (inflamed) is best understood as a reference to sexual desire and passion. It adds to the overall characterization of the opponent as unable to control his emotions and his subjugation to a mere *anthrōpos*. Such intensity of feeling spurs him on and results in unreasonable actions, including the current trial. His relationship with the woman undermines his masculinity and thus his social legitimacy before the judges.[40]

The speaker hints that the opponent was originally free from his affliction and a reasonable man, whom he endorsed as a judge (and who supported the speaker's own tribe at the Dionysia) (4.3–4). While he includes this detail to emphasize the absence of any previous animosity, the detail also highlights how his desire for the woman has affected and changed him. Not only is it difficult for him to act with self-control, but he becomes susceptible to a woman's influence. The focus of the speaker's critique is not that his opponent keeps or spends too much on an enslaved sex laborer, as is a common complaint against opponents in other speeches and comedy (e.g. Aischin. 1.42; Ar. *Wasps* 1354–1359), but that he is too rash in his actions and vulnerable to the manipulations of the sex laborer because of the state he is in. The speaker privileges *duserōs* as the defining quality of his opponent in order to showcase his incapacity for self-mastery, thereby reducing his credibility and feminizing him given the importance placed on self-control as a masculine virtue. The negative characterization is consistent with the sociopolitical discourse on masculinity in Athens more broadly.[41]

Another example of an Athenian losing himself in a relationship with a sex laborer is Olympiodoros in pseudo-Demosthenes 48. The speech details a dispute over an inheritance awarded to Olympiodoros. The plaintiff in this trial, Kallistratos, claims that he is owed a portion of the estate and that Olympiodoros originally promised to share it with him but then reneged on the arrangement. Near the end of the speech, he draws attention to Olympiodoros' freeing of a sex laborer as a way to question his opponent's stability and character ([Dem.] 48.53–54):

> For, fellow jurors, this man Olympiodoros has never married an Athenian woman in accordance with your laws; he has no children and has never had any, but having purchased freedom for a *hetaira*, he keeps her at his home. She is the one ruining [*lumainomenē*] us all and impelling [*poiousa*] him into a higher state of lunacy [*mainesthai*]. For how is he not insane [*ou mainetai*] if he thinks it unnecessary to honor any of the things that he promised and readily agreed upon and swore to?

29

Kallistratos emphasizes the madness of Olympiodoros with the use of *mainesthai*, a forceful verb indicating a person not at all in control of his senses. It is a term used to describe the madness induced by an external force like wine (*Od.* 18.406, 21.298) or even a god (*Il.* 6.132; Hdt. 4.79; Paus. 2.7.5). In this case it is again passion for a sex laborer that destabilizes the mental state of the opponent. As in Lysias 4, Olympiodoros' infatuation is abnormal. He is described as "being out of his mind [*paraphronōn*] as no man ever was out of his mind, under the influence of a female sex slave [*gunaiki peithomenos pornēi*]" ([Dem.] 48.56). He should be helping his poor relations rather than spending money on freeing the sex laborer and keeping her in expensive clothes and jewels (48.55). The speaker emphasizes further that all Olympiodoros' friends and relatives consider him melancholy (*melancholan dokōn*, 48.56). *Melancholos* is a technical term indicating an excess of black bile (*cholē melaina*) in the body. In Hippocratic medicine, the four humors had to be balanced; an excess of any one humor required immediate attention (*Diseases* 4.1). Untreated, the excess humor could cause disease, including mental illness: *Epidemics* connects being mad with an excess of black bile (5.1.2). The speaker intends the verb *melancholan* to suggest a mental disease has put Olympiodoros under the influence of this woman.[42] His freeing and continued support of her is the result of his mind's disease, brought about by *erōs*. These accusations come at the end of the speech; Kallistratos intends them to affect the jurors' opinion of Olympiodoros and his mental state. Not only is he incapable of controlling his desire; he is in fact driven mad by it. It leads him to dishonor agreements made with other citizens, even those who are kin, and renders him vulnerable. Here again a speaker uses his opponent's association with a sex laborer to critique his masculinity and diminish his social legitimacy.

NARRATING AN *ANTHRŌPOS*

The dispute in the courts is between the accuser and the defendant, but the original quarrel involved at least three individuals: two men and a sex laborer. Could the unnamed woman have had any interest or involvement in the dispute? As Steven Johnstone tantalizingly asks, "Is it possible that this case originated less in aristocratic male rivalry than in a woman's assertion of her own interests?"[43] Although the speech provides only a glimpse of her viewpoint, she probably had various complaints against the speaker: he rejects any assertion that she was freed (4.12, 14), and the opponent appears to have argued that he tried to abduct her from his home (4.5). Disputed claims about status as well as abuse at the hands of a client are cited in other speeches as conflicts that arose between sex laborers and their clients. Apollodoros says that Neaira left Phrynion on account of his treatment of her. When she returned to Athens he tried to claim her as his personal slave despite her status as freed ([Dem.] 59.40). The speaker of Lysias 3 claims that Theodotos hated Simon and refused to associate with him because of the treatment he received at his hands (Lys. 3.31). We can only speculate on the unnamed woman's personal conflicts with the defendant, but he himself does not hesitate to incorporate her into his arguments and concluding remarks. In his account, she oscillates between being an object of pleasure and a subject who manipulates the two men.

Although Greek has a variety of terms for sexual companions, including the euphemism *hetaira* (companion), the speaker simply refers to her as *anthrōpos* (woman; person), a disparaging term given the absence of social markers, and a common way to refer to enslaved or formerly enslaved women in the orators.[44] Its use in this speech leaves the woman's juridical status unclear but, more important, highlights her social insignificance. I stress this latter aspect of the term by rendering it "nobody" in some of my translations. It also obscures her exact relationship with the two men, one of whom appears to be treating her as a long-term companion rather than a mere sex slave. Other terminology elides her position further and stresses her status as enslaved. The speaker refers to her as *doulē* (slave: 4.19) and offers her up for torture like an enslaved person (4.17). He calls her *pornē* twice, once in collocation with *anthrōpos* (4.9) and once with both *doulē* and *anthrōpos* (4.19).[45] In both cases the use of *pornē* is pejorative and emphasizes her status as a sexual commodity.[46] It is never a neutral term in oratory and is commonly reserved for the end of a speech as a direct attack on a woman, even one supposedly working as a sex laborer.[47] The regular references to money (4.8, 9, 10, 12, 16) and the mention that she was shared in common (4.1, 10, 16) further identify her as a sexual commodity as opposed to a companion. The language aims to vilify and alienate her from the judges and positions her as an object to be enjoyed without any consideration in the dispute.

In the opening section of his argument as we have it, the speaker refers to "the business concerning the woman [*ta peri tēs anthropou*]" (4.1) and suggests that she is the main reason behind an *antidosis* (exchange of property) with him (4.2). Few details are provided, so it is not clear which of the two men was the challenger in this exchange and thus who was commissioned to undertake the liturgy and whether or not the woman was part of that exchange. Stephen Todd suggests the phrase *di' ekeinēn* (because of her) highlights "her central rôle as object of the dispute." If enslaved, she would have been part of the property exchanged and thus possibly the reason for the *antidosis*. A successful challenge might have brought her fully into the property of one of the men, thereby ending their joint arrangement or alternatively might have ensured unimpeded access to her for both men. It is unclear exactly how the *antidosis* would have brought about either result, and for this reason some editors have suggested removing the preposition *dia* (*di'*) and taking the demonstrative *ekeinēn* with *antidosin* instead of as a reference to the woman. Todd favors accepting the manuscript reading "as a piece of deliberately manipulative illogicality."[48] If freed, she would not have been part of the exchange, but *di' ekeinēn* is still difficult to interpret. There is some ambiguity in the use of the preposition, and the ambiguity could hint that she was somehow responsible for the exchange. Did she gossip about the wealth of one man to the other?[49] Did she encourage the exchange out of spite? Without the narrative portion of the speech, events surrounding the *antidosis* remain elusive, but as the argument progresses the speaker's version of the dispute takes into account the woman's agency and even slyly positions her as an actor in the dispute.

The speaker pulls the woman into the trial with the challenge to have her testify to events using the procedure of *basanos*. The opponent refused the request, but the speaker uses his refusal as an opportunity to attribute their animosity to her behavior (4.16–17).

> This woman was owned in common [*koinē*], since we both equally [*homoiōs*] provided the funds [*argurion*]. And she has specific knowledge of this. It is on account of her [*dia tautēn*] that all the disagreements [*ta prachthenta*] have happened between us. You will not be unaware that I was at a disadvantage in having her tortured, but I did not shrink from this danger. For she very clearly cares more deeply [*peri pleionos . . . poiēsamenē*] for him than for me and has wronged [*ēdikēkuia*] me with the help of this man [*meta men toutou*], but she has never committed a wrong against him [*oudepōpote eis touton examartousa*] with my help [*met' emou d'*].

The speaker represents the woman simultaneously here as their shared property and an active player in their discord. The use of *dia* in this case suggests the woman is responsible for their disagreements, and her involvement is stressed by the particles used to describe her. He admits that she favored the opponent over himself (*peri pleionos touton ē eme phainetai poiēsamenē*) and in doing so provides her with a point of view. He also claims the woman crossed him. Todd's translation of *meta men toutou*, along with Lamb's, stresses that she "joined him," the opponent, in wronging the speaker.[50] The active feminine participle *ēdikēkuia* (having wronged) to describe the woman, with the emphatic pronoun *eme* (me), stresses her offense against the speaker and positions her as an active subject in the conflict. I translate *meta men toutou* as "with the help of this man" to highlight the extent of autonomy the speaker allows her here. *Examartousa* (committing a wrong) also positions the woman as subject, and the contrast created between the opponent and himself with *meta men toutou . . . oudepōpote . . . met' emou d'* (with him . . . but never . . . with me) underscores her choice in deciding to wrong one man but not the other.

The woman's personal involvement in the dispute is hinted at earlier in the speech as well. The speaker argues that it is her fault that his opponent is so inflamed with passion (*hupo tēs anthrōpou parōxummenos*, 4.8, discussed above). The use of the genitive of personal agent highlights her responsibility for his mental state. He also accuses her of stringing them both along: "And she at one moment says [*phēsi*] that she prefers me [*hē de tote men me*], at another him [*tote de touton*], since she wants to be desired by us both" (4.8). It's one of the rare instances in oratory when a woman, and an enslaved woman, at that, is given a voice and provided with a point of view.[51] The detail underscores the emotional labor demanded of a sex laborer, who, regardless of her own feelings, had to please every client.[52] The speaker uses her words as proof that she was an active player in a love triangle and as an example of her dishonesty. It sets up her culpability and even responsibility behind their quarrel. The full passage includes a syntactical inversion: "and *he wants both things [amphotera bouletai]*, to not return the money and to keep the woman. . . . and she says she prefers me and then him, since *she wants to be loved by both men [bouloumenē hup' amphoterōn erasthai]*." Stephen Todd calls it striking, in that each phrase evokes a different individual and in doing so invites the listeners to compare two equally absurd desires.[53] The chiasmus assimilates not only their wishes but also the woman and the opponent as desiring subjects. In doing so, it feminizes the opponent while emphasizing dishonesty as a trait they share. The use of *hē de* introduces her as a party in the dispute, and *bouloumenē* (wanting) emphasizes her subjectivity and autonomy, subtly influencing the judges' perception of her role in the quarrel.[54]

The suggestion of blame begins in the next section. After the drunken brawl, the speaker claims his opponent made a dramatic show of his injuries (4.9):

> But my opponent here has come to such a level of insanity [*barudaimonias*] that he is not ashamed to call his black eye physical trauma and to be carried around on a stretcher [*en klinēi*], feigning a terrible state on account of a sex-slave nobody [*heneka pornēs anthrōpou*], whom it is possible for him to have all to himself once he has paid me my money.

The opponent may have appeared before the court on a stretcher, or perhaps he was previously carried through town to show his injuries to the magistrate, or simply carried around after the confrontation in the same way that Arkhippos was, in another fragment of Lysias, after his whipping at the hands of Teisis and his slaves. In that speech the speaker describes how the bearers pointed the victim out to the crowds, who became enraged at the sight of his injuries.[55] The speaker of Lysias 4 downplays the conflict and his opponent's wounds by suggesting that the wounds were faked and that the fight occurred on account of a "sex-slave nobody," but *barudaimonia* also suggests that the opponent has become unhinged and is in a vulnerable state. The situation is more complex than a simple brawl over a sex laborer after a night of drinking. The emphatic inclusion of the woman, *heneka pornēs anthrōpou*, also invites speculation.[56] The woman emerged as a personality with a viewpoint in the passage immediately preceding (4.8), and so it becomes unclear here whether the woman is merely the object of the brawl, the reason for the opponent's behavior, or the architect of the episode. The short phrase suggests simultaneously that she motivates his behavior and actively influences it, thus discreetly implicating her in the opponent's actions. With this comment the speaker implies to the judges that she played a role in their dispute in addition to being the object of it. The use of *pornē* makes her involvement all the more disturbing, stressing as it does her low status as well as her role as a sexual commodity.

The speaker credits the woman's role in the trial more strongly near the end of the speech, when he claims that he is placed in such grave danger owing to a lowly sex laborer and enslaved nobody (*dia pornēn kai doulēn anthrōpon*, 4.19). The use of *pornē*, *doulē*, and *anthrōpos* together leaves no doubt about the speaker's vilification of the woman and highlights the absurdity of his situation at being on trial. Once again *pornē* comes first, putting the emphasis on her role as a sexual commodity, and is intended as a disparagement. With this emphatic attribution he presents her to the judges as unworthy of any consideration but at the same time suggests her direct connection to a dispute for which he risks losing his civic rights. He ends this section with *dia toutous* (on account of them); whereas Lamb translates the phrase using "these men," Todd is more ambiguous, "these people."[57] We should not be too quick to dismiss the woman's inclusion here. *Toutous* must refer to the opponent and the *anthrōpos* together, since no others are mentioned as parties to the dispute. It suggests that the woman and his opponent are both equally to blame for the danger he now faces. By highlighting the woman in his closing remarks and lumping her and the opponent together, the speaker likely heightened concern among the judges about the extent to which the opponent was subject to her manipulations. As a contrast, he is careful to demonstrate that he himself has kept the relationship in perspective and treated her as an enslaved person should be treated. The repeated use of *chrēsthai* (use, enjoy: 4.1, 13), a verb for sexual intercourse with a sex laborer, in connection with his own association with her, emphasizes her sexual exploitation by stressing her status as a commodity to be enjoyed.[58] Unlike his opponent, he remained in control of himself and also the relationship and thus fell outside her influence.

UNDER THE INFLUENCE (OF WOMEN, NOT WINE)

Through the portrait of his opponent's relationship with a sex laborer the speaker not only denigrates his opponent's masculinity but subtly exploits social anxiety over the influence such women can yield. The exploitation of common social anxieties around the influence of women in male affairs is an effective rhetorical strategy.[59] In Athenian law, evidence of female influence was a valid reason for annulling a will (Dem. 46.14):[60]

> Everyone ... shall be permitted to dispose of his own property, however he wishes, if there are no legitimate male children, unless [he disposes] on account of insanity [*maniōn*], senility [*gērōs*], drugs [*pharmakōn*], or illness [*nosou*], or under the influence of a woman [*gunaiki peithomenos*], and is out of his mind [*paranoōn*] on account of one of the preceding, or [he disposes] while under constraint by duress or detention.

This law lists female influence alongside mental illness (including insanity and senility) and the negative effects of drugs or disease.[61] Their grouping effectively equates female influence with these other ailments and thereby constructs female influence as a type of impairment. Being under the influence of a woman is a sign of weakness, specifically a mental incapacity. The Greek participle *peithomenos* is stronger than simply "influence," suggesting someone who is under the control of a woman, someone who carries out a woman's demands. The inclusion of *gunē* in the law suggests an underlying bias in society more broadly against listening to women in matters of substance. The law evokes a negative stereotype suggesting that female sway is responsible for bad decisions and even dangerous, something that should be feared.

Although *gunē* suggests female kin, speakers broaden the law to include sexual companions, who also had direct access to the personal affairs of men through their intimate relations with them.[62] The speaker of pseudo-Demosthenes 48 (discussed above) describes Olympiodoros as under the influence of his sexual companion (*gunaiki peithomenos pornēi*). (See [Dem.] 48.56.) He parrots the law in describing the sex laborer's hold on Olympiodoros while both increasing the listeners' anxiety and degrading the woman with the use of *pornē*. A syncopated form of the law follows to drive home the speaker's point: "Solon established as law that all actions that anyone undertakes at the instigation of a woman [*gunaiki peithomenos*], especially her sort [*toiautēi*], be invalid." In this rendering, the law references only female influence and is expanded to include all acts, not just wills, and to be concerned primarily with sex laborers.[63] Another example of a woman condemned for her influence is Antigona, a renowned *hetaira* turned sex trafficker, in Hypereides' *Against Athenogenes*. In this speech Antigona brokered a transaction between two men, the Athenian Epikrates and Athenogenes, an Egyptian merchant.[64] Epikrates purchased from Athenogenes three enslaved laborers and the perfumery in which they worked. (See chapter 4.) Once the transfer had taken place, Epikrates discovered that the business was riddled with debt, for which he was now responsible. He attempts to invalidate their contract by citing the law dealing with wills and then highlighting Antigona's influence in the drawing up of the contract.[65] He claims that he was swayed by Athenogenes' *hetaira* in completing the transaction (*ego tēi Athēnog[eno]us hetairai epeisthēn*) and now wants the contract invalidated (17–18). Once again the speaker interprets the law to apply to any action undertaken at the instigation of a woman and uses the woman's status as a sex laborer to frame the influence as even more egregious.[66]

In the current speech, Lysias 4, the speaker is more subtle. He does not cite or imply any specific law in his arguments. But his characterization of the sex laborer raises the issue of female influence and shifts the focus from himself as the perpetrator of wrongdoing to a female sex laborer. In contrast to the opponent, he argues that they were not personal enemies and that their disagreements center on the woman. Although only a fragment of the speech is extant, it is enough to suggest the speaker attempted to exploit the same social anxiety surrounding female influence, particularly in the case of sex laborers. At two key points relating to the trial, when the speaker accuses the opponent of feigning his injuries and when he asks for the judges' pity, he refers to her as *porne* (4.9, 19). The term is both degrading and inaccurate. It appears the woman has been living with the opponent as his personal *hetaira* or even *pallake* (long-term partner).[67] At the start of the speech the speaker questions why, if he had indeed overpowered his opponent at his home, he did not then take the woman from his house, suggesting she was living there (4.5). Her situation as a live-in companion may have allowed the speaker to arouse anxiety among the judges about what she was doing in such a position. Johnstone's playful discussion of the grievances the woman had against the speaker as an aggrieved party raises possibilities that may have also occurred to the judges.[68] They would also have been aware that, as Todd comments, "in practice she may well have some capacity to influence the outcome of the dispute."[69] Her behavior toward the two men caused some level of conflict that resulted in the trial and put the speaker at risk, but it also hints at her ability to manipulate the opponent, who is overly amorous of her, in particular. The references to her as *doule* and *anthropos* stress her status as enslaved and non-Athenian as well as female and develop any influence she exerts as triply troubling. We will see this topos developed further in chapter 2, where a female sex laborer named Alke convinced an Athenian to recognize her son and introduce him into his phratry and then robbed him of his wealth (Isai. 6.21, 48). The verb *peithein* is once again used to characterize female influence and invoke the law.

A COMMON STEREOTYPE

The sex laborer of Lysias 4 is not a unique character in Attic oratory. She exhibits qualities that mirror female sex laborers in other lawcourt speeches, like Alke in Isaios 6 (chapter 2), Neaira in pseudo-Demosthenes 59 (chapter 3), and Antigona in Hypereides' *Against Athenogenes*. These portraits recall the sex laborers of Attic comedy, a trope even in Old Comedy.[70] A poignant example is Philokleon's address to the flute girl whom he has stolen away from a symposium in Aristophanes' *Wasps*. Philokleon expects gratitude for having rescued the performer from the other symposiasts: "return the favor [*charin*] for this to this here penis" (1347). But he recognizes in advance that she will not oblige him and will instead string him along, just as she has done with many men before him. He presents her as ungrateful and untrustworthy, not bound by the usual quid pro quo of *charis*.[71] Philokleon's complaint, "You will deceive me and taunt me greatly. For you have done just this to many others already" (1349–50), also fuels the speaker's accusation in Lysias 4 that the unnamed *anthrōpos* manipulated him along with his opponent by feigning affection for one and then the other lover (4.8). Philokleon also suggests that the flute girl will please him in order to obtain her freedom (1351–1353). By invoking her manumission (and maintenance) Philokleon comments on the self-interest of such women whose only motivation is personal gain.[72] The characterizations of the sex laborers in forensic speeches depend on such stereotypes: the mere mention of a *hetaira* or *pornē* would conjure such associations in the minds of the listeners. The enslaved status of the women, which compelled them to perform these roles, and the power dynamic behind these relationships are conveniently subsumed under the comic stereotype.

Speakers could also rely on the inclusion of *hetairai* figures in comedy to fill out any story lines around the sex laborers in their speeches. Although the dramatic role of the sex laborer in Aristophanic comedy was limited: a mute character on stage primarily for other characters to grope and enjoy (e.g., Ar. *Ach.* 989–999, 1198–1231; *Lys.* 1114–1188; *Peace* 894–904; *Thesm.* 1160–1231; *Wasps* 1326–1449),[73] Aristophanes' contemporary Pherekrates included a *hetaira* figure as a character in the plots of a number of his plays: *Kitchen, Forgetful One/Thalatta, Petalē,* and *Tyranny.* According to Athenaios, his *Korianno* was named after a *hetaira* (Ath. 13.567c). Its plot included an old and young man, possibly a father and son, in dispute over a *hetaira*, likely Korianno herself (Fr. 77–79 *PCG*). Jeffery Henderson credits Pherekrates with popularizing the character type in his "domestic comedy" and inventing the "hetaira comedy," since his characters and plotlines seem to have provided the groundwork for a new genre of comedy.[74]

By 410 BCE other playwrights, starting with Theopompos, developed plots centering on *hetairai.* Diokles' *Thalatta* may even be a rewrite of Pherekrates' play.[75] Judging by the female names used as titles, playwrights of Middle Comedy (ca. 390–320 BCE) continued to incorporate *hetaira* figures: *Chrysis, Malthrake,* and *Melitta* by Antiphanes; *Anteia* by Eunikos or Philyllios; *Nannion* and *Plangon* by Euboulos; *Double-Lais* by Kephisodoros; *Neaira* and *Nannion* by Timokles.[76] Titles that reference the foreign backgrounds of female characters are possibly also about women working in the sex trade.[77] Mask types catalogued by Julius Pollux are further evidence that this character played an increasingly important role in comedy in the fourth century BCE: he lists six mask types for the *hetaira* figure in his typology of forty-four comic masks.[78] As Henderson points out, "the legacy of hetaira-comedy was its creation of women who, because of their non-citizen status, could safely be portrayed as both objects and subjects of erotic desire; who could be shown interacting with men or even dominating them; who could exemplify the negative 'iambic' traits of bibulousness, gluttony, masturbation, drug-use (especially aphrodisiacs), preoccupation with fine clothes and jewellery, . . . greed, and disruptive effects on males."[79] There are echoes of my discussion of the unnamed *anthrōpos* in Lysias 4 as simultaneously sexual object and social agent in Henderson's comments here.

Such comedy provided ample material for the orators to exploit in their speeches. In comic plots, a young man falls in love with a sex laborer (Antiphanes' *Zakynthios*); a father and son compete for the attentions of a sex laborer (Pherekrates' *Korianno*; Theophilos' *Flute Lover*); a sex laborer escapes the brothel life with the help of a young man (Alexis' *Hippiskos*); sex laborers turn out to be legitimate children and eligible for marriage (Antiphanes' *Didymai/Aulētris*).[80] A fragment of Antiphanes features a young man in love with a *hetaira* living and working in his neighborhood (*Hydria* 103K). Though the passage alludes to the negative stereotype of such women already known from Old Comedy, it also suggests a new characterization for sex laborers.[81] The young man describes his love as *astē* (free citizen female) but without guardian or relatives. In addition to being free, he describes her as possessing virtue (*aretē*). The portrait differs to the more typical *hetairai*, whom the young man complains sully the name "companion" with their habits. The young man's comment, which singles his *hetaira* out from others, implies that the negative portrayal is the more expected type but it also reinforces suspicion and mistrust of the character, whose intentions may not be transparent. These plots highlight the disruptive force of the *hetaira* figure along with her unstable status and hint at the complexity of her character type.

The later, Hellenistic playwright Menander plays with the audience's expectations of the *hetaira* type, even using her to resolve the plots of some of his plays, but the attitudes of other characters likely invoke earlier comedy.[82] In his play *Epitrepontes*, the character Habrotonon appears on stage discouraged by her client's lack of interest and the disgust she feels at having to endure the unwanted attentions of other symposiasts. She admits that she had hoped to encourage the young man who hired her to fall for her and free her. As the play progresses and she learns about an abandoned infant who may be the son of her client lover, she concocts a plot to trick him into admitting the son is his own (511–515). Her fellow slave recognizes her intentions as another way to gain her freedom (538–540) and admires her scheming ways (535, 555–560).[83] Although the play changes course when Habrotonon discovers that the mother of the child is the wife whom her client has abandoned (and she begins to use her skills to bring her paying lover and the young woman back together), duplicity and self-interest explain her initial actions in the play. From such sources, we get a glimpse of the *hetaira* character on stage in the fourth century BCE. She is increasingly central to the plot, but her cunning and intrigue continue as important character traits. At the same time, she is a volatile figure who can be good or bad for the other characters.

The emergence of the sex laborer as a focal character in Attic comedy likely influenced the incorporation and characterization of such women in oratory. The sex laborers of the lawcourts are not simply signs of an opponent's extravagance, but they also play a central role in events related in the narratives. Such narratives mirror comic storylines: young men are overly amorous of sex laborers (Lys. 4; Isai. 3; [Dem.] 59); old men are bamboozled by them (Isai. 6; [Dem.] 48); enslaved sex laborers escape the brothel (Isai. 6; [Dem.] 59); sex laborers play clients off against each other (Lys. 4; [Dem.] 59); sex laborers desire their freedom (Lys. 4; [Dem.] 59); and sex laborers "marry" citizens (Isai. 3, 6; [Dem.] 48, 59). As in comedy, the plots are complicated, with their twists and turns, and the identities of sex laborers are unstable.[84] Judges and jurors would be familiar with the character type from the theater and anticipate their schemes and power to influence based on the plots of plays. Comedy thus facilitated the task of the orator by perpetuating stereotypes and completing plotlines only hinted at in their speeches. As Brenda Griffith-Williams comments, "their willingness to accept a story they heard in court may have been influenced by what they had seen on stage as much as by their experience of real life."[85] For many of the jurors and bystanders, comedy was their only exposure to such women.[86] Although they may have been familiar with the *pornē* in the brothel and on the streets, the sex laborer who mixed with citizens at elite symposia and was kept in expensive clothes and jewelry was beyond their immediate circle.

The portraits of female sex laborers in oratory likely entertained their audiences, like the comic portraits, but the orators use such characterizations and plots to new purpose. In the context of the lawcourts plots involving the female sex laborer become sinister, promoting her as a troubling, threatening, and even dangerous figure. The orators are not interested in lampooning or exploring the character type or in creating a happy ending but instead reshape the comic portraits in their narratives to create anxiety and uncertainty in their audiences. As we will see in subsequent chapters, the female sex laborer beguiles young and old alike, influences her male associates, steals from the family wealth, usurps the role of citizen wife, offends the gods, and is always foreign. It was the comic context that provided traction for the speaker's portrait of the unnamed *anthrōpos* in Lysias 4.

CONCLUSION

In Lysias 4 the main constraint for analysis is the fragmentary nature of the speech. Nevertheless, specific anxieties are discernible in this speech based on the female gender of the sex laborer. Mentions of the woman are not merely in passing but are calculated inclusions. Through regular references to her, the speaker hints that his opponent is victim to a woman's schemes and will, even as he remains reticent about the details of her involvement. The vocabulary stresses the opponent's helplessness, calling him *duserōs* (love-mad: 4.8), associating him with *barudaimonia* (insanity: 4.9), and describing him as inflamed with passion (*parōxummenos*, 4.8) and abnormal in his desires (*enantiōs tois allois*, 4.8). The *daimōn* component in *barudaimonia* (4.9) plays on his infatuation with the woman, suggesting that she is what has unhinged him.

By focusing on the mental state and vulnerability of the opponent, the speaker overlooks any vulnerability of the woman herself and instead imbues her with agency and highlights her untrustworthy character.[87] The speaker insinuates the woman is manipulative when she plays the two men off against each other (4.8) and reveals her to be a threat when she wrongs him himself (4.17). Her portrait oscillates between a piece of property to be enjoyed and a player with a personal interest in the conflict. The speaker hints at her direct involvement through the prepositions *hupo* (by), *dia*, and *heneka* (on account of) (4.2, 8, 9, 19). In fact, the speaker seems even to blame her for the trial itself when he states that he risks losing everything on account of a *doulē* and *pornē* (4.19), a direct reference to the woman as the motivating force behind the opponent's charge. Through such tactics he deflects attention from his own actions and arouses anxiety about the woman's influence over the opponent and her role in the dispute, even in the trial itself.

Portraits of sex laborers were familiar to the judges of the court from the comic stage. This type became a stock character over time and probably appeared in a speaking role as early as Pherekrates' *Korianno*. The sex laborer was already a known comic type when Lysias wrote this speech, in the early fourth century BCE. His portrait of the unnamed *anthrōpos* is a precursor to the more extensive portraits of Alke in Isaios 6 and Neaira in pseudo-Demosthenes 59. Any similarities among these three portraits, however, are best explained by the impact of comedy, which provided a stereotype as well as plotlines. A speaker could rely on his audience's familiarity with such comic tropes to influence reactions to his speech and even fill in blanks in the narrative. The portraits in oratory are more sinister than in the comic genre since the sex laborers introduced by the orators remain foreign and disrupt the status quo to varying degrees. This character type was also used to critique an opponent's masculinity and enabled the more positive portrayals of wives that appear in this same genre, as discussed in chapters 2 and 3. In oratory, female sex laborers' associations with citizens disrupt the social fabric, in contrast to citizen kinswomen, who are used to create and maintain bonds between citizens and households within the polis.

---— TWO ——

IN THE *OIKOS*

ISAIOS 6, *On the Estate of Philoktemon*, offers a much more developed portrait of a sex laborer than does Lysias 4. Rather than a case of physical violence heard by the Areopagus, the dispute was over property and played out in the popular courts, where narrative digressions were more permissible. The trial stems from a dispute over the legitimate heir of Euktemon, a wealthy Athenian who died at the age of ninety-six (6.18). His estate consisted of considerable wealth and property in Athens and Attika (6.60), including farms, houses, a bathhouse, livestock, specialized slaves (6.33–34, 38), and building complexes (6.19, 20). He had three sons, Philoktemon, Ergamenes, and Hegemon, as well as two daughters (6.10), one of them a widow by the time of the trial (6.51). The division of the estate should have been straightforward, but the sons predeceased their father, and all died childless. Although his two daughters were still living, daughters were not able to inherit the paternal estate in Classical Athens. Philoktemon, the last of the sons to die, had most likely adopted his nephew Chairestratos, making him eligible. But Euktemon appears to have had two surviving sons from a second marriage. Under Athenian law, these sons would legitimately inherit everything. The disagreement eventually led to the delivery of this court speech at a trial in 364 BCE.[1]

Although the opponents identify an Athenian woman, Kallippe daughter of Pistoxenos, as the mother of these young men (6.13), the speaker claims that the mother is a well-known sex laborer by the name of Alke and suggests that the father is not Euktemon at all but a freedman named Dion (6.20). The speaker focuses his strategy on the questionable origins of these two sons (6.17). He emphasizes Alke's role as a sexual companion, first as a *paidiskē* (young sex slave) in a brothel and then as a personal companion to Euktemon, and skillfully uses her movements and networks to problematize the sons' identities. He presents her as the mastermind behind the claim on the estate and in this way puts a woman and a sex laborer at the center of a familial dispute. In this chapter, I explore the attitudes and anxieties regarding female sex laborers in the Athenian household and the concept of family, and I further tease out some of the topoi introduced in chapter 1.

UNRAVELING THE DISPUTE

The buildup to the current action was complex. Near the start of the speech we learn that upon Euktemon's death a distant relative named Androkles claimed the widowed daughter in marriage as an *epiklēros* (heiress), identifying himself as the nearest next of kin.[2] In the case of no surviving sons, Athenian law required a daughter to marry such kin, and the resulting male offspring became heir to the estate.[3] This law kept wealth in the male line and ensured the survival of the paternal *oikos* (household, property). The immediate family, however, argued that Philoktemon had adopted his nephew Chairestratos in his will, making him sole heir (6.8). But Chairestratos had not officially claimed this status before now.[4] Androkles then claimed the estate on the grounds that Euktemon had two surviving sons by another wife (6.12, 45, 57), and therefore contested Chairestratos' claim through a *diamarturia* (protestation) in court (6.43–44).[5] Chairestratos countered by charging Androkles with perjury in a *dikē pseudomarturiōn* (private suit for bearing false witness, 6.10, 58). This particular speech, delivered by a family friend (6.1–2),[6] is in support of Chairestratos' action.[7]

As with most ancient Athenian legal cases, we do not know the outcome of the trial. It is possible that Chairestratos lost his claim, if we may judge from a later dedicatory inscription by a Chairestratos son of Phanostratos of the deme Kephisia (*IG* II[2] 2825.11). If he had won, he presumably would have been the son of Philoktemon, not still "of Phanostratos."[8] Regardless, the speech offered much to give the jurors pause.[9]

A TALE OF TWO HOUSES

The speaker's narrative of Euktemon's intimacy with Alke is presented as an uncomfortable moment in the history of the family. The telling appears intended to develop discomfort in his audience, since it exploits unease surrounding Athenian concepts of *oikos* and polis, and the role of the enslaved, aliens, and women in the household. The speaker clearly draws on an ideal of the Athenian family as nuclear when he focuses on what constitutes Euktemon's *genos* (descent group, clan).[10] He constructs two gene-

── IN THE *OIKOS* ──

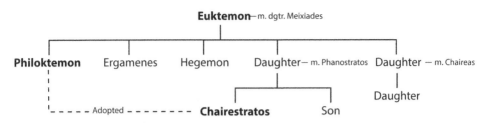

FIGURE 2.1. *Family Tree I: Euktemon. Prepared by Tina Ross.*

alogies, one for a legitimate family and the other for an illicit one, obfuscating what appears to be a complex family history including a divorce, remarriage, and half-siblings. The legitimate family is identified with Euktemon's immediate kin from his first marriage (fig. 2.1). The speaker claims that Euktemon lived with his wife in an *oikia* (house, family) with their children, three sons and two daughters. The wife's lineage is stressed: she is the daughter of Meixiades of the deme Kephisia (6.10), the same deme as Euktemon's.[11] According to the speaker, the wife, along with the three sons and two daughters, are known to all Euktemon's *prosēkontes* (relations), to Euktemon's phratry members, and to many of his demesmen (6.10). They have the recognition of all levels of Athenian society, attesting to their status and legitimacy as *astoi* (townspeople), as a *genos*, and as Athenian citizens. Given Euktemon's status, he likely held a sacrifice and marriage feast for the members of his phratry at the annual Apatouria immediately after his wedding to Meixiades' daughter to legitimate this marriage in his community.[12] In addition to rituals (such as the child-naming ceremony the *amphidromia* or the *dekatē*) recognizing his children as part of his *oikos*, at another celebration of the Apatouria he would have offered a sacrifice on behalf of each new son. Like all citizens, he would have enrolled his sons in his phratry with the offering of the *koureion* (a sacrifice on the boy's account) when they came of age at eighteen. Such membership qualified them for membership in his deme and the accompanying privileges of Athenian citizenship.[13] The speaker comments that relatives, phratry members, and many demesmen are willing to bear witness to their identities (6.10):

> For, fellow citizens, all the relatives [*pantes hoi prosēkontes*] and members of his phratry and many members of his deme [*tōn demotōn hoi polloi*] know truly that Euktemon, the father of Philoktemon, had these children: Philoktemon, Ergamenes, Hegemon, and two daughters, and that their mother, whom he married, was the daughter of Meixiades of Kephisia. And they will be witnesses for you.

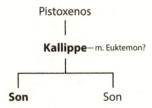

FIGURE 2.2. *Family Tree II: Kallippe. Prepared by Tina Ross.*

His comments highlight that these sons have participated in important rituals and have been accepted by his kin, phratry, and deme as Athenians. These witnesses are crucial evidence of the family's standing and their status as Athenians. The daughters, moreover, both married citizens: one Chaireas and the other Phanostratos (6.6). Their marriages and subsequent offspring bring further legitimacy to the members of Euktemon's *genos*, including his wife, their mother, since only daughters with Athenian citizen status could legally marry Athenian citizens. The daughter married to Phanostratos (also of Kephisia) had two sons, the elder being the nephew Chairestratos, who has brought forward this case of perjury against Androkles and presents one claim to the estate.

The second household, in contrast, is unknown and unfamiliar. It centers on a young man introduced into Euktemon's phratry as Euktemon's son, put forward as a claimant to the estate by Androkles and Antidoros (6.47; fig. 2.2). The importance of this youth's younger brother in the trial is not clear, but he too may have been recognized as legitimate and may thus have qualified for a portion of the estate (6.30, 36).[14] The speaker makes everything about this second family a cause for unease, beginning with its unfamiliarity (6.11):

> But that [Euktemon] married some other wife who bore him these sons no one [*oudeis*] knows about at all, and no one ever heard about during [Euktemon's] lifetime.

Their status as *astoi* and thus Athenian is uncertain, since they lack the support of witnesses to verify their identities (6.11). *Oudeis* (no one) contrasts markedly with *pantes hoi prosēkontes . . . kai hoi phrateres kai tōn demotōn hoi polloi* (all the relatives, ... and phratry members, and the majority of the demesmen), who attest to the first family of Euktemon (6.10). Androkles first claims the mother was born to an Athenian *klērouchos* (holder of an allotment of foreign land, colonist) on Lemnos, without further details.[15]

He later identifies the mother as Kallippe daughter of Pistoxenos (6.12–13). No demotic is provided for Pistoxenos, and no one seems to know who he was, but if he was indeed a *klērouchos*, it might be reasonable that his family was not well known at Athens.[16] The story verges on scandal (the speaker refers to it as *anaideia*, "beyond decency") and untrue: Pistoxenos left Kallippe with Euktemon when he went to fight in Sicily (whence he did not return), and under Euktemon's guardianship she gave birth to her two sons. Neither Euktemon's *oikeioi* (close relatives) nor his *therapontes* nor *oiketai* (enslaved members of the household) from either household are able to verify that she was married to Euktemon or under his protection (6.16).[17] Unlike the first family, there are no *prosēkontes* (relatives) and *sungeneis* (kin) able to testify to her identity as *astē*, and thus the status of the sons as Athenian is questionable (6.15, 64).[18] Aside from no record of a marriage feast or other public services on her behalf, the speaker claims that there is no evidence of a tomb for Kallippe, nor of Euktemon and these sons performing rites at any grave (6.65; cf. 3.77–80). Kallippe could not be less socially visible, and thus her identity and legitimate status could hardly be more questionable.[19]

The speaker provides an alternative version of the sons' origins even more salacious than the account of Kallippe (fig. 2.3). He identifies Alke, a sex laborer and sexual companion to Euktemon, as their mother.[20] According to the speaker, a freed person named Dion was the father of her two sons, not him (6.20):

> A freed person by the name of Dion was carrying on a relationship [*sunēn*] with [Alke] while still living in the *sunoikia*, and she claimed he was the father of these boys. And Dion raised them as his own [*kai ethrepsen autous ho Diōn hōs ontas heautou*].

The verb *sunēn* (from *suneinai*, "be together"), used here to refer to the relationship between Alke and Dion, commonly signifies a temporary sexual relationship (like one with sex laborers) and is not used to indicate a stable legal relationship like marriage.[21] And indeed Dion eventually had to leave Athens for Sikyon and did not take Alke and the children with him (6.20).[22]

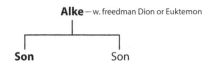

FIGURE 2.3. *Family Tree III: Alke. Prepared by Tina Ross.*

But the speaker also claims that Dion brought the boys up as his own while he remained in Athens. *Ethrepsen* (from *trephein*, "bring up," "raise") indicates that he both supported and raised the boys and furthermore acknowledged their paternity. The vocabulary stresses a familial commitment to the boys and signals to the audience that he was well known in some circles as their father during this period.

When Dion left town, Alke became intimately involved with Euktemon after he put her in charge of another of his *sunoikiai* (multiple-occupancy housings, tenements), this time in the Kerameikos. The speaker claims this Alke convinced Euktemon to acknowledge at least one of her sons as his and to introduce him into his phratry (but the speaker claims no members are willing to verify this: 6.64). He also promised this son a piece of land, but otherwise no rituals were observed for either of Alke's sons. The speaker stresses that Euktemon was not acting with his full mental capacity when he recognized the boy (6.21). The makeup of this *oikos* is confusing, being full of speculation and even intrigue. The household members have not received the full recognitions normally required to legitimize citizenship, and in the speaker's account the real mother is enslaved, or at best a freed person; such a status would exclude the boys from citizenship regardless of the identity of their father. As we consider these family trees, the networks become smaller as the women gain prominence.

The language of the speaker reinforces differences between Euktemon's first household and his household with Alke. Whereas the wife is the mother, whom he married, as well as a *gunē* (wife) and Meixiades' *thugatēr* (daughter), Alke is regularly referred to as a mere *anthrōpos*, without known kin and not part of an official *oikos*. (See chapter 1.) She is, in turn, regularly named, whereas women in the first household are referred to only periphrastically, with the names of male kin.[23] Alke lacks a *kurios* (guardian) to watch over her and keep her under control. In contrast, men represent and accompany these other women in all their dealings. The son Philoktemon challenged his father about introducing new family members to his phratry (6.21–24). When the mother and daughters visited Euktemon's corpse upon his death, they were accompanied by male kin. The speaker refers to the women's action in attending to the body as *eikos* (fitting, right: 6.41). The mother and daughters remain silent in the text, never associated with verbs of speaking.[24] They willingly follow the lead of their *kurioi*, demonstrating appropriate subservience and the dynamic of a well-ordered *oikos*. In contrast, Alke is not at all submissive. She does not play a secondary role to the men but is instead in control of events, manipulating first Euktemon (6.21) and then Androkles and his associates (6.29). Ac-

IN THE *OIKOS*

cording to the speaker, she persuades and convinces; she is the one scheming and plotting to obtain Euktemon's wealth.[25] The speaker, furthermore,
associates Alke with transgressive behavior through the verbs *hubrizein*
(insult), *tolman* (dare), and *kataphronein* (disdain), describing her actions,
moreover, as *paranomia* (lawlessness: 6.48). Her household represents an
inversion of the norm and is as a result an abomination.

MOVING THROUGH THE CITY

In contrast to the unnamed woman in Lysias 4, the speaker provides a personal history for Alke.[26] He begins his narrative on her at 6.19 with a reference to Peiraieus and continues to privilege place whenever he introduces
a change in her circumstances. Each time the geographical and the physical
location are dominant features of the narrative (6.19, 20, 39):

> There was a freedwoman of [Euktemon's] who oversaw his *sunoikia* in
> Peiraieus and who kept young sex slaves. One of those she acquired had
> the name Alke, whom indeed I believe many of you know. And this Alke,
> once purchased, sat for many years in her brothel [*kathēsto en oikēmati*],
> but by the time she was older she had left the brothel [*apo men tou oikē-
> matos*]....
>
> Then Euktemon set up this woman [*tēn d' anthrōpon tautēn*], Alke,
> to manage his *sunoikia* in the Kerameikos, near the postern gate, where
> wine is sold....
>
> But even when Euktemon died, they became so emboldened that with
> Euktemon lying dead inside [*endon*] they kept guard over the house-
> hold slaves [*tous men oiketas*] lest one of them might inform his two
> daughters, his wife, or any of his close relatives. And with the help of this
> woman [*meta tēs anthrōpou*] they carried off the property from within
> [*ta de chrēmata endothen*] to the house next door [*eis tēn homotoichon
> oikian*], which one of them, that man Antidoros, occupied as a renter.

By locating Alke in three main areas of Athens (Peiraieus, the Kerameikos,
and the *astu* [city]) and in three main spaces (an *oikēma*, a *sunoikia*, and
an *oikia*, respectively), the speaker depends on common associations with
these places to influence his audience; but by building on such associations
he is also able to develop unease in his audience. With each change of location Alke's social networks also shift, and her identity becomes more and
more unstable. In placing her in these areas of the polis and plotting her

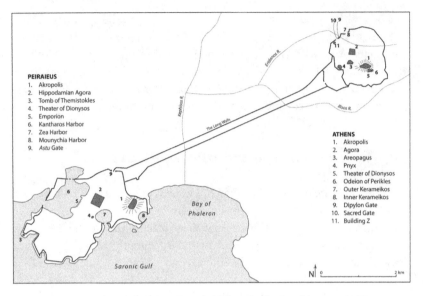

FIGURE 2.4. *Map of Peiraieus and Athens in the fourth century BCE. Drawing by Tina Ross, adapted from Conwell 2008: 234, fig.4.*

movements in tandem with her social networks, he develops her character as threatening. Because of her mobility Alke becomes a locus of anxiety for Athenian concepts of *oikos* and polis and for the roles of enslaved persons, non-Athenians, and even women in these places.

When first introduced, Alke is in a brothel in Peiraieus, a unique locale in the Athenian imagination (fig. 2.4).[27] As the major port, Peiraieus was a point of entry for *xenoi* (foreigners), whether enslaved or free, including itinerant populations of traders and other travelers.[28] In addition to being a hub for trade, it was also an industrial center, featuring shipbuilding, shield factories, sword factories, a bedstead factory, and a limestone quarry (e.g., Dem. 27.24–25).[29] Given its important commercial associations, it had a more varied demographic (both economically and socially) than other demes of Attika, with one of the largest populations of metics, resident aliens who made Athens their permanent home.[30] The inhabitants included a large number of enslaved and freed persons. The large and varied population suggests that *sunoikiai* outnumbered individual *oikoi*.[31] Peiraieus' location by the sea, its distance from the *astu* of Athens, and the composition of its occupants placed it at the margins of Athenian imagination and identity, explaining besides its popular association with non-Athenians, lowlifes, and mobile populations, as well as the easy access there to sex laborers and cheap hotels (Ar. *Peace* 164–165; Dem. 32.10; Aischin. 1.40).[32] Sitta von Reden refers to a "rhetoric of otherness" surrounding Peiraieus.[33] The speaker of Isaios 6 exploits the area as a peripheral space in the polis, at a safe distance from the *astu*, and constructs Alke's location there as appropriate and unremarkable, given her status as non-Athenian and enslaved.

Alke had arrived in Peiraieus as a *paidiskē* (young sex slave) sold to a freedwoman in charge of a *sunoikia* of Euktemon.[34] Her purchase price could have been considerable, since we hear of *paidiskai* being sold for three hundred drachmas each (Hyp. *Ath.* 2). The use of *nauklērein* (literally, "run a ship"; metaphorically, "manage") in reference to the freedwoman suggests that she was Euktemon's agent and manager and that his employment of her may even have included running the brothel.[35] The freedwoman trained Alke in the sex trade and trafficked her (as well as other girls). The speaker claims she sat in an *oikēma* (little room: 6.19), a term likely referring to the small rooms wherein sex laborers serviced customers (cf. Hdt. 2.121; Aischin. 1.74; Din. 1.13; Ath. 13.569d) and hence commonly indicating a brothel.[36] At some point Alke may have gained her freedom, although her status as freed is never specified. The speaker provides no indication of when it happened or who purchased freedom for her, but a possible scenario is that Euktemon freed Alke before he moved her to the Kerameikos with the task of managing another of his properties.[37] This *sunoikia* was located in a wine district and so was likely near other venues of entertainment and leisure. It was possibly another locale including brothel workers, like the freedwoman's business in Peiraieus where Alke herself first worked.

Like Peiraieus, this area was known for its wine taverns as well as the sex trade.[38] It covered a large area of Athens, stretching from the northwest corner of the Agora to beyond the city walls.[39] The walls and city gates that cut through the Kerameikos defined it as a liminal space, existing both within and outside the city. As an important entry point to the *astu*, the region likely included hostelries, making it popular with travelers. The famous Building Z, for example, is located here, nestled between the walls and the Sacred Gate.[40] By the mid-fourth century BCE (in its third phase), Building Z was a hostelry, a tavern, and possibly a brothel.[41] (Building Y, located a short distance from Building Z, has been identified as another tavern and possible hostelry.)[42] According to the speaker, the *sunoikia* that Alke managed was located in the Kerameikos in a wine district near the postern gate (Isai. 6.19). (Hermann Lind attempted to identify Alke's *sunoikia* with Building Z3, but the chronology of the structure makes the identification unlikely.)[43] This location once again places Alke in an entertainment district, but now she is at the very boundary of the *astu*. With this situation, she has moved closer to the center of Athens, but she is still somewhat at the periphery and limited in her social networks.

A consequence of the move to the Kerameikos is Alke's physical proximity to Euktemon. He begins to visit her regularly, but his time with her takes him away from his family. He eventually abandons them altogether to live with her full-time (6.21). Upon his death, Alke is found within the intimate space of his *oikia*, with the legitimate family barred from entering to view and prepare his body for burial (6.39–40). While Euktemon lies dead inside, Alke helps Androkles and Antidoros remove as much as they can, so that the house is almost empty of material goods. Euktemon's household is now the very opposite of Ischomachos' well-ordered house as described in Xenophon's *Oikonomikos* (8.1–10), in which the wife keeps everything secured in place and orderly, with the wealth visible and easily accessible.[44] The property has been depleted. The household slaves are unable to perform their duties in the *oikos*, including informing relatives about Euktemon's death. When the wife and daughters finally do gain entrance, they are told it is not their role to care for Euktemon's corpse (6.38–42). The speaker hints through their exclusion that it is Alke who will perform this ritual.

The speech has chronicled Alke's personal history as a migration through various entry points of the polis to the intimate space of an Athenian *oikos* within the *astu*, and it has highlighted this movement as a disruption of social as well as physical boundaries. In this way the speaker constructs a topography within the speech that highlights Alke's transgressions but also problematizes the flow of persons between the *oikos* and the polis. Alke, despite her identities as woman, enslaved, and non-Athenian, becomes firmly located in Euktemon's *oikos*. She inhabits a place of significance to the social organization of Athens and becomes part of an important social network in possession of ritual agency.

DISRUPTING THE HOUSEHOLD

Alke's ability to move from Peiraieus to the *astu* has been disastrous for the ideal family the speaker constructs within this speech. She is the cause of "many evils" for them, perhaps evoking the infamous Helen and the many sufferings she brought to the Greeks. The speaker offers up a vivid image of Euktemon spending time with Alke in the *sunoikia*, even taking meals with her, while his wife and daughters wait at home for him.[45] The language is forceful (6.21):

> And her settlement there [*katoikistheisa entauthoi*], jurors, was the start of many evils [*pollōn kai kakōn*]. For Euktemon, visiting regularly to collect the rent, was spending a lot of time at the *sunoikia*, and at times even ate with this woman [*meta tēs anthrōpou*], abandoning [*katalipōn*] his wife [*tēn gunaika*], his children [*tous paidas*], and the home [*oikian*] he was living in [*ōikei*]. Although his wife and sons disapproved, nevertheless he did not cease, but eventually began to live there [*ekei*] full-time, and he was reduced to such a state [*houtō dietethē*] by drugs [*hupo pharmakōn*], disease [*hupo nosou*], or some other means [*hup' allou tinos*] that he was persuaded by her [*epeisthē hup' autēs*] to enroll her elder son in their phratry under his own name.

The speaker claims that Euktemon abandoned his wife and children, referring to them as *tous paidas*, even though the children appear to be adults by this time. The intensity of *katalipōn* (abandoning), communicated by its prefix, hints at Euktemon's permanent forsaking of his legitimate family and the *oikia* (physical house) in which they lived to live instead with Alke (labeled *anthrōpos* here). His move does not represent the creation of a new *oikos*, since he cannot set up such a household with an *anthrōpos*, someone without family connections and social status.[46] But the disruption still goes to the core of the household, affecting membership in the *genos* itself. After a time Euktemon agreed to introduce to his phratry Alke's eldest son, whom the speaker has just claimed Dion fathered. Although the son Philoktemon protested, he eventually conceded. That concession presents a problem for the trial, but the speaker finesses it by claiming Euktemon threatened to marry and recognize more children as legitimate if Philoktemon did not comply (6.22).[47] In the speaker's account Alke's child became a member of their phratry and was promised a farm (6.23), as if he were a legitimate son and worthy of Athenian citizenship along with its accompanying privileges. Alke successfully disrupted the family unit with her influence. But her actions are more sinister still. By convincing Euktemon to recognize her sons as his own, she incorporated non-Athenians into his *genos*.

Alke not only manipulated Euktemon so that he would introduce her son to his phratry, disrupting the familial line; she is also presented as having plotted to take the family's wealth. The speaker describes Euktemon as under her sway (*epeisthē hup' autēs*, 6.21) to explain why he agreed to register her son in his phratry against the wishes of his son Philoktemon. The use of passive-voice forms of the verbs *diatithenai* (reduce, arrange, manage) and *peithein* (persuade) highlights how far Euktemon was under her influence. He is now subject to Alke, and the voice of the verb stresses this shift. But the speaker also accuses his current opponents of acting under her guidance and working with her when they plot to rob Euktemon of his property (6.29, 38, 55).[48] Wyse suggests "cringing before, truckling to" as possible translations for *hupopeptōkotes* in *hupopeptōkotes hoide tēi anthrōpōi*: literally, "these men here, having fallen under the power of the woman" (6.29). The verb *hupopiptein* emphasizes Alke's dominance over these men as well.[49] In league together they persuaded Euktemon to annul his will, which the speaker claims had restricted Alke's son to a single farm (6.23, 27, 29). They next convinced him to sell some of his property to hide his net worth. Athens had no official records of personal property, which was classified as visible (*phanera* or *emphanēs*) and invisible (*aphanēs*). Visible property was whatever was openly on view, such as land, whereas invisible property was just that—invisible to neighbors, fellow citizens, and, of significance here, alienated family members.[50] According to the speaker, Euktemon liquidated more than three talents' worth of his assets (in land, buildings, livestock, and enslaved persons; 6.33–34). These transactions allowed Alke and her associates to obscure the value of the estate, prevented the legitimate family (set to inherit the real property) from obtaining their full inheritance, and enriched Alke's sons, who now acquired this newly created invisible (i.e., in-cash) wealth (6.30).

In the speech Alke is an effective manipulator of Euktemon. She takes advantage of his vulnerable mental state as soon as he begins living with her.[51] The speaker attributes any reduced mental capacity to possible disease or some other cause, but he also suggests that Alke may have controlled him with *pharmaka* (drugs: 6.21). Esther Eidinow suggests the use of *pharmaka* as a marker of dangerous women. Other examples of historical women associated with *pharmaka* include a scheming wife and a *pallakē* (Antiph. 1.14–19), a healer by the name of Theoris of Lemnos (Dem. 25.79–80), and a priestess named Ninon (Dem. 19.281). Three of the women were accused of wrongdoing and punished.[52] Alke's motivation would have been Euktemon's easy manipulation. The speaker later describes how Alke and her associates exploited his old age and senility (6.29), not even relenting when he was bedridden and incapacitated with old age (6.35). Verbs relating to scheming (*epibouleuein* and *kataskeuazein*, 6.35, 38, 61) characterize their relations with him, and it is clear from the use of language like *sunepitithentai* (they join in attacking) and *meta tēs Alkēs . . . sunepibou-leusas* (having plotted together with Alke) that Androkles and the other opponents united with Alke in conspiring to obtain Euktemon's property (6.29, 55).[53] The strongest condemnation of her comes at section 48, where she is described as "the one who destroyed [*hē diaphtheirasa*] Euktemon's reason and gained control [*enkratēs genomenē*] of much of his property." In other words, the speaker presents Alke as the ringleader and main threat to Euktemon and his family. *Enkratēs* (in possession of authority), commonly expected of men but not women, here again contrasts Alke with the female members of the legitimate family of Euktemon by masculinizing Alke and revealing the extent of her influence.

The speaker emphasizes at the start of his narrative that Euktemon was *eudaimōn* (fortunate) prior to meeting Alke.[54] He had a sizable property, children, a wife, and was well off in other respects too (6.18). He lived to the remarkable age of ninety-six, and although he was predeceased by his sons, at least one, Philoktemon, died an honorable death fighting the enemy (6.9). His wife and daughters remained to care for him, and he had two grandchildren, including a grandson, adopted by Philoktemon, who could carry on his family line.[55] They had ample wealth, since they were able to undertake liturgies, with family members having served as *triērarchos, cho-rēgos*, and *gumnasiarchos*. They counted among the three-hundred class, the richest class of Athenians (Dem. 18.171), but they did not begrudge paying the special war tax and spent their wealth for the benefit of the city, as Athenians expected, not wasting it on themselves (6.5, 38, 60–61).[56] Despite performing these costly services, Euktemon and his son Philokte-mon had continued to increase their wealth, thereby ensuring stability for their household for future generations (6.38). But this narrative suppresses the fact that Euktemon and his wife were likely divorced long ago and the children fully grown adults in households of their own by the time Alke came along. By developing this portrait of an ideal *oikos*, the speaker turns Alke's movements into transgressions despite there being nothing illegal or even unusual about keeping an alien woman as a sexual companion in one's home.

The speech stresses that Euktemon would have remained *eudaimōn* if it had not been for Alke, attributing to her the troubles that befell him in the last decades of his life. His narrative on her relationship with Euktemon begins as follows (6.18–19):

> In his old age he had major trouble [*sumphora*], which caused ruin [*elu-mēnato*] to his entire house and destroyed [*diōlese*] much of his wealth

and put him in conflict with his closest relatives [*tois oikeiotatois*]. By what cause and how these things happened, I will explain in the most concise manner I can.

The reference to *sumphora* (misfortune: 6.17, 18), elaborated to be ruin to his entire household, a loss of wealth, and ill will between himself and his *oikeiotatoi*, "his most intimates" (the immediate members of his family), affixes responsibility to Alke for the family's change in circumstance. The orator Hypereides similarly blames the *hetaira* Antigona for the downfall of a household in the deme Cholleidai (*Ath.* 3).[57] The verb choices, *lumainesthai* (ruin) and *diollunai* (destroy utterly), highlight the scale of the family's misfortune. As indeed the speaker observes, Euktemon's troubles were not small (6.18). The net worth of his property was greatly reduced (6.38), and his once-idyllic family was torn apart after he became involved with the *anthrōpos* Alke, an alien without family connections and an enslaved sex laborer. It is the speaker's portrayal of a once-ideal *oikos* and its decline that establishes Alke's movements and locations as transgressive and produces anxiety concerning her and those like her among the jurors. The narrative constructs Alke as out of place, and her presence has troubling outcomes, including a serious loss of wealth for an Athenian *oikos* and the displacement of its members.

DESTABILIZING THE POLIS

Alke's actions are not limited to Euktemon's household, however, but have consequences for the entire polis, since as a member of Euktemon's phratry her son is now eligible for membership in a deme, and thus full status as an Athenian citizen. Alke disrupts the entire citizen body, not just Euktemon's *oikos*, when she convinces him to recognize her son as his own. The fate of Euktemon's household, as the speaker frames it, should be a concern for the entire citizen body. It is within this context that the speaker narrates a final incident involving Alke. He begins the account with an open attack on her (6.47–48):

> And she, who destroyed [*hē diaphtheirasa*] Euktemon's reason and gained control [*enkratēs*] of much of his property, so abuses her position [*hubrizei*] with the help of these men that she is disdainful [*kataphronei*] not only of the members of Euktemon's household [*oikeōn*] but also of all

the city. After you have heard just one example you will easily recognize her disregard for law [tēs ekeinēs paranomian].

As the speaker notes, Alke's association with Euktemon has had damaging results for Euktemon and his household, but her refusal to accept her lot and her disdain for him and his family also spills over to the city. Her depletion of his property reduces the liturgical capability of the household as well as its ability to contribute resources to the polis in times of emergency. Her behavior also puts the polis at risk. The speaker accuses Alke of having attended a festival for citizen wives, the Thesmophoria, despite not being eligible to participate given her status and her scandalous past (cf. [Dem.] 59.73). He alleges that she took part in the procession as well as the sacrifice in honor of the two goddesses, Demeter and Persephone, and viewed the secret rites. Once again the language is forceful and conveys Alke's arrogance and sense of privilege (6.49–50):

> The mother of these boys, although being enslaved [ousa doulē] and having always lived scandalously [hapanta ton chronon aischrōs biousa], who should not have passed into the sacred precinct [eisō tou hierou] or viewed any of the sacred items within, during the sacrifice to these two goddesses [Demeter and Persephone] dared [etolmēsa] to join in the religious procession [tēn pompēn], enter the sacred area [eis to hieron], and see what she was not permitted to see.

The speaker labels Alke doulē here.[58] It is the only time he refers to her with this term in his entire speech, more commonly preferring the designation anthrōpos. But by highlighting her enslaved status the speaker is able to escalate her transgression for his audience: a sex slave disregarded the law and joined in a sacred procession and a ritual restricted to free Athenian women.

Alke's offense was serious, since the Thesmophoria ensured the success of the polis by promoting fertility for the land and among individual households.[59] The festival likely took place on the Pnyx (Ar. Thesm. 655–658),[60] a hill southwest of the Agora and west of the Akropolis and the location of the regular Assembly of citizen males.[61] Once a year, Athenian women took over this meeting place with their festival. They celebrated over a three-day period with a procession, fasting, sacrifices, feasting, and drinking. The women appear to have lived on the Pnyx for the duration. The focus on fertility, including human reproduction, the breeding of livestock, and the regeneration of crops, made the festival essential to the survival of the polis. Alke's attendance at the Thesmophoria violates a key religious festival, since in addition to the performance of secret rites, unlike other festivals, only legitimately married Athenian women were permitted to take part. Their participation marked their status as citizen wives.[62] Alke's involvement usurps such status and represents an intrusion into an intimate ritual space of the *astu* from which noncitizens were normally barred.

The speaker includes her intrusion at the Thesmophoria, which is not related to the immediate issue at hand, for its emotional and psychological impact. Because participation was limited to *astai* who were also wives and mothers, Alke's involvement is a desecration and hints at not only her usurpation of female citizenship but also her audacious disregard for law and, by extension, the polis itself. As well as highlighting her daring and transgressive nature, her placement within this ritual space threatens the well-being of the Athenian community. Not honoring the requirements of the ritual or performing it as required by law could result in catastrophe for an individual household and even the entire polis. According to the speaker, her offense led to the *Boulē* passing a series of decrees (6.50).[63] Although the speaker requests that a document be read out to the court, he does not discuss the particulars of any decree, but he strongly suggests that Alke violated sacred law and thus risked offending the goddesses by her presence. Although the speaker's main interest is her effect on his friend's household, he uses this episode to strengthen the connection between the *oikos* and the polis, *genos*, and *dēmos*. It is only through Alke's connection to Euktemon and his household that any transgressions against the polis and *dēmos* become possible for her. The narrative exposes the fragility of these important institutions, since Alke does not simply occupy these places but also seemingly performs important social roles and rituals connected with these social spaces.

DANGEROUS CREATURES

While Alke's role as a sex laborer is fundamental to the identity ascribed to her, the speaker avoids labeling Alke either *pornē* or *hetaira*.[64] Without such labels, she is not affixed to a particular type of space, as the *pornē* is to the streets and the *porneion* (brothel), the wife and *pallakē* are to the *oikos*, and even the *hetaira* is to the *sumposion* (drinking party).[65] This choice contrasts with other ancient authors, who typically prefer such terminology. Instead, the speaker refers to her as *anthrōpos* throughout, stressing her enslaved status and her lack of local kin ties (hence emphasizing her non-Athenian status). Her identity as a sex laborer embodies enslaved, alien, and female. This intersection of status, ethnicity, and gender increases the perception of her as a threatening figure, especially within the context of the *oikos*.[66] The role of the other within the household and through it to other social spaces was a definite cause for apprehension, since citizenship depended on membership in a household. The speaker's narrative on Alke provided much for the jurors to think about in this regard. She appears to have been living with Euktemon like a citizen wife and even claiming that status through the performance of ritual.[67] Her influence in the *oikos* resulted in Euktemon's desire to have her son legitimized. Her power over Euktemon also led him to liquidate much of his property. According to the speaker, Euktemon appears no longer in control of his *oikos* at the end of his life. Instead, he suggests it is Alke who has power over the wealth and membership of his household. Her intimacy with Euktemon affected the stability of his *oikos* and by extension of the polis, since Alke had at least one of her sons recognized as a citizen and performed important religious rituals, despite her enslaved and alien status.

The carefully constructed narrative exploits a series of social anxieties common to other texts: concern about the influence of women within the household more generally; angst surrounding the role women play in determining membership in the *genos*, phratry, deme, and polis; and unease regarding the relationship between sex laborers and the household. The speaker not only exploits unease by characterizing Alke as truly an outsider (to both the *oikos* and the polis) but also builds on apprehension concerning the influence of women more generally, as we observed for Lysias 4. Archaic and Classical Greek literature displays a mistrust of women's motives and loyalties within the household. Aischylos' Klytaimnestra (*Ag.*) and Euripides' Medea (*Med.*) are extreme examples of this wariness. But even Homer's Penelope (*Od.*) had to be tested by Odysseus upon his return. Semonides' bee woman, who is presented as the ideal wife, also requires vigilance to ensure she remains trustworthy (Semon. 7). As discussed in chapter 1, evidence of female influence was a valid reason for annulling a will (Dem. 46.14).[68] This law reveals an underlying bias in society more broadly against heeding women. In this trial, the speaker suggests that Euktemon was mentally incapacitated and subject to the influence of a woman when he disposed of his property before his death. Alke, of course, is not just any woman but is and was an enslaved sex laborer and foreigner, and as she is such, the speaker focuses social anxiety about female influence within the *oikos* on the sex laborer rather than the wife. In her role as a sexual companion, she has the potential to develop intimate relationships with clients and as a result has the opportunity to manipulate such paying lovers and by extension their households. Alke's status as a sex laborer also enabled her movements around the city, from Peiraieus to the Kerameikos, creating the spatial volatility that enabled her entrance into the *oikos* and from there into the *astu*.[69]

Concern about the effect of such women on household wealth is a common theme of comedy (e.g., Ar. *Wasps* 1352–1359) and appears in several other court orations. In another speech of Isaios', the speaker comments on young men bringing financial ruin on themselves through infatuation with *hetairai* (Isai. 3.17). Demosthenes lists *hetairai* among Apollodoros' extravagances: he wastes money freeing such women, wears fancy clothes, goes about with a retinue of slaves, and has a decadent lifestyle (Dem. 36.44–45). The speaker in pseudo-Demosthenes 48, also discussed in chapter 1, claims that his opponent, Olympiodoros, has wasted the family wealth by freeing a sex laborer. He now keeps her in expensive clothes and jewels while his sister and niece live in poverty, deprived of capital that should rightfully be theirs ([Dem.] 48.53–55). Olympiodoros is bewitched and deranged through his association with this woman, and this association, like Euktemon's, disrupts the legitimate distribution of wealth. The speaker argues that the woman is driving Olympiodoros to act as he does and thus is ruining the family. The very same verb, *lumainesthai* (ruin), is used to describe her effect on the family unit. In other words, he suggests that the sexual companion has significant influence over Olympiodoros in his use of wealth.[70] Anxiety in Isaios 6, however, goes beyond the sex laborer as a drain on household finances as in these other examples. Euktemon may be wasting money on Alke, but what the speaker emphasizes is her attempt to control the wealth of his *oikos*. He argues that it was only after Alke became intimately involved with Euktemon that his troubles started. Alke was not a threat when she was enslaved and in the brothel, but once unbounded by that space she was able to penetrate Euktemon's *oikos*, disrupt its composition, and deplete its wealth. From there, she gained citizenship status for her son and attempted to usurp the privileges of *astai*, legitimate female members of the polis and *astu*. The complex reality of familial configurations in Classical Athens and the lack of documentation identifying legitimate family members enabled the speaker to arouse suspicion about Alke and her relationship to the surviving sons.[71]

In this narrative, general unease about women focuses on the sex laborer. The wife and daughters, in contrast, are productive members of the household and thus play an important role in the *oikos* (and the polis) and *can*

IN THE *OIKOS*

be trusted.[72] In contrast to earlier texts that frequently present wives and daughters as the weak link, here they become a line of defense against the corruption and contamination of the household. They offer continuity, are central to the family unit, and maintain important family and polis rituals. The typical blame discourse lobbed against such women in Archaic and earlier Classical texts is absent, replaced by a discourse of risk centered on the sex laborer.[73] Once Alke moved out of the brothel, she became troubling because of her lack of a *kurios* (male guardian) who could control and contain her. Even when associated with Euktemon she is portrayed as outside the bounds of his authority. In such circumstances, cultural stereotypes associated with the female nature, like being untrustworthy, manipulative, and deficient in self-control, have free rein. The speaker presents Alke as dangerous and threatening on three levels: to individuals, to households, and to the polis. Anxieties centering on the threat that enslaved persons, aliens, and women pose to the democracy come together in the identity of the sex laborer within Alke's story, given her association with all three groups.

CONCLUSION

Isaios 6 shares a number of similarities with Lysias 4. As discussed in chapter 1, the portrait of Alke draws on a comic stereotype of the sex laborer and borrows from its plotlines. As Brenda Griffith-Williams comments, "it is possible that Isaios deliberately shaped his story to meet the theatregoers' expectations."[74] Key components of Alke's portrayal, as with the unnamed *anthrōpos* of Lysias 4, are her possession of agency and her influence over her partner. Even if the specific facts of the two women's lives may be fictions, both speeches offer a rare glimpse into the possible lives of marginal women in the Athenian household and polis. The types of disputes are very different, as were the courts in which they were heard, but the incorporation of sex laborers in the narratives alters how the disputes played out by focusing the judges' or jurors' attention on these women instead of on the issue at hand. They become smoke screens that obscure the facts of the case while other concerns are brought to the fore. But the differences are also noteworthy. The speaker of Isaios 6 presents a detailed narrative of Alke's life and her relationship with Euktemon, an inclusion the popular courts allowed. He downplays the role of Euktemon in the familial dispute and instead portrays him and his household as victims of her plotting. The portrait of Alke does not test Euktemon's worth as a citizen even though it denigrates the speaker's opponents for their involvement with her. Rather than questioning Euktemon's relationship with Alke, the speaker relies on his audience's sympathy for the old man and directs any negative emotion against Alke and her associates. These differences allow for the emergence and development of more complex themes, including the place of sexual companions in Athenian households and the limitations on identifying legitimate members of an *oikos*.

Alke's mobility as a sex laborer makes her a dangerous and troubling figure and exposes the vulnerabilities of the *oikos* and polis. Her transgressions are social as well as spatial, with her social mobility a direct result of her spatial instability. By highlighting spatial instability, the speaker questions the place and role of sexual companions, and by extension enslaved persons, non-Athenians, and even women, in the household. It is reasonable for Athenians to have access to the sex market, yet the speaker's narrative on Alke arouses anxiety about the sex laborer's access to the more intimate spaces of the polis (the *astu* and *oikos*) by focusing on the outcomes of her association with Euktemon and his *oikos*. There was not likely to be consensus among his audience on the appropriate conduct for such relationships, but many would have been anxious about the potential longlasting effects of such women on households and the city.

The speaker increases the anxiety surrounding Alke by normalizing an ideal household as a particular type of place where one physically lives with an Athenian woman and children. It is only by constructing such an *oikos* that Alke gets marked as transgressive and thus dangerous. But by plotting her movements around the city and locating her in a variety of physical spaces and social networks, the speaker also destabilizes concepts of family and household and marks the relationship of the *genos* to the polis as troubling. The seeming facility with which Alke moved around the polis develops unease about women, enslaved persons, and non-Athenians more generally and marks their presence in many spaces as troubling. Although such women were a regular presence in Athenian households, the female sexual companion presented risks to the polis more generally on account of this association with the *oikos* and exposed the weaknesses behind the conferring of Athenian citizenship. At the same time, the narrative shows the importance of citizen women to Athenian households and the polis, a theme more thoroughly explored in the next chapter.

THREE

PART OF THE FAMILY

THIS NEXT SPEECH, pseudo-Demosthenes ([Dem.]) 59, *Against Neaira*, was likely delivered between 343 and 340 BCE.[1] It differs from the other speeches examined so far in that it is definitely part of a *graphē*, a public suit, and has two speakers: Theomnestos brought forward the charge, the *graphē xenias* (for being an alien: i.e., posing as a citizen), and delivered the *prooimion*, but Apollodoros, his brother-in-law, presented the narrative and arguments, as well as the closing remarks. Together they accuse Stephanos of having set up a household with an alien woman (Neaira) and of having given an alien woman (Phano) in marriage to a citizen as if she were Stephanos' legitimate daughter. The penalties for both were severe, since a child could be invested with the privileges of citizenship only if it was the issue of a marriage between citizens. According to the speakers, Stephanos has sidestepped the laws and has made noncitizens into citizens. If the jurors agree, Stephanos will be required to pay a fine of one thousand drachmas, a significant amount of money ([Dem.] 59.16–17). But he will lose much more: Neaira will be sold into slavery, and the legitimacy of his children (three sons and one daughter) could possibly be challenged. Since he twice married Phano to Athenian citizens as his legitimate daughter, if she is proven an alien, Stephanos will be stripped of his citizenship and have all his property confiscated ([Dem.] 59.52).[2] Successful prosecution in a *graphē xenias* had the potential to wipe out his entire *oikos*.

As a public prosecution, in contrast to the private trial behind Isaios 6 and possibly Lysias 4, any male citizen could launch a *graphē*, since such lawsuits were brought on behalf of the community.[3] That being the case, the defendant if convicted was guilty of crimes against the citizen body and polis rather than against another citizen or *oikos*. Although Theomnestos justifies the launching of the suit on account of an enduring animosity with Stephanos that put his extended family at risk, the speech of Apollodoros avoids any mention of himself or his own household. Instead, the trial against Neaira focuses on her status and relationship to the larger social group and its institutions, including marriage and cult, and not her impact on an individual *oikos*, as was the focus of the narrative on Alke in Isaios 6. Whereas citizenship and its performance were simply hinted at in Isaios 6, especially with Alke's attendance at the Thesmophoria, they dominate Apollodoros' speech. His speech also introduces a new topos: the body. In this chapter I expand the discussion of the previous chapters to explore how Apollodoros uses the identity of a sex laborer to exploit anxieties around female citizenship, the performance of ritual, and sexuality.

CITIZEN RIVALRY

The trial is the result of a long-standing dispute between Stephanos and Apollodoros. Theomnestos specifies the cause of their hostility in his opening and puts the blame on Stephanos, who launched a series of lawsuits against Apollodoros. He first disputed a decree that Apollodoros put before the Assembly relating to the use of surplus funds and won a judgment ([Dem.] 59.4–5). He then suggested a fine of fifteen talents as penalty that, according to the speaker, Apollodoros would have been unable to pay (59.6). As a debtor to the state, his family would have been thrown into poverty (59.7–8). The jurors appear to have taken pity on the household and decided on a fine of one talent instead. Stephanos also brought Apollodoros before the Palladion on a charge of having murdered a freedwoman (59.9–10).[4] But in this instance he was unsuccessful in securing a conviction. Theomnestos brings the current prosecution forward as revenge for these actions (59.1, 11–12), but he makes clear that the interests of the polis are served in the event of a favorable verdict, since that outcome will ensure that citizen privilege remains intact (59.13). Although he would not be in court if his family had not suffered so, it is to the benefit of every citizen that he now finds himself as the accuser in this public trial.

The dispute is between men, since Theomnestos emphasizes that it is Stephanos who has done them wrong (59.1), but the focus shifts to women as in Lysias 4 and Isaios 6. The life of Neaira and the marriages of Phano dominate the narrative and the argument of the speech. Theomnestos, in fact, names Neaira in his opening sentence as the one indicted. It was not possible for Neaira to be the one to answer the charges, since regardless of their status women were not speakers in a court of law. Instead, it was regularly a *prostatēs* (protector) or *kurios* (guardian) who faced and responded to any charge relating to a woman under his protection.[5] In this case, the *graphē xenias* applies to citizen men just as much as to alien women, since they too suffer a penalty in any conviction, as outlined above. Apollodoros chooses to put the focus on Neaira, but it will be Stephanos who will answer to these charges of *xenia* (59.118–120). He also chooses to focus on sexual labor in his narrative with Neaira and even Phano as the daughter of a sex laborer. He uses such status to confirm them as *xenai* (alien women) and mark their marriages as illegal but also to brand the women dangerous.

FAMILY TIES

Theomnestos introduces his speech with important references to family and marriage. Although he has brought forward the *graphē* alone, he stresses the collective suffering of his family at the hands of Stephanos: "for we were being gravely wronged by Stephanos, and we were being placed in extreme danger by him." The "we" is immediately defined as including his brother-in-law, his sister, and his wife (59.1) but grows to include all his nieces (59.13; cf. 7). His brother-in-law is Apollodoros son of Pasion, who will soon take over the prosecution speech. He is married to Theomnestos' sister, and their daughter is Theomnestos' wife (59.2). The family connections between the two speakers could not be more intertwined and intimate; they are *oikeioi* (59.2, 13), but the emphasis is clearly on their legitimate status. Theomnestos introduces their marriage alliances with a discussion of Apollodoros' family history and how Apollodoros came to be a citizen.[6] He was not born an Athenian but was granted citizenship along with his father, Pasion, an ex-slave (although this fact is suppressed in the narrative), as a gift of the people. In agreement with this *dōrea dēmou* (gift of the *dēmos*), as Theomnestos characterizes it, Theomnestos' father offered Apollodoros his daughter in marriage (59.2). Apollodoros, in return, treated the entire family well, as is indicated by the choice of *chrēstos* (upright, good)—a word connected to *chrēsimos* (useful, deserving)—to describe him, and surely a nod to the benefits of his earned citizenship and status in the community.[7] As Theomnestos tells it, Apollodoros offered his own daughter to him because of this quality and his desire that they all should prosper together.

Pasion's grant of citizenship and the legitimate marriages of Apollodoros and Theomnestos outlined in the opening provide an important framework for the larger speech and argument.[8] These opening details are particularly significant, since they contrast with Neaira, who stands accused of wrongfully usurping citizen privilege in her relationship with Stephanos.

Stephanos, in turn, is portrayed as granting citizenship himself without the consent of the people by living with her (an ex-slave like Pasion and Apollodoros himself) and recognizing her children as his own. This family offends the gods in its violation of citizenship law and mockery of legitimate marriage (59.13). Stephanos' activities also threaten legitimate households, like Theomnestos'. Stephanos was not satisfied with obtaining a conviction against Apollodoros with a *graphē paranomōn* (prosecution for proposing an unconstitutional law); he even attempted to ruin his entire family with the sentencing. According to Theomnestos, Stephanos urged the court to fine Apollodoros fifteen talents for his action when his estate was worth at most three (59.6–7).[9] Levying such a fine would have pushed Apollodoros and Theomnestos into extreme need and poverty (59.6). Apollodoros would not have been able to pay the fine, and the result would have been his disenfranchisement, with no marital prospects for his children (59.8).[10] It would have brought shame and misfortune (59.11) and an end to both their *oikoi*. Theomnestos recounts how Apollodoros was brought to the brink of ruin (59.9) and marks Stephanos with violent vocabulary like *anairein* (destroy: 59.9), *epibouleuein* (plot against: 59.11), and *aphairein* (deprive: 59.13). Apollodoros and his family, by contrast, are associated with active and passive verbs denoting their victimization: *paschein* (suffer: 59.1, 12), *adikeisthai* (be wronged: 59.11), and *anarpazesthai* (be ruined: 59.8).

Theomnestos' discussion of the sufferings that he and his extended family endured does not simply bespeak a desire for the jurors' pity and sympathy but is a justification for the trial as well as his revenge (59.13):

> And just as this Stephanos here tried to snatch my family members [*tous oikeious*] from me despite the laws and your decrees, thus I have come forward to prove to you that [Stephanos] is living with an alien woman against the laws [*xenēi men gunaiki sunoikounta para ton nomon*], has introduced the children of others [*allotrious de paidas*] to the members of his phratry and deme, and has given in marriage the daughters of *hetairai* as if they were his own [*hōs hautou ousas*]; and having committed impiety against the gods, he has taken away the authority of the *dēmos* to grant citizenship to whomever it wishes.

This statement, coming near the end of his introduction, cements the contrast between the two households: the first a legitimate *oikos* almost brought down, and the second a fraudulent one usurping Athenian privileges and threatening the privileges of others. It points, furthermore, to important themes in the upcoming speech of Apollodoros—marriage, family, citizenship, and even piety—while emphasizing the reciprocal relationship between them. With the reference to *hetairai*, it is also the first mention of sexual labor, which plays a central role in Apollodoros' narrative and arguments. The first *oikos* is in fact two households, as it includes Theomnestos, his wife (who is also his niece), his sister (wife of Apollodoros), Apollodoros (his brother-in-law), and another niece (Apollodoros' daughter). It appears that Apollodoros has no sons, and that lack may explain the close relationship with Theomnestos: his wife may, in future, be an *epiklēros* (female heir), or Apollodoros may be intending to adopt Theomnestos.[11] The second *oikos* includes Stephanos, Neaira (sexual companion, live-in partner, or wife), Phano (the daughter), two living sons, and one son deceased. Both Theomnestos and Apollodoros identify the children as the children of Neaira, but only the daughter, Phano, plays a role in the narrative.

Theomnestos establishes the legitimacy of his own household and Apollodoros', leaving it to Apollodoros to demonstrate the fraudulent nature of Stephanos' *oikos*. After a reading of the law on *xenia* and its summation, Apollodoros begins with a narrative of Neaira's life. It starts long before she meets Stephanos in a brothel in Corinth: Neaira was one of seven *paidiskai* purchased by a freedwoman by the name of Nikarete and put to work in the sex trade throughout Greece (59.18). Nikarete pretended that her girls were her daughters (59.19) and claimed that they were free rather than enslaved. Neaira, it turns out, has a history of posing as family and usurping status when no such legitimacy was merited. But why does Apollodoros have to reach back so far into the past? As Cynthia Patterson observes, Neaira was probably in her fifties at the time of the trial and had likely been living with Stephanos in quietude (and obscurity) for twenty or so years.[12] If she was currently known to any jurors, it was likely in connection with Stephanos' household and not as a sex laborer from Corinth as Apollodoros claims. Indeed, Rebecca Kennedy has recently argued that she may have been a working girl but a different sort of one. Perhaps she was a freedwoman who looked after Stephanos' household and even took care of his children growing up in the absence of a wife and mother.[13] Perhaps she was a long-standing sexual companion of Stephanos, as Apollodoros intimates Stephanos will claim. Or perhaps she was indeed his legal and legitimate wife. The uncertainty surrounding her story and her relationship to Stephanos' household remains in place at the end of the speech.[14]

Phano's story is easier to parse. Although Apollodoros identifies her as the daughter of Neaira, he provides no evidence or witness testimony to confirm such status.[15] She was, instead, likely a legitimate daughter of Stephanos.[16] Apollodoros mentions a dowry of thirty minas (59.51–52) and agrees that she twice married citizens as a legitimate daughter (59.50, 72). A second marriage was not unusual for Athenian women, who would be expected to remarry after divorce or widowhood if still of marriageable age. Further evidence of her Athenian status was that in her first marriage she had borne a son to one Phrastor, who then enrolled the son in his phratry (59.59–60). Phano also had a prominent position in Athenian cult, performing important rites at the Anthesteria (59.74–78) in her role as *Basilinna*, a public office open only to citizen women. These are the facts that remain intact once one strips away Apollodoros' charges. It is curious that Apollodoros says so little about the sons, even though he claims they were also children of Neaira. They were fully grown by the time of the trial and had been recognized as citizens in their phratry and registered in the deme of Eroiadai.[17] The proofs of their legitimacy would not have been so easily stripped away, since males, unlike girls, were regularly recognized publicly by official bodies in multiple phases of their lives.[18] We do not know how Stephanos narrated his own family history and thus recounted events to the jurors, since only the account of Apollodoros is extant. Nor do we know whether Theomnestos and Apollodoros secured a conviction and were thus convincing in their representation of Stephanos' marriage and *oikos* as unlawful.

THE LIFE OF A SEX LABORER

Apollodoros attempts to prove that Neaira is a *xenē* by showing that she was enslaved in the sex trade. It is the main argument that he uses against her. He begins by calling her a *paidiskē* (young sex slave: 59.18), the same term used of Alke (Isai. 6.19), and tells his audience that a freedwoman by the name of Nikarete had purchased her for this purpose. Neaira was one of seven girls whom Nikarete acquired. Apollodoros claims that Nikarete trained her girls skillfully (*paideusai empeirōs*). The verb chosen, *paideuein*, is used of the education of children more generally and suggests the girls learned specialized skills like music and dance as part of their training and thus catered to a more elite clientele. Nikarete is presented as skilled at her profession, eventually making a profit from Neaira by selling her for the mighty sum of thirty minas (59.29). Neaira's original purchase price is not offered, but the orator Hypereides names another sex trafficker, Antigona, who purchased a *paidiskē* for three hundred drachmas (*Ath.* 2).[19] Antigona is described as the most successful *hetaira* of her day before turning to trafficking (*Ath.* 3), and it may be that Nikarete is also assumed to have begun her career in the sex trade as a trafficked woman.

Neaira's story has a similar trajectory to the story of Alke discussed in chapter 2 and is as gripping as anything found in the Athenian theater. Cynthia Patterson remarks that it begins "like the plot of New Comedy and continues with numerous dramatic twists and turns as well."[20] In a reversal of the comic plot, however, in which a sex laborer turns out to be wrongfully enslaved and able to legitimately marry, Neaira is exposed as masquerading as a wife and playing the role of a citizen despite being a "sex slave." What is noteworthy about her story is her progression from enslaved sex laborer to so-called citizen wife (59.18–49). She began her career in Corinth as a young enslaved girl under Nikarete. She associated with the rich and famous of Greece: actors, poets, wealthy metics, and elite citizens.[21] After some years Nikarete sold her for a profit to two young men, who kept her as their personal sex slave. They eventually allowed Neaira to buy her freedom from them (for twenty minas) on condition that she never work again in Corinth.[22] The alternative was to sell her back to a *pornoboskos* (sex trafficker: 59.30). An Athenian by the name of Phrynion used his own wealth and contributions collected from her other former clients to purchase her freedom in a third-party transaction.[23] She returned with him to Athens but soon moved to Megara to shed herself of his abuse. In Megara she met another Athenian, Stephanos, who enabled her return to Athens, where he acted as her *prostatēs* (protector).[24] Phrynion found out and immediately claimed Neaira as his runaway slave. Stephanos intervened, however, and after arbitration, Neaira was declared *autē hautēs kuria* (guardian of her own person: 59.46).[25] The settlement required that she split her time between Phrynion and Stephanos. Eventually, however, Phrynion disappeared. Neaira had been permanently living with Stephanos in his *oikos* with children for some time (possibly over twenty years) before the present charge was brought forward.[26]

Although Neaira belongs to Nikarete and works in her brothel along with other girls, she is most commonly associated with the private homes of clients and the *sumposion* (symposium), the all-male drinking party in which men gathered to drink wine and enjoy themselves. It was an occasion of leisure, and women, as flute players, dancers, and sex laborers, were commonly part of the entertainment. Symposia took place in private houses in the *andrōn*, frequently a specialized room with an off-center door separated from the rest of the home by an antechamber. Despite the domestic location, wives did not attend such events. Symposiasts reclined on couches, played games, and drank wine out of *kulikes* (drinking cups). A

FIGURE 3.1. *Red-figure cup by the Brygos Painter, 490–480 BCE. British Museum. 1848,0619.7. Drawing by Tina Ross. Accessed via britishmuseum.org.*

dinner often preceded the drinking (Xen. *Symp.* 2.1; Pl. *Symp.* 176a). Neaira accompanied Nikarete to such parties from a very young age. She is described as wining and dining like a *hetaira* at the house of Ktesippos during the Greater Panathenaia in the company of visitors to the city (59.24). She is also part of the *sumposion* at the home of the Athenian Chabrias to celebrate his victory in the chariot race at the Pythian Games (59.33).[27] Apollodoros includes her presence at such parties in his speech to reinforce her status as a *hetaira* and enslaved. Claude Calame argues that "the distinguishing mark of a *hetaira* of classical Athens was that she took part in banquets for men."[28] As another speaker tells it, "married women do not go with their husbands to dinners and do not consider dining with strangers" (Isai. 3.14). Neaira's presence at the *sumposion* is central to her identity not just because it contrasts her with wives but also because many Athenians would have experienced such parties or at the very least would have been familiar with its entertainments and the women found there.[29] Drinking ware from the fifth century BCE depict such women sharing couches with the symposiasts, reclining and drinking alongside the men at such events (fig. 3.1). The close quarters meant the women were available for fondling and other intimate activities with the symposiasts. Neaira's presence in such places calls into question any status associated with her living in Stephanos' *oikos*.

Although Apollodoros claims she is like a *hetaira* (*hōs hetaira ousa*, 59.24, 25, 28, 37, 48, 49) in her habits and the places she frequents, Neaira's portrayal differs from characterizations of such women in other texts. Instead of being associated with gift exchange and working to obscure her exact relations with men, so important to James Davidson's definition of the *hetaira*,[30] and as we saw in the case of Xenophon's Theodote in the introduction, Apollodoros highlights early on exactly what Neaira's role as a sex laborer entailed (59.20):

> I will prove to you that this Neaira here was owned by Nikarete [*Nika-retēs ēn*] and worked with her body [*kai ērgazeto tōi sōmati*] for pay [*mistharnousa*] and was available to anyone who wanted [*tois boulomenois*] to have sex with her [*autēi plēsiazein*].

This statement is filled with important vocabulary that Apollodoros returns to throughout his narrative. All the traits that the *hetaira* normally aims to conceal are openly on display. She has an enslaved background: she was enslaved to Nikarete (also 59.18, 23, 108, 118) as well as others and at various points is called a *doulē* (59.29, 85). She works with her body (also 59.22, 36, 49, 108) and is paid for her services (also 59.23, 26, 108). No mystery surrounds her transactions. Her paid encounters are for the purpose of sex. Her body is bought and sold for pleasure like every other sex laborer's. Despite outlining a wealthy clientele for her, Apollodoros' emphasis is on Neaira's open accessibility. She is indiscriminately available to all who want her (*tois boulomenois*). Kate Gilhuly remarks on how the language of her availability echoes democratic law and an active citizen in the democracy.[31] Theomnestos and Apollodoros use forms of *boulesthai* (be willing) to indicate the right of all Athenians to vote on the use of an administrative surplus (59.4), to determine citizenship (59.13, 88), to bring forward a public suit (59.16, 90), to acknowledge the right of citizens, whether as individuals or as jurors, in enacting justice (59.12, 86, 88; cf. 80), and to recognize the supreme authority of the *dēmos* (59.88). The specific phrase *ho boulomenos* is not unique to this text. "Whoever wishes" seems to have been a formulaic phrase of the democracy, indicating citizen privilege and engagement (Aischin. 1.23; 3.220).[32] The use of *hoi boulomenoi* to describe Neaira's paying lovers equally appears to suggest Neaira is a privilege available to each citizen to use as he chooses.[33] Such availability contrasts not only with the exclusive *hetaira* but with the female citizen, sexual access to whom was restricted to her current or future husband. Indeed, there were severe penalties for having sexual relations with another citizen's wife, daughter, or sister (59.66).[34]

Two episodes in the narrative stand out for modern readers and likely did for the Athenian jurors as well, though for different reasons. In the first instance, Apollodoros comments on the age at which Neaira began working as a sex laborer. Nikarete had brought her to Athens with Metaneira during the Eleusinian Mysteries (59.22):

> And this Neaira here accompanied them, since she was already working with her body [*ergazomenē men ēdē tōi sōmati*], despite being quite young [*neōtera*] not yet having reached sexual maturity [*dia to mēpō tēn hēlikian autēi pareinai*].

Apollodoros provides the jurors with surprising detail about her age. His choice of vocabulary is particularly significant. *Neōtera*, which I have translated as "quite young" and Murray translated as "young as she was," Kapparis as "still too young," Bers as "not yet fully grown," and Carey as "though she was too young," suggests a minor.[35] Its meaning is heightened by the qualification *dia to mēpō tēn hēlikian autēi pareinai* (literally "on account of her not yet having reached sexual maturity"). *Hēlikia* is a hard term to translate, given that it refers to an appropriate stage of life based on one's age. For Athenian females it would indicate an appropriate age for marriage and reflect their (present or soon to come) fertility.[36] Citizen women, at least among the elite, were normally married by age fifteen or as young as twelve.[37] Based on these descriptors, Apollodoros suggests that Neaira was much younger, likely prepubescent. I suggest Neaira could have been any age between seven and eleven.[38] This realization is shocking to the modern reader, who recognizes that Neaira was not responsible for working at such a young age. It was instead Nikarete's decision and at her discretion. The Athenians had some laws about sex with minors and trafficking minors (Aischin. 1.13–15), but such laws relate to free individuals, and Apollodoros has stressed from the beginning that Neaira was enslaved. Regardless of her exact age, the use of *hēlikia* seems intended to shock the jurors. It suggests that there was something unnatural about Neaira given that she was working in the sex industry at such a young age. With these details, Apollodoros presents Neaira as having not just the body, but also the nature of a sex laborer and so expressly suited to her profession.

Apollodoros' description of Neaira with Phrynion is another point in the narrative that some scholars read sympathetically.[39] But once again we may be applying modern values when extracting such a reading. Why would Apollodoros want to elicit sympathy for Neaira, whom he wants the jurors to condemn? Although he describes Phrynion as extravagant and depraved (and infamous for it; 59.30), his portrayal mirrors Neaira's since the same descriptive language, *polutelēs* (59.36) and *aselgēs* (59.114), is gradually applied to her. Her time with him in Athens is key to her portrait and worth quoting in full here (59.33–34):

> Coming back here with her, he used her lewdly [*aselgōs*] and with reck-lessness [*propetōs*]. He took her all over [*pantachoi*] with him, to din-ners, wherever he was drinking; he always partied hard [*ekōmaze*] with her, and openly had sex [*sunēn*] with her everywhere [*pantachou*] when-ever he wanted [*hopote boulētheiē*], making a public display of his sexual license to onlookers. He went to many different homes with her to party, even the home of Chabrias of Aixone when he took first at the Pythian Games in the archonship of Socratidas with the four-horse chariot that he had bought from the sons of Mitys the Argive, and returning from Delphi he held a victory celebration at Kolias. And many there had sex with her in her drunken state [*polloi sungignonto autēi methuousēi*] while Phrynion was asleep—even Chabrias' slaves [*hoi diakonoi*] who had served up the meal.

Phrynion makes such a show of his sexual access to Neaira that, as Rosanna Omitowoju observes, even the enslaved attendants are comfortable to have sex with her at a drinking party without fear of punishment.[40] What to modern sensibilities is an extreme case of sexual violence is offered as fur-ther support that she was readily available for sex with everyone.[41] Anyone of any status is allowed to penetrate (and has penetrated) her body. There is no critique of those assaulting her.[42] Apollodoros intends to raise the dis-gust of the audience toward her with this example.[43] The added detail that she was drunk reinforces what little control she has over her own body.[44] At this point (and at the actual trial) Neaira is no longer enslaved in the sex trade, but Apollodoros continually reminds the audience of her past work as a sex laborer and stresses her status as enslaved in order to arouse hostility at her usurpation of citizen privilege. To Apollodoros, the sugges-tion of violence is unproblematic (it appears hardly noticed, in fact) and its presence simply reinforces the accessibility of her body and her identity as a sexual commodity.[45] It also highlights her insatiability, as Christopher Carey stresses, since in this instance others have sex with her for free.[46] The anecdote once again suggests her natural fit to this profession.

LIKE MOTHER, LIKE DAUGHTER

Phano's story, in contrast, is more discreet. She is not directly labeled a *paidiskē* or *hetaira*, but status as a sex laborer is alluded to through her association with Neaira. Apollodoros creates suspicion about Phano as soon as he introduces her (59.50):

> This Neaira here's daughter, whom she brought with her to his home as a small child and whom at that time they were calling Strybele, but now they call Phano....

As he does with Neaira, Apollodoros employs the direct use of her name, Phano, to suggest a familiarity or notoriety that adds to suspicion about her character since Athenian women were rarely referred to by their forename.[47] The reference to a name change from Strybele to Phano also hints at dubious status, since it alludes to the practice of providing nicknames for *hetairai*.[48] At the same time the name Phano suggests a tactic to cover up her past status by connecting her linguistically to Stephanos.[49] According to Apollodoros, she came to Athens with Neaira from Megara and so was not a daughter of Stephanos but was masquerading as one. He is careful not to refer to her with the patronymic "the daughter of Stephanos." She is instead "the daughter of Neaira" or even more glaringly "the daughter of that Neaira" to emphasize her lack of social legitimacy. Her nomenclature echoes Neaira's own upbringing as a daughter of Nikarete (59.18–19). The connection to Neaira, in the context of Apollodoros' narrative, marks her as the daughter of a *hetaira*, and Theomnestos' opening statement that Stephanos was illegally giving daughters of *hetairai* in marriage to citizens becomes a clear reference to Phano (59.13). The same accusation of being the daughter of a *hetaira* is used against a woman named Phile in a speech by Isaios to discredit her eligibility as an *epiklēros* (female heir). The speaker of this speech regularly refers to her as *ex hetairas* (from a *hetaira*) and depends on the mother's portrait to discredit the daughter's character.[50] Here again the mother is associated with the *sumposion* as well as general revelry not appropriate to wives (Isai. 3.11–14).

An emphasis on matrilineage was a topos of sexual labor, with daughters suspected of sexual profligacy or even carrying on the profession of their mothers.[51] Apollodoros encourages his audience to compare Phano's character and lifestyle with Neaira's directly as the passage continues (59.50–51):[52]

Stephanos gave her in marriage to an Athenian husband, Phrastor of Aigilia, as if she were his own daughter, and gave a dowry of thirty minas with her. But when she came to the home of Phrastor, who was a hard-working man and had carefully scraped together his livelihood, she did not learn to adapt to Phrastor's ways but longed for the habits of her mother and the degeneracy of her household [*ezētei ta tēs mētros ethē kai tēn par' autēi akolasian*] since, I believe, she had been raised in such indulgence [*en toiautēi . . . exousiai*]. And Phrastor, seeing that she was neither modest [*oute kosmian ousan*] nor wanted to obey him, and at the same time having learned without doubt that she was not the daughter of Stephanos but of Neaira, . . . divorced the woman [*tēn anthrōpon*].

Although this dowered marriage to an Athenian citizen affirms Phano's status, Apollodoros manipulates his narrative to stress her similarities to Neaira and obscure the reasons behind the divorce. Curiously, Phano's dowry is the exact amount paid by Timanoridas and Eukrates for the exclusive use of Neaira (59.29). She has the same habits and even lifestyle as her mother. Apollodoros claims that Phano longed for the dissolute lifestyle of her mother's house. The term *akolasia*, which Konstantinos Kapparis translates as "loose morals," suggests the potential for sexual misconduct in particular.[53] Apollodoros also alludes to the lavishness of Phano by contrasting her with her husband, whom he describes as frugal, and describes her as not respecting his manner of living as an Athenian wife should. He comments that she was unruly for him and not *kosmia*, as was expected of Athenian women. The female relatives of another speaker, in contrast, behave so moderately (*kosmiōs*) that they even avoid being seen by their own male relatives (Lys. 3.6), and Apollodoros may be using the same term to hint that Phano was flirtatious.[54] Although she is not accused of any impropriety here, the potential for it lurks.

Apollodoros also implies that Phano was practicing her mother's trade. He claims that Stephanos caught a man from Andros named Epainetos having sex with Phano and proceeded to blackmail him as a *moichos* (adulterer). He attempted to extract thirty minas from him (59.65), again the same amount paid for Neaira (59.29). Epainetos, however, threatened to indict Stephanos for wrongful confinement (59.66). He argued that his association with Phano was not *moicheia*. He had been invited into the house, and Neaira knew about his relations with the daughter. While there he paid them a lot of money and supported the household (59.67), just like some of Neaira's clients had done when she was working under Nikarete (59.29).

Epainetos is clear about what was going on: "this place, the house of Stephanos [*tēn Stephanou oikian*], was a brothel [*ergastērion*]; this was their business [*tēn ergasian tautēn*], and they were very well off [*autous euporein malista*] from it." According to Apollodoros he supported his innocence by producing a law that forbid accusations of adultery in such cases (59.67).[55] Although the dispute was resolved without an indictment, Apollodoros states emphatically that "this Stephanos, aware that he would be exposed as pimping [*pornoboskōn*] and being a sycophant, agreed to arbitration" (59.68).[56] Apollodoros manipulates what was probably a legitimate case of adultery to suggest that Stephanos and Neaira were actively trafficking Phano for sex.

Phano's narrative is circumspect, but sexual labor still casts a shadow over her life and status. Apollodoros associates her with Neaira to connect her to the sex trade and being foreign, thus rendering her two marriages illegal. In turn, her illegal marriages become further proof of Neaira's illegitimate status, since only the daughter of an *astē* (female citizen) could marry another citizen.

COME FROM AWAY

Apollodoros' narrative stresses that Neaira and Phano come to Athens from elsewhere. Neaira's story begins as a *paidiskē* in Corinth. She first visits Athens at the expense of the wealthy metic Lysias, who houses her along with Nikarete and Metaneira at the house of an Athenian friend, Philostratos of Kolonai. They came for the Eleusinian Mysteries, but Neaira is there to work (59.21–22). She later returns with Simos of Thessaly for the Greater Panathenaia and joins him at symposia. They lodge at the house of another Athenian, Ktesippos of Kydantidai (59.24). An influx of visitors, including itinerant sex laborers, would have been common (and expected) at festival time. But residency in the city soon follows. After Neaira gains her freedom, she moves to Athens with Phrynion, who takes her everywhere with him, to drinking parties and dinners, as his *hetaira* (59.33). She soon leaves Phrynion and moves to Megara, where she continues in the sex trade (59.35–36). Her next entrance into the city is with the Athenian Stephanos. This time, however, there is a narrative shift: she takes up residence in his *oikos* and comes as a *gunē* (wife) with three children, whom Stephanos promises to enroll in his phratry (59.38–39).[57] Apollodoros offers no actual proof of the last two statements and instead reports them as an intimate conversation between Stephanos and Neaira that some jurors might

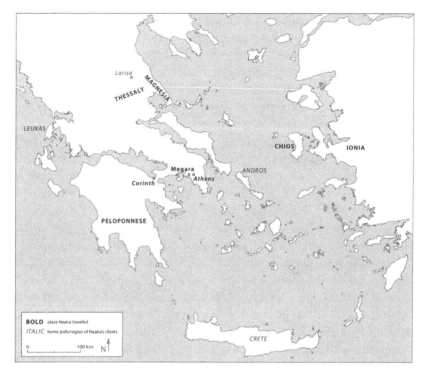

FIGURE 3.2. *Map of Neaira's travels and client base. Prepared by Tina Ross.*

see through, but the back-and-forth between Corinth, Megara, and Athens as a sex laborer establishes her alien status and raises a red flag regarding her relationship to Stephanos' household, where she has been living for years.

Neaira's presence in Stephanos' household is troubling because she has traveled all over Greece. Apollodoros focuses on her movement when he asks, "Where has she not gone for her daily wage?" and responds that she has worked her way around the entire world (59.108). Athens is not her hometown. But neither is Corinth, Megara, or any of the many other towns that Apollodoros moves her through. These are merely places where she stops to work. This fact contrasts with legitimate wives, whom Perikles' citizenship law required to be *astai*, from the *astu*, the local area.[58] They are affixed to place, specifically Athens and Attika. Their immobility provides a contrast to Neaira.[59] Whereas the wives, daughters, and mothers of the jurors are found at home (59.110), Neaira is found everywhere. Her work required her to progress through the Greek landscape, including the Peloponnese, Thessaly, Magnesia, Chios, and Ionia (59.108; fig. 3.2). Christopher Carey is skeptical about her ability to have traveled to all these places, although Konstantinos Kapparis suggests it may have been possible.[60] It is not important to Apollodoros to show that she worked at these various locations. By mentioning such regions near the climax of his speech, Apollodoros emphasizes her motion. Like Alke in chapter 2, Neaira is mobile, but on an entirely different scale, because it is the city she infiltrates, not simply a single *oikos*. Her mobility emphasizes her lack of place and in turn her enslaved status, since enslaved persons have no claim to any home.[61] Her connection to places like Thessaly and Ionia establishes her as exotic and foreign. It is not simply her dislocation that Apollodoros hopes to stress in this way, but these named locations also seem specifically chosen. Their very geographies help shape her identity.[62]

Apollodoros begins his narrative in Corinth with Neaira working for Nikarete, and Corinth is the location most commonly mentioned for her.[63] He states that she worked openly in Corinth, where she was *lampra*, "a celebrity" (as Christopher Carey appropriately translates the term; 59.26).[64] Her association with Corinth in her capacity as a *hetaira* is repeated three more times (59.30, 32, 36). Placing Neaira's past in Corinth marks her, since Corinth was renowned in antiquity for its sexual commerce. It was the home city of Laïs, a *megalomisthos*, a high-earning sex laborer in the fifth century BCE. According to the geographer Strabo the city was famous for its sanctuary to Aphrodite, which had over a thousand *hierodouloi* (sacred slaves) working as *hetairai* at the temple (8.6.20).[65] The symposiast Ulpian in the *Deipnosophists* claims that such women were dedicated to Aphrodite's temple to pray for the salvation of Greece during the Persian Wars (Ath. 13.573c–574a). Archaeological evidence for such a temple remains elusive, but the city's association with sexual labor more generally is well attested. Pindar suggests that Corinth's association with the sex industry goes back at least as far as the Late Archaic and Early Classical periods (Fr. 122 SM).[66] According to Kate Gilhuly, the Athenians in particular associated Corinth and Corinthians with the sex trade.[67] To them, it was not simply one business of many, as in other cities, but its primary business. Aristophanes makes references to sex laborers at Corinth in his play *Wealth* (149–152). Another comic playwright, Alexis, claims that sex laborers were so important in Corinth that they celebrated their own festival in honor of Aphrodite (Ath. 13.574b–c, 389K). Corinth's association with the sex trade was in fact so strong that the place name itself became a linguistic marker of sexual commerce. Philetairos (Fr. 1 *PCG*) and Poliochos (Fr. 5 *PCG*) both have plays entitled *Korinthiastēs*, commonly translated "whoremonger," "pimp." *Korinthia korē* (girl of Corinth) indicated a woman who was trained in pleasing a man sexually (Pl. *Resp.* 3.404d). The verb *korinthiazein* (act like a Corinthian) meant either *hetairein* (be a *hetaira*) or *mastropeuein* (be a pimp), depending on the context (Hesychius; *korinthiazomai* in Ar. Fr. 354K).[68] Isthmias, a nickname for a female sex laborer, was derived from the geographic location of the city and was the name of one of Neaira's supposed contemporaries ([Dem.] 59.19; Philetairos Fr. 9 *PCG*). Corinth as a place of sex slaves and sex trafficking was embedded in the Athenian imagination. Its position at the crossroads of commerce between Italy and Asia and the Peloponnese and mainland Greece recalled to Athenians the accessibility and promiscuity of a sex laborer's body itself.

Megara, by way of which Neaira and Phano come to Athens (59.35–38), was considered another hotbed for the sex industry, with famous *hetairai* coming from this city as well.[69] Like Corinth, this city was well known for its sex trafficking: Jeffery Henderson comments that "pandering was an especially 'Megarian' calling."[70] The comic poet Kallias identifies a class of sex laborers known as *Megarikai sphinges*, "sex slaves of Megara" (Fr. 28 *PCG*), highlighting their large number.[71] In Aristophanes' *Acharnians*, a Megarian wants to sell his piglets, but actually his daughters in disguise, to the comic hero Dikaiopolis (729–817). He puns on *choiros*, "piglet," also a term for prepubescent female genitals, and calls himself a *choiropōlēs*, "pig dealer" (818).[72] He tells Dikaiopolis that they are excellent offerings to Aphrodite and will develop into fine *kusthos* (an obscene term for women's genitals: 782, 789). The references to "skewered on the spit" (*ton odelon ampeparmenon*, 796) and their love of chickpeas (*erebinthous*, 801) and figs (*ischadas*, 802), both evocative of the male genitals, further suggest sexual play.[73] The common association of Megara with sex trafficking makes the passage entertaining and provides a context for these double entendres as well as the use of the obscenity *kusthos*: Dikaiopolis is purchasing sex, not simply food, from the Megarian, who is acting as a pimp here. Neaira's located history in both Megara and Corinth develops a geographical identity that reflects her promiscuity, affirms her involvement in the sex trade, and identifies her as foreign.

BRINGING IT BACK HOME

If in the end Apollodoros is unable to convince the jurors that Neaira and Phano were sex laborers and thus alien, he has at least shown that they are not fit to be Athenian wives. And according to Apollodoros, the women of Athens would agree. At the end of his speech he invokes the wives of the jurors with a glimpse into the reception jurors will receive upon returning home (59.110–111):

> And what should each one of you say when you go home to your own wife, or daughter, or mother, after having acquitted her, when she asks you, "Where were you?" You respond, "We were in court," at which she will immediately ask, "Concerning whom?" It is clear that you will say, "Neaira" (Will you not?), "that although being an alien, she is unlawfully setting up a household with a citizen [*xenē ousa astōi sunoikei para ton nomon*] and that she has given her daughter, although caught with a *moichos* [*memoicheumenēn*], to Theogenes, the King Archon, and this same one has carried out the sacred rites on behalf of the city and was given to Dionysos as a wife," and describing other details concerning the charges against her ... upon having heard [these] they will ask, "And what did you do?" and you yourselves will say, "We acquitted her." Thereupon the most virtuous of women will be furious with you [*sōphronestatai tōn gunaikōn orgisthēsontai humin*], since you judged this one [*tautēn*] worthy to share equally with them [*autais*] in the privileges of the city and its sacred rites [*metechein tōn tēs poleōs kai tōn hierōn*].

The passage transports the listeners into their very own homes. It begins with one woman (a wife, daughter, or mother) asking the questions and ends (nightmarishly) with the juror confronted by a group of women together— presumably all his female kin or perhaps even the collective female citizenry.[74] According to Apollodoros, they would be angry at Neaira's position in Stephanos' *oikos* and her daughter's ritual role. It is interesting that he credits Neaira with Phano's marriage to Theogenes here, when legally it would be the father who contracted such alliances. But it puts the focus on Neaira and perhaps speaks to the fact that women may have understood themselves to play a part in the marriages of their daughters. It is another of the many privileges that they might consider Neaira has stolen from them. It is not simply that Neaira and Phano inhabit a citizen household; they also play the part of citizen wives. They perform social and ritual roles restricted to female citizens that in fact define female citizenship, but also female responsibilities as citizens and thus as recognized members of the polis.[75] The singular accusative at the end of the passage (*tautēn*) positions Neaira as the main impostor, despite not detailing the sacred activity that she performed. Apollodoros instead appears to conflate Phano's offenses with Neaira's own, constructing what Cynthia Patterson and Barbara Goff refer to as "a fictional two-headed monster" "of sexual *and* ritual depravity."[76]

In conjuring their female kin in this way, Apollodoros puts a spotlight on female citizenship. He suggests that, like male citizens, women had obligations associated with their status as Athenians, and he describes these as a share in the affairs of the polis as well as religious matters. Barbara Goff reads this passage as confirmation that female ritual roles equate to male political roles. Athenian women "are depicted as having a stake in the exclusivity of the city and in the claims of citizens against the incursions of non-citizens, which they articulate on the grounds of 'public ceremonials and religious rites.'"[77] Josine Blok has argued more strongly that all public roles, including the performance of ritual, were key to both male and female citizenship. The verb *metechein* (share) is central to the Athenian concept of citizenship.[78] Pseudo-Aristotle uses it when he defines citizen privilege as a share in the *politeia* (*Ath. Pol.* 42.1). The same verb is found in Demosthenes 57, a speech challenging the decision of a deme to disqualify a member from citizenship. In addition to his descent from *astoi* (57.17, 46) and his rightful share in inheritance (57.46), the litigant affirms his citizen status by his share in both *hiera* (sacred rites) and *koina* (common affairs: 57.26, 54). Apollodoros uses this same verb in reference to the privileges of male citizens (59.28) and the privileges granted the Plataians (59.92). His conception of female citizenship is very specific.[79] He comments that women share in *tōn tēs poleōs kai tōn hierōn* (the things of the polis as well as religious matters) to indicate an obligation to the city and its sacred rites. He is particular in distinguishing polis and *hiera*. It is not immediately clear what *tōn tēs poleōs* refers to, since Athenian women did not participate in the Assembly, courts, and administrative offices, but *hiera* is again a focus. Ritual participation is key to female citizenship in other speeches and includes serving in cultic offices, like overseeing the Thesmophoria (Isai. 8.19–20). Kate Gilhuly separates out the cultic roles from the role of wife in her provocative analysis of this speech, but Apollodoros in fact presents the two as integral.[80] As with Alke, Neaira and Phano's usurpation of the ritual roles of female citizens is possible only through their social position in an Athenian *oikos*.

By describing the women with the superlative *sōphronestatai* (most virtuous), Apollodoros differentiates citizen women from Neaira and her daughter in their very natures and reputations. He suggests that *gunē* indicates not only status but also particular qualities. *Sōphrosunē* as the primary virtue of women goes back to the Archaic period. Helen North considers the full range of meanings for the term, including moderation, good household management, sexual loyalty, and obedience.[81] Literary and funerary uses of the concept in the Classical period show that Athenians valued demonstrations of *sōphrosunē* by women and considered it an important virtue for them to emulate.[82] Apollodoros exploits the jurors' familiarity and expectation with this ideal when developing portraits of Neaira and Phano by making the concept of *sōphrosunē* an important marker of *astai*, the Athenian wives, daughters, and mothers evoked in the passage.[83] Throughout the speech, verbs indicating sexual relationships with women, both within and outside the bonds of marriage, abound: *gamein* (marry), *sunoikein* (live with), *ekdidonai* (give in marriage), and *echein gunaika* (take a wife) to refer to legal marriage versus *plēsiazein* (have sex with), *chrēsthai* (use, enjoy), *sungignesthai* (join with), *suneinai* (be with), and *porneuein* (have sex for money) for relationships with Neaira and Phano.[84] Such sexual terminology is crucial to Apollodoros' portraits of women and in the distinctions he draws between them. This vocabulary highlights the importance of sexual behavior to the concept of *sōphrosunē* and citizenship in this speech.

Apollodoros' discussion of the laws governing *moicheia*, which at first appears to be an unnecessary digression, reinforces this connection and links sexual virtue with the maintenance of legitimate status and privilege (59.86):[85]

> But the laws [*hoi nomoi*] forbid only those women [*tais gunaixi*] with whom a *moichos* was caught from entering the public temples [*eis ta hiera ta dēmotelē*]. But if she ever enters and disobeys the law, she is to endure whatever punishment anyone wants to inflict except death, and the law granted anyone happening upon her the right of punishing her for her violations. Because of this, the law allowed that she suffer the worst maltreatment [*hubristheisan*], except death, with no recourse to justice [*mēdamou labein dikēn*], in order that pollution [*miasmata*] and impiety [*asebēmata*] not occur in the temples and to instill suitable fear in women [*tais gunaixi*] to be *sōphrones* [*tou sōphronein*] and do no wrong but behave appropriately in the home [*dikaiōs oikourein*], teaching that, if she does any such wrong, all at once she will be cast out of her husband's household [*ek te tēs oikias tou andros*] and the city's temples [*ek tōn hierōn tōn tēs poleōs*].

The passage punctuates the end of the narrative on Phano. I agree with Konstantinos Kapparis that it confuses and diffuses Apollodoros' argument about her exact status, since only sex with *astai* constituted adultery, but I note that it benefits his argument besides by highlighting the importance of female *sōphrosunē* not just to personal relationships and households but also to the temples and thus the city more broadly.[86] It demonstrates connections not only between *oikos* and polis in ritual but also between women's sexual and ritual roles. Not only is the female adulterer no longer a member of her husband's household, banished from his home; she is no longer allowed to attend public festivals as a spectator or to perform a ritual role in civic cult. The stress on temples as belonging to the city, like the house in the case of the husband, suggests her complete banishment from the polis more generally. With a lapse in sexual virtue a woman loses all the privileges and responsibilities that she has as an Athenian citizen. It is equivalent to banning a male citizen from the Assembly and lawcourts, a female kind of *atimia*.[87] Status as *astē*, it turns out, is worth less than sexual virtue.

Apollodoros plays with feminine ideals to construct sexual virtue as an important civic value for women and thus a further requirement of female citizenship beyond simple birth and marriage to a citizen. The jurors' familiarity with *sōphrosunē* and their expectation that citizen women be *sōphrones* provide a context for the interpretation of the speakers' accusations against Neaira and Phano and for the judgment of their status. This contrast that Apollodoros has been developing for his audience is laid bare in its final usage, in his concluding remarks to the jurors (59.114):

> And so let each one of you consider that you are casting your vote on behalf of your wife [*huper gunaikos*], on behalf of your daughter [*huper thugatros*], on behalf of your mother [*huper mētros*], on behalf of the city, the laws, and our sacred rites [*huper tēs poleōs kai tōn nomōn kai tōn hierōn*], lest these women be shown to be held in equal regard with this sex slave [*tautēi tēi pornēi*], or lest women who have been raised with much fine virtue [*meta pollēs kai kalēs sōphrosunēs*] and care by their relatives and have been betrothed according to the laws [*ekdotheisas kata tous nomous*] be shown to share in equal rights [*en tōi isōi phainesthai metechousas*] with one who has often each day joined with many men [*pollakis pollois hekastēs hēmeras sungegenēmenēi*] and in many offensive ways [*pollōn kai aselgōn tropōn*], as each man desired [*hōs hekastos ēbouleto*].

This passage is the only instance of *pornē* in the text in direct reference to Neaira.[88] The term *pornē* (like its masculine equivalent, *pornos*) is rare in Attic oratory. It appears only seven times in the corpus, always in lawcourt speeches, and only when the orator is attempting to arouse the *odium* and *indignatio* of his audience.[89] It highlights both Neaira's formerly enslaved status and her sexual commodification, and emphasizes the speaker's contempt for her, contempt that he wishes to transfer to the jurors also. It is

83

in strong contrast to his use of the terms *gunē, thugatēr,* and *mētēr,* none of which Apollodoros employs as descriptors for Neaira in his text. Apollodoros also opposes "having been lawfully betrothed" (*ekdotheisas kata tous nomous*) with "often having joined with many men each day" (*pollakis pollois hekastēs hēmeras sungegenēmenēi*). The switch from a passive to a middle participle stresses their difference even more, since Apollodoros could have chosen a verb that emphasized Neaira's role as a trafficked commodity, as he does with Phano. Finally, he contrasts sexual virtue (*meta pollēs kai kalēs sōphrosunēs*) with sexual profligacy (*meta pollōn kai aselgōn tropōn*) in order to highlight Neaira's sexual promiscuity and degeneracy in her role as a sex laborer.[90] All such tactics employed by Apollodoros stress as sexual disparities the differences between Neaira and the women associated with the jurors. Once again a form of *metechein* appears (share in equal rights: *en tōi isōi . . . metechousas*). In addition to marking out citizen women's special status, it stresses Neaira's wrongful assimilation to them.

LOOKING TO THE POLIS

Apollodoros' focus on ritual as the enactment of female citizen status and privilege dissolves the boundaries between household and city. His detailed account of the impiety of Neaira's daughter, Phano, in performing the role of *Basilinna* at the Anthesteria is pivotal to his overall argument. This three-day feast was a wine festival to celebrate the beginning of spring. It honored Dionysos and marked the readiness of the wine from the previous harvest.[91] The *Archōn Basileus,* the "King Archon," who oversaw all cultic ritual for the polis, played an important role during the Anthesteria, with his wife as *Basilinna* performing part of the ritual on the second day of the festival.[92] In addition to sacrifices, the *Basilinna* oversaw the oath taken by the *Gerairai* (venerable women) upon their appointment to office. The oath suggests the women oversaw sacrifices at two other festivals in honor of Dionysos, the Theoinia and the Iobakcheia (59.78).[93] The *Basilinna* also underwent a ritual marriage to the god Dionysos.[94] The marriage took place in the Boukoleion, located in the Agora not far from the Prytaneion, and thus in a central part of the city. It may have been proceeded by a "marriage" procession from another sanctuary, the Limnaion, the location of which is now unknown. The *Basilinna* performed the ritual on behalf of the entire polis and became the city's link to the god to ensure its prosperity and the god's favor. The *Basilinna* was thus an important civic role for citizen women under the democracy, who were all eligible to serve

84

in this ceremonial position, given that the *Archōn Basileus* was decided by lot, a fact noted by Apollodoros (59.75).[95]

Stephanos married Phano to Theogenes while the latter was serving as the *Basileus*, and this meant that Phano became the *Basilinna* at the Anthesteria that year. Apollodoros spends time commenting on the rites, described as *hagia* (holy) and *semna* (solemn: 59.77, 78), in order to point out the sacrilege resulting from Phano's position in this role. He emphasizes how the Athenians passed a law requiring the *gunē* (wife) of the *Basileus* to be not only *astē*, but also faithful to her husband as well as a *parthenos* (a pubescent girl inexperienced in sex) when she married him (59.75). Apollodoros has made clear that Phano's status and behavior are in direct contrast to these requirements: Phano is not Athenian but the daughter of Neaira (whom he claims is a sex laborer), she was previously married to Phrastor, and she was the object of an adulterous relationship with the *xenos* Epainetos (59.72). His emphasis is Phano's character as much as it is her alien status. He claims that after the festival the Areopagus investigated who Theogenes' wife was, and to avoid being charged with impiety himself, Theogenes claimed that he had been unaware of Phano's actual status and immediately divorced her to prove it (59.80–83).

The use of a plural perfective participle of *asebein* (*ēsebēkotes*, "having committed impiety": 59.77) to punctuate Phano's wrongful performance of the rites suggests collective responsibility and implicates Neaira (and also Stephanos) in her actions.[96] Theomnestos referenced Neaira's impiety (59.12) and Stephanos' impiety in his opening (59.13), and Apollodoros directly refers to Neaira's impious behavior toward the gods throughout his speech (59.44, 107, 109, 117). The discussion of the Anthesteria becomes evidence of the impious acts for which Apollodoros argues Stephanos and Neaira both deserve punishment (59.74). Phano's religious crime is in fact their crime. Near the end of his speech Apollodoros goes one step further and conflates Phano and Neaira in this episode. He asks the jurors to punish Neaira for her impiety against Dionysos and adds Phano only in the second reference (59.117): "Will you not punish this Neaira here for having committed impiety against the same god and the laws, both the woman herself and her daughter?" In the case of Phano and Neaira in particular, their identities intertwine in the accusation of *asebeia*. The episode adds a divine dimension to the trial and highlights the importance of the case to the well-being of the entire city.[97] If the jurors do not punish Neaira, her impiety will become their crime (59.109).

Apollodoros reinforces the severity of the case with the mention of an actual charge of impiety against a hierophant at Eleusis, one Archias

(59.116–117).[98] In addition to other charges, Archias sacrificed a victim on the sacred hearth during the Haloa, a day when sacrifices were not permitted.[99] Moreover, such sacrifices were to be performed by the priestess, not the hierophant. Archias was charged, convicted of impiety, and punished (59.117).[100] An important detail, according to Apollodoros, was that the sacrificial victim had been an offering on behalf of the *hetaira* Sinope (59.116). Yet it was Archias who paid the penalty, despite his position and the pleas of his family. Apollodoros' closing comment on the case, "You punished him because he was reputed to have done wrong [*doxanta adikein*]" (59.117), replaces *asebein* with *adikein*, obscuring what his crime was and hinting that he was wrongfully punished. As highlighted by Esther Eidinow, the sacrilege happened at Sinope's request and thus through her influence. The mention of another *hetaira* in connection with impiety surely resonated with the jurors and added support to Apollodoros' argument against Neaira. The stories of Sinope, Phano, and Neaira expose the threat to the city posed by such women, who easily traverse civic and ritual boundaries without punishment.[101] It also warns the jurors about the consequences when impious women are not punished: someone else (or the city) may pay the penalty for them.

Over the course of his speech, Apollodoros has slyly brought the charges around to impiety. His closing remarks highlight a shift from the laws (59.115) to the gods (59.126):

> On the one hand, fellow judges, seeking vengeance both on behalf of the gods, whom they have treated with such irreverence [*ēsebēkasin*], and then on behalf of myself, I have placed these individuals on trial and submitted them for your vote. And you must, considering that the gods against whom they have transgressed [*paranenomēkasin*] will take note of how each of you votes, vote for justice [*ta dikaia*] and punish them foremost on behalf of the gods and then on behalf of yourselves, and having done so you will appear to everyone to have judged this public trial well and justly [*doxete pasi kalōs kai dikaiōs dikasai tēn graphēn*], in which I indicted Neaira for living in marriage with a citizen although being an alien [*xenēn ousan astōi sunoikein*].

Although there was a public prosecution in such cases, the *graphē asebeias*, Apollodoros preferred the *graphē xenias* for this trial. Still, the focus on *asebeia* was well chosen. The Athenians prosecuted a number of women on such charges of impiety in well-known cases, including Aspasia, the companion of Perikles (Plut. *Per.* 32), and the sex laborer Phryne (Plut.

Mor. 849e; Ath. 13.590d–e, 591e).[102] Both were acquitted, likely in no small part because of their involvement with elite Athenian males (Perikles and Hypereides). Demosthenes mentions two other trials with the expectation that they will be familiar to his audience: those of Ninon (Dem. 19.281; scholia 495A, 495B [Dilts]) and of Theoris (Dem. 25.79–80).[103] These latter women were found guilty and suffered the death penalty as punishment. In the case of Theoris, her entire family was executed along with her. In three of the examples sexuality and impious actions are again connected: Aspasia and Phryne worked in the sex industry, and Ninon supposedly administered love potions to young boys.[104] Aside from Aspasia's, these trials occurred in the mid-fourth century BCE. Although the dates are uncertain, it is possible that even Phryne's trial occurred before Neaira's.[105] They suggest a deep-rooted anxiety about women's activities and their impact on the polis. It is possible that Apollodoros' mention of *asebeia* in relation to Neaira would trigger the jurors' memories of such trials and even anger them further that certain types of women (*hetairai*, for instance) perform ritual roles unlawfully and yet escape punishment.[106]

A DISCOURSE OF RISK

Theomnestos and Apollodoros both present Neaira's usurpation of privilege as a threat to the social fabric by characterizing her, in her relationships to the city, its laws, and its gods, as *hubrizousa* (haughty), *kataphronousa* (disdainful), and *asebousa* (impious).[107] By having established a faux household with Stephanos, Neaira treats the polis with contempt (*hubrizousa*, 59.12, 107); but by overstepping social boundaries, she also commits an outrage (another sense of *hubrizein*) against the city and its citizens every time she acts on behalf of Stephanos' *oikos*.[108] Through membership in Stephanos' household, Neaira automatically gains access to civic cult and obtains citizenship for any children. But her position as a wife in the polis is *para tous nomous* (illegal: 59.13).[109] Based on Apollodoros' speech, Neaira's identity as a former slave and an alien establish her as a threatening figure whose actions destabilize Athenian *oikoi* and the polis. It is her identity as a sex laborer, however, that makes her dangerous, since it has enabled her to travel between cities and infiltrate citizen households.

Neaira's disregard for law and her treatment of the gods puts the polis at grave risk. But her acquittal would in itself be a further risk, one that Apollodoros warns against. Quite simply, her acquittal will disrupt the social fabric and embolden others to do wrong because they will no longer fear punishment (59.77): it would be fatal to the good order and stability of their polis by disrupting traditional institutions like marriage and patrilineal inheritance, and by overturning the female status quo, including important social values and hierarchies.[110] Apollodoros warns the jurors about what the lasting effects of her acquittal would be (59.111–112):

> And to the many women lacking in good sense, you clearly grant the right to do whatever they wish [*ho ti an boulōntai*], since you and the laws have granted impunity. For you will show yourselves to be neglectful and careless and to approve of [Neaira's] way of life [*tois tautēs tropois*]. So it was much better for this trial not to have happened than, with it having taken place, for you to acquit her. For there will now be license for sex slaves [*pornai*] to marry whomever they wish [*sunoikein hois an boulōntai*], and to claim that their children are the children of whomever they happen to meet. Your laws will lack authority [*akurioi*], but the lifestyle [*hoi tropoi*] of *hetairai* will gain authority [*kurioi*] [for them] to do whatever they wish [*ho ti an boulōntai*].

He argues that there will no longer be any reason for women to strive to be *sōphrones*, and men will no longer be able to identify their legitimate offspring. The *tropoi* (lifestyle) of *hetairai* will prevail instead. This passage also highlights the loss of authority of the laws and the impotence of male citizens in their control of women if sex laborers marry and have children with whomever they wish. The use of *kurioi* (authority) and its opposite, *akurioi*, evoke the authority of males over females, since Athenian women were subject to a *kurios* (male guardian) throughout their lives. In this new world order that Apollodoros conjures for the jurors, what Joseph Roisman describes as "a nightmare, topsy-turvy world" and "feminine anarchy," *hetairai* usurp that authority and overturn the institutions that depend on it.[111] The repeated use of *ho ti an boulōntai* (whatever they wish) hints at the newly gained autonomy and privilege of such women at the expense of everyone else, including the male citizens.[112]

This obtainment of citizen privileges will lead to the collapse of important social, civic, and ritual boundaries that keep the polis stable. Apollodoros cautions that many poor daughters of citizens will remain unmarried, and free women will no longer have a distinct status (59.113):

> And with the law losing its authority [*akurou genomenou*], most certainly the work of sex slaves [*pornai*] will fall to the daughters of citizens [*eis tas tōn politōn thugateras*]. On account of a lack of resources many

would not be able to be married. And the privilege of free women [*to de eleutherōn gunaikōn*] will fall to *hetairai* if they gain permission to have children in whatever manner they wish [*hōs an boulōntai*] and to participate in sacred offices, sacrifices, and honors in the city [*teletōn kai hierōn kai timōn metechein tōn en tēi polei*].

According to Apollodoros, citizen women have a special place within the institutions of the polis, indicated again by the verb *metechein* (share in; cf. 59.111). Neaira's acquittal will compromise that position. Poor women receive help from the state with their dowries, and certain roles are restricted to citizen women. But in the new social order, poor citizen girls will do the work of the lowest grade of sex laborer, and *hetairai* will perform the most important functions of free Athenian women. The importance of the female citizen will be overturned. Overlooking the place of a *hetaira* within a citizen *oikos* has consequences for all citizens, for all levels of society, and for every sphere. Neaira and her daughter do not simply put individuals at risk with their influence and actions; their influence and actions also threaten the relationships within and between *oikoi*, the polis, and the divine realm, and thus have social as well as divine consequences.

A TOUCHSTONE FOR CITIZENSHIP

Terms for female citizens, *astē* and *politis*, commonly appear in this text, highlighting female citizenship as an essential component of the argument. *Astē* is the more common term and what appears to be used in law (59.16–17). In this speech, it occurs more than any other term for women, appearing twenty times.[113] It is used in combination with *gunē* and *kata tous nomous* (according to the laws), stressing the connection between female status and legitimate marriage (59.58, 63). In her analysis of the speech, Cynthia Patterson argues for the importance of such marriages to the stability of the democratic polis, since both Theomnestos and Apollodoros stress the importance of citizenship and its fulfillment through marriage.[114] In addition to Apollodoros' own gift of citizenship, followed by his legitimate marriage as narrated by Theomnestos, the text includes a discussion of the granting of citizenship to the Plataians in the late fifth century BCE (59.94–106).[115] Apollodoros reminds the jurors of the extreme circumstances that led to the incorporation of Plataians into the Athenian populace as citizens, *politai*. It was only after generations of Plataian support, beginning with the Battle of Marathon (59.94–95) and the Plataians' loyalty to the Athenians during the Peloponnesian War (59.102), that citizenship was granted to them upon the loss of their city (59.103–106). Full citizen rights and thus full participation in the democracy, however, would be granted only to the next generation born from legitimate marriage with an Athenian *astē* (59.106).

The integration of the Plataians into the citizen body is also a tale of caution, since it was only after much careful consideration and deliberation by the *dēmos* regarding the loyal acts of the Plataians that the Athenians granted them citizenship. Each Plataian underwent a *dokimasia* (scrutiny: *dokimasthēnai en tōi dikastēriōi*, 59.105) to determine his Plataian status and to verify whether or not he was *philos* (friend) to Athens. It is no small detail that Apollodoros notes this scrutiny took place in a *dikastērion* (lawcourt: 59.105, 106). By noting this location, Apollodoros invites the jurors to scrutinize Neaira thoroughly in the same way in the current trial.[116] In short order he asks them to observe her *opsis* (physical appearance), confirming that she is present in the courtroom but also that her past is written on her person, as they carefully consider whether or not she is guilty of transgressing the laws (59.115).[117] The granting of citizenship to the Plataians and their subsequent ability to be legitimately married to *astai* highlights the importance of women to civic status. It provides an essential backdrop to Neaira's unlawful place in Stephanos' household and her resulting status in the polis, since Neaira is neither *astē* on account of ancestry nor *politis* through a grant of citizenship by the *dēmos* (59.107).[118] Her marriage to Stephanos destabilizes the concept of citizenship, disrupts the meaning of citizen privilege, and dilutes the citizen body.

Before concluding, we can now turn to the most commonly quoted passage from this speech, but with more context included (59.122).

> For living together in marriage [*to gar sunoikein*] is this: whenever a man produces children and enrolls his sons in his phratry and deme and betroths his own daughters to husbands. We have *hetairai* for the sake of pleasure [*hēdonēs heneka*], *pallakai* for the daily care of our bodies [*tēs kath' hēmeran therapeias tou sōmatos*], and wives for the lawful production of children [*tou paidopoieisthai gnēsiōs*] and to have a trustworthy guard for the things inside [*tōn endon phulaka pistēn echein*].

Since Apollodoros' speech highlights the status and position of *astai* within the polis in their role as citizens and in the determination of citizenship, he is very concerned to enforce distinctions between women. Such distinctions, he argues, are necessary for social stability. In his speech, it is lifestyle and inner qualities that arise as the most important indicators of any difference: traits that he claims are easy to uncover with an examination of women's habits and way of life. It is the use of the female body that becomes the touchstone for marriage and thus female citizenship, as he outlines for the jurors in this passage. These remarks follow Apollodoros' challenge to Stephanos to hand over Neaira's slaves for torture (Thratta, Kokkaline, Xennis, and Drosis), a practice known as *basanos* (literally, "touchstone": 59.120–121).[119] This context suggests Apollodoros' comments are also a test. Although he begins by referencing proofs of marriage as children, the enrollment of sons in a phratry, and the betrothal of daughters, the touchstone of legitimacy is how male citizens use and value female bodies: sex for pleasure, sex for companionship, sex for the production of legitimate children.[120] This breakdown is not likely meant to be prescriptive, in that a man may associate all three types of sex with his wife, or pleasure with a *pallakē*, or even regular companionship with a *hetaira*, but to highlight what defines the primary social functions of these women within the household (cf. 59.118–119).[121]

Apollodoros' remarks point to the vulnerability of the *oikos* and polis, since there was no official scrutiny of female status. Yet the polis, as discussed above, relies on legitimate marriage in its determination of status and its conferring of privilege. The *oikos*, in turn, relies on the status and trustworthiness of women to ensure its legitimacy. Scholars commonly understand *tōn endon* in the passage as material possessions and thus household economy.[122] But such readings may rely too much on Xenophon's *Oikonomikos*, in which the wife is responsible for household management of slaves and goods.[123] *Endon* is a term that can also signal female plotting and even be evocative of the location of adultery.[124] In the context of Apollodoros' speech, *tōn endon* may best be understood as the integrity and sanctity of the *oikos*, not just its material well-being. After all, all the women identified (*hetaira, pallakē,* and *gunē*) can be found within the Athenian household,[125] but the absence of a *sōphrōn gunē astē* means there is no guarantee that the household and its membership are legitimate.[126] In this way, Apollodoros evokes men's fears about the sexual loyalty of women and exploits Athenian anxiety about how to recognize *astai* (legitimate women) and legitimate marriages among them when a variety of living arrangements were in fact possible. He suggests that it is only through scrutiny of the sexual behavior of women that true loyalty and legitimacy can be uncovered. This being so, the scrutiny of women should be a concern not just for individual members of households but for the entire polis.

CONCLUSION

As discussed in chapter 1, the portrait of Neaira draws on many of the same stereotypes present in Lysias 4 and Isaios 6. Like the women in these other speeches, Neaira advances her personal interests through scheming and deception. In her case, she is accused of masquerading as Stephanos' wife and unlawfully promoting her children despite being an alien and having been enslaved. But the fact that the trial is a public one requires Apollodoros to broaden the scope of her wrongdoing to the community. His speech dissolves any boundaries between the *oikos* and the polis. Through their inclusion in Stephanos' household, Neaira and Phano are able to participate in civic institutions and enjoy the privileges of Athenian citizenship. Themes of female influence, family, and household still prevail, but the emphasis moves to marriage, citizenship, and cult. Neaira's identity as a sex laborer intersects with status, sexuality, and gender and accordingly is central to Apollodoros' discussion of female privilege and participation in the democracy.

Neaira becomes a threatening figure because she is not restricted to a particular social category or legally beholden to a male partner or other authority. She behaves as she desires without being subject to a *kurios*, the laws of a polis, or even the gods. In her role as sex laborer, she easily moves between cities and individual households, where her presence disrupts household membership and corrupts the citizen body through her offspring. Like Alke in Isaios 6, Neaira is characterized by mobility. Her ability to cross social and civic boundaries, as Esther Eidinow emphasizes, also suggests that other boundaries, like the supernatural, are open to her.[127] And this makes her even more dangerous. Apollodoros' speech, like Lysias 4 and particularly Isaios 6, exploits the sex laborer as a locus of anxiety for women's status, roles, influence, and privilege within the household and polis, exposing the fragility of these institutions vital for the well-being of Athenian democracy. The complex arrangements of Athenian households and the absence of scrutiny regarding female citizens left those institutions exposed.

Neaira's identity as a sex laborer plays a pivotal role in unmasking the vulnerabilities of important institutions to outsiders and enables Apollodoros to scrutinize female sexuality and sexual virtue while still upholding the democratic *oikos* more generally. His speech demonstrates that female citizenship included being able to marry an Athenian male, to have legitimate children who would become eligible members of the polis, and to participate in civic cult. His discussion of Neaira and her daughter becomes an exploration of the female citizen ideal. Even if the law, with few exceptions, requires a citizen to be born from a female citizen in a legitimate marriage, Apollodoros argues that such birthright is not enough for a woman simply to claim status as *astē*. A female citizen needs to embody particular qualities and perform her citizenship in a particular way.[128] Crucial to his idea of female citizenship is *sōphrosunē*, an important attribute of free women associated with the household dating back to the Archaic period. With this speech, Apollodoros develops sexual virtue along with female citizen status as essential to the democracy and polis in myriad ways, including the performance of ritual. It is through Apollodoros' exploration of the alien sex slave that the importance of female citizens and female sexuality to the democratic polis come to the fore. The focus on sexuality and *tropoi* (lifestyle) also distinguishes this speech from the previous speeches. Aischines' speech *Against Timarchos*, the topic of chapter 5, likely influenced Apollodoros' approach.

FOUR

SAME-SEX DESIRE

WHILE THE PREVIOUS chapters discussed female sex laborers in Attic oratory, the orators also tell of disputes involving male sex laborers.[1] Here again we hear of home invasions and public brawls, plus the drunken pursuit of boys.[2] The focus of this chapter is Lysias 3, *Against Simon*, a speech that, like Lysias 4 (chapter 1), focuses on a clash between two citizens over a sex laborer as part of a legal dispute, but in this case the sex laborer is male. Like the speaker of Lysias 4, the litigant of Lysias 3 defends himself in a *graphē* or *dikē traumatos ek pronoias* (intentional wounding) against the accusation that he physically attacked his opponent.[3] The extended accounts of Lysias 3 and 4 offer an opportunity to consider the intersectionality of gender, slavery, and sexual labor to be taken up in the concluding chapter. Together they expose social tensions surrounding male versus female sexual labor as well as anxiety over male desire. As seen in chapter 1, character becomes an essential element of the argument and closely connects to the development of *pathos* in the speech.[4] We sympathize with the defendant and his troubles. Yet it is also through the dramatic character portrayals in Lysias 3 that social tensions surrounding sexual labor, specifically that of male sex laborers, as well as anxieties surrounding the male body and desire take shape.

THE CHARGES AND THE DEFENSE

Likely delivered shortly after 394 BCE, Lysias 3 presents the arguments of the defense against a formal charge of *trauma ek pronoias* (intention to do physical harm).[5] This trial takes us back to the court overseen by judges drawn from the Council of the Areopagus. The speaker defends himself against the accusation that four years earlier he harmed Simon by striking him on the head with a potsherd. He focuses on *pronoia* as premeditation and attempts to prove that he did not intentionally seek out and wound his opponent.[6] As discussed in chapter 1, intention did not require premeditation, but the speaker emphasizes such forethought as an important criterion to obscure the actual charge against him. Claiming that he never planned any attack, he argues that Simon was instead plotting against him. The speaker thus presents himself as acting in self-defense against the planned attacks of his opponent and remains reticent about Simon's injuries. His speech aims to produce doubt in the judges about the facts of the case and who harmed whom. Although the accuser likely had witnesses to support his claim, the speaker deflects attention away from the facts by focusing on the nature of Simon's relationship with the boy Theodotos.[7] The relationship is essential not only to Simon's character portrayal but also to the development of *pathos* in this speech. By focusing attention on Simon's treatment of Theodotos, the speaker is able to leave Simon's actual injuries unaddressed and evade the question of the use of a weapon, the potsherd.

IN DISPUTE

The defense against a charge of intentional harm was not the only lawsuit the speaker of Lysias 3 found himself involved in. He had recently lost a case resulting from an *antidosis* (exchange of property) over the performance of a liturgy. The speaker claims that it was only when Simon heard about that ruling that he launched his own suit (3.20). He implies that Simon was using this loss to his own advantage in launching a trial at this particular time, since he is only now seeking redress for injuries sustained four years ago (3.39). According to the narrative, the men came into conflict over a young male sex laborer named Theodotos, who at the time of the trial is living with the speaker (3.33). In his defense, the speaker argues that the dispute is absurd and not worthy of the judges' attention. He also claims it is unjust, since Simon himself is the one who should be on trial (3.1). References to being wronged and to the desire for justice are common tropes in the speech.

The dispute involves three individuals: the unnamed speaker as defendant, Simon as prosecutor, and Theodotos as the sex laborer in question. The speaker suggests that he himself is a beneficial member of society and admits he aspires to appear *chrēstos* (useful), as one who is indispensable to the community (3.9).[8] He is not shy to admit that he regularly uses his wealth to perform public services in the form of liturgies (3.47). In addition to his being of the liturgical class, the wealthiest class of citizens, Stephen Todd suggests that the speaker is unmarried based on the fact that he mentions a sister and nieces living in his home but makes no mention of a wife (3.6).[9] It is not certain from the evidence, however, that he has never been married. In contrast, Simon appears younger and less wealthy than the defendant.[10] The speaker informs the judges that Simon valued his own property at two hundred and fifty drachmas (3.24), but his statement is likely consciously misleading. As argued by Todd and Christopher Carey, it is probable that Simon's net worth is higher, based on the facts not only that he is claiming a loss of three hundred drachmas for Theodotos (3.22) but also that he appears to have served as a hoplite under the taxiarch Laches (3.45).[11] The minimum net worth of a typical hoplite was normally 2,000–3,000 drachmas.[12]

Theodotos is a youth, as is indicated by the term *meirakion* used to describe him throughout. (See further on the significance of this term below.) His status, in turn, is ambiguous, since he is referred to as a Plataian upon his initial introduction to the judges (3.5). This designation suggests he is free and possibly even Athenian, since in 427 BCE the Athenians granted citizenship to a group of Plataians who had fled to Athens after their city was captured by the Spartans during the Peloponnesian War ([Dem.] 59.104–106). Citizenship extended to their descendants.[13] But at section 33 the speaker lets slip Theodotos' probable status as enslaved. He suggests that he would not have plotted to attack Simon and his thugs with just *to paidion* (the boy) to assist him, since not only would Theodotos be ineffectual in any confrontation, but he would also be liable under torture to denounce the speaker for any wrong committed.[14] The use of *basanizomenon* (under torture) indicates the enslaved status of the youth, since *basanos* (torture) was a common procedure for extracting evidence from an enslaved person to support the arguments in a case and was rarely used on free individuals.[15] Although agreeing that Theodotos works in the sex trade, scholars remain divided on whether he was a citizen, a metic (resident alien), or enslaved, with the majority assuming enslaved status.[16] According to Nick Fisher, it is not possible to ascertain his exact status based on this speech, and Stephen Todd admits that "some of the difficulties of interpretation may arise not simply because Theodotos' status could itself have been unclear, but also and precisely because Lysias could be deliberately muddling the issue."[17] I suggest that maintaining such ambiguity is in fact part of his rhetorical strategy, since it is to the speaker's advantage that the judges remain unclear as to the boy's status.

The cause of the initial disagreement appears to have been a breach of contract. Although the speaker argues against the existence of any formal agreement, it appears that Simon hired Theodotos for three hundred drachmas per *sunthēkai* (contract: 3.22).[18] The contract presumably guaranteed his exclusive sexual enjoyment of Theodotos as a live-in rent boy.[19] Christopher Carey argues that Simon's account is likely the true one, given that the speaker does not demand witnesses to any contract or repayment of money but instead relies on argument from probability in his rebuttal.[20] The terms used, *sunthēkai* (3.22) and *sumbolaion* (3.26), while indicating a formal agreement, do not require a written contract, and so Simon may not have had any documentary evidence to support his claim. A verbal contract sworn before witnesses was equally binding. Christopher Carey points out that such agreements were likely difficult to enforce, since "witnesses to its making may not always be available ... and witnesses to its breach would often be difficult to come by, unless the breach involved leaving a shared home ... or some other public action." He comments further that if Theodotos was enslaved, then the contract was not legally binding, since an enslaved person could not make such a contract, but presumably any disagreement in such a case would be taken up with the person's owner.[21] Even if Theodotos was of enslaved status, he may have had some independence in attracting clients and negotiating contracts, similar to those skilled in a craft and living apart from their owners.[22] Another speaker suggests that his opponent, Athenogenes, sent the enslaved boy he was enamored with to set the terms for his use (Hyp. *Ath.* 23–25). Whatever the arrangement with Simon, Theodotos eventually took up with the speaker (3.31). In similar fashion, Timarchos in a speech of Aischines abandons one lover for another, and the jilted party, Pittalakos, gets into a dispute culminating in a physical altercation with Timarchos and his new lover, Hegesandros (Aischin. 1.58–59). In the current case, Simon's reaction was to demand the return of Theodotos or the money he had spent. The disagreement led to a series of physical assaults. It is the head wound sustained in the last altercation that is the reason for the current charge.

The speaker reconstructs events leading up to the trial as follows. He refers to a home invasion and numerous street fights. In the prelude to the first violent confrontation, Simon went searching for Theodotos, even invading the speaker's home (3.6–7). Upon finding out where the speaker was dining, he immediately went there and called the speaker outside. As soon as the speaker appeared, Simon and his gang began to beat him (3.8–9). After the attack the speaker realized it was not safe to stay in Athens, and so he and the boy left the city for a time (3.10). The second fight broke out upon their return. In this case, Theodotos was staying next door to a house rented by Simon. On this particular afternoon, the speaker claims Simon set lookouts on the rooftop watching for Theodotos (3.11). He also filled his house with his friends, who ate and drank while waiting for the youth to appear. On an impulse, the speaker visited Theodotos at this location, and in short order they left the premises together. As soon as they stepped outside, Simon and a number of his friends, now drunk, jumped them and tried to drag the boy off (3.12).[23] The boy managed to escape, however, and the speaker then fled the scene. But Simon and his friends pursued the boy and caught up to him hiding in a fuller's shop. A fight broke out in the shop and spilled into the street, with Simon and his gang dragging the boy off (3.15–16). At this point the speaker happened upon them again and decided he had to help the boy. Another fight ensued, in which they all received injuries (3.17–18). In this version, the assault in which Simon was injured occurred after a pursuit near the house of Lampon.

Simon, in contrast, appears to claim that he was severely beaten outside his front door (3.27–28). In response, the speaker presents Simon as the aggressor and argues that he plotted to abduct Theodotos. He in turn was only trying to protect the boy and defend himself (3.11–12). He claims that he was trying to avoid any kind of conflict, and his narrative is carefully crafted to support this viewpoint.[24] The proof section stresses the speaker's unpreparedness for any fight. He claims that he was alone with Theodotos and thus without friends or slaves to aid him in a fight against Simon and his gang (3.33). The speaker likely exaggerates his innocence.[25] James Davidson argues that the speaker was probably the assailant and the one in search of Theodotos when the fight broke out. I agree that the speaker is not being totally honest in his recounting of events, but Davidson's comments that Theodotos was in fact the speaker's personal slave and living at Simon's house as a runaway have no support in the text and remain intriguing conjectures only.[26] The speaker claims many times that the boy remained with him (3.10, 31, 33), and it would have been easy for Simon to produce witnesses to support a claim that the boy was with him, but the speech nowhere indicates Simon disputed the speaker's assertion (3.28–31). Still, the speaker may have been out to provoke Simon, since upon their return to Athens he installed the boy right next door to the house Simon was renting.[27] Stephen Todd considers him a provocateur for flaunting "his conquest in his opponent's face."[28] But understandably the speaker suppresses any baiting of the opponent, given his portrayal of himself as avoiding trouble.

Despite arguing that he himself is the victim of Simon's aggressive behavior, the speaker states that he could not bring himself to denounce him, since he thought it *deinon* (incredible) to prosecute someone in court for fights over boys since the penalty was so severe (3.40, also 43, 48).[29] He questions whether the courts are the appropriate place for resolving such quarrels by playing up the comic elements of their encounters. For example, in the first attack Simon summoned the speaker outside and immediately attempted to strike him. But the speaker defended himself and managed to fend him off. Simon then moved to a safe distance and began to throw rocks at the speaker, but he missed him and instead hit Aristokritos, one of his own supporters, in the forehead (3.8). With these details the speaker presents Simon as a ridiculous figure and likely aroused laughter among the judges.[30] In the second attack, Theodotos easily escapes his initial abduction by slipping out of his cloak (3.12). After a chase, a chaotic fight ensues. The speaker highlights the disorderliness of it for the judges by labeling it a *thorubos* (tumult, confusion) and, as Christopher Carey observes, by employing a string of genitive absolutes to describe the action.[31] According to the speaker everyone, even the bystanders who came to help them, got his head bashed, not just Simon (3.18). As Carey aptly comments, "Monstrous as Simon's conduct is, there is a hint of farce about the whole situation."[32] The comic elements downplay the seriousness of the attack and question whether their dispute over the boy and their personal enmity is worthy of the council's time and consideration.[33] The chaos also broadcasts to the judges that it would be difficult to determine who harmed whom.

DESIRING CITIZENS

As is typical of Lysias' speeches, characterization plays a significant role.[34] In Lysias 3, the speaker develops his own *ēthos* (character) for the court in his opening, as is typical in forensic oratory, but admits to being in an uncomfortable situation.[35] He states that he would not be freely disclosing any facts if he had not been forced by Simon to do so (3.3). He knows he takes a risk in admitting this relationship and in placing Theodotos at the center of the dispute between Simon and himself, given the negative attitudes toward serious relations with sex laborers as evidenced in other speeches.[36] He is well aware of this bias and admits that his actions may appear *anoētoteron* (rather foolish) to the judges, especially given his age (3.4, 9, 10). He is clearly not a youth but a middle-aged man (3.4) and is expected to be in control of his emotions and desires.[37] The orator Aischines suggests Athenians considered a man over forty to be *en tēi sōphronestatēi hautou hēlikiai* (in the most temperate period of his life: 1.11). Before admitting to his desire for Theodotos, using *epithumein* (long for) in a sexual sense, the speaker claims that out of shame he is embarrassed to relate the events surrounding his dispute with Simon (3.3).[38] As Christopher Carey argues, his embarrassment likely stems from the fact that it is normally younger men who are susceptible to being overpowered by sexual desire and reduced to fighting over sex slaves.[39] His opponent likely exploited this stereotype in his prosecution speech by playing up the speaker's age to brand him ridiculous (3.31).[40] To counter this image, the speaker presents himself as a respected, modest, trustworthy citizen (3.9), a benefactor of the city (3.47), as well as a person whom his judges and any bystanders can sympathize with (3.4) and should pity (3.48). He claims he never sought out trouble with Simon or any other person, and in fact went to great effort to avoid conflict with his opponent (3.9, 13, 30, 32, 40). He comments repeatedly that he is himself the party wronged (3.3, 9, 15, 18, 20, 36, 37, 40, 47).

In speaking of his desire for Theodotos, he appeals to the judges, in this case the Councilors of the Areopagus, to look kindly upon him. He tries to downplay any focus on his age by arguing that what is significant is how one reacts in the face of such desire (3.4):

> Knowing that all men fall victim to *epithumia* [*epithumēsai*], the most virtuous [*beltistos*] and self-controlled [*sōphronestatos*] person would be the one who is able to endure his misfortunes [*sumphoras*] with the utmost propriety [*kosmiōtata*].

The speaker credits the ideal individual, the *beltistos . . . kai sōphronestatos*, with *kosmiōtata* (most orderly conduct) even in the face of adversity. As Christopher Carey argues, the context suggests that *sumphorai* represent the misfortunes of love.[41] (Cf. Xen. *Cyr.* 6.1.31–37.) One aim of the speech is to demonstrate that the speaker himself has acted with the utmost propriety.[42] He stresses being *agathos* (*beltistos* is used as the superlative) and *sōphrōn* because these two qualities have significance in Athenian society. Both adjectives, *agathos* (virtuous) and *sōphrōn* (moderate), are common in Greek literature, including other oratorical texts, in reference to the ideal citizen. *Kalos kagathos* (beautiful and good), for example, became a common way to indicate a model citizen.[43] An important virtue for the male citizen, like the female citizen, was *sōphrosunē*, which, in the case of men, signified moderation and self-restraint.[44] In Classical Athens, it became a democratic value as well, opposed to *hubris* (excess), which came to be associated with undemocratic and even tyrannical behavior.[45] Because *agathos*, *sōphrōn*, and *kosmios* frequently describe conduct, they gained civic significance, and, as Stephen Todd points out, are similar to the modern concept of the law-abiding citizen.[46] The fact that conduct in this speech relates to feelings for a young boy imbues the terms with an erotic dimension. The speaker thus sets up an exemplar of civic virtue and hints with the rest of his speech that despite his longing for the boy he acted with self-restraint. Any shortcomings are blamed on Simon, who at times, he claims, hampered his ability in this regard (3.4). He calculatingly positions his relationship to desire in this way, since he indicates near the end of the speech that Simon has in fact accused him of being compelled by *epithumia* (3.31).

The speaker depends on his audience's sympathy for being in love when he argues that all men experience desire (3.4). Hypereides uses a similar strategy in his speech *Against Athenogenes*.[47] In that speech, the speaker, Epikrates, wanted to buy freedom for a boy he was enamored with, but instead Athenogenes convinced him to purchase the boy along with his father and brother and the perfumery in which they worked.[48] Once he acquired ownership, he discovered that the perfumery was almost five talents in debt (*Ath.* 9), and he was unable and unwilling to pay it.[49] Although Epikrates acknowledges that he willingly entered into the contract (*Ath.* 8), he argues that Athenogenes misrepresented the size of the debt (*Ath.* 9–10). As a result, he considered the contract to be unfair and argued it should not be binding (*Ath.* 13). He portrays himself as a man in love inexperienced in the world of business and claims that his passion for the boy made him trust Athenogenes and his accomplice, Antigona (*Ath.* 2), and rendered him incapable of reviewing the details of the agreement carefully (*Ath.* 8).[50] He states that he would never have purchased the perfumery if it had not been for his desire for the boy (*Ath.* 2). He details how Athenogenes coached the boy to agree to his freedom only if his father and brother were also freed (*Ath.* 23) and how Athenogenes convinced him that purchasing them all as enslaved was the best way to ensure that the boy did not have other lovers (*Ath.* 4). Hypereides depends on the jurors' fellow feeling "for men defeated by eros," as Joseph Roisman characterizes it, and David Whitehead observes that Lysias' client makes a similar appeal in his trial.[51] In contrast to the speaker of Lysias 3, however, Epikrates displays no embarrassment at spending a large sum of money to gain control of an enslaved youth as his own personal sex slave. This difference highlights the variable and complex attitudes toward the Athenian sex market.

The speaker's main argument in Lysias 3, however, details Simon's conduct, not his own. Stephen Todd highlights how vocabulary related to anti-social behavior and negative mental states, including *hubris*, *paranomia* (lawlessness), and *mania* (madness), dominate his portrait. The claim that

Simon was attracted to Theodotos suggests that desire was what motivated Simon to behave in such a disorderly manner and so violently toward the speaker, the boy, and others. Joseph Roisman argues that the Athenians thought sexual desire could threaten a man's masculinity, hamper him in his role as *kurios*, kin, and citizen, and endanger the polis. He points to Ischomachos' warning in Xenophon's *Oikonomikos* that a certain type of love for boys is hard to overcome and can turn into an obsession (Xen. *Oec.* 12.13–14).[52] In this speech the emphasis on drunken behavior (Lys. 3.6, 12, 18, 19, 43) both day and night likely made Simon's inability to control himself in the face of other appetites, like sexual pleasure, more credible to the judges. His *mania* appears to be the result of an internal incapacity (3.7). It suggests that his desire for the youth results from a lack of *sōphrosunē* rather than an external force that possesses him.[53] As Christopher Carey suggests, it is an emotional disturbance rather than a clinical madness that drives him, and such a condition must elicit condemnation rather than sympathy.[54] Xenophon, in fact, explicitly positions *mania* in opposition to *sōphrosunē* (Xen. *Mem.* 1.1.16). The focus on *hubris* in the speech further disassociates Simon from the ideal citizen.[55] He is demonstrating not simply a lack of propriety in his desire for the boy but also dangerous undemocratic tendencies.[56]

Rather than showing him sympathy, the speaker condemns his opponent for experiencing the very same emotion as himself, *epithumia*. In doing so he exploits two very different views of surrendering to desire.[57] He hints that although their presence in court relates to past competition for the youth, it is their demonstrated abilities to control their desires (or not to) that should now concern the judges. The speaker emphasizes this difference at the very start of his narrative with a direct contrast that becomes the framework for the rest of the speech.[58] It is the first introduction to Theodotos, the love interest of both men. Whereas the speaker characterizes his own relationship with Theodotos as based on reciprocity, Simon's contact with the youth, in contrast, highlights how the youth was forced to submit to Simon (3.5):

> We both longed for [*epethumēsamen*] Theodotos, a Plataian lad [*meirakiou*], and whereas I resolved that he be well disposed to me [*einai moi philon*] with my good treatment of him [*eu poiōn auton*], my opponent here thought he could force him [*anankasein auton*] to do what he wanted [*bouloito*] through abuse [*hubrizōn*) and unlawful methods [*paranomōn*]. It would be an enormous task to narrate all the abuses [*kaka*] this boy has endured at his hands [*hup' autou*].

The language relating Simon's relations with the youth is the exact opposite of the relationship Theodotos has with the speaker. The contrast is between *einai moi philon* (be well disposed toward me) and *anankasein auton* (force him): that is, between a willing and an involuntary partner. The subject and object position of the youth in each respective phrase strengthens the contrast, as does the specific language describing his treatment. Whereas the speaker hoped to win the youth's favor by treating him well (*eu poiōn*), Simon attempted to force the youth's compliance using abusive and even unlawful tactics (*hubrizōn kai paranomōn*).[59] The orderliness that the speaker highlighted as crucial to men who are *sōphrones* is absent in the case of Simon. *Hubrizōn* and *paranomōn* also suggest that Simon's treatment of Theodotos was unreasonable, whatever Theodotos' status. It includes attempting to abduct the youth (3.11), dragging the boy around (3.12), seizing the youth by force (3.15), and perhaps even sexually assaulting the youth (*anomōs kai biaiōs hubristhenta*, 3.17).[60] Near the end of the speech, Simon is labeled *akosmotatos* (most disorderly: 3.45) putting him in direct contrast with *kosmiōtata* of the opening and with the speaker (3.4).[61] Such strong language likely piqued the interest of the judges while also causing discomfort, and this tension in regard to Simon's behavior persists throughout the speech.

MAPPING DESIRE

The speaker begins with events at his own home. Focusing on his household is likely a direct rebuff to Simon's accusations and credibility (a *tu quoque*, as Todd characterizes it), since Simon is charging the speaker with attacking him outside his own front door (3.27).[62] The speaker, in turn, details how a drunken Simon invaded his home (3.6–7):

> For upon learning that the youth was with me, he went to my house by night while drunk [*methuōn*]. After knocking down the doors, he entered the women's quarters [*gunaikōnitin*] even though inside were my sister and nieces, who have lived so decently [*kosmiōs*] that they might even feel shame at being seen by their male relatives. This man, moreover, came into such *hubris* that he refused to leave until the bystanders and his companions drove him out by force [*biai*], since they thought he was behaving terribly [*deina poiein*] by entering among young orphaned girls. And so far was he from repenting of these violations [*tōn hubrismenōn*] that upon finding out where we were dining he behaved most

abominably and most astonishingly [*atopōtaton pragma kai apistotaton*], unless someone were familiar with his madness [*manian*].

The passage moves quickly through a series of violations that amplify each other as the passage progresses. Simon arrives uninvited, at night, in a drunken state. Since drinking wine was commonplace in Classical Athens, *methuōn* highlights Simon's being unable to control himself under its influence and is a regular descriptor for him in this speech.[63] He enters the home forcibly by breaking down the doors. Once inside, he searches everywhere for Theodotos, despite the fact that the speaker is not at home. Moreover, he shows no consideration for the female occupants.

In a case of another home invasion, Demosthenes recounts how Meidias and his brother burst into his *oikia* and issued a challenge for an exchange of property over a trierarchy (Dem. 21.78–80). In recounting the episode Demosthenes focuses on the foul language they used in front of his sister, who at the time was still a young girl, and the abuse they uttered against his mother, as well as himself and all of them together. Demosthenes claims the entire city heard about their *aselgeia* (reprobate behavior) and describes the event as *ta hubrismata* (insolent acts) against him. The presence of female members of the household intensifies the transgression of Meidias and his brother and magnifies the insult to Demosthenes' honor. In another example, the speaker of Demosthenes 47 carefully notes that he entered his opponent's home only because he knew that he was not married and would not encounter any female kin inside (47.38). He also claims that a passerby did not enter his home despite the cries from inside because he, the *kurios*, was not present (47.60). In contrast, his opponents had no qualms about entering and harassing the women and even violently abusing an elderly freedwoman who was living with them (47.52–61).[64] The speaker uses Simon's behavior to similar purpose. It is not simply that he surprises the women at home alone, with only enslaved household members to aid them, but that he enters the *gunaikōnitis*, regularly rendered "the women's quarters" or "women's rooms" in modern translations. But once among the women, he refused to leave until his companions and the bystanders who had gathered at the commotion drove him out. It is his refusal to leave that is stressed as evidence of his *hubris*.[65]

Paul Millett observes that "transgression of the threshold is regularly manipulated in law-court speeches in order to discredit opponents," and Christopher Carey identifies invasions of the *gunaikōnitis* as a topos.[66] Athenian and Greek houses more generally were inward-looking, with rooms organized around a central court only accessible from the outside by a door. Windows seem to have been high up, to keep outsiders from looking in. Restricted sight lines and access into the Greek house suggest a focus on domestic privacy.[67] But they did not have a specific area of the house restricted to female use. Instead of being secluded, women more likely avoided interaction with non-kin males in the household by scheduling activities around visits from outsiders and being flexible in regard to where they carried out their activities.[68] In Lysias 3 the speaker's concern is not so much an actual physical space of the house but, as James Davidson argues, what the term *gunaikōnitis* signifies to the judges.[69] Not being a common term, its ideological implication is more critical in that it highlights the importance of upholding separation between a male citizen's female kin and other males and thus underscores the unapologetic disregard Simon has for common social conventions.

The passage also stresses the virtue of the women by claiming that they lived so decently that they even felt shame at being seen by male relatives. Their discomfort among even male kin emphasizes the extent of their virtue. Their description as decent along with their portrayal as uncomfortable at being seen highlight their virtue as sexual virtue. There is also a symbiosis between the women and the house, with the term *gunaikōnitis* accentuating Simon's invasion as not simply an intrusion but a sexual transgression.[70] His treatment of the women is described as *deina poiein* (terrible behavior) and his actions are *hubris* (*eis touto ēlthen hubreōs*, 3.7) and described as gross violations (*tōn hubrismenōn*). Rosanna Omitowoju wonders if perhaps "we are supposed to infer [personal or sexual violence] … because it is just not possible to describe it explicitly in such a context."[71] The speaker refers back to this episode a number of times (3.23, 29), and the use of the present participle *phoitōn* (visiting: 3.29) even implies that Simon went by the speaker's house more than once in search of Theodotos.[72] As the first encounter the speaker narrates, it sets the judges' expectations for the rest of the speech and anticipates Simon's transgressions against the youth as sexual as well.

In contrast, the confrontations between the speaker himself and Simon are described as occurring in public spaces like laneways and shops. The speaker highlights the arbitrariness of the confrontations and stresses their visibility, since the majority of encounters occur on city streets and in broad daylight. In the first confrontation (3.8), the speaker was dining out with Theodotos. The speaker is not specific about where, but he is most likely at a friend's house.[73] An important detail here is that the incident began with Simon summoning the speaker outside into the street: "Having called me outside [*ekkalesas gar me endothen*], as soon as I exited [*exēlthon*], he tried to strike me." With *endothen* the speaker emphasizes that he was inside and not already on the street. His choice of verbs, both of which include the prefix *ek* (out [of]), also stresses his departure outside onto the street.

In the second confrontation (3.11–18), the incident in which Simon claims he sustained his injuries, the emphasis is on the attempted abduction of the youth. By this time the boy was staying at the house of Lysimachos, most likely a friend of the speaker's. The speaker probably kept the youth there out of respect for his female relatives.[74] This house, however, was very close to where Simon lived. The speaker uses its location to stress intent on the part of Simon, who, he claims, watched for the boy from his rooftop as part of a plan to abduct him (3.11).[75] According to the current narrative, the speaker's arrival on the scene is *kairos*, a word that highlights the randomness of his appearance but also characterizes it as fortuitous and timely given Simon's plan. On the day of the incident, the speaker was returning from Peiraieus and while passing the house decided to drop in. When Simon observes the speaker and Theodotos emerging from Lysimachos' into the street, he and three of his companions attempt to drag the boy away. The speaker does not say where, but the context suggests that they were attempting to take the youth back to Simon's house. Theodotos, however, escaped their grasp and after running off attempted to hide in a fuller's workshop. The speaker also abandoned the scene. Simon and his gang pursued the boy into the fullery and dragged him kicking and screaming into the street (3.15), whereupon Molon (the fuller) and some bystanders tried to come to the youth's aid (3.16). But they were unsuccessful in protecting the boy, whom Simon's gang continued to drag off. According to the speaker, they were outside Lampon's house when he happened upon them all by chance (3.17). It was thus here that his own fight with Simon occurred.

Stephen Todd wonders how familiar the speaker's audience would have been with these names, but the speaker presents the details as if they are well-known parts of town (3.11–18).[76] Even if the actual locations remain unknown to the modern audience, the narrated topography, regardless of how sparse, is essential to his defense. Through his use of the cityscape, the speaker both widens the dispute to include a fuller and bystanders, whom he claims were victims as well as witnesses, and removes the conflict from outside Simon's front door (3.14), where Simon claims he was savagely beaten (3.27), to other locations in the polis. Such details also allow the speaker to highlight Simon's attempted abduction and treatment of the youth as serious offenses in the eyes of other residents.

DAMAGED BODIES

In stark contrast to the injuries Simon claims he suffered are the abuses Simon enacts on the youth Theodotos. One of the first references describes his conduct with the boy as *kaka* (abuse: 3.5). Throughout the narrative and the accompanying argument, the speaker continues to refer to the relationship with formidable language. He describes Simon as forcing the boy (*anankasein*, 3.5), as treating the boy with *hubris* (*hubrizōn*, 3.5, 17, 26), and as breaking the law (*paranomōn*, 3.5, 17) in his use of the boy. Not only is much of Simon's behavior described as *deina* (despicable: 3.1, 7, 9, 16, 17, 37) in the case of Theodotos; it is also beyond the law (*paranomia*, 3.10; *anomōs*, 3.17; *paranoma*, 3.37) and involves the use of force (*bia*, 3.15; *biaiōs*, 3.17). Forms of the verb *hubrizein* commonly describe Simon's conduct toward Theodotos (3.5, 17, 23, 26). The intensity of this vocabulary conveys that Simon's behavior was beyond what was often tolerated among young men and excused because of their age.[77] The speaker, moreover, differentiates the suffering of the boy from his own by employing more moderate vocabulary, like committing wrong (*exēmartēken*, 3.5), doing wrong (*adikēsas*, 3.15), and conspiring (*epibouleusas*, 3.15) to describe his own victimization by Simon in these same contexts. Only near the end of the speech does he suggest *hubris* in relation to himself as well (3.34, 40). In this way, the speaker directs attention away from Simon's physical injuries in their current dispute and toward the mistreatment of the youth instead.

The emphasis of the narrative becomes the boy's physical body. *Sōma* (body) occurs once in the text, in the final encounter, in which Theodotos defends himself: *peri tou sōmatos amunomenou* (3.18). This phrase translates simply as "defending his body," but the preposition *peri* denotes more specifically that his body is what the struggle is about; he is "fighting for his body." The same passage depicts the speaker as defending himself as well, but without this specific detail of the body. Stephen Todd translates the first phrase as "defending his own life," and it certainly seems like the speaker is aiming to convey that more is at stake for the boy than for others in the fight. In the context of the narrative, however, the boy is likely defending his body against the threat of sexual abuse and assault. Sexual violence is hinted at with Theodotos' very first mention. The speaker claimed Simon tried to compel the boy with *hubris* and without regard for law to do what he wanted (3.5). Although the speaker is vague about what Simon actually did with the boy, the choice of *epethumēsamen* (we desired) to introduce this behavior confirms the activity as sexual. The focus on Simon's compulsion of the boy through *hubris* and lawlessness suggests sexual behavior that is both violent and deviant. The body of the youth here is stressed with mention that the boy suffered abuses *hup' autou* (at [Simon's] hands).

This theme of sexual violence overhangs the narrative. In section 12 of the speech, although both the speaker and Theodotos are again surprised by Simon and his gang, the speaker concentrates on the attack against the youth. With three others, Simon attempts to abduct him:

> Then these men, drunk by now [*ēdē methuontes*], jumped us. And some of his companions did not wish to join in the assault [*sunexamartein*], but this Simon here and Theophilos, Protarchos, and Autokles were starting to drag the youth [*heilkon to meirakion*]. Then the youth threw off his cloak and, fleeing, ran away. And I, believing he would escape,... departed via another street, leaving the scene [*apiōn*].

The speaker specifically says that they were dragging the youth away (*heilkon to meirakion*). The verb *helkein* frequently connotes sexual violence (or at least the prelude to such violence). Lysias in another speech uses this same verb to describe the treatment of an enslaved female (1.12), and Aristophanes uses it in describing sexual violence against wives (Ar. *Lys.* 160). But the term is also used with such connotations to indicate males on the verge of sexual assault (Ar. *Eccl.* 1066, 1087, 1093).[78] In the current situation, the speaker's use of *helkein* suggests that Simon and his gang were dragging the boy back to Simon's house, where he would receive further abuse in the form of sexual violence, but the boy manages to escape their grasp and run off.

It is after the boy's successful abduction from the fuller's shop that the speaker comes across them again. They now appear to be carrying out a violent sexual assault against the boy (3.17):

> And I, thinking it terrible [*deinon*] and shameful [*aischron*] to look on as the youth [*neaniskon*] was so lawlessly [*anomōs*] and violently [*biaiōs*] subjected to their *hubris* [*hubristhenta*], grabbed hold of him. But these men, when asked why they were committing such lawlessness [*parenomoun*] against him, refused to say, but releasing the youth [*neaniskou*] they started to beat [*etupton*] me.

The speaker elides the boy's enslaved status by calling him a *neaniskos* (young man) here, a term to describe free Athenian youths at their coming of age (also 3.10). *Anomōs* and *biaiōs* make clear that the assailants do not simply engage in insulting or arrogant behavior but also enact their *hubris* directly upon the body of the youth. The passive participle *hubristhenta* in turn stresses the actions in relation to the youth's body and creates unease about what he is enduring. Are they simply beating him, or are they in fact attempting to violate the boy sexually? It seems significant that in contrast the speaker chooses the verb *tuptein* (beat), a verb without any sexual overtones, in relation to the attack on himself in this same passage. The verbs *hubrizein* and *tuptein* are also distinguished in section 23, and although there the context is more generic, since the passage lists the particulars of Simon's conduct, it effectively separates out *hubris* from the beatings they received, from Simon's participation in a *kōmos*, and from his forced entry among citizen women in their own home. Whereas *hubreōs* and *hubrismenōn* previously described his invasion of the speaker's home (3.7) and the verb *hubrizein* is eventually used (in passive-voice forms) in relation to the speaker himself without sexual overtones (3.34, 40), in all the other examples with Theodotos (3.5, 17, 26) it suggests some kind of sexual violence and may be alluding to such sexual conduct against Theodotos here in section 23 as well.[79]

The speaker's emphasis on Simon's *hubris* against Theodotos has a further significance. In addition to being antithetical to the conduct of *sōphrones*, there was a specific charge in Classical Athens for hubristic and lawless behavior, including sexual assault. Any citizen could bring forward a *graphē hubreōs*, a public prosecution for *hubris*, on behalf of another citizen or even on behalf of someone of enslaved status.[80] As a *graphē*, the procedure highlights the social concern surrounding *hubris* and removes it from the private realm. Such a procedure reveals how great a cause of anxiety treating others with *hubris* and *paranomia* (both highlighted in Simon's case) was at Athens.[81] Although the speaker is defending himself against a charge by Simon, his frequent references to Simon's *hubris*, combined with his *paranomia*, suggest Simon was ripe for a charge of dishonoring others in a *graphē hubreōs*. The speaker does in fact comment near the end of his speech that Simon should be on trial for his life (3.44).[82] The reference to *thanatos* (death), a penalty commensurate with the *graphē hubreōs*, hints at this specific procedure.[83] The speaker likely has no intention of launching such a suit and likely expected that no other citizen would either. The common pattern in the orators is to allude to the procedure but to prosecute with a *dikē* instead.[84] The importance of the *graphē hubreōs* seems largely rhetorical. Alluding to the *graphē* was an effective way to denote the seriousness of an offense and, as Nick Fisher notes, to incite anger among jurors and induce them to convict and assess a heavy penalty under another procedure. In this particular case, the speaker uses *hubris* to bias the judges against Simon's prosecution and question its legitimacy. As the speech progresses, the speaker no longer distinguishes between himself and Theodotos but conflates their mistreatment (3.38, 46) and eventually describes his own victimization as *hubris* as well (3.40). This strategy deflects any wrongdoing on the speaker's part back to Simon. Although unlike other courts the Court of the Areopagus limited discussion before it to events specific to the pending charge (3.44), the speaker slips in noteworthy commonplaces against Simon, like perjury (3.24, 28, 31, 35), cowardliness, unruly behavior, insubordination, and his resulting dismissal while on campaign (3.44–45).[85] But it remains *hubris* that dominates in his portrayal of his opponent.

LOVING BOYS

Although the speaker openly admits his *epithumia* (3.5) for and association with the youth, he is less eager to divulge details about the relationship and prefers "to allow the status of [his] own affairs to be inferred rather than specified."[86] Sex with a paid sex laborer was an accepted practice, but such relationships were subject to scrutiny. Too much passion for sex laborers or forming strong bonds with sex laborers was frowned upon, and the orators use such relationships to besmirch an opponent's reputation.[87] The orator Aischines, for example, attributes a major flaw to Misgolas, an otherwise respected citizen: he has an addiction to young cithara players (Aischin. 1.41), whom James Davidson refers to as "a special group of sex-slaves, ... the closest male equivalent to female courtesans."[88] The equivocal language (and absence of detail) in the narrative suggests some discomfort on the part of the speaker in admitting his continued relationship with a male sex slave.[89] (Cf. Hyp. *Ath.*) The fact that citizen boys were freely available for courtship complicates the practice of male sexual labor. Since boy beloveds were available for courting, the choice to hire male sexual partners might appear questionable and make the judges and bystanders apprehensive, since unlike courtship sexual labor is based not on reciprocity but on personal indulgence and sexual gratification. By the middle of the fourth century BCE, the orator Aischines links purchased sex with *hubris* and describes the purchaser as a *hubristēs* (Aischin. 1.15, 137). As James Davidson puts it, "Greek Love was one thing. Homosexual Lust was something else entirely."[90] To return to the example of Misgolas, it seems to be his predilection for cithara boys that renders his relationship with Timarchos disturbing. It suggests something unsavory about his sexuality. Aischines also calls out other citizens who merit the label *agrioi* (savage) as household names for their profligate pursuit of boys (Aischin. 1.52).[91]

It may be in anticipation of similar attitudes that the speaker seemingly obscures the fact that Theodotos is a sex laborer, instead characterizing him as wrongfully subjected to ill treatment and unlawful behavior, as if he were an *erōmenos* (beloved).[92] In describing his relationship with the boy, the speaker never refers to money, avoids all mention of terminology frequently used to indicate a sex laborer or a client, and never refers to Theodotos as working for pay.[93] In fact, he instead appropriates vocabulary surrounding the pederastic love relationship to describe his association with the youth. Theodotos is regularly referred to as a *meirakion* (youth: 3.4, 5, 6, 10, 12, 15, 18, 22, 26, 29, 31, 32, 35, 37), which marks the common age for *erōmenoi*, just around puberty.[94] When the speaker comments that he treated the boy well (*eu poiein*), he implies that he offers gifts, not payment, as if courting him.[95] Christopher Carey suggests he "probably glosses over a financial arrangement" with such language.[96] Most remarkably he refers to the boy as *philos* toward him, hinting that the boy is his beloved (3.5). *Philia* (love, friendship) represents a relationship built on loyalty, trust, and reciprocity, and thus once again is more appropriate to a pederastic love relationship than to sexual labor.[97]

Stephen Todd suggests the speaker positions his relationship with Theodotos "within a more respectable nexus of aristocratic homosexuality based on gifts and favours" signified by the term *charis* (reciprocity; gratitude).[98] In such relationships, the *charis* expected of the *erōmenos* is commonly loyalty. Although Theodotos has little characterization himself (in the words of Christopher Carey, he "never emerges as a personality"),[99] his portrait does suggest devotion to the speaker, who makes clear that Theodotos wants nothing to do with Simon (3.31) and was not trying to play one man off against the other to his own advantage like the sex slave in Lysias 4 discussed in chapter 1. He suggests throughout that the youth preferred to be with him and always behaved appropriately in this relationship. If Theodotos was of enslaved status, he would of course not be able to participate in a relationship built on *charis*.[100] The speaker's main aim is to show that he himself has acted with only the utmost propriety in his dealings with the boy.[101] In this way, he romanticizes the arrangement that he has with Theodotos by drawing on (but also constructing) an ideal model of pederasty.[102] His proclivity to moderation promotes the Athenian view that the *erastēs* (lover) of a youth had to exhibit self-control in his conduct with his *erōmenos*.

In comparison, coercion characterizes Simon's relationship with Theodotos: "he thought he could force [*anankasein*] [the boy] to do whatever he wanted [*ho ti bouloito*]" (3.5).[103] Any relationship Theodotos has had with Simon, the speaker argues, has been through compulsion, not based on *philia* and reciprocity.[104] Simon did not attempt to win the boy's favor by treating him well (*eu poiōn*), as the speaker claims to have done himself (3.5); quite the opposite: he treated the youth terribly (*poiein deina*, 3.26). The contrast between *eu* (well) and *deina* (terribly) could not be more distinct. Stephen Todd suggests that "the function of the euphemism [*eu poiōn*] will presumably have been to distinguish the speaker's relationship with Theodotos from Simon's claim at 22 to have paid him."[105] But it also points to a different way of treating the youth. As noted above, Simon was not averse to using physical force to get his way with Theodotos (3.15, 17, 37). He compelled the boy without regard to law (3.5). Even strangers recognized the *deina* behind Simon's treatment of Theodotos and attempted to step in to protect him (3.16). In contrast to the speaker's idealized association with the boy, the vocabulary chosen for Simon's appears designed to suggest abuse and arouse discomfort. According to the narrative, Simon appears to lack all control in his encounters with Theodotos and experiences no shame at his behavior toward him. Whereas the speaker presents himself as an ideal *erastēs* (and citizen), Simon displays a hubristic *epithumia* that both is excessive and disregards all convention in the use and treatment of the boy (and others).

The speaker's rejection of a payment or any contract is an opportunity to play up Simon's *hubris* against the boy and raise questions about their relationship (3.26):

> He says that he paid the money lest he appear to be treating him terribly [*deina poiein*], if without having any contract [*sumbolaion*] he dared to subject the youth to such *hubris* [*toiauta etolma hubrizein to meirakion*].

What his *hubris* entails is never specified, but it is clearly sexual. Stephen Todd points out that the age and status of the boy is crucial to understanding what the speaker insinuates with the term here.[106] Although a contract would be legal in various scenarios, without one Simon had no claim on the youth. If Theodotos was a minor and a citizen, as Todd points out, Simon would be guilty of purchasing sex illegally, for which the penalties were severe (Aischin. 1.13).[107] Nick Fisher interprets *hubris* (in Aischines 1) as sexual relations that are painful for the partner and may even cause physical harm. He concludes that its use implies a lack of concern for the sexual partner.[108] Xenophon assumes such sexual abuse is associated with tyrants

(Xen. *Hiero* 1.31–38). The judges' reading of *hubris* here would likely vary, and it is to the speaker's benefit to keep his insinuations vague and open to speculation.

Although Simon claimed that he purchased the boy as a sexual companion (*to hetairēsonta ... emisthōsato*, 3.24), a perfectly legal transaction in Classical Athens, the speaker argues instead that Simon abused a *meirakion* (*etolma hubrizein to meirakion*, 3.26). By employing *meirakion* in this context he exploits the variable attitudes that existed around purchasing sex from boys and courting them, despite the normalcy of both practices in Classical Athens. As James Davidson emphasizes, it is "the distinction between commodity exchange and the exchange of gifts, between payments and presents."[109] Commodities are measurable, comparable, and given a specific value. What is being exchanged is very clear to both purchaser and seller, even when the commodity is sex: price could indicate time or a specific person or even involve a particular body part. The transaction is immediate and final. In contrast, gifts build social networks and establish an ongoing obligation with the receiver, who is expected to repay the debt at an unspecified future time. Rather than a single event, a gift triggered a cycle of exchange. Images of courtship show lovers bestowing gifts on youths as a way to win their favor: fighting cocks, hares, strigils, hunting dogs, cats, and even deer and foxes.[110] Such gifts were personal, with no immediate expectation of sex. But the line between sexual labor and courtship was slippery (Ar. *Wealth* 149–159).[111] The speaker of Lysias 3 elides both practices in his narrative and argument to confuse the judges about the wrong committed and to vilify Simon. By obscuring Theodotos' status and profession the speaker is able to press at the limits of acceptability in Simon's treatment of the youth.

By muddying Theodotos' juridical status and questioning Simon's claim to have hired him under contract, the speaker plays with the boundaries that separate youths from sex laborers and may make judges and bystanders feel ill at ease. The language surrounding Simon's association with the boy, centering on *hubris* and *paranomia*, is alarming and suggests behavior inappropriate even in the case of enslaved persons, including sex slaves. By arousing discomfort among his peers the speaker hopes to succeed in his defense. His strategy both exploits and magnifies underlying anxieties about male sexual labor and courtship. It was not any anxiety specifically about allowing anal intercourse, however, as David Halperin argues; it was instead about the ability to compel a boy or sex laborer (through payment) to do as you desired, as the speaker emphasizes in the case of Simon (3.5) and, as we shall see (chapter 5), as Aischines stresses in the case of Timarchos' lovers (Aischin. 1.41, 55, 70).[112] It was this dynamic of payment, played up in Aischines' speech *Against Timarchos*, that made male sexual labor discomforting and created anxiety around the male sex laborer's body and its sexuality.[113] The speaker obscures his own relationship with Theodotos in the narrative, never mentioning actual payments or contracts, as a way to garner sympathy for his plight, but in that same narrative he vilifies Simon's association with the boy, with the result that the mention of Simon's claim to money owed and thus to purchasing sex only adds to his offensive treatment of the boy and his negative portrait as hubristic in his response to desire.

CONCLUSION

Lysias 3 is unique in that, in contrast to the characterizations of sex laborers and their clients examined previously, the speaker of this speech recounts in detail his own relationship with a sex laborer. He is careful to avow his restraint in the face of desire by suggesting that he has maintained his composure despite his *epithumia* for Theodotos and in the *sumphorai* that have befallen him (3.4). He recognizes that being in control is what his audience values, and he hints that he is such a person, despite his opponent's characterization of him as foolish in his behavior toward the youth (3.31). He realizes that he may appear this way given his age but argues that while everyone is prone to foolishness when in love, the *beltistos* (best) and *sōphronestatos* (most moderate) men are able to endure it *kosmiōtata* (in the most orderly way: 3.4). He implies he was successful in doing so until Simon pulled him into court. He thus associates himself with being *agathos* and *sōphrōn*, important traits for the good citizen in Classical Athens under the democracy.[114] Both qualities suggest a relationship beneficial to the city and to its citizens. The use of *chrēstos* further emphasizes this theme (3.9). He does no wrong to the city and its citizens (3.47). Even his pretension to *charis* promotes him as an ideal citizen.[115] What is key to his speech is how his construction of desire fits into his picture of a model citizen.

In the case of Simon, a lack of self-control is manifest in his drunken brawls (3.6, 12, 18) and in the descriptions of him as hubristic and subject to *mania* (3.7). As Stephen Todd notes, almost everyone in the speech experiences shame at his actions at some point, but never Simon.[116] Most shameful of all is his conduct with the youth Theodotos. The speaker makes clear at the very start of his narrative that Simon is violent and forceful in his relationship with him, using strong verbs imbued with social and legalistic meaning: *anankazein, hubrizein, paranomein* (3.5, 12). His actions toward the boy, furthermore, are described as *kaka* (3.5) and *deina* (3.16, 26). *Hubrizein* is even modified with *anomōs* (unlawfully) to suggest a serious accusation of *hubris*. Simon's conduct contrasts with the controlled and moderate behavior of the speaker but also hints that he is a threat to the social fabric and to democracy more generally. Simon behaves in a manner contrary to what is expected of the ideal male citizen in the face of desire, and that contrast begins to expose his deficiencies as a citizen and to question his social legitimacy. The trial reveals a complex attitude toward desire as well as sexual labor, especially in the case of male sex laborers, since the speaker garners sympathy for his *epithumia* at the same time as he vilifies his opponent for this very same emotion. The speech also moves toward a sense of citizenship based on particular qualities and their performance as opposed to civic action alone (cf. Lys. 21.19), anticipating the portrayal of Timarchos in Aischines 1, the topic of the next chapter.

FIVE

CITIZEN SEX SLAVES

WHEN AISCHINES ACCUSED Timarchos of having worked as a sex laborer in a speech delivered in the popular courts, Timarchos was an established politician. He had played an important role in the Council, participated in important embassies, proposed more than a hundred decrees, and commonly served as a prosecutor in the courts.[1] Unlike the sex laborers of the previous chapters, he was an active citizen well known to the jurors who faced him at the trial. The case is not a dispute over a sex laborer but a *dokimasia tōn rhētorōn* (scrutiny of public speakers). It accuses a male citizen of having practiced the profession as a youth. The allegation is one of four made against Timarchos: he is also accused of mistreating his mother and uncle, being a coward, and squandering his patrimony.[2] Aischines makes these accusations to demonstrate Timarchos' unsuitability for public life and thus prevent him from being able to speak in the Assembly and bring further court actions.

Although Aischines highlights four transgressions, he chooses to focus much of his speech on proving Timarchos was working as a sex laborer. In doing so he fashions a sexual ethics of citizenship that tests Timarchos against the ideal citizen and marks him as deserving the penalty of *atimia* (loss of civic rights). Aischines constructs an identity for Timarchos as a *pornos*, uniting this identity with a particular lifestyle and values that he promotes as antithetical to Athens as a democracy. He uses this identity to mark the boundary between the ideal citizen and others, including those not worthy of citizenship. Aischines depends on the jurors' familiarity with Timarchos' erotic popularity as a youth (Dem. 19.233), and he furthermore exploits unease concerning citizens' bodies, social ambivalence around pederasty and male sexual labor (as in chapter 4), as well as distrust of rhetors more generally. With this chapter, I expand on themes considered previously (in chapters 3 and 4) with sharper focus on the body, sexuality, gender, and citizenship as problematized in relation to sexual labor. The common association of sex laborers with enslavement, alien status, and being female, along with their dependence on others, challenged Athenian standards of masculinity, and the instability of the sex laborer's status, discussed in previous chapters, contradicted the permanency of other social categories in the polis and paved the way for Timarchos' disenfranchisement.

BODIES IN COURT

Like the trial against Neaira, the case is a *graphē* (public suit) heard before a popular court. Aischines brought it forward in 346/345 BCE in retaliation against his political rivals. Timarchos along with Demosthenes had recently prosecuted Aischines for misconduct on the embassy to conclude a peace agreement with Philip II of Macedon. The charge was that Aischines had accepted bribes from Philip to betray Athens' interests. Aischines immediately launched this suit against Timarchos, charging him with being unsuitable for public life because of a scandalous past. Based on the public prominence of Timarchos, the trial likely attracted a large crowd in addition to the speakers, defendant, and jurors, providing Aischines with a large audience. The actual speech as published by Aischines presents a complicated but entertaining and even shocking narrative with its inclusion of love triangles, gambling houses, and stories of embezzlement.[3] It begins with the reason for the trial, outlining why Aischines himself is bringing the charge and why the trial is of public concern (1.1–5); then there follows a discussion of a series of laws supposedly relevant to the case and the technicalities of the procedure under way (1.6–36).[4] The jurors are next presented with a detailed discussion of Timarchos' private life, his financial status, and his public career (1.37–116). Aischines then relays arguments he says will be part of the defense and refutes these one by one (1.117–176). He then exhorts citizens to *aretē* (virtue) and ends with an appeal to uphold the laws for the benefit of the young (1.177–196).[5]

The charge against Timarchos falls under the *dokimasia tōn rhētorōn* (scrutiny of public speakers), which disallowed citizens who exhibited cowardice, abused their parents, mismanaged personal finances, or worked as sex laborers from speaking in the Assembly (1.28–32).[6] This being a trial before a popular court, the jury included a broad cross-section of Athenian society, many of them familiar with Timarchos' speeches in the Assembly.[7] Speaking was an important privilege of Athenian citizenship under the democracy (often touted as the most important privilege). As Aischines himself makes clear, any male citizen, regardless of status, is free to speak in the Assembly (1.23, 27). And any citizen is free to demand a scrutiny of the speaker.[8] Aischines associates Timarchos with all the offenses listed during the course of his speech (and as Nick Fisher notes, he likely only includes a select list here), but he condemns Timarchos based only on the last two, mismanagement of patrimony and working as a sex laborer.[9] The bulk of his argument, however, centers on the latter charge (1.57–76).

Accusations of working in the sex trade are not directed uniquely against Timarchos. In fact Aischines hints at just such a tactic against Hegesandros, another citizen, in this same speech: Hegesandros regularly attacked Aristophon of the deme of Azenia in the Assembly until Aristophon threatened to call for Hegesandros' scrutiny (1.64). References to Hegesandros and Leodamas in Aischines' speech suggest sexual labor may have been the focus of this procedure (1.69–70, 111).[10] Diodoros, in an earlier speech of Demosthenes, claims Androtion has been making illegal proposals because of his (past) status as a sex laborer (Dem. 22.21–24), but he only threatens to bring suit. Andokides too in his speech *On the Mysteries* alludes to the court's familiarity with such charges against Epichares, one of Andokides' accusers (And. 1.100). Aischines' charge against Timarchos is not exceptional, but the fact that such a scrutiny went to trial appears to have been rare.[11]

CITIZEN BODIES

Near the end of his speech, Aischines links an acquittal of Timarchos to a disruption of *eukosmia* (good order) for the next generation (1.191–192), a term that Andrew Ford argues he uses to indicate decent or decorous behavior, but that, more important, is crucial to social stability.[12] With this term Aischines links back to the start of his speech, where he attributes the lawgivers' first concern to *nomoi . . . peri eukosmias*, giving *eukosmia* primacy under the democracy (1.22). As we shall see, the concept of *kosmia* is highlighted in a variety of contexts in this speech, with *eukosmia* important for children, rhetors, women, the city itself (1.8, 22, 34, 183, 192), and its opposite, *akosmia* (disorder), used to describe the life of the sex laborer (1.189).

Aischines also argues that Timarchos' acquittal will overturn the educational system (1.187). Rather than setting the young on a path to virtue, a wrong vote by the jurors will have a corruptive force, with more insatiable youths seeking out pleasures above all else, in the manner of Timarchos. Aischines also implies that youths emulating Timarchos instead of *aretē* will encourage tyranny and be the downfall of the *dēmos* (1.190–191). The threat that an acquittal poses to the stability of Athenian society can be found in the epilogue of earlier speeches (e.g., Lys. 1.47, also at 36) and was employed by Apollodoros in his speech, *Against Neaira* ([Dem.] 59.113–115); its focus here on young males recalls the charges of corrupting the youth brought against Socrates in the late fifth century BCE. In fact Aischines mentions the philosopher in reference to Demosthenes, who had brought some students to this trial to hear him speak (1.173).

Nick Fisher suggests that the threat posed by the growing power of Macedon and the political discord at Athens stimulated debates over civic institutions and likely also the appropriate education of the young.[13] Indeed, the educational system would be restructured by the laws of Epikrates in 335–334 BCE. Although Aischines avoids mention of the current political situation in his speech, he clearly exploits such divisions when he conjures up the young male relatives of the jurors and demands to know what the jurors will tell their sons when they question them about the outcome of the trial upon their return home (1.186–187):

> In what frame of mind will each of you head home [*oikade*] from the lawcourt? For the one you are judging is not obscure [*aphanēs*] but known to all [*gnōrimos*]. And the law on the scrutiny of the orators is not petty, but very important [*outh' ho nomos ho peri tēs tōn rhētorōn dokimasias phaulos, alla kallistos*], and it should be expected that boys and young males [*tois paisi kai tois meirakiois*] will ask their kinsmen how the case was decided. What then, indeed, will you say, you who are invested with authority [*kurioi*] to vote, when your sons [*hoi humeteroi paides*] ask you whether you convicted or acquitted him?

This passage shares similarities with Apollodoros' invocation of the mothers, wives, and daughters of the jurors in pseudo-Demosthenes 59.110 and likely influenced that speech directly.[14] Both are striking because they ask jurors to consider the response of groups that have no public voice in Classical Athenian society.[15] In this case, Aischines reminds his audience that the *paides* (boys) and *meirakia* (youths) will wish to know the outcome of the case. In referring to their young male relatives, he employs vocabulary specific to institutions that provide an important context for the speech: *paideia*, but also pederasty and citizenship.[16] Their mention takes the jurors back full circle to the start of Aischines' speech, where he out-

120

lines the laws protecting the bodies of these young males from unwanted suitors and sexual exploitation (1.7–17). With this move Aischines plays on Athenian anxiety about the young male kin in their charge.

By highlighting the interest of these two groups in the outcome of a *dokimasia tōn rhētorōn*, Aischines also links the trial to citizenship more generally, since boys and youths also underwent a scrutiny. As the jurors were well aware, *paides* and *meirakia* were subject to a *dokimasia* when they reached the age of majority, referred to by scholars as the *dokimasia eis andras* (for manhood) or the scrutiny of ephebes, which determined their status as citizens.[17] Through pseudo-Aristotle we know that the youth first appeared before his deme, where he submitted to a physical inspection, provided evidence of his free status, and verified the citizen status of his parents (on both sides: [Arist.] *Ath. Pol.* 42.1–2).[18] A physical inspection was done to determine the candidate was the right age (*hēlikia*) for citizenship (42.1). In a comic account in Aristophanes' *Wasps*, boys' *aidoia* (genitals) are referenced (578), suggesting the boys appeared naked, but it is not definite that the lines refer to the actual scrutiny in the demes. If not of age, then the candidate is returned to the class of boys without queries into his status or that of his parents. The physical exam is an important part of the process, since if the *Boulē* determines in its scrutiny that the candidate is not of the correct age for citizenship then the deme is fined.

Aischines' reference to male youths taking an interest in the *dokimasia tōn rhētorōn* also dramatizes recent social unease about who is legitimately a citizen and deserving of citizen privileges.[19] Shortly before this trial, Demophilos proposed a review of the citizen lists to the Assembly (346/345 BCE), who voted in favor of a scrutiny of each citizen (1.77, 86; cf. Dem. 57.49). This scrutiny, known as the *diapsēphisis*, required every citizen to submit to a vote from his deme regarding his status as citizen. The procedure likely mirrored the procedure of the *dokimasia* of ephebes mentioned above. Presumably in the case of the decree of Demophilos it was primarily parental status and a person's status as free that needed reverifying. We know that Euxitheos was struck from his deme list during these scrutinies and launched an appeal in the lawcourt contesting the decision (Dem. 57.66–70).[20] Euxitheos spends much of his speech verifying the citizen status of each of his parents and the legitimacy of their marriage. His status as *astos* (citizen) depends on his birth, and no mention at all is made of having undergone a physical inspection.

In contrast, Aischines' recounting of these same scrutinies makes no reference to a consideration of parental and personal status, and highlights instead the physical body, the *sōma* (1.77):

Scrutinies [*diapsēphiseis*] have happened in the demes, and each of us has allowed a vote about his *sōma* [*peri tou sōmatos*] [to determine] who is truly Athenian [*Athēnaios*] and who is not.

As Susan Lape has argued, Aischines' reference to this recent event in his speech encourages the jurors to consider their role in judging Timarchos as no different from their recent evaluation of the citizen status of members of their demes.[21] By emphasizing *sōma* (body) here Aischines also refocuses the procedure so that the body (its physical appearance and appetites) becomes the most important criterion of Athenian citizenship. When *genos* (birth) is finally mentioned (1.79), it is immediately eclipsed with a reference to *epitēdeuma* (personal habits): "if, just as on birth, so on lifestyle, Timarchos had to submit to a vote on whether or not he is guilty of the charge ... I am absolutely certain that you would vote against him." The *hōsper ... houtō* (just as ... so) construction assimilates personal habits with birth as something that is equally deserving of scrutiny.[22] Through this parody of the *diapsēphisis*, the vote on Timarchos parallels the vote on citizenship. Aischines thus confuses and conflates the *dokimasiai* on citizenship and the *dokimasia tōn rhētorōn* to his own advantage (1.77–78).

TIMARCHEAN BODIES

The focus on the physical body and its appetites as sites of social legitimacy is central to the approach Aischines employs against Timarchos—what Susan Lape labels a "physiognomic strategy."[23] Aischines begins his narrative on Timarchos with the spectacle of his body, displaying it to the "gaze of citizens."[24] He reminds the jurors how just the other day Timarchos threw off his himation with his theatrics in the Assembly, revealing his *sōma*, suggesting that he was in fact inviting his own scrutiny (1.26):

Indeed those men felt shame [*ēischunonto*] at speaking with their arms exposed, but this one here, not long ago, but recently, threw off his cloak [*thoimation*] and began to perform the moves of the pankration [*epankratiazen*] naked [*gumnos*] in the Assembly; and his body [*to sōma*] was in so terrible and shameful a condition [*houtōs kakōs kai aischrōs diakeimenos*] from drink and sordid living [*hupo methēs kai bdelurias*], that levelheaded men hid their faces [*eu phronountas enkalupsasthai*], feeling ashamed [*aischunthentas*] for the city that we use such individuals as advisers.

Aischines poses a direct contrast here between this body of Timarchos and the modest bodies of the noble ancestors of the democracy: Perikles, Themistokles, Aristeides, and Solon. He has only just commented that these past rhetors were so *sōphrones* (virtuous) that they considered it overbold, immodest, to speak in the Assembly with their arms bared (1.25). He invites his audience to contemplate a statue of Solon at Salamis in which Solon is portrayed in his customary manner of addressing the people, with his arm inside his cloak.[25] Aischines highlights this stance as a sign of modesty. In contrast to this *schēma* (comportment; public persona) of Solon, Aischines describes Timarchos as *gumnos* (naked), an exaggeration, for speaking without a cloak. The reference to the pankration, an all-out fighting match with few rules, conjures a lively speaker gesturing aggressively in his addresses and even suggests Timarchos had an unusual and eccentric manner of speaking.[26] Aischines' emphasis on the degenerate state of Timarchos' body (indicated by *kakōs* and *aischrōs*) from drinking and *bdeluria* (sordid living) also contrasts with these other bodies as *sōphrones*.[27] These comparisons highlight an ideal of citizenship as visibly written on the body and encourage the jurors to inspect Timarchos' person and conduct as they listen to him defend himself in court. (Cf. [Dem.] 59.115.) Indeed, *sōphrosunē* and the related term *metrios* are prominent concepts against which Timarchos is measured throughout the speech.[28] Comments on his past performances might also unbalance Timarchos as he stood up to address these same jurors.[29]

At the time of the trial Timarchos was no longer a young man, and Aischines exploits what Christopher Carey observes may have been simple signs of aging to suggest that Timarchos' gluttony, gambling, and hiring of women (1.42, 65, 95–96, 105, 115) are the cause of his degenerate state.[30] A concern with personal consumption is not distinctive to this speech, but as others have noted, the extent of the focus in a lawcourt speech is exceptional.[31] Joseph Roisman labels Aischines 1 "the most glaring example of criticism of yielding to pleasures."[32] Central to Aischines' discussion is the terminology of enslavement: *douleuōn* (being enslaved to: 1.42) indicates his habits as addictions, as Rosalia Hatzilambrou highlights, and designates his dependence on his appetites.[33] Susan Lape argues more strongly that by characterizing him as enslaved Aischines "rules out any possibility that Timarchus is simply a hedonist."[34] His dependence on others in the fulfillment of his addictions by serving as a sex toy directly ties his desires to his role as a sex laborer and highlights what Susan Lape identifies as a psychological motive for this lifestyle. But Aischines pushes the analogy with slavery even further to manipulate his audience's reaction to Timarchos and tarnish his social authority.[35] Although terminology relating to slavery is common in Classical thought to denote deficiencies in self-control, including in relation to a lover's desire, Aischines' use adds to the social anxiety he develops with his narrative, since it presents Timarchos like a person enslaved in his relationships as well.[36] The opposition of free versus enslaved, so crucial to Athenian self-identity, becomes an opposition between free versus *pornos* in this speech (1.123).[37] Aischines plays with that familiar contrast to stress the enslaved status of the *pornos*, thereby eliding the variable status of sex laborers, who could be enslaved, freed, or free. The contrast heightens the previous and upcoming invective of Aischines in referring to Timarchos as *pornos* (1.70, 130, 157).

Such terminology also links him linguistically with the prohibitions against the enslaved listed in the closing sections of the speech. These laws prevented enslaved individuals from exercising at gymnasia and courting boys (1.138–139). According to Aischines, they enforced distinctions between enslaved and free by limiting the public spaces and sexual activities available to enslaved individuals.[38] In doing so, he teases out Timarchos' slavish addictions as relevant to a discussion of his worthiness as a speaker in the Assembly. Timarchos' citizen status acts as a cover for his slavish nature and activities, but this character flaw, once exposed, calls his presence in other civic spaces into question. While Timarchos outwardly claims privilege as a free citizen, he is merely a *pornos* in his daily habits. Rather than a *pornoboskos* (sex trafficker), his enslaver is his appetites.

It is also Timarchos' use of this *sōma* that Aischines problematizes.[39] *Sōma* in fact occurs twenty-seven times in the text, most commonly in reference to Timarchos' body and its misuse.[40] Nick Fisher comments on its collocation "with *hybris* and words for shame" in particular, and this contrasts with other bodies described as pure.[41] Timarchos is accused multiple times of shaming his body (1.40, 54, 70). Aischines also describes how Timarchos sold himself for money (1.40), worked with his body for hire (1.40, 52), received money (1.41, 53, 58), was a kept man (1.51), suffered what others chose to do, and did not hesitate to submit to their desires (1.41). By listing these activities, even though he never details exactly what they entailed (cf. 1.45, 55, 59, 73, 76), he emphasizes that there were no limits to what Timarchos would endure. It is his willingness to tolerate such behavior in exchange for payment that Aischines stresses and exploits for his audience as disturbing: what James Davidson characterizes as being "gay for pay."[42] Timarchos' only concern is for the material reward. In contrast, references to the purity of the body required for priesthoods (1.188), to personal protections under the law (1.5), and to describe the body subjected to scrutiny by the deme (1.77), as noted above, also employ *sōma*. The result is a vivid contrast between Timarchos' *sōma* and its treatment and the valued *sōma* of the citizen more generally. In other words, as we saw in the case of Neaira, it is a particular body that is worthy of citizenship.

What Aischines aims to demonstrate with his narrative is that Timarchos lived the life of a *pornos*: it is this particular identity that Aischines depends on, not simply his body as insatiable, penetrated, or feminized, to win his case.[43] Rosalia Hatzilambrou argues convincingly that the charge of having worked as a sex laborer brought coherence to Aischines' arguments by uniting Timarchos' failings in a single identity.[44] He refers to Timarchos' activities with Misgolas and Hegesandros in particular and more generally using middle forms of *porneuein* (to prostitute: 1.52, 70, 119, 154, 155, 159, 188, 189). In section 74, he even compares Timarchos to the apparently well-known assemblage of *pornoi* working out of small rooms near the Agora. He misleadingly focuses the charge and the trial (and thus the jurors' attention) on sexual labor when he imagines the herald's final pronouncement to the court: "the pierced token for the one who thinks Timarchos has sold himself as a sex slave [*dokei peporneusthai Timarchos*] and the solid for the one who thinks he has not" (1.79). Aischines also works to affix permanently the label *pornos* to Timarchos by suggesting its use as a popular diminutive for him: "Which Timarchos? The *pornos*?" (1.130, also 70; cf. 123).[45] He presents "Great Timarchean sex slaves" (*pornous megalous Timarchōdeis*, 1.157) as a well-known comic reference to Timarchos.[46] The joke identifies "Timarchean" as a particular class of *pornoi*, and Aischines completes the joke by naming Timarchos the *klēronomos* (successor, heir apparent) to the business (1.157).[47] Finally, he equates him with those who willingly sell themselves for sex (*tous d' hekontas peporneumenous*), suggesting his meretricious nature (1.188). He is not working in the sex trade out of necessity.

As other scholars observe, instead of proof the speech relies on *phēmē* (rumor) to support Aischines' charge that Timarchos worked as a sex laborer.[48] No evidence of witnesses, of Timarchos paying the *pornikon telos* (prostitution tax: 1.119), or of negotiated contracts with a client (1.160) backs up Aischines' allegation; but a definition strategically placed amid his narrative of Timarchos' past relationships makes clear exactly what a sex laborer is (1.52):

> Passing over these coarse men [*tousde tous agrious*], Kedonides, Autokleides, and Thersandros, I mention only those in whose houses he took up, having hired out his body [*memistharnēkota auton epi tōi sōmati*] not

only at the house of Misgolas but also at the house of another and again another and going from this house to yet another. Indeed clearly he is no longer simply one who has been kept as a sexual companion [*hētairēkōs*] … but one who has prostituted himself [*peporneumenos*]. For a person who practices this with many and for pay [*ho gar eikēi touto kai pros pollous prattōn kai misthou*] is, it seems to me, guilty of this.

Although Aischines elides any difference between being a companion and being a *pornos* in his discussion of the law (see below), here he presents the two as distinct (also 1.51). Someone who prostitutes himself does not discriminate but goes with anyone, does things for payment, and is clearly not faithful or loyal to any one partner.[49] Timarchos embodies this definition: his sexual partners, both named (Kedonides, Autokleides, Thersandros, Misgolas, Antikles, Pittalakos, Hegesandros) and unnamed, are not restricted to citizens, but include *emporoi* (traders), *xenoi* (aliens), and even an *anthrōpos dēmosios* (public slave: 1.40, 54). He has not only had many sexual partners, but chooses them based on their ability to pay. *Argurion* (silver: i.e., money) is the reason he takes up with Misgolas (1.41). Pittalakos is attractive to Timarchos because he again has plenty of money and can act as the personal *chorēgos* (financier) of Timarchos' bad living, summed up as *bdeluria* (*chorēgon tēi bdeluriai tēi heautou*, 1.54). Hegesandros is also flush, and Aischines implies here that it is once again the money that Timarchos goes for, since Hegesandros needs few words to convince him to leave Pittalakos (1.56–57).

In the narrative Timarchos moves repeatedly from one man's house to another's and is generously compensated for the use of his body. Aischines emphasizes access to Timarchos' *sōma* for a price, with no limits, it seems, to what one could buy or even who could buy him. In doing so, he commodifies Timarchos' associations in a society that, as Aristotle observes, viewed *charis* (reciprocity) as the best way to organize personal relationships within the polis and distinguish relations between free persons from transactions with enslaved persons (Arist. *Eth. Nic.* 1132b35–1133a4).[50] As Aischines tells it, *argurion* defines Timarchos' relationships instead of such reciprocity. Although the narrative begins with Timarchos' past, the inclusion of contemporary events in the Assembly and the theater throughout the speech that reference his sexuality obscures the range of time Aischines covers and implies Timarchos continues in these same sorts of relationships through adulthood.

BODIES IN PLACE

Place also plays a prominent role in this speech. Aischines moves his audience through civic space (*Ekklēsia, Agora, gumnasion*), domestic space (*oikia*), urban spaces of leisure (*kubeion, porneion, sunoikia, oikēmata*), and even secluded areas around the Pnyx. His text presents a colorful picture of an urban landscape for Classical Athens. But his detailed cityscape focuses on Timarchos' presence or absence and through the body of Timarchos highlights the place of the male citizen within that landscape. Although he depends on his audience's knowledge of the city, he also assigns new meaning to familiar spaces. Aischines thus employs place as an important strategy in disrupting Timarchos' networks despite his prominence as a public speaker at Athens.

Aischines begins his attack with Timarchos located in the *Ekklēsia*, on the Pnyx, a common sight; but Timarchos' presence there violates the practices of the Assembly (1.22). Aischines claims there are laws of order, emphasizing the idea of *eukosmia* (good order) as akin to *sōphrosunē* (self-control) first and foremost, and indeed Ford translates the phrase "the laws of virtuous conduct."[51] Despite his audience's familiarity with the procedures of the Assembly, he reminds them of the sacrifice and prayers offered at the start of each meeting. According to Harpokration (s.v. *katharsion*), the ritual involved the sacrifice of piglets to purify and cleanse the Assembly of pollution. By mentioning these practices Aischines highlights the Assembly as a sacred space (1.23). It is important for Aischines that his reference to the purification ceremony attaches *sōphrosunē* to place, much as with the case of people. Aischines also reminds the jurors of the protocols in place for speakers. Once the issues for discussion are made known, the herald invites members to the *bēma* in order of seniority, based on age.[52] Aischines emphasizes in his speech that any citizen is allowed to address the Assembly but also that under some circumstances certain citizens are disqualified from speaking (1.23). He seems to suggest that it is only those lacking in virtue who are disqualified from this privilege.

In addition to highlighting the Assembly itself as *sōphrōn*, he names distinguished past speakers (Perikles, Themistokles, Aristeides) and highlights their status as *sōphrones*. At the same time he provides his first direct mention of Timarchos (1.25), whom he contrasts with Aristeides in particular. He also includes Solon in his list of model speakers and compares Timarchos to all four ancestors (1.26). The mere mention of these noble ancestors well known to the Athenians constructs the Assembly as a place of nostalgia associated with democratic ideals of citizenship. Timarchos is

SEXUAL LABOR IN THE ATHENIAN COURTS

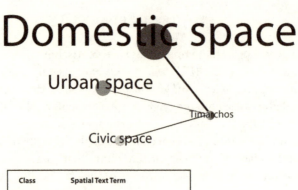

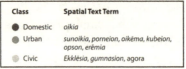

Class	Spatial Text Term
Domestic	*oikia*
Urban	*sunoikia, porneion, oikēma, kubeion, opson, erēmia*
Civic	*Ekklēsia, gumnasion, agora*

Drawn for publication by Tina Ross

FIGURE 5.1. *Spatial Networks for Timarchos, I: Graph of classes of spatial text terms associated with Timarchos in Aischines 1. The size of a node and its label represents the frequency of that class of terms' occurrence in the text. An edge links Timarchos with each class. The thickness of an edge represents the frequency of the connection with Timarchos. Prepared by Esther Knegt using Gephi (Bastian, Heymann, and Jacomy 2009).*

presented in a dramatic contrast establishing him as out of place in such a gathering. His life and habits make a mockery of the Assembly, which Aischines has just presented as a *sōphrōn* space. In fact in section 42 of the speech, Timarchos is emphatically *ho miaros houtos* (this polluted one). In the current passage (1.26, quoted above), Aischines describes those in attendance as covering themselves (*enkalupsasthai*) for shame at the sight of him. The verb implies they used their *himatia* to veil their faces, thereby affecting a weighty gesture that removed him from their view but also indicated their disapproval.[53] Aischines clearly constructs the Assembly as a space associated with particular values, and these values and the people who populate the Assembly define it as a place in the democracy and determine who can and cannot participate.[54]

Yet Aischines' spatial emphasis is, surprisingly, the private house, with the term *oikia* overrepresented in this speech, given its subject matter, but also compared to fourth-century BCE oratory in general. Figure 5.1 represents the dominant position of domestic space within the text based on textual frequency. The term *oikia* itself appears twenty-two times in Aischines 1. It is important that it is not Timarchos' paternal *oikos* that is the focus of such mentions. Instead it is Timarchos' presence in the *oikoi* of others. The displacement of the paternal *oikos* within the text foreshadows Timarchos' own displacement from the polis. Any mentions stress its loss. Although Timarchos was from a very wealthy family, if we believe Aischines he now has nothing left: no *oikia*, no rooming house (*sunoikia*), no land (*chōrion*); not even slaves (*oiketai*) or loans.[55] Even his family ties have become tenuous. Timarchos' mother and an uncle appear in the narrative, but only to be mistreated by their son and nephew (1.99, 103–104). Although Demosthenes references children of Timarchos (Dem. 19.283), Aischines makes no mention of them or their mother in the speech as we have it.

To judge from the account in Aischines, the family had plenty of resources to finance liturgies and benefit the city besides taking care of all household members.[56] Their property included houses, country estates, and workshops in addition to movable property like furniture, enslaved persons, and livestock (1.97).[57] Arizelos, Timarchos' father, had full control of the paternal estate, since one brother had died and the other was blind (1.102). Under Timarchos, however, the property is woefully mismanaged, and family members are terribly wronged. Aischines claims that Timarchos sold all his assets, just like he has sold his body—a constant refrain in the speech—to satisfy his own pleasures (1.96, 105). Nick Fisher rightly questions the accuracy of such statements, claiming if not land, Timarchos must have had some liquid assets.[58] But such statements allow Aischines to claim that there is no longer even any residence associated with Timarchos. His lack of place facilitates his *atimia*, loss of citizen privileges within the polis, since citizenship was tied to household membership, as status was to landownership.[59]

But even before Timarchos reached this state, his relationship with his father's household was problematic. The *oikia* (house) is referred to as the house of his paternal ancestors throughout the narrative. The term *patrōios* indicates the genealogy of the *oikos* and the responsibility of each of its members for its continuation. Yet, whenever Aischines makes mention of the *patrōia oikia* it is commonly to comment on Timarchos' absence. It is not simply that he is physically absent, however, but that he has in fact forsaken his father's house. Aischines repeats more than once (1.42, 47, 75) in his narrative that Timarchos abandoned his home as a *meirakion*. For instance (1.42):

> And this foul one [*ho miaros houtos*] felt no shame in forsaking his paternal home [*eklipōn men tēn patrōian oikian*] and living at the house of Misgolas [*diaitōmenos de para Misgolai*], who was neither a friend of his father [*oute patrikōi onti philōi*], nor his own age, but at the home of a

129

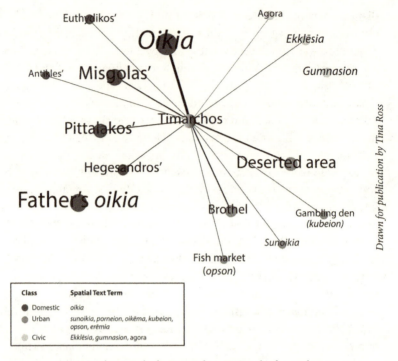

FIGURE 5.2. *Spatial Networks for Timarchos, II: Graph of spatial text terms associated with Timarchos in Aischines 1. The size of a node and its label represents the frequency of that term's occurrence in the text. Nodes are spatially grouped and colored according to the classes of fig. 5.1 (Domestic, Urban, Civic). The thickness of an edge represents the frequency of each term's connection with Timarchos, and if there is no edge to Timarchos, the term is mentioned to exclude Timarchos. For example, Timarchos is said to never be in his father's oikia (node near bottom left of the diagram), so there is no edge, and the size of the node indicates that this is mentioned relatively often. Prepared by Esther Knegt using Gephi (Bastian, Heymann, and Jacomy 2009).*

stranger [*par' allotriōi*], older than himself, and although being in the prime of his youth [*hōraios ōn*], at the home of one without restraint [*par' akolastōi*] in these affairs.

His use of *eklipōn* (forsaking) here and of forms of *kataleipein* (leave behind) in other passages suggests the complete desertion of his father's *oikos* and renders Timarchos' presence at the houses of others even more troubling.

As figure 5.2 illustrates, his father's *oikos* is positioned outside his spatial network. Aischines does not locate him in his paternal home as expected and where he should in fact belong as a citizen of the polis, but instead moves him between the households of strangers (*allotrioi*) as represented here. The narrative first locates Timarchos at the house of a doctor (Euthydikos) in Peiraieus (1.40). Peiraieus is also the first location for Alke's sexual labor in Isaios 6 (chapter 2). As the major port of Athens, Peiraieus served a transient population, and indeed Aischines mentions the presence of both *emporoi* (traders) and *xenoi* (foreigners) as visitors to the house. The status of Euthydikos is not explicit, but the lack of a demotic suggests he was not an Athenian. It was in this location, according to Aischines, that Timarchos first offered himself up for sale, indiscriminately serving such customers. Timarchos is said to be just past boyhood at this time, and it is unclear whether his father was still alive.

He soon moved from Euthydikos' to the house of Misgolas, the son of Naukrates of the deme of Kollytos (1.41, 50).[60] Although Athenian, Misgolas is not *philos* (a friend) to Timarchos' father but *allotrios* (a stranger) to the family (1.42, quoted above). He had met Timarchos in Peiraieus at Euthydikos' residence and offered him a sum of money to move from that physician's house to his own *oikia*. Aischines presents Misgolas as well known for leisure, surrounding himself with singers and cithara players.[61] He also describes him as *akolastos* (lacking in restraint: 1.42). Once he has Timarchos in his own house and out of sight he uses him in any way he desires. Misgolas' house is presented as a place without paternal oversight, a house of excess and unsavory habits. In this context Aischines stresses how Timarchos, in the prime of his youth and thus at his most vulnerable, abandoned his father's house (1.42; cf. 1.47).

Unlike Alke and Neaira, whose permanency in an *oikos* is threatening, it is Timarchos' movements between households that Aischines has concerns about (1.51):

> Moreover, Athenians, if this Timarchos here had remained at Misgolas' house and had not gone on to another man's house, he would have acted more moderately [*metriōtera*], if indeed any such behavior is moderate [*metrion*], and I would not have dared to bring any other charge than what the lawgiver openly references, only that he has been kept as a companion [*hētairēkenai monon*].

If Timarchos had stayed at the house of Misgolas, rather than going from household to household, his behavior would have been considered somewhat moderate, modest, decent, or even more tolerable, depending on how one interprets *metriōtera* here.[62] *Metrios* is both quantitative and qualitative. It was an important social (and democratic) value, and its use here stresses Timarchos' failure to live up to expectations.[63] For after Misgolas, he goes to live with Antikles son of Kallias of the deme Euonymon (1.53). No details are provided except that Timarchos was taken up by Antikles after Misgolas sent him away because of his extravagance. From here Timarchos moves in with Pittalakos, who was or once had been a public slave (1.54).[64] It was here, at Pittalakos' house, that Hegesandros first met Timarchos and immediately enticed him to his own home with money (1.56–58, 64). By specifying different locations, Aischines emphasizes Timarchos' transitory state within the polis as well as the indiscriminate nature of his movements. In contrast to citizens more generally, paternity and familial duty do not connect Timarchos with *oikia*, nor does loyalty; instead, it is *argurion* (silver) that binds him to a space.

Aischines is also vague in his discussion of the places Timarchos moves between, simply associating Timarchos with many different *oikiai* (1.40, 52). Although Aischines thus specifically identifies certain houses with a specific owner and thus sexual partner, other *oikiai* are simply associated with *heteros* and *allos* (1.51, 52) or designated *allotriai* (1.75). There is no definitive number given to the houses Timarchos inhabits and spends his time at. In addition to *oikiai*, he is found lunching unchaperoned in a *sunoikia* with some aliens as a youth (1.43). Aischines assumes the jurors know of the gambling den where Timarchos meets Pittalakos but hints he would not expect to find any of them there (1.53).[65] Even if they are expected to know where Timarchos has been, they are not expected to be frequenting such places themselves.

Aischines also suggests that the general citizenry associate Timarchos with illicit activity in the desolate areas around the Pnyx (1.81–84, 90). Timarchos had apparently brought forward a proposal in the Athenian Assembly regarding the dilapidated houses and derelict cisterns in that region.[66] Aischines is not interested in the details of the proposal and instead emphasizes the reaction of those assembled to the suggestion that Timarchos was familiar with the *erēmiai* (deserted areas) and *topoi* (places) of the Pnyx. This area was geographically distinct from the rest of the city, located away from the Agora on its own hill on the other side of the Areopagus (fig. 5.3). Although used as the meeting place of the Assembly and the location for the Thesmophoria festival, at other times it was devoid of activity and known as a quiet area.[67] Aischines reminds the jurors that at the mention of *erēmiai* and *mikron analōma* (little expense) the assembled crowd applauded and laughed, making it hard for the speaker to continue. Although the double entendres of the complete passage remain obscure to modern

FIGURE 5.3. *Map of the Pnyx and vicinity in the fourth century BCE. Drawing by Tina Ross, adapted from John Travlos in Lang 2004: 2, fig. 1. Accessed via ASCSA.net, Agora Excavations.*

readers, we may assume that Aischines uses this anecdote to suggest Timarchos lurks around deserted areas of the polis offering cheap tricks to any he encounters.[68] The secretive nature of such places suggests indecent activity that decent citizens would feel shame at witnessing or even hearing about, signaling that Timarchos has something to hide.[69]

Indeed, the activities Timarchos engages in, like the many places he inhabits, remain obscure throughout the narrative. What went on at Pittalakos' place Aischines refuses to say (1.55). Aischines again hesitates to be more explicit about what happened between Hegesandros and Timarchos when they were home alone together (1.70). Aischines assures the jurors that they do not actually need to see in order to know, since without looking inside they are all familiar with, for example, what goes on inside a brothel (1.74–75). Although Aischines cites his own shame in not being more specific, by not detailing what goes on inside he exploits anxiety about other *oikoi* and what other citizens can actually know about the goings-on at one another's homes.[70] By leading jurors to various houses through the repeated use of *para* and *hōs* he invites them to envision what went on inside but leaves that largely to their own speculation.[71] In the case of Hegesandros, he directly engages the imagination of the jurors with reference to *bdeluria* (disgusting behavior) and drunkenness (1.70). Such obscurity allows the jurors to imagine all sorts of behavior but also creates uncertainty about Timarchos' intentions, since Athenian males are expected to be out in the open and in civic space, not doing things in secret and behind closed doors like tyrants.[72]

Timarchos' erotic relationships do not take place in the open at the *gumnasion*. Like his paternal *oikos*, the *gumnasion* is not part of his spatial network. (See fig. 5.2.) This omission contrasts with Aischines himself. He strategically marks the gymnasium as the context for his own liaisons when he suggests his opponents will critique him for being a pest and many times an *erastēs* (lover) at gymnasia (1.135). *Erastēs* distinguishes Aischines from Timarchos' partners.[73] Its use and the location of his own erotic affairs are not random: athletics were central to Greek eroticism and concepts of masculinity.[74] In the Classical period, gymnasia were clearly defined locales and likely popular with more than simply elite Athenians ([Xen.] *Ath. Pol.* 2.10). We know of three public gymnasia: the Academy, the Lyceum, and the Cynosarges (Dem. 24.114). The familiar peristyle of the Hellenistic period was not always present, since all that was required was a large open area and a grove of trees for shade (Ar. *Clouds* 1005–1008).[75] Since they were in the open air, the activities within were visible to all. Even the Classical period's *apodutērion*, the area designated for undressing and anointing with oil, was spacious and open. In addition to offering exercise space, gymnasia functioned as schools and offered social spaces for boys, youths, and men.[76]

The mere mention of gymnasia suggests Aischines has nothing to hide and provides an important backdrop to his discussion of his own relationships as *dikaion* (just: 1.136) and his own desire as *sōphrōn* (controlled) and *ennomos* (lawful: 1.140). Such comments highlight the openness and visibility of his associations compared with those of Timarchos, which occur out of view in private houses and deserted areas of the polis. The gymnasium is where boys and youths regularly (and legitimately) spend their time as citizens in training.[77] At gymnasia *erōmenoi* (beloveds) were courted by *erastai* (lovers), and normalized and accepted sexual relations occurred.[78] Pederastic relationships were easily overseen here and were thus open to scrutiny. Aischines purposely appears to avoid any reference to Timarchos' status as an athlete practicing in gymnasia, yet his fame as a beautiful youth likely grew from his visible presence at such venues.[79] Removing Timarchos and his lovers from this public place and relocating them in private homes marks their associations as something different, as secretive and suspect, and thus even deviant. For in contrast to gymnasia, Classical houses were designed to shield the occupants from view with their high-placed windows and internal courtyards.[80]

The Assembly and gymnasium literally introduce and conclude Aischines' detailed discussion of Timarchos in the urban landscape, and this positioning highlights his habits in private houses as antidemocratic and suspect. The frequent mention of *oikia* also feminizes Timarchos, since it was women who regularly spent their time indoors. Words like *echein* (have, keep: 1.41, 54, 64, 95), *analambanein* (take up: 1.43, 52, 53, 54, 57, 58), and *diaitasthai* (live with: 1.42, 47, 50) to describe Timarchos' relations with his lovers reinforce this identification, since men commonly live with wives, *hetairai*, and even *auletrides*.[81] It comes as no surprise that Aischines eventually refers to Timarchos as the wife of Hegesandros, albeit through the words of another (1.110–111; cf. 1.185):

> Pamphilos, when there was an assembly, stood up and said, "Athenians, a man and a woman [*aner kai gune*] are stealing a thousand drachmas from you." And when you expressed amazement how a man and a woman and what the story was, after a short time he said, "Are you ignorant of what I am saying? ... The man [*ho men aner*] is the now-infamous Hegesandros, ... who was previously wife [*gune*] of Leodamas; and the woman [*he de gune*] is this Timarchos here."

David Halperin and others interpret the passage as a reference to anal penetration.[82] Yet feminizing Timarchos as guilty of female crimes (1.185) and labeling him "wife" in his relationship with Hegesandros might just as likely refer to his insatiable appetites resulting from a deficiency in *enkrateia* or to his economic dependency, James Davidson argues, since such traits were also commonly associated with women.[83] Even if Aischines does intend to suggest the position Timarchos takes in sexual intercourse here, it does not mean that a sexually passive role like anal penetration is the focus of his speech and concern or of his accusations of *hubris*. (See below.) Through his movements and occupation of space Timarchos resembles a *hetaira* and *gune*.[84] Pamphilos' comment simply gives voice to what Aischines hopes the jurors will freely interpret. The anecdote is also strategic. Since women were not legally eligible to attend assemblies, the affinity questions Timarchos' fitness to attend and speak at assemblies as well. Aischines faults Timarchos for his presence in the homes of strangers and yet through his speech also relegates him to such networks by visibly removing him from the Assembly and feminizing him.[85]

Aischines very consciously exploits social space throughout his narrative as a means of emphasizing Timarchos' deviance and displacement in the polis. A popularly referenced section of this speech against Timarchos showcases Aischines' sense of space as embodied (1.123–124):

> For neither rooms nor residences [*ou gar ta oikēmata oud' hai oikēseis*] provide names for their occupants, but rather the occupants render names to the places [*tois topois*] based on their personal activities [*tōn idiōn epitēdeumatōn*]. For where many men inhabit one house, having rented it and divided it up among themselves, we call it a rooming house [*sunoikian*], but where one person lives, a single dwelling [*oikian*]. And if a doctor [*iatros*] settles into one of the workshops facing onto the street, it is called an *iatreion*. But if he vacates it and a metal worker [*chalkeus*] takes over this same workshop, it is called a *chalkeion*; if a fuller [*knapheus*], a *knapheion*; if a wood worker [*tektōn*], a *tektoneion*; and if a pimp and his sex slaves [*pornoboskos kai pornai*], from their very business [*tēs ergasias*] it is called a *porneion*. So you [Timarchos] have created many brothels [*polla porneia*] with your unscrupulous transactions [*tēi tēs praxeōs euchereiai*].

The passage reveals his construction of place within the narrative by stressing the role of occupants and activities over the actual physical space. The same space can become the place of the doctor, the metal worker, the fuller, the wood worker, or even sex slaves. Aischines emphasizes that it is the associations that define the space as a place. When occupied by a doctor, for example, it becomes a medical practice, by sex slaves, a brothel. There is a definite dynamism between self and space in this argument that renders each the embodiment of the other. This slippage between the body and place is what James Davidson refers to as the "body = building metaphor." He observes how the passage echoes the career of Timarchos, which began at the house of a physician (1.40), with the rented space paralleling the hired body of Timarchos.[86] The *topoi* (places) that the defense demands as proof of Timarchos' activities as a sex laborer skillfully become an analogy for Timarchos' body, with both indiscriminately hired out. Timarchos is just as promiscuous as the spaces he moves through. With this argument Aischines conflates all kinds of spaces, including *oikoi* and *porneia*, to claim that Timarchos himself transforms space into brothels because of his unscrupulous transactions. (Cf. 1.127.) At this point in the speech, Aischines warns that Timarchos' behavior infects everywhere he goes, and for this reason it is critical that he be disenfranchised before he pollutes the democracy further. Timarchos' association with the *porneion*, in turn, marks the end of a downward spatial trajectory and completes his transformation into a *pornos*, one who turns cheap tricks with multiple customers in a single day and is frequently enslaved, female, and foreign. While he constructs normative spaces, like the Assembly or the house of Timarchos' father, that uphold the democratic status quo and its accompanying values, he also develops places of deviance through his narrative of Timarchos' activities and movements.

SŌMA AND POLIS

Aischines had already pointed out at the start of his narrative that Timarchos' behavior should be a concern to the jurors because it has implications for the city, not just Timarchos himself. When Timarchos moves from lover to lover and place to place for a price, he shames not only his own body, but the city more broadly (*kataischunōn to sōma to heautou kai tēn polin*, 1.40; cf. 65). The two are invariably linked. His personal activities make him a threat to the city and its citizens: "What would he not sell, if he has trafficked in his own body's abuse [*tou sōmatos hubrin*]? Whom would he pity, if he has had no pity for himself?" (1.188). In this way Aischines emphasizes a connection between *sōma* and polis, and thus private behavior and public acts. As Giulia Sissa observes, the personal mirrors the political: how a man treats family, his wealth, and his body becomes the predictor of how he will behave when entrusted with the business of the city.[87] Through such comments Aischines taps into public mistrust of civic institutions brought on by the ever-increasing threat of Macedon. He mentions accusations of bribery in the Assembly and lawcourts (1.86–87), and there were also allegations of bribery against Aischines himself.[88]

Timarchos' label as a sex laborer also contrasts with an idealization of citizenship and the identity of the citizen as *kalos*, *agathos*, *sōphrōn* (self-controlled), *metrios* (moderate), and *katharos* (pure: e.g., 1.6–11, 25, 31, 42, 81, 188), one who is restrained and socially beneficial to the community. The qualities associated with Timarchos the *pornos* are the opposite of these. He is *aselgēs* (degenerate), *bdeluros* (repulsive), *hubristēs*, and even *miaros* (polluted: 1.42, 54). The terms not only identify him as the opposite of the productive citizen, but that polarization also suggests he is dangerous and even threatening to the community. Such language leads Susan Lape to conclude that Aischines was attempting to shift focus from Athens' external affairs to an enemy within by reconfiguring moral standing as the most important quality of the Athenian citizen.[89] Although many of these terms were common in differentiating between citizens, as we saw in Lysias 3, Aischines' discussion of Timarchos destabilizes traditional concepts of citizenship based on status and suggests a particular code of conduct, an ethics of citizenship, against which citizens are measured.

The use of *bdeluros* and *bdeluria* (repulsiveness) are particularly significant in this regard and dominate in Aischines' descriptions of Timarchos and his activities when otherwise rare in oratory, as Giulia Sissa notes.[90] Aischines connects Timarchos with this particular attribute seventeen times, using it throughout the speech to describe Timarchos and his activities. He first uses it in section 26, quoted near the start of this chapter, in connection with the adverbs *kakōs* (terribly) and *aischrōs* (shamefully) and in contrast to *sōphrōn* used to describe more noble ancestors like Solon in section 25.[91] Early on, Aischines develops *bdeluros* as the polar opposite of *kalos* and *agathos*, traits of a true citizen (1.31):

> [Solon] believed that to hear the recommendations of a good and noble man [*para men andros kalou kai agathou*], even if delivered exceedingly poorly and simply, would be beneficial [*chrēsima*] but that to hear the proposals of a repulsive person [*para de anthrōpou bdelurou*], who has used his own body absurdly [*katagelastōs men kechrēmenou tōi heautou sōmati*] and recklessly consumed his family property [*aischrōs de tēn patrōian ousian katedēdokotos*], would not be profitable, even if spoken very well.

The *anthrōpos bdeluros* (repulsive person) is not fit for the full privilege of citizenship and the right to address the Assembly—a privilege reserved instead for the *anēr kalos kai agathos* (good and noble man). This contrast, between *kalos kai agathos* and *bdeluros*, is central to Aischines' concept of citizenship. The use of the generic *anthrōpos* (a term devoid of status and used for persons lacking citizenship, including freed and enslaved persons) versus *anēr* (used commonly for men with social status) adds to the contrast.[92]

Aischines identifies a *bdeluros* person here as someone who uses his own body in an absurd way and shamefully wastes his ancestral wealth, the two offenses of Timarchos focused on in his speech (1.37–76, 97–105, respectively). At the same time, *bdeluros* and its noun, *bdeluria*, are affixed to Timarchos' identity as a *pornos*, appearing in connection with its verbal cognate, *porneuein*, more than any of the other actions associated with Timarchos. The final reference comes at the end of the speech (1.189–190):

> Indeed, who among you does not well know the repulsiveness of Timarchos [*hē Timarchou bdeluria*]? Just as we recognize those in training [*tous gumnazomenous*], without being present at the *gumnasion*, from seeing their physical condition [*tas euexias autōn*], so too we know those who have prostituted themselves [*tous peporneumenous*], even if we do not witness their deeds [*autōn tois ergois*], from their insatiate appetites, daring, and personal habits [*ek tēs anaideias kai tou thrasous kai tōn epitēdeumatōn*]. For the one despising the laws and decency [*tous nomous kai tēn sōphrosunēn*] possesses a certain disposition [*echei tina hexin tēs psuchēs*] that is recognizable from the dissoluteness of his way of life [*ek tēs akosmias tou tropou*]. You could find a great many cities that have come to ruin from such men [*ek tōn toioutōn anthrōpōn*].

The emphasis of Timarchos' *bdeluria* here is the fact that he has worked as a sex laborer. Appetites and lifestyle, not payments, are stressed as evidence of working in the sex trade at this point. James Davidson argues that Timarchos' "whoring" is parallel to his wasting of his estate—both are the means of financing his insatiable appetites.[93] But Timarchos' relationship to sexual labor is not only economic. In this quote, *anaideia* (insatiate appetite) identifies (and drives) sex laborers. Their boldness also gives them away. Rather than this profession simply financing Timarchos' lust, greed, and gambling, these habits stem from his *hexis tēs psuchēs*, "the condition of his inner being": his "soul," as Susan Lape and others translate the term *psuchē*.[94]

The choice of *hexis* (condition), when *psuchē* would suffice, links back to *euexia* (good condition) used to identify those regularly at the *gumnasion* and suggests that a citizen's inner disposition is mirrored in the material body and its habits. The *tropos* ascribed to the sex laborer is summed up as *akosmia* (disorder) in opposition to the desired *eukosmia* of *paides* (1.8), rhetors (1.34), women (1.183), and the city (1.192), which the laws attempt to protect (1.22).[95] With his narrative, Aischines hints Timarchos has had a particular disposition since boyhood (1.39). It is this temperament that renders his body ready and willing for anything (1.41–42, 57). It also leaves his body insatiable. It is because of his disposition that Timarchos truly deserves the label *pornos*. According to Laura McClure, verbs more commonly indicate males practicing sexual labor, focusing on it as a trade as opposed to an identity, and so Aischines' use of *pornos* signified Timarchos was at core a sex slave (1.130; cf. 123).[96] By the end of the speech Timarchos' identity as a sex laborer embodies all that is disturbing about his *sōma*. Notably, *bdeluria* also heads the list of Timarchean qualities that Aischines claims produce the worst (*kakistos*) and least beneficial (Fisher's rendering of *alusitelestatos*) citizen (*politēs*, 1.105).[97] Aischines effectively uses the sex laborer's body to problematize Timarchos' role as citizen in the democracy.

ACCUSATIONS OF *HUBRIS*

Aischines also adds a new character flaw to the portrait of the sex laborer: *hubris*. In contrast to Theodotos (chapter 4), who is described as *hubristhenta* (Lys. 3.17), and Androtion, who submits to *hubristai* in exchange for payment (Dem. 22.58), Timarchos is not a victim of the *hubris* of others, except once during his relationship with Pittalakos, a public slave.[98] Instead, Aischines claims emphatically that Timarchos is guilty of *hubris* in relation to his own *sōma* (1.108, 116, 185, 188). Although *hubris* is a broad term indicating arrogant, antisocial behavior, in Aischines' speech, as in Lysias 3, *hubris* commonly references sexual transgressions (1.15, 29, 87, 137, 141, 163). In a legal context it refers to an array of offenses against the honor of another person for which the perpetrator could be prosecuted in a *graphē hubreōs*.[99] What exactly Aischines means by *eis to sōma to heautou* (against his own body) has been the topic of scholarly debate. David Halperin argues for *hubris* as a reference to his submission to anal penetration, whereas James Davidson takes a more general view of Timarchos' offense and focuses on the commodification of his body. Nick Fisher suggests that he endures sexual acts that are physically painful to his person.[100] Although the specific act behind his *hubris* remains speculative, the references imply that Timarchos takes an active role in his dishonor by not treating his body, a citizen body the lawgivers legislated to protect (1.5), as it should be treated.

Timarchos' *hubris* may best be read in relation to Aischines' discussion of the law against *hubris* that protected children, women, and men, whether free or enslaved, from hubristic acts against their persons (1.15).[101] The account of the law follows a summary of the laws against the illegal procuring of children (1.13–14). Aischines' interest in the law against *hubris* also relates to sex trafficking: he specifies *hubris* against *paides* as the hiring of a boy for money. In this way, he specifically links the law to the trafficking of children. Next he discusses the *graphē hetairēseōs* (1.19–21), a suit against any citizen who held public office (including religious offices), acted as an ambassador, brought prosecutions to court, or addressed the Assembly after working in the sex trade.[102] In this case he specifies that the law was relevant to *meirakia* (youths). Aischines is likely limiting a procedure that was relevant to citizens of any age acting as sex laborers—in what Nick Fisher identifies as a desire to provide "a carefully graduated schema" of laws for each age class up to full adulthood—to explain the procedure he chooses, the *dokimasia*, in his case against Timarchos.[103] Aischines' discussion of the law also conflates different types of sexual labor. (Cf. 1.51–52.) Stephen Todd and Nick Fisher suggest that *hetairēsis* refers to working as a male escort similar to a *hetaira*, who was kept and not paid per sexual transaction.[104] But as we witnessed in Apollodoros' speech, *Against Neaira*, Aischines' *hetairos* is indistinguishable from the *pornos*: the phrase *eis ta heautōn sōmata examartanontōn* (doing wrong against their own bodies: 1.22) emphasizes the physical aspect of the relationship and suggests the jurors should be concerned about what goes on in such relationships. At this stage, responsibility for any mistreatment belongs to the escort instead of any procurer or client. Aischines concludes his discussion of the laws with the *dokimasia tōn rhētorōn* (discussed above), which he connects with citizen males, *Athenaioi* (1.22). He again conflates *peporneumenos* (having worked as a *pornos*) with *hētairēkōs* (having served as a sexual companion) when he explains that male citizens working in either role are banned from speaking in the Assembly as a matter of public trust, because a citizen who commits *hubris* against his own body (again stressing the physical component) might easily betray the interests of the city (1.29). In this case the wrongs against the body have become *hubris*.

Although Athens did not have a body of law dealing with sexual labor, Aischines presents these laws and procedures as a coherent body of Solonian legislation when it is more likely they were introduced independently over the course of the fifth century BCE.[105] But by grouping together a series of laws that relate to purchasing or working as a sex laborer and embedding the law of *hubris* among them Aischines misleadingly associates activities around the sex trade with *hubris*. Giulia Sissa comments on the "rhetorical forcing" of the connection in a society for which engaging in the sex trade, although precluding one from public service or an advisory role, was not in itself a punishable offense.[106] These laws frame Timarchos' *hubris* as not unique but central to his identity as a *pornos*. Such *hubris* questions his suitability for the privilege of citizenship in light of the *graphē hubreōs*. In discussing the law Aischines claims that anyone who is *hubristēs* (a person who commits *hubris*) is not fit to be a *sumpolitēs* (fellow citizen: 1.17). And indeed, Timarchos is eventually labeled *hubristēs*, at which point his *hubris* against his own body is assimilated with *hubris* against others (1.108).

SEX LABORERS AND *ERŌMENOI*

An important context for Aischines' argument is pederasty, the relationship between an *erastēs* (lover), normally an older male youth, and an *erōmenos* (beloved), a prepubescent boy. The relationship was indeed sexual, although Greeks considered it an effective way to mentor younger citizens and thus an important phase of adolescence.[107] Aischines himself admits in court to enjoying the role of an *erastēs* with youths and highlights the excellence of this type of relationship, referring to it as *erōs dikaios* (a "just love": 1.136). Many scholars argue that the association of such a relationship with the symposium and the gymnasium brands it as an elite practice.[108] If that is correct, its discussion in a speech in a popular court (1.136–140), with jurors mainly from among the non-elites, seems risky and not likely to garner any sympathy. Thomas Hubbard suggests Aischines may have edited his speech to include this discussion prior to publication and once the trial was long over, since his readers would be from among the elite.[109] Giulia Sissa argues that Aischines crafted his speech for two different audiences with the discussion of pederasty geared to a minority of elites among the jurors.[110] Susan Lape regards the inclusion as self-serving: she concludes that Aischines inserted a lengthy discussion of *erōs* to defend his own activities with youths and distinguish himself from the behavior of Timarchos. He uses the speech and the trial to disassociate pederasty from the elite and craft it as a democratic tradition.[111] Others, following Nick Fisher, argue that the current speech is evidence that pederasty had become a widespread practice by the fourth century BCE.[112] James Davidson agrees and argues that the concern was not with pederasty per se, but with the increasing commodification of same-sex relationships as "the market in handsome males seems to have become more obvious, more visible, more talked-about" at Athens.[113] It was this available market that enabled Aischines to reframe Timarchos' relationships.

A quantitative measure of the Athenian sex trade is not possible from the available data. But if we assume the text as we have it is close to what Aischines presented to the court, as Fisher does, the characterization of Timarchos depends to some extent on the ubiquity and visibility of sexual labor at Athens as well as on widespread acceptance of the practice of pederasty, whether limited to the elite or open to Athenians more generally, while also playing upon social anxiety around the pederastic relationship.[114] Comparisons between beloveds and female sex laborers can be found as far back as the Archaic period, and concern about relationships with youths surfaces in the mid-fifth century BCE in the comedies of Aristophanes.[115] In *Wealth*, boys are compared to Corinthian *hetairai*, with the emphasis on the line between the legitimate exchanges behind pederasty and the commodified transactions of the sex laborer (149–159). When the motivation is economic gain, there is no loyalty in relationships with lovers, and the boys like *hetairai* instead exploit lovers' affections to personal advantage. These types of boys are not *chrēstos* (good), but according to the comic poet they become known as *pornoi*. They have no qualms about whom they have sex with and will even stoop to sex with an old woman so long as the compensation is right (981–986). Gender adds to the comic effect, since it is unlikely women had access to the sex trade as clients.

The old woman as a character also highlights the commercial exchange, since presumably no youth willingly has sex with an old woman (in the ancient Athenian mind, at least).[116] The character Chremylos emphasizes the venal aspect of the relationship even as the old woman reminisces about the young man's affection for her (1006–1024). The old woman's description of their relationship includes requests for money so that the young man can buy himself cloaks, shoes, and so on, instead of waiting for gifts of her choosing. Any hint of *philia* is only feigned, since the young man drops the woman once he no longer needs financial help (992–1002). Particularly interesting is the use of *bdeluros*: the old woman originally called the youth a *meirakion philon* (975), appropriating language associated with courtship (see chapter 4), but when the boy no longer needs her and rejects her cakes, he is *ho bdeluros* (the disgusting one: 993). Although the term is not limited to this play and context, Aristophanes' more common use still suggests reprehensible behavior, and Aischines may be alluding to a comic precedent with its use in his speech.[117]

Similarities between Timarchos and this other young man suggest Aischines was playing with common stereotypes and anxieties going back to the fifth century BCE. As discussed in chapter 1, the portraits of female sex laborers were familiar to the jurors through Middle Comedy. Although male sex laborers are less frequent, their sexual labor is still alluded to. As in Aristophanes, there is anxiety that centers on distinguishing between pederasty and sex for sale and the commodification of personal relationships. A passage from Ephippos' *Sappho* hints a young man is sexually trafficking himself when he contributes nil toward the food at dinner (Fr. 20 *PCG*). Instead of paying his fair share outright, he spends the night with the host.

Athenaios comments on its resemblance to Aischines' argument against Timarchos and points out how Ephippos' passage closely parallels a passage of Aischines (Ath. 13.572c–d). The second line of Ephippos' fragment is corrupt, and so I quote two different translations:[118]

> Whenever a young man enters a house [*oikon*] of another in secret and lays his hands on the food without contributing a share [*asumbolon*], you can be certain he pays his dues during the night [*tēs nuktos*].

> When a young man, going out, learns to eat another man's fish [*opson*] and puts a hand that pays no share [*asumbolon*] to the food, you must believe he pays his reckoning in the night [*tēs nuktos*].

Whether the amended text refers to a house or to fish, both link to the corresponding passage in Aischines with their references to dining in exchange for sex (Aischin. 1.75–76):

> Or what ought we to call it when a young man—an exceptionally beautiful one—abandons the house of his father and spends the night [*nuktereuēi*] at the homes of other men, dines on expensive dinners without contributing a share [*asumbolon*], keeps the most expensive flute players and *hetairai*, and gambles without paying anything himself, but another does so on his behalf? Are divinations needed to explain these activities? Is it not crystal clear that the one making such demands on others must himself, in exchange for these, provide certain pleasures to those who are spending their money?

Both authors emphasize the missing contribution with *asumbolos* (not contributing to the cost) and to imply that the recompense is of a sexual nature employ a similar euphemism suggesting transactional sex: *didonai . . . tēs nuktos logon* (pay his due during the night) in Ephippos and *nuktereuēi* (spends the night) in Aischines. As Nick Fisher points out, although Ephippos was a contemporary of Aischines, the date of his play is uncertain, and so it is impossible to establish which was written first and thus whether one was a direct allusion to the other.[119] Even if the passages are not based on a character type, they hint at the suspicion and gossip surrounding young men dining unaccompanied outside the home and play on the slippage between legitimate courtship and paid sexual labor.[120]

A fragment of Alexis (also attributed to Antiphanes) corroborates such an attitude. A character labels another dinner companion a *pornos* because he always avoided leeks whenever they dined together in order not to foul his breath for his evening lover (Ath. 13.572c, Fr. 244 *PCG*). This passage also seems to allude to sexual favors in exchange for dining at the expense of another. In this case contempt is stressed, however, as opposed to suspicion. Although male sex laborers and beloveds were not commonly represented in comedy or present on stage as characters, their mentions suggest that as early as the fifth century BCE they were the butt of jokes that depended in their jesting upon attitudes of suspicion toward transactional sex and apprehension around courtship.

Aischines was able to rely on his audience's familiarity with such comic tropes in his speech against Timarchos. He, like Lysias before him (see chapter 4), exploits ambivalence around the pederastic relationship and sexual labor in describing Timarchos' relationships. As he nears the end of his speech, he asks his audience whether they would classify Timarchos with those who have been loved as beloveds (*eis tous erōmenous*) or those who have sold themselves for sex (*eis tous peporneumenous*, 1.159). With this question he makes the distinction between the *erōmenos* and *pornos* a central feature of his argument. But it is unlikely that his audience would easily have agreed on what exactly an appropriate love with an *erastēs* was and what made it sexual labor.[121] Aischines himself makes clear that the defense will try to argue that Timarchos was in fact simply a popular *erōmenos* on account of his exceptional beauty and that he is now being prosecuted because of these good looks and past popularity (1.126, 133–134; Dem. 19.233). In anticipation, Aischines emphasizes that it was not simply Timarchos' beauty and admiration that were the problem: he points to contemporary Athenians of all ages (naming past and current *erōmenoi*) famous for their beauty and courted by many *erastai*, but who were the *sōphronestatoi* (most *sōphrōn*) and thus were never once confused with those working in the sex trade (1.155–157). In contrast, the *homotropoi* (kindred spirits) of Timarchos are infamous for their activities in the sex trade and profligate lifestyles (1.158–159).

Aischines develops the contrast further by idealizing pederastic relationships in his speech and connecting them with good civic action, what Victoria Wohl terms a "socially productive erotics."[122] Anticipating and appropriating the arguments of the defense (1.132), Aischines suggests that the intimacy between Harmodios and Aristogeiton also has democratic significance because it resulted in their noble and brave actions on behalf of the polis against the tyrant Hippias and his brother, Hipparchos (1.140).[123] He comments on the lovers' *aretē* and their important role as civic benefactors. He describes their *erōs* for each other as *sōphrōn* and *ennomos* (lawful), even presenting it as the essential component of their education that prepared them for their noble action, the assassination attempt against Hippias (514 BCE). With this example and by associating pederasty with democratic lawgivers like Solon (1.138–139), Aischines not only presents pederasty as the ideal relationship of male citizens regardless of their social status but politicizes it as an important democratic institution.[124]

Harmodios and Aristogeiton were well known to Athenians, who commemorated the tyrannicides in common drinking songs (Ath. 15.695a) and more formally with a civic cult and statue group.[125] The *dēmos* also approved a decree allotting special privileges to their descendants, including dining free in the Prytaneion.[126] Aischines presents the pair as exemplars of the positive actions that come out of the pederastic relationship, but their erotic attachment was not the primary emphasis of their idealization in texts of the Classical period. The skolia stress the democratic and heroic nature of their actions, with little attention to the erotic element.[127] Nonpopular accounts, however, are critical of the details of the attack. According to Herodotus, the actions of the pair did not liberate Athens but only increased the suffering of Athenians until the Alkmaionids were able to free them from the tyranny (Hdt. 5.55, 6.123). In Thucydides' analysis, the assassination attempt was the result of a disagreement between elites. He stresses their motivations as personal (jealous rivalry for Aristogeiton and an insult to Harmodios) rather than attributing altruistic and democratic incentives to their actions (Thuc. 1.54–59; cf. [Arist.] *Ath. Pol.* 18–19).[128] Only Plato idealizes the role of *erōs* and *philia* in the downfall of the tyranny and in doing so equates pederasty with democratic freedom (*Symp.* 182c). Aischines' speech suggests the sexual aspect of the relationship was common parlance by the fourth century BCE, and this awareness enabled Aischines' manipulation of the myth in his attack on Timarchos. His version appears unique in that it effectively conflates the pederastic element with the popular version of events and promotes pederasty as a democratic sexuality that he puts front and center in his attack on Timarchos.

Aischines also invokes the poets as witnesses to the two types of *erōs* he develops in his arguments: what exists between *tous sōphrones* versus the *erōs* involving *tous akrateis* (the incontinent) and *tous hubristas* (terms associated with Timarchos earlier in the speech; 1.141). He begins with the relationship between Achilles and Patroklos in Homer, presenting it as another ideal example of pederasty.[129] Aischines again highlights excellence (*aretē*, 1.146) but emphasizes fidelity and loyalty in this case as the most important characteristics of a *sōphrōn* love (1.145, 147). The bond between the two lovers was so strong in fact, Aischines explains, that Achilles opted to join Patroklos in death rather than keep on living (1.150). As in the example of Harmodios and Aristogeiton, Aischines credits their erotic fidelity to each other with enabling Achilles to be the hero he was at Troy, since without it he would not have killed Hector and would have returned home to die in obscurity (1.145).[130] Aischines also invokes Euripides. He quotes lines from an unnamed play in support of his view that a *sōphrōn* love produces *aretē* in the lovers (1.151). Nick Fisher suggests that Aischines purposefully suppresses the name of the play (*Stheneboia*) and skips the immediately preceding lines on bad *erōs*, which would in many ways further support his point, because the play centers on marital *erōs*, not pederasty, with adultery being the unchaste love alluded to.[131] Aischines clearly identifies the second, longer quotation as from Euripides' *Phoinix*. He presents the lines as evidence that you can judge the nature of a man's erotic life by his daily habits, his associates, and how he manages his business affairs, but he expands his interpretation of the text to argue again for an erotics of public life: private *erōs* is intimately tied to public actions (Aischin. 1.152–153).[132] It is the *sōphrōn erōs* of the pederastic relationship that most benefits Athens and the democracy.

Aischines' point in idealizing the pederastic relationship is that Timarchos and his lovers contrast with these models and instead engage in meretricious acts. Throughout the narrative he works hard to construe Timarchos' associations as the polar opposite of such a relationship. Aischines argues that Timarchos' relationships depended on *argurion* and *misthos*, as opposed to *charis* (gratitude), central to the pederastic relationship, which depended on gift exchange.[133] The *erastēs* courted the *erōmenos* with presents, and the beloved reciprocated with *charis*.[134] Such gratitude includes a sexual element, but also loyalty to the *erastēs*. Unlike the pederastic relationship, however, Timarchos' relationships lack such fidelity and true reciprocity. Timarchos offers no loyalty to a lover and instead accepts monetary payment from whomever can afford him. His motivation is the satisfaction of addictions to which he is enslaved (1.42, 95–96).[135] These addictions further contrast him with the *erōmenos*: Timarchos, as we have seen, inhabits an uncontrollable and excessive body, whereas the *erōmenos*, the beloved, is valued for his restraint and moderation (1.137, 139).[136] Aischines makes a direct comparison between pederasty and sexual labor and in doing so politicizes sexual labor as well (1.137):

> I mark out loving the beautiful and virtuous [*to men eran tōn kalōn kai sōphronōn*] as a condition of a humanitarian and reasonable nature [*philanthrōpou pathos kai eugnōmonos psuchēs*], but behaving licentiously by

hiring someone for money [*to de aselgainein arguriou tina misthoumenon*] is an act of an insolent and uneducated man [*hubristou kai apaideutou andros ergon*]; further, I say that to be loved without being corrupted is honorable [*kalon*], but having sold oneself for sex in excitement for a fee [*to d' eparthenta misthōi peporneusthai*] is shameful [*aischron*].

The passage repeats key vocabulary employed throughout the speech and very familiar to Aischines' listeners by this point: *kalos, sōphrōn, aselgainein, hubristēs, porneuein, misthos, aischros*. It tags many of the negative qualities and habits already attributed to Timarchos and associates the idealizing terminology with the pederastic relationship. Whether hiring a sex laborer or being purchased as one, the individual is not the ideal citizen, who instead is identified as either the *erastēs* or the *erōmenos*. Everything Aischines has detailed prior to this point connects Timarchos with sexual labor as the one who is hired. And it is only within the context of pederasty that we recognize the full implications of this argument. In contrast to the pederastic relationship, Timarchos' relationships do not produce good citizens working to better Athens and strengthen the democracy but give rise to the *hubristai* who threaten the democratic polis. As James Davidson explains it, the speech conflates "a new world of commoditized homosex and democratic paranoia about politicians getting into bed with one another literally and figuratively" to create the "prostitute politician," who looks only to his own advantage.[137]

It is not simply what Davidson claims, that "there is something fundamentally undemocratic about politicians having friends," but that, according to Aischines, the type of friendship has an impact on the democracy.[138] Rather than noble actions that benefit the city, Timarchos is presented as engaging in actions not merely of no advantage to the city or his own family but even potentially harmful (1.106). He accepted bribes and engaged in blackmail when serving as a public auditor, and he sexually corrupted free men's wives in his tenure as *archōn* (chief officer) on Andros (1.107).[139] As an elected official he embezzled and extorted citizens again (1.113–114).[140] Timarchos does his greatest damage to the democratic city when in partnership with others. Aischines claims that while Timarchos was a member of the *Boulē* he conspired with Hegesandros, who was serving as treasurer, to steal a thousand drachmas from the city treasury.[141] Aischines describes them acting together *mala philetairōs* (with much devotion to each other). But instead of idealizing their relationship the term emphasizes the negative consequences of their type of erotic attachment (1.110). By focusing on sexual labor Aischines is able to arouse suspicion around any associates in Timarchos' circle with his accusations, including those, like Hegesandros, who will come to his defense (1.71). Their relationships become disruptive and have a negative impact on the city and on individual citizens. Timarchos' actions, especially on Andros, echo the behavior of tyrants and directly contrast him with the tyrannicides Harmodios and Aristogeiton, hinting at his antidemocratic disposition and the need for his immediate expulsion.[142] Timarchos himself in no way resembles Harmodios in relationship with Aristogeiton, as Demosthenes' defense speech may claim (1.132), but represents the exact scourge that their pederasty helped to purge.

CONCLUSION

A prominent topos in Aischines 1 is sexual labor, which connects with a variety of other themes, including the body, pederasty, citizen privilege, and civic community. Physical *topoi* also predominate. Aischines skillfully manipulates the urban landscape to question Timarchos' relationships and alienate him from his own city. He rhetorically links sexual labor with *hubris*, primarily sexual in this speech. His accusation that Timarchos directs it against his own body is shocking and perhaps even more a cause for discomfort to the jurors than Simon's treatment of Theodotos in Lysias 3 (chapter 4). Even more so than that speech, Aischines 1 advances such sexual *hubris* as antidemocratic. As suggested in his *prooimion*, it is specifically the protection and thus treatment of *sōmata* that differentiate democracies from tyrannies and even oligarchies (1.5)—both of which the Athenians were very familiar with. Aischines has advanced Timarchos' trafficking of himself to problematize Timarchos and his relationships with others and the polis, not just his own body and appetites. His failings do not simply question his masculinity and trustworthiness as a rhetor in the Assembly but place him in opposition to the ideal citizen, who is *kalos*, *agathos*, and *sōphrōn*. They undermine his social legitimacy more generally and present him as a threat to social stability.

Timarchos and his sexuality are commonly referenced in scholarly discussions of passivity, penetration, and *kinaideia*, normally defined as the disposition of an effeminate and sexually deviant male.[143] But the speech is vague about what Timarchos did with his sex partners, and although the nouns *kinaidos* and *kinaideia* both occur in the speech (1.131, 181), they describe Demosthenes, not Timarchos.[144] Aischines associates the term with *anandria* (lack of manliness) and luxurious and delicate clothing more appropriate to a woman than a man (1.131). He regularly uses this descriptor for Demosthenes in other speeches, where he develops the concept further (2.23, 88, 99, 151). In Aischines 1, the *kinaidos* is distinct from Timarchos: even when employed in the same sentence it is emphatically associated with Demosthenes (1.181). Timarchos' deviance and insatiability are instead tied to his role as *pornos*. In the same way that he uses *kinaidos* as a lifestyle and identity for Demosthenes, Aischines employs *pornos* to indicate a lifestyle and personality for Timarchos. His concern is not to show that Timarchos has practiced a profession—no concrete proofs like witnesses, contracts, or the *pornikon telos* are offered—but to show that he embodies an identity. Through this identity Aischines is able both to feminize Timarchos and mark him as slavish while also commodifying his relationships.

Aischines 1 shares many similarities with Apollodoros' speech, *Against Neaira* (chapter 3), and likely directly influenced it. The body is a focal point of both speeches. Aischines and Apollodoros clearly connect citizenship to particular qualities and place an emphasis on the citizen as a particular kind of body. As we have seen, Timarchos is associated with *bdeluria, aselgeia, hubristēs,* and *aischrōs,* terms that signify opposition to an ideal citizen and justify his loss of citizen privileges. As with Timarchos, *aischrōs* and *aselgeia* describe Neaira's activities and contrast her with an ideal female citizen who is *sōphrōn*. Both use sexual labor to maintain their extravagant lifestyles at the cost of others. The expensive lifestyles highlight their insatiability and further develop the sex laborer as a tool to map out the boundaries between those who deserve citizen privileges and civic honors and those who do not. With both speeches the sex laborer becomes a locus for Athenian anxieties around citizenship, privilege, and sociopolitical institutions.

Through his portrait of Timarchos as *pornos*, Aischines destabilizes what being a citizen in a democracy means. It is not simply engaging in civic acts, like attending assembly, serving as a juror, advising the city well, serving in the military, respecting other citizens, or performing liturgies. It is a life lived in a particular way. His argument sufficed to convince the jurors to convict Timarchos, who suffered *atimia*, total loss of citizen rights, as Demosthenes tells us (Dem. 19.257, 284–286).

CONCLUSION

BY DECIDING TO FOCUS every chapter on a specific lawcourt speech, I have been able to highlight the complex uses of sexual labor in each but also to present sexual labor as a topos of the orators. All the speeches discussed involve sex laborers and include extended narratives on the sex trade, regardless of the type of trial, whether a *graphē* or *dikē*. Lysias 3 and 4 center on charges of intentional wounding and frame the disputes around competition for the affections of a sexual companion. In each case, the relationship with the sexual companion is used to develop the characters of the disputants. Isaios 6 is part of a dispute over an inheritance and attempts to discredit the legitimacy of a claimant to an estate by associating his birth with a sex laborer named Alke. In this speech, the speaker develops the character of the sex laborer as a disruptive force in the *oikos*. Aischines 1 and pseudo-Demosthenes 59 move the discourse beyond the *oikos* by contesting an individual's citizen privileges. In the first case, Timarchos is charged with wrongfully asserting his right to address the Assembly because of past behaviors, including working as a *pornos*, whereas in the second Neaira is accused of masquerading as a citizen wife as part of an attack on Stephanos, despite her having been an alien sex slave and ineligible for marriage with a citizen. In each case, a sex laborer is crucial to the litigant's narrative, but the points of tension shift with considerations of gender.

CITIZEN HOUSEHOLDS

Because of their profession, sex laborers were available for hire to anyone who desired them. The orators stress this fact with their use of *ho boulomenos* (the one wanting) to refer to clients and with their focus on commercial exchange in the sex laborers' interactions. But the number of configurations surrounding sexual labor in Classical Athens, along with the variety and flexibility around relationships with them, meant that the lives of sex laborers did not present a predictable pattern. Sex laborers were found on the streets, in brothels, at symposia, and in *oikoi*. A female sex laborer's connection with an *oikos* could be fleeting, as when accompanying or entertaining men at a symposium. Associating with men at the *sumposion* in fact defines the *hetaira* (Isai. 3.14; [Dem.] 59.24, 48). She might also temporarily occupy an *oikos* with her paying lover for a set period. Athenians kept sex laborers at a second residence, sometimes the *oikos* of a friend ([Dem.] 59.22; Lys. 3.11), or housed them in their own *oikoi* (Lys. 4.2, 5; [Dem.] 59.29–30), sometimes even with other female family members present (Antiph. 1.14–15; [And.] 4.13–14). In other cases, associations with *oikoi* might have a more permanent nature and the appearance of respectability or even legitimacy. Apollodoros presents such permanency in the case of Neaira, who was living with Stephanos at the time of her trial. Alke seems to have maintained a connection with Euktemon for more than a decade, and he apparently passed away while living with her. The unnamed woman in Lysias 4 may have been living with the accuser as a *pallakē*.

Both Neaira and Alke began their careers enslaved in brothels under the management of freedwomen. The orators exploit the ease with which these women were able to enter *oikoi* and obscure the category of wife to create anxiety in the jurors judging their trials. As discussed in chapter 2, the sex laborer Alke gained control of a family's wealth as a result of her close relationship with Euktemon, the household's *kurios*. As the speaker describes it, Euktemon abandoned his family to live with Alke, a formerly enslaved brothel worker from Peiraieus. She used her position to gain recognition for her sons as well as wealth. As long as Alke remained in the brothel as a sex slave in Peiraieus, she posed no threat to Euktemon's family and by extension the polis. But as a sex laborer (despite being female, foreign, and enslaved), she was able to move about the city and even inhabit a citizen's *oikos*. Neaira too is presented with a colorful past before settling down in the home of Stephanos. Like Alke's, Neaira's children (if we believe Apollodoros) also gained citizen status. The speakers of Isaios 6 and [Demosthenes] 59 exploit concerns about associations with sex laborers and increase apprehension by presenting Alke and Neaira, like the *anthrōpos* of Lysias 4, as influencing their male partners. The speakers also show how the sex laborers' relationships have consequences for the stability and integrity of the *oikos*.

—————————— CONCLUSION ——————————

CITIES AND SANCTUARIES

The women's location in individual *oikoi* facilitates the infringement of other boundaries (including social and civic) in the polis, since the household mediated between its members and citizen status as well as civic participation: household membership was required for membership in a deme and participation in political and religious spheres. As a consequence of the representation of these households the orators destabilize social and civic institutions as well as democratic society more generally. According to speakers, the children of Alke and Neaira gained recognition as citizens. Because of their intimate association with individual households Alke and Neaira also participated in cult restricted to citizen wives. Apollodoros emphasizes that an acquittal of Neaira in a *graphē xenias* will indicate approval of her ways and encourage all women to do as they please ([Dem.] 59.111). It will make it legal for *pornai* to marry citizens and to claim any citizen as the father of their children, while citizen girls will become *pornai* to gain a larger dowry (59.112–113). If Neaira is acquitted, sociopolitical institutions will be open to outsiders, and the privileges of citizenship will be eroded. The discourse that Apollodoros develops around her life as a sex laborer highlights the risks posed to the democracy. He presents her conviction as necessary to maintain order in the polis.

The speakers further develop apprehension among the jurors by exploiting instability in their portraits of sex laborers. A common feature is the unstable identity of the sex laborer, who moves between houses and men and has no fixed status, being enslaved, freed, foreign, or even free. The orators themselves are often elusive about such legal status. In some cases, the lack of certainty is because of the perspective of the narrative. For example, the speaker of Isaios 6 would be reluctant to discuss how Alke got her freedom if it were Euktemon who purchased it for her, given the negative association around freeing such women ([Dem.] 48.53–56). The speaker of Lysias 3 is ambiguous about the status of Theodotos on account of his embarrassment at his continued relationship with him. Narrating their changeable circumstances, like Alke's and Neaira's, highlights the unease around sex laborers, whose affection is easily purchased, who have little obligation to loyalty, can be enslaved, freed, or free, might inhabit a brothel, or cohabit with a citizen in his *oikos*. It is such instability that makes the sex laborer not only so useful in these attacks but also threatening. Their status and relationships can be difficult to pin down. Moreover, such uncertainties, as seen in the narratives on Alke and Neaira in particular, exploit tensions around the risks the enslaved, freed, and female members pose to the integ-

SEXUAL LABOR IN THE ATHENIAN COURTS

rity of *oikoi* and by extension the polis given the importance of households to citizen identity and to participation in the religious, political, and legal realms of the democracy.

BODIES COMPARED

An important site of contention in the discourse on sexual labor is the physical body. As early as the Archaic period, being Athenian came to be directly connected to the physical body and free status. Solon's reforms of 594 BCE included the *Seisactheia* (shaking off of burdens), which canceled all debts and freed Athenians in bondage both at home and abroad (Sol. 36W 3–12). Later Athenians connected Solon and his reforms with the start of the Athenian democracy, and as a result the free physical body was intimately tied to Athenian identity under the democracy. An important feature of citizenship was that the bodies of citizens were not subject to torture as enslaved persons could be. The orators rely on this privileged position of the citizen body in their speeches and construct the sex laborer in opposition to this as a body enslaved. Even after sex laborers are freed, as in the case of Neaira and possibly the unnamed woman in Lysias 4, speakers continue to refer to them with *doulē*, permanently attaching the terminology of enslavement to them. The terminology associated with Alke is more subtle, but *doulē* is used in her final appearance and the regular use of *anthrōpos* evokes her enslavement narrated at the start. In such cases, the orators distance the jurors from the sex laborer by referencing their enslaved status, but it adds to the anxiety surrounding them when masquerading in a privileged position, as Alke and Neaira do. Aischines also, despite Timarchos' free citizen status, attempts to challenge his reputation and social standing with the terminology and imagery of slavery. His addictions and identity as a *pornos* both feminize and render him slavish.

The Greek word *sōma* is a focal point of Aischines' speech *Against Timarchos*. It commonly appears in descriptions of Timarchos as a sex laborer. Aischines' concern is how Timarchos' body is used. He accuses Timarchos of employing *hubris* against himself in engaging in sex as a sex laborer. His body is associated with *bdeluria*, *aselgeia*, *hubristēs*, and *aischrōs*. These qualities are brought into focus through his identity as a sex laborer, and stress his inability to control his body, a key character trait of the male citizen. *Sōma* is also common in pseudo-Demosthenes 59, and in this case highlights the availability of Neaira's body, which anyone who wishes can have access to so long as he can afford her price. In her case, it is the accessibility of her body that is stressed as a cause for anxiety. Unlike the citizen wife, Neaira's identity as a sex laborer depends on her not being *sōphrōn*. Like Timarchos, *aischrōs* and *aselgeia* apply to her, but her body further lacks the exclusivity essential to female citizen bodies and maintained through marriage. As a sex laborer, anyone can penetrate her in any way he likes.

FEMALE PRIVILEGE

With their portraits of sex laborers, the orators effectively bring focus to the privileges and obligations of citizens, particularly female citizens, and hint at their subjectivity. Apollodoros in his speech, *Against Neaira*, affirms that, like male citizens, women had obligations associated with their status as Athenians. He describes these as a share in the affairs of the polis as well as religious matters ([Dem.] 59.111). The verb used, *metechein* (share), is the same one found in Demosthenes 57, a speech challenging the decision of a deme to disqualify a member from citizenship. The litigant associates citizen status with descent from *astoi* (Dem. 57.17, 46), rightful share in inheritance (57.46), and participation in *hiera* and *koina* (57.26, 54). Pseudo-Aristotle uses the same verb to indicate the privilege of citizenship. He states that only those born from *astoi* on both sides share in the *politeia* (*Ath. Pol.* 42.1). In the context of Apollodoros' speech, female citizenship is very specific. He comments that women share in *tōn tēs poleōs kai tōn hierōn* (the affairs of the polis as well as religious matters) and suggests an obligation to the city and its sacred rites.

It is not immediately clear what *tōn tēs poleōs* (Dem. 59.111) refers to, since Athenian women did not participate in the Assembly, courts, and administrative offices. Perhaps Apollodoros is referring to the fact that women would marry and have children as their main contribution to the polis, since it was these children who became enrolled as citizens. Neaira, of course, is accused of illegally marrying a citizen and passing off her children as legitimate. In other words, she is accused of masquerading as a female citizen by living with Stephanos and allowing her daughter to be married to citizens. *Tōn hierōn* connects civic cult with citizenship. Apollodoros also accuses Neaira and her daughter of violating the Anthesteria by participating despite their fraudulent status. It is in this context that we can better understand the inclusion of the episode of Alke at the Thesmophoria near the end of Isaios 6. By participating in these festivals, Phano, Neaira, and Alke perform the role of female citizens despite, according to each speaker, not qualifying for citizenship. Through the discussion of these women's impious acts, however, we see that female citizenship was essential to the democracy and the polis in myriad ways, including the performance of ritual. It is thus with the narratives on sex laborers that female citizenship takes shape for the modern audience: through these tales of illegal relationships and wrongful participation the obligations of female citizens as well as the appropriate performance of female citizens' responsibilities come into focus.

A NEW KIND OF CITIZEN

Sex laborers are useful to the orators not only for their alien and enslaved status but also because they challenge sex and gender norms familiar to their audience. They exist between the categories of male and female. Female sex laborers inhabit spaces unavailable to citizen women, like the symposium, and gain a level of independence not recognized for citizen women in their narratives. Neaira leaves Phrynion and escapes to another city when she tires of their relationship. Neither she nor Alke is permanently tied to a household, partner, and *kurios*. Male sex laborers exist outside the sociopolitical structures available to male citizens, like the Assembly, the *gumnasion*, and even the *sumposion*, and are characterized by their dependence on and submission to others. Timarchos relies on his lovers to support his habits and will submit to their demands in the fulfillment of his pleasures. Precisely because sex laborers threaten gender norms and represent an alternative model of sexual relations the orators can play with expectations of citizen behavior and challenge social legitimacy with these portraits.

Both Aischines and Apollodoros expand the understanding of citizenship with these narratives by focusing on citizenship as an embodiment of particular values, not simply status and a share in civic institutions and rites. It is not just that Alke, Neaira, and Phano are not *astai* when they participate in civic ritual but that they live shameful lives (*aischrōs biousa*, Isai. 6.49; *toiautē ousa*, [Dem.] 59.72). They contrast with the *sōphrosunē* exhibited by citizen women. Not only do they not meet the qualifications, but they have not behaved as Athenian women should. Apollodoros' narrative imbues the term *gunē* with specific qualities, not simply status as an *astē*. Such an understanding of *gunē* brings added significance to *hē anthrōpos*, which indicates not only enslaved and formerly enslaved status and a lack of kin but also the absence of qualities expected of Athenian women.

Aischines' discussion of sexual labor also depends on ideals of citizenship that he constructs for his audience. He provides little proof that Timarchos has engaged in the sex trade, offering neither witnesses nor evidence that Timarchos paid the venal sex tax, and instead focuses on how he behaves. Timarchos does not merely engage in the sex trade but, like Alke and Neaira, lives a shameful life (Aischin. 1.90, 118, 127, 129, 195). His manner of living contrasts with the life that is *katharos* (pure: 1.48) and *chrēstos* (beneficial: 1.179), which Aischines associates with the ideal citizen crucial to the democracy in a vision of citizenship that stresses particular qualities over status and the spectacle of citizens' bodies. Like Demosthenes, Timarchos would likely have been very surprised by the outcome of the trial. He had performed many services on behalf of the polis, including serving as an ambassador, and had been honored with offices and a priesthood. Since citizens were regularly scrutinized before taking up such roles and upon completing their terms, Timarchos' record of participation indicates his success in past reviews. Aischines' victory rests on his discussion of Timarchos' supposed private conduct, which Aischines attributes to his identity as a *pornos*. He affixes a label to Timarchos' reputation as a beautiful youth and known fondness for indulgence. Whereas other orators accuse opponents of a lack of restraint and stress the consequences of such behavior to the polis (Lys. 21.19; Dem. 18.294–296), Aischines is unique both in focusing his speech on such incontinence and in associating it so closely with the identity of the sex laborer.

(EN)GENDERING SEXUAL LABOR

Examining these speeches together allows for some interesting observations and generalizations about sexual labor in Athenian society overall. The speeches develop and exploit common social attitudes to be as convincing as possible in court. Different anxieties are played up in the speeches based on the gender of the sex laborer as female or male. In the case of male sex laborers, the prime site of disquiet is the body. As seen in chapter 3, Simon is violent toward Theodotos and forceful in his relations with him. *Anomōs* (unlawfully) and *biaōs* (by force) to describe his acts of *hubris* make clear that the violence is physically enacted on Theodotos' body (Lys. 3.12). Through such language the speaker exploits social apprehension about the appropriate sexual use of the male body as well as the appropriate expression of desire in the case of same-sex relations. The speaker's evasiveness about his own involvement with Theodotos and his hubristic portrayal of Simon evoke unease and suggest common tensions around paying males for sex. The trial of Simon anticipates discomfort with the portrayal of Timarchos in Aischines 1. Aischines is reluctant to name what goes on between Timarchos and his lovers, but he is specific in labeling that behavior hubristic. He repeatedly accuses Timarchos of treating his own body with *hubris* (Aischin. 1.108, 116, 188) in allowing various lovers to do whatever they like with him for payment (1.41–42, 55, 70). The tensions these orators create around the body and its appetites also reflect on the pederastic relationship and civic masculinity under the democracy. Both purchasing a male sex laborer or performing that labor expose deficiencies that conflict with the expectations for citizens and even pose risks to the community.

Commercial transactions identify a female sex laborer like Neaira, but there is less concern about what that payment buys and no anxiety around purchasing sex with female sex laborers. Only in the closing arguments of his speech does Apollodoros problematize payment and sex acts specifically ([Dem.] 59.108). Nor are the orators concerned about the treatment of the female sex laborer and any violence she may be subject to. In contrast to the portrayal of Theodotos in Lysias 3, there is only silence around the physical treatment of the women in Lysias 4 and Isaios 6. These sex slaves are instead blamed for the disputes and identified as behind the actions of the lawsuits. The speakers stress the loss of autonomy of the paying lovers, who easily fall victim to their schemes and will. In pseudo-Demosthenes 59, Apollodoros expresses no concern about the harsh treatment of Neaira in her relationship with Phrynion. He is specific about his conduct toward her, claiming that he took her everywhere and openly had sex with her wherever he went. His sexual display resulted in enslaved persons and others having intercourse with her when she was drunk and he was asleep. But rather than arousing anxiety and condemnation at her abuse, the episode stresses her accessibility and aims to distance the jurors from her. Although Apollodoros claims Neaira abandoned Phrynion on account of his violent abuse of her, it is Neaira who claims it was *hubris*, not Apollodoros. His added detail that she absconded with some property of Phrynion's works to negate and render invisible any violence against her. In these speeches, the anxiety exploited instead exposes to varying degrees the vulnerability of the polis, *oikoi*, and opponents to such women.

A cause for anxiety for both types of labor in these speeches is its location. In Aischines 1, Aischines moves Timarchos' relationships out of public view into the private dwelling. The speech begins with Timarchos on the Pnyx in an assembly and subtly removes Timarchos from there and other civic spaces to spark social anxiety about his association with the polis and its institutions. The focus is on the *oikia*, the physical space of the house, not its networks, not even as the location of symposia. Aischines uses the invisibility of these relationships and transactions to trigger concern around Timarchos' presence in the Assembly and public offices. Male citizens were subject to official scrutiny through *dokimsiai* and informal scrutiny at the *palaistra* and gymnasium. The secrecy associated with Timarchos' relationships poses a risk to the polis and its institutions. Even his public encounters occur in isolated and deserted areas of the city. Timarchos' movement from one *oikia* to another identifies him as a sex laborer while developing distrust around him.

In the case of Neaira, her initial location is the *oikos* of Stephanos, since she is regularly described as living with him. The *oikia* in this speech is more than simply physical space for their encounters; it is the locus of social and familial networks. The household as a gateway to the polis is cause for anxiety. This theme is also played up in Isaios 6, where Alke's movements infringe upon the *oikos* and provide social mobility to her and her children. Yet in order to demonstrate that Neaira and indeed Alke are alien sex slaves, the speakers begin their narratives in brothels and at symposia, locations not meant for citizen women. Whereas Aischines moves Timarchos into the house and out of view to question his relationships, Apollodoros moves Neaira in the opposite direction for the same reason. The sites of these relationships contradict the appropriate locations of citizens, associated with the Agora, Assembly, *sumposion*, and *gumnasion* in the case of males, and the *oikos* and sacred precinct in the case of females. The representation of sexual labor depends on a gendered idealization of space in the *oikos* and polis and on gendered patterns of movement.

MAPPING SEXUAL LABOR

I hope that by the end of these pages it has become clear that oratory, despite its interactions with other genres, provides a unique discourse on sexual labor. These narratives on sex laborers connect to varying degree with important sociopolitical institutions, including marriage, the household, pederasty, citizenship, and the education of the young. The logographers present these institutions as ideals when they are in fact muddled by the makeup of Athenian households, the variability of sexual relationships, the absence of official records to affirm birth, status, and social networks, and disparities in education. According to the orators, however, an Athenian could easily recognize a legitimate wife, family, courtship, and citizen, and conversely those who violated such roles. The orators create points of tension in their speeches by drawing upon and further developing such ideals, which in turn expose the limits of these institutions, which required constant reexamination and affirmation.

The portraits of sex laborers are a key element of such discourses because they exist at the boundaries of such institutions and have the potential to dissolve them. They were a common presence in Athenian society, even as members of the household, the basic unit of the Athenian polis and the gateway to Athenian privilege. The intimacy of both female and male sex laborers with citizens might resemble other relationships, like marriage, the foundation of the household, or pederasty, a practice associated with *paideia*. Their labor was not illegal in Athens, but attitudes around that labor were variable and complex, intersecting with concerns of gender, status, sexuality, the body, family, and community. With these portraits of sex laborers the orators expose the permeability of established institutions and cultivate unease (and perhaps even fear) among their listeners around social legitimacy. By developing the sex laborer as a threatening figure, the orators underscore social anxieties already present among the Athenian citizenry, and project them onto a specific group, which was otherwise diverse. It is also with these portraits that orators explore citizens' roles in the polis and define essential qualities of the citizen, both male and female, along with democratic values of community. Sexual labor mapped across Athenian society and culture in myriad ways.

A HISTORY OF SEX LABORERS

These speeches work only because of the ubiquity and visibility of sex laborers in Classical Athens, yet we end not learning much about the sex laborers themselves. The orators tell us very little about the actual experiences of individuals in the sex trade. Although they employ terminology suggestive of a diverse trade in everyday Athens, from enslaved brothel workers to freed or free live-in companions, they regularly elide any differences by reducing the profession to payment, slavery, working with one's body, and by constructing the sex laborer's body as excessive. At the same time, their stories acknowledge that sex laborers could be mothers, were daughters and sons, desired to better their lives and, where possible, those of their families. They might even enjoy intimate bonds with some of their clients. What the orators construe as manipulative behavior from a different perspective suggests the potential agency of sex laborers in their re-

160

lationships and the emotional labor required of them. Female sex laborers had greater opportunities for social mobility than did their male counterparts, who more quickly aged out of the profession. Despite the legality and social acceptance of sexual labor, the lives of sex laborers remained precarious and subject to violence. More than anything, the orators reveal the complex networks and ambivalent attitudes that sex laborers navigated in their daily lives.

NOTES

INTRODUCTION

1. See, for example, E. Cohen 2015; Glazebrook 2011a, 2011b. An accessible overview of sexual labor in the ancient sources is Robson 2013: 67–89; in law, Kapparis 2018a: 193–206.

2. On the independent *hetaira* (frequently referred to as a courtesan figure), see Davidson 1997: 109–136.

3. See, for example, Christ 2006, Ober 1989, Roisman 2005.

4. An exception is Wohl 2010.

5. On the importance of storytelling in forensic oratory, see Gagarin 2003, 2019.

6. Todd made this point more than thirty years ago (1990c), but it is still a common approach to the orators.

7. See Arist. *Rh.* 1356a1–4. On *ēthos* of the speaker, see Arist. *Rh.* 1356a4–8, 1366a23–28, 1377a20–28. On the opponent, see Arist. *Rh.* 1417a3–8, 1417b27–28, 1417a36-b2. On *pathos*, see Arist. *Rh.* 1356a20–25, 1428a36–38. For further discussion, see Carey 1994; Hunter 1994: 101–110; G. Kennedy 1994, 1964; Russell 1990; Tempest 2007. On the rhetoric around sexuality specifically, see Glazebrook 2014a.

8. I follow Christ 2006: 19–20; Herman 2006: 150–154; Ober 1989: 43–49; and Roisman 2005: 1–6 in taking this view.

9. Glazebrook 2005, 2006, 2012, 2014a.

10. Glazebrook 2011a, 2015a, 2016a.

11. Davidson 1997, Gilhuly 2009, Kurke 1997.

12. For a critique, see Corner 2011.

13. Fisher 2001.

14. Kapparis 2018b.

15. E. Cohen 2015.

16. Dover 1978: 19–109. Also Foucault (1985), who brought the penetration model, closely following Dover, to those outside the Classics community in *The History of Sexuality*, volume 2.

17. Halperin 1990: 96–101.

18. Whereas Dover and Foucault both recognize the silence around anal penetration

in ancient Greek texts, Davidson (2001: 37–47) argues that they interpret such reticence as sexual repression and discomfort/anxiety with the practice in the case of citizen boys. For a critique of Davidson's (and others') understanding of Foucault, see Ormand 2014.

19. Davidson 2007: 455, 446. See also his discussion (1997: 112–116) of Aischines 1.

20. Scott 1986. Important early work in Classics includes Richlin 1992a, Winkler 1990, Wyke 1998, and Zeitlin 1995. Also note the collections by Foxhall and Salmon (1998a, 1998b) and Richlin (1992b).

21. Michel Foucault's *Histoire de la sexualité*, published in three volumes between 1976 and 1984, was equally embraced and rejected by classicists. The volumes were published in English in 1978, 1985, and 1986, respectively, as *The History of Sexuality*. Volume 2, *The Use of Pleasure*, covers ancient Greece. For his influence on classicists, see Halperin 1990 and the collection by Halperin, Winkler, and Zeitlin (1990). For criticism of Foucault, see Davidson 2011, Foxhall 1994, Richlin 1991, and as well the collection by Larmour, Miller, and Platter (1998).

22. Roisman 2005.

23. Blok 2017: 11, 182–186.

24. See, for example, Alcock 2002, Alcock and Osborne 1994, and Cole 2004. See also the collection by de Jong (2012). On the "spatial turn" in Classics, see Eckerman 2014 and further the introduction in Gilhuly and Worman 2014. There is an expansive bibliography on space and place. Major works include Harvey 1996, Lefebvre 1991, and Tuan 1977.

25. Millett 1998. Blanshard (2014) considers how orators crafted a unique place for their audiences and manipulated aspects of the physical environment surrounding them to their advantage. See Tuan 1991 on the role of speech and the written in the creation of space.

26. De Bakker 2012b.

27. Davidson 2011. See also Nevett 2011 and, on the household in particular, Nevett 1995, 1999.

28. Cresswell 2004, 1996.

29. For an overview, see Cresswell 2011.

30. Cresswell 2011: 552–554. On movement as differentiated, see Adey 2006, Cresswell 1996. On gender and mobility, see Hanson 2010, Law 1999, and the collection by Uteng and Cresswell (2008).

31. Konstantinou 2018: 9.

32. A concise overview of the legal system is Carey 1997: 1–25. Also Phillips 2013: 26–43.

33. Lanni 2006: 75–114.

34. The most common number of jurors was 500. By the 380s, an odd number (so, for example, 201) was preferred. The change was possibly to prevent tie votes (Dilts, schol. Dem. 24.9); however, from early on the Athenians had established that ties ruled in favor of the defendant. See Boegehold 1995: 34.

35. For a concise summary of Greek currency and its economic value, see Fisher 1976: xi. The pay of three obols is based on inscriptional evidence for the building records of

NOTES TO PAGES 10-11

the Erechtheion. Skilled laborers received six obols (one drachma). For a detailed discussion, see Loomis 1998: 104–108.

36. In Aristophanes' *Wasps*, the jurors are all old men, but the increase in jury pay likely broadened participation in the fourth century BCE. For a summary of different views on the makeup of the jury, see Todd 1990a. Todd himself (1990a: 169) argues that such pay did not benefit artisans and shop owners, but favored farmers, who might be a diverse group of the "poor, fairly poor, fairly well off, or rich" (although the proportion of each is not calculable).

37. For discussion, see Mirhady 2007.

38. For such trials, see MacDowell 1978: 61–62.

39. For a detailed discussion of procedure from initiating a lawsuit through to the outcome of a trial between 410 and 340 BCE, see Boegehold 1995: 30–36. By the fourth century BCE, metics seem to have been able to initiate trials, but their cases were heard in a special court, with the exception of *emporikai*. Their crimes as well as crimes against them were subject to different penalties. See Kamen 2013: 47–49, Phillips 2013: 23–24, Whitehead 1977: 92–94. On *emporikai*, see Cohen 1973: 93–95, Lanni 2006: 152–153.

40. Boegehold 1995: 30–31.

41. Noncitizen women, poor and impoverished women, and widows are possible exceptions, suggesting it was more a matter of convention than statutory law in the case of free women. See Gagarin 1998: 48–49; further Kapparis 2021: 2–4, 105–121.

42. On Athenian women, see Foxhall 1996: 140–149; Gagarin 1998; S. Johnstone 1998; Kamen 2013: 91; and Kapparis 2020 and 2021. And on the enslaved, see Mirhady 1996; Gagarin 1996; S. Johnstone 1998; Kamen 2013: 13–14.

43. Because these speeches were published, there is the possibility that many speeches had been adapted before publication. See Hall 1995: 41; Worthington 1991. Herman (2006: 153) suggests that such rewriting only strengthens the speeches' relevance for sociocultural history, since orators would surely have revised them to make them more convincing to an audience by adapting the less well-received arguments and expanding the points that secured a victory or, at the very least, received a positive response from the audience.

44. See W. Thompson 1970; Wyse 1904: 488. For a contrary interpretation that questions what we can conclude from the inscription, see Griffith-Williams 2017: 55 n. 22.

45. *Hēliaia*, Odeion, Parabyston, and the Stoa Poikilē (Boegehold 1995: 9); see also Boegehold 1995: 1–9 on the variety of terminology identifying each of these courts.

46. Dikastic equipment was found in Building A. On possible identifications, see Boegehold (1995: 11–16), who suggests that Building A was the *Hēliaia* and Building B the Parabyston, identifying Buildings C and D as new courts of the last quarter of the fourth century. On the site reconstruction of these buildings, see Townsend 1995: 104–113, but note that their fig. 8, the reconstructed drawing of Building A, shows exterior walls all the way up with one entrance and no windows: this does not fit with the presence of bystanders, who might be outside the building behind the *druphaktoi* (fences or railings) yet still expected to hear the goings-on inside. Few actual structural remains were found in situ: blocks remain in two separate areas, and there are stretches of foun-

165

dation trenches on three sides as well as some possible traces of an entrance. There may have been more entrances, or perhaps the walls were not complete on the north side. Townsend (1995: 105) also suggests that the terracotta water channels standing on end and sunk into the floor of Building A were not for the court's ballot boxes but for wooden boxes storing dikastic equipment like the bronze ballots.

47. Boegehold 1995: 32–33.

48. Such audiences appear common throughout the life of the courts: Ar. *Acharn.* 915; Antiph. 6.21–24; Isai. 5.20; Aischin. 3.55–56; Dem. 25.98; Dein. 1.30, 2.19. On by-standers and physical structures outside the courts, see Boegehold 1995: 192–201.

49. See further Millett 1998: 212–217.

50. See Bers 1985; Hall 1995: 43–44; Sato 2019. Plato refers to this as *thorubos* (*Laws* 876b, 959b). For a comic example, see Ar. *Wasps* 623–627, 912.

51. See, for example, Aischin. 2.5; 3.56, 207; Antiph. 6.14; Dein. 1.66, 2.19; Dem. 19.196, 30.32 (cf. 54.41), 45.6, 58.31; Hyp. *Dem.* 22. On speakers engaging the jurists, see Aischin. 1.159; Dem. 18.52, 23.18–19. On the popularity of the lawcourts, see Ar. *Knights* 1316–1318 and schol. *ad* line 1317. See further Bers 1985: 8–10, Sato 2019.

52. Note also Ar. *Wasps* 550–551, 562–570, 579–586.

53. Bers 1985: 14–15; Hall 1995: 44. Bers, although allowing *thorubos* for the Palladion and the Delphinion, has reservations about the Areopagus court, calling it "the august court" but not discounting the possibility of heckling in this court altogether.

54. Garner 1987: 95, 97–99. See Hall 1995 with further bibliography. Note Goldhill 1999: 1–29 on democratic Athens as a "performance culture," specifically p. 25 on the lawcourts.

55. See Arist. *Rh.* 1403b24–30; see also 1403b16, 1404a1–8. Note the comic example of Ar. *Knights* 347–349. On the importance of performance for orators, see Hall (1995: 46–49), who notes voice, pitch, volume, pace, and gestures. For comic examples cited by Hall, see Ar. *Wasps* 562–570, 579–586.

56. Hall 2006: 362.

57. Harding 1994 focuses on the influence of Old Comedy on language and carica-tures in such speeches as Lysias 24 and Demosthenes 22, *Against Androtion*, but also (pp. 211, 213) references similarities to New Comedy. He does not consider Middle Comedy at all, given the fragmentary nature of the evidence, but the influence would probably have continued. See also Hall (1995: 56–57) on the general use of humor.

58. See Sidwell 2014: 67. Aischines, Demosthenes, and Lykourgos also cite the tragic poets Euripides and Sophocles, and Green argues this practice reflects reperformances of their plays that the orators expected the jurors to have seen (1994: 50–51).

59. See further Kapparis 1999: 44.

60. Scafuro 1997 is an interesting study of the influence of legal procedure on New Comedy.

61. In what follows, I provide a summary of Henry 1985: 13–31 and offer only a few examples for the reader. See Henry for more examples and further discussion.

62. LSJ s.v. *choiros*; Henderson 1998: 147 n. 94.

63. See Henderson 1998: 157 n. 99.

NOTES TO PAGES 14–21

64. See Robson 2009: 137. For the view that such figures objectified women and reinforced Athenian patriarchy, see Zweig 1992: 85.

65. Cf. Ariphrades Paphlagon also in *Knights* 1284–1286, 1399–1405. Euripides is critiqued for his corrupt style (*Frogs* 1325–1328; Plato Comicus, *Sophistai* 134K).

66. Lysikles (*Knights* 763–766), Cleophon (*Knights* 805), Perikles (Eupolis, *Philoi* 274K; Kratinos, *Cheirons* 241K; Kallias, *Pedetai* 15K). For more references with discussion, see Henry 1985: 13–15.

67. Ancient scholars, like Athenaios, refer to Old, Middle, and New Comedy. Aristotle, however, refers only to Old and New Comedy. As a result, modern scholarship remains divided about the accuracy of Middle Comedy as a distinct phase of Attic comedy. See Sidwell 2000: 247–250; 2014: 68–70.

68. See the detailed discussion in Henry 1985: 33–40.

69. For further examples, see Henry 1985: 34 n. 65, 36.

70. Henry 1985: 36–40.

71. See Glazebrook 2005, 2006.

72. Griffith-Williams 2017: 46–47. C. Patterson (1994: 207) likens Neaira's story to a plot of New Comedy.

73. Griffith-Williams 2017.

74. Gilhuly 2009, Hamel 2003, Miner 2003, C. Patterson 1994.

75. Glazebrook 2005, 2006.

76. Blok 2017. On Athenian women as citizens, see also Campa 2019, Goff 2004, C. Patterson 1987.

77. See, for example, E. Cohen 2006, Davidson 2007, Phillips 2007.

78. Dover 1974, 1978; Halperin 1990.

79. Davidson 1997, Sissa 1999.

80. Lape 2006.

81. See Witzke 2015.

82. See, for example, the work of the philosopher Shannon Bell (1994).

83. Leigh 1997.

84. Miner 2003: 29–30 and Kapparis 1999: 409 on [Dem.] 59.114.

85. On the slavish connotations, see E. Cohen 2006: 102–103. On servile invective in oratory, see Kamen 2020: 69–74.

CHAPTER 1: UNDER THE INFLUENCE

1. For examples, see Dem. 54.14; Isai. 3.13; Lys. 3.43.

2. For a general overview of the types of relationships and arrangements sex laborers found themselves in, see Glazebrook 2016b: 705–708.

3. On the procedure see Phillips 2007 and 2013: 85–86, 88–90. Also Todd 2007: 281–84. Most scholars argue such cases were always public cases, but Todd argues for the existence of both a *graphē* and a *dikē*.

4. Explanations for the condition of the speech include: (1) only the proof and epi-

167

NOTES TO PAGES 22–25

logue were commissioned; (2) what we have is the second of the two speeches delivered to the Areopagus; (3) that this speech is a postclassical rhetorical exercise based on Lys. 3; and (4) that the speech was damaged before its inclusion in the Palatinus manuscript. See Todd 2007: 349–351, who himself opts for number 4.

5. Speech titles regularly contain the name of one of the litigants, but for other speech titles of Lysias that lack such details, see Lys. 7, 17, 21.

6. As an authentic speech of Lysias, it would date between 403 and ca. 380 BCE, the span of Lysias' speechwriting career. See G. Kennedy 1994: 65; Usher 1999: 55.

7. For the Areopagus I use "judges" to refer to the members of the council who oversaw the case. In contrast, I use "jurors" (chapters 2, 3, 5) to refer to members of the popular court.

8. For details and bibliography see Todd 2007: 350 n. 12.

9. On their differing characterizations, see Kapparis 2018b: 242–243.

10. See also Todd's (2007: 347–348) overview of the parallels and differences.

11. Todd (2007: 350–351) counters views that the speech is merely an exercise or that only this portion of the speech was commissioned of Lysias and concludes that the speech "has suffered mutilation at some stage."

12. As Todd (2007: 366–367) mentions, the speech is confusing with regard to who made the request and the actual outcome and procedure of the *antidosis*. On the *antidosis* as a procedure, see Phillips 2013: 25–26.

13. I have argued elsewhere that *eleuthera*, in contrast to *aneleuthera*, is a way to refer to an enslaved person freed via the *prasis ep' eleutheriai* and that such an individual was freed without obligations to an ex-master. See Glazebrook 2014b. Todd (2007: 378, 379) notes here that the opponent seems to claim sole ownership in contrast to the speaker's claim to joint ownership. Spatharas suggests she had been freed by him prior to the trial (2006: 96). Marshall (2021) rightly observes that the outcome of the trial will also determine her status.

14. Carey 1989: 109–110; Todd 2007: 282–283.

15. Phillips 2007: 86–87.

16. Phillips 2007: 84. Further, Phillips 2013: 46.

17. Todd 2007: 281–282.

18. On harmful intent as the criterion, see Loomis 1972; Spatharas 2006: 105–106; Phillips 2007: 85–87, 99. By contrast, on premeditation as the criterion, see Carawan 1998: 223–225; Hansen 1981: 14–15.

19. Phillips 2007: 82–83.

20. "But the joint ownership itself is asserted rather than argued" (Todd 2007: 379).

21. The testimony of enslaved persons was permissible only under torture. On the procedure, see Gagarin 1996; Hunter 1994: 91–94; Mirhady 1993–1994, 1996, 2000, 2007b. Refusing to turn a slave over or accept an opponent's slave for torture is commonly exploited as confirmation of the opponent's argument. But there are multiple reasons why an individual might not accept any such challenge, not least of all affection for a slave.

22. See Glazebrook 2014b and compare Kamen 2014.

168

NOTES TO PAGES 25–31

23. Scholars refer to this procedure as a kind of third-party sale. On the procedure and examples, see E. Cohen 2015: 55; Glazebrook 2014b; Kamen 2014; Kapparis 1999: 232–233. See Cox (1998: 188–189) on the arrangements in this speech in particular, but the reconstruction she provides is perhaps more definitive than the speech allows. See Todd 2007: 366–367 and note 13 in this chapter.

24. Todd 2007: 371. Compare Lys. 1.23, 3.6–7.

25. See Todd 2007: 372 n. 19. On the use of pottery as a weapon, see further Naber 1905: 74; Todd 2000b: 53.

26. Compare the use of *pronoia* (including its verbal form) in Lys. 3.28, 29, 34, 37, 41, 42, 43; Todd 2007: 331.

27. Todd 2007: 373. See Lys. 3.43; Dem. 21.36, 54.14. Cf. Spatharas 2006: 90.

28. Phillips 2007: 89.

29. On the importance of visible injuries, see also Dem. 40.32–33, [Dem.] 47.41, and Aischin. 2.93; 3.51, 212. For discussion, see O'Connell 2017: 46–47. Also Spatharas 2006: 102.

30. See Todd 2007: 379. Note that 4.10 marks the speaker's first explicit claim to have contributed to the cost.

31. See the discussion in Todd 2007: 366, 375.

32. Roisman 2005: 168.

33. Lamb 1930: 99; Todd 2007: 357.

34. Wohl 2002: 171–172, 188–191, 197.

35. On love as an affliction and even madness, see Carey 1989: 94–95; Dover 1974: 125, 137–138, 210–211; Roisman 2005: 168; Thornton 1997: 33–35.

36. Compare the use of *paroinos* in the account of an enslaved woman's treatment at the hands of symposiasts in Dem. 19.198. See further Todd 2007: 374. Although alcohol can be an excuse for bad behavior, it is also evidence of the violent tendencies and excessive habits of an opponent. On drinking, see Davidson 1997: 36–69; Roisman 2005: 167, 170–173.

37. Roisman 2005: 167–168. For another example, see Aischin. 1.58–59. On drinking and sex see Davidson 1997: 213–215.

38. Lamb (1930: 99) translates "irritable state," and Todd (2007: 357) chooses "surliness," but these renderings seem too moderate in the context. Montanari s.v. *barudaimonia*: "insanity Lys. 4.9."

39. See Fisher 2001: 171.

40. See Marshall (2021) on the speaker's exploitation of "emotional attachment" in this speech.

41. See Davidson 1997: 139–182; Roisman 2005: 163–176.

42. Cusset (2014) argues that in Menander *melancholia* is a disease associated with lovesickness in particular (174) and concludes that it refers to violent emotion as opposed to simply madness (177), negatively affecting the individual's relation with the group (178).

43. S. Johnstone 1998: 221–222.

44. Gagarin 1997: 116 (in reference to Antiph. 1.17) and Hunter 1994: 73 on the term

169

NOTES TO PAGES 31–35

in oratory. Todd (2007: 366) translates it "slave-girl" in this speech. See further Sosin 1997: 75–77. Dickey (1996: 152–153) stresses its insulting intention when used to address those known to a speaker.

45. E. Cohen (2015: 47–48) highlights the ambiguity of her status and uses this speech to question whether *pornai* were always enslaved.

46. Kapparis (1999: 409; 2021: 168) argues that the term disparages the woman, who was a long-standing sexual companion of the opponent. Also Spatharas 2006: 92-93.

47. See [Dem.] 48.56, 59.114. On *pornē*, see Glazebrook 2005, Miner 2003. Note that Miner (23) also suggests *pornē* indicates a young sex slave, but the orators appear to use *paidiskē* for that. See [Dem.] 59.18; Hyp. *Ath.* 1; Isai. 6.19.

48. See Todd 2007: 366–367. Cf. Spatharas 2006: 88–89. For a new reconstruction of the events of the exchange, see Marshall 2021. On *antidosis* generally, see Phillips 2013: 25–26.

49. I thank Thomas Hubbard for this provocative suggestion during my talk at the University of Texas.

50. Todd 2007: 363; Lamb 1930: 105.

51. On the paradox of female voices in oratory, see Gagarin (2001), who discusses nine examples of female speech. Only one example incudes a slave—a conversation between an Athenian woman and an enslaved sexual companion (Antiph. 1.15–16). The other examples include Athenian (Lys. 1.12–13; 32.11, 12–17; [Dem.] 47.57, 55.24; [Dem.] 59.110–111), metic (Hyp. *Ath.* 1–4), and freed (Lys. 1.16) women. Gagarin (169) notes the use of "standard forensic speech and commonplace forensic argument" in five of his examples and suggests that the passages were written to support the trial and not to convey the actual words of a female speaker. Instead these passages provide needed proof for the arguments and convey a stereotype. Even when the speech is "nontechnical," it supports the speaker in these ways. Bers (1997: 145–146) argues that in some cases the words are likely accurate as to what was said. He argues for less of a distinction between the forensic and the common speech. Another example of a conversation with an enslaved female is Lys. 1.19–20.

52. For a good discussion of emotional labor and sexual labor in the ancient context, see Levin-Richardson 2019. She draws on the work of Sanders (2005) and Wharton (2009).

53. See further Todd 2007: 373–374. He also points to a discrepancy in the woman's actions between 4.8 and 4.16 in the speaker's account of events, but it is unlikely that the judges noticed it in an oral delivery.

54. *Boulomenos* is commonly associated with the democratic right of male citizens. See, for example, the opening of Aischin. 1 with discussion in chapters 3 and 5.

55. Carey 2007: Lys. Fr. 279.6.

56. The word order is unusual and stresses a causal effect. Smythe §1700, "*on account of, for the sake of, with regard to*, usually postpositive." The preposition *peri hetairas* seems more common to signify simply fighting over a girl (Dem. 54.14; Lys. 3.43).

57. Lamb 1930: 105; Todd 2007: 363.

58. See Spatharas 2006: 93–94; Todd 2007: 366, 374, 379. Todd also cites Ste. Croix 2004: 66. For other examples see Dem. 24.197; [Dem.] 59.29.

170

59. See also Griffith-Williams 2019: 61–64, 67–68.

60. Trans. Phillips 2013: 251. See also Plut. *Sol.* 21.3–4 and [Arist.] *Ath. Pol.* 35.2, quoted in Phillips 2013: 252.

61. See further Arnaoutoglou 1998: 1–2; Phillips 2013: 251–252.

62. Antiph. 1.14–15; [Dem.] 25.56–57; Men. *Sam.* See Cox 1998: 171–189.

63. Also see Kapparis 2018a: 196.

64. The name of the speaker is not definitive but is conventionally used in discussions of this speech. On the speech, see Whitehead 2001.

65. Whitehead (2001: 313) sees this argument as the speaker's most effective strategy for winning his case.

66. Whitehead (2001: 314) concludes that the contract becomes invalid because "it was made under the influence of a woman less reputable than a wife."

67. See Kapparis 1999: 409. For the suggestion that she is a *pallakē*, see Todd 2007: 375.

68. S. Johnstone 1998: 221–222.

69. Todd 2007: 374.

70. See further Henry 1985: 13–31; Robson 2009.

71. On *charis*, see chapter 5 below.

72. Cf. Habrotonon in Men. *Epit.* 535, 538–540.

73. The accessibility of these figures suggests their identity as *pornai*. On these characters see Ruffell 2014: 160–161; Robson 2009: 137; Taaffe 1993. Zweig (1992: 78–81) argues a nude sex laborer likely appeared on stage in these roles.

74. Henderson 2000: 144; O'Higgins 2003: 128–131; Hughes 2012: 35. For the idea of two separate tracks of comedy in the fourth century BCE (i.e., satirical versus non-iambic plot-based), see Sidwell 2014: 72–75.

75. Henderson 2000: 138–139. For a catalogue of plays with *hetairai* up to 380 BCE, see Henderson 2000: 147. See also Storey 2011: 412; Ruffell 2014: 160.

76. Ath. 13.567c; O'Higgins 2003: 128. It was not common to name citizen women openly. See Schaps 1977. On *Neaira*, see the introduction.

77. Hughes 2012: 35.

78. See Ruffell 2014: 154, fig. 7.4; Green 1994: 63–84; Sidwell 2014: 63. For illustrations of the *hetaira* mask type, see Webster and Green 1978: 23–25.

79. Henderson 2000: 140.

80. See Henry 1985: 36, 38–39.

81. See Henry 1985: 34, 36–38, for other examples of positive portrayals in this period.

82. Ruffell 2014: 156–158.

83. Modern commentators have remarked, sometimes disdainfully, on her incentive: Rosivach 1998: 100; Traill 2008: 225. Ruffell (2014: 157) argues "mercenary motivations and actions were expected" of this character type.

84. See Patterson 1994 on [Dem.] 59 and Griffith-Williams 2017 on Isai. 6.

85. Griffith-Williams 2017: 46. Hall (2006: 19) focuses on a character role "from its imaginative creation to the moment it transcended the moment of performance to become in its own right an active ideological influence on public discourses beyond the theatre."

NOTES TO PAGES 40–46

86. Henderson 2000: 140.

87. On the vulnerability to violence of sex laborers in Classical Athens, see Glaze-brook 2015a: 91–95.

CHAPTER 2: IN THE *OIKOS*

1. The date is provided at 6.14: fifty-two years from when the Sicilian Expedition set sail (415 BCE).

2. It is unclear whether he claimed her as Euktemon's *epiklēros* or Philoktemon's. See Edwards 2007: 95 n. 1.

3. See Phillips 2013: 217–218, 232–243.

4. On the procedure for adoption by will, see Wyse 1904: 484–485, 491–492.

5. On questions regarding the age of the sons, see Wyse 1904: 500, 512. The older son is said to be not yet twenty, but the chronology and timing of events suggests the elder son may have been twenty-seven at the time of the trial.

6. Some scholars suggest Aristomenes of Poros as the speaker, based on *IG* II² 1609.82. See Griffith-Williams 2017: 46 and n. 11.

7. On the common use of this procedure in inheritance disputes, see Scafuro 1994: 171, 172–178.

8. See W. Thompson 1970; Wyse 1904: 488. For a contrary interpretation that questions what we can conclude from the inscription, see Griffith-Williams 2017: 55 n. 22.

9. I use "jurors" to indicate those reviewing cases in the popular courts, as here, and reserve "judges" to refer to the members of the Areopagus overseeing the homicide court (chapters 1 and 3).

10. The members of an *oikos* regularly included extended family, like widowed or un-married female relatives and aging parents, enslaved persons, and (sometimes) female sexual companions and their children. On the complexity of the Athenian *oikos*, see Cox 1998. A good summary is Edwards 2007: 5–10.

11. Philoktemon, his son, has the demotic *Kēphisieus*. Euktemon must belong to the same deme, since it is the father's deme that determines the son's eligibility for Athenian citizenship (6.3).

12. Later sources describe the *gamēlia* as a sacrifice, a feast, or a donation. See Wyse 1904: 363–364. Cole (1984: 236–237) argues it was a sacrifice followed by feasting. On identifying female citizens, see Isaios. 3.79–80 and Dem. 57.68–70. For discussion, see Scafuro 1994: 162–164, 167–169 with reference to this speech, Isaios 6.

13. See Scafuro 1994: 158–159, 162. On the *koureion* and the importance of enroll-ment in the phratry to citizenship, see Cole 1984: 233–235. On admission to the deme, see [Arist.] *Ath. Pol.* 42. It is possible that every deme had a registry of its members. See Scafuro 1994: 161.

14. For scholarly discussion concerning their likely legitimacy see Wyse 1904: 486 and *APF* 563. Cynthia Patterson (1994: 52; also 114) comments: "Whether the two were

172

NOTES TO PAGES 46-50

in fact the legitimate offspring of a second marriage is a matter of controversy.... Certainly, they were marginal to this wealthy family."

15. See Wyse 1904: 498-499.

16. See also Edwards 2007: 103 n. 16.

17. See Wyse (1904: 502) on the difficulties of whose slaves are being referred to in this passage.

18. A *genos* collected witnesses through a variety of communal events (as discussed above) in order to maintain the legitimate status of its members and have proof of this status. "Everyone knew that, and everyone gathered witnesses.... Witnesses to one's Athenian status were the most important witnesses one could have" (Scafuro 1994: 165, 170). See [Arist.] *Ath. Pol.* 42 and below on Perikles' citizenship law.

19. Cf. Isai. 3.79-80. Cox (1998: 179) suggests that the uncertainty surrounding the mother of these boys could be explained by an early death.

20. Cf. Isai. 3.6-17, where a female claimant to an estate (an *epiklēros*) is said to be the daughter of a *hetaira* and thus illegitimate. The accusation of having children by or being the son of a *hetaira* is a common form of invective in other Attic speeches: Aischin. 2.177; Dem. 22.61; [Dem.] 25.80; Din. 1.71. See also Ath. 13.577b, 592a, 592d, 592e, 589c. See further Griffith-Williams 2017: 42; Ogden 1996: 189-199.

21. See Glazebrook 2005, 2006; Wyse 1904: 506.

22. See Wyse (1904: 506-507) on his possible legal situation.

23. On naming conventions for women, see Schaps 1977.

24. Despite the feminine virtue of being silent before men, women are sometimes given voice in the orators. Note for example Dem. 29.26, 33, 56; 39.3-4; 40.10-11; [Dem.] 59.110-111; Lys. 32.11-17. See further Gagarin 2001 and chapter 1 above.

25. Contra Roisman (2005: 41), who downgrades the extent of her plotting. On scheming women in inheritance suits as a topos credible to Athenian audiences, see Griffith-Williams 2019: 61-64.

26. Even if more of Lysias 4 were extant, the details would likely remain sparse given that the trial took place before the Court of the Areopagus. Note that we know of Alke only from this speech and cannot verify the details of her life, so we must be cautious in what we can know about her. On portraits of women in oratory, see Glazebrook 2005, 2006; Roisman 2005: 32-38.

27. Demetriou (2012: 192-193) argues that it was very much like a colony, having been relocated here on a grid plan, despite being a deme of Athens. See also von Reden 1995: 27.

28. See Garland 1987: 83-92 and Demetriou 2012: 193-195 on the complexity of its administration as compared with other demes.

29. See further Garland 1987: 68-69.

30. See Demetriou 2012: 196-205, 228; Garland 1987: 58-62, 72-73, 101, 105; Whitehead 1986: 83-84. For consideration of the cosmopolitan nature of emporia, including Peiraieus, and the effect of such multiculturalism on law, religion, and material culture of emporia, see Demetriou 2011: 266-270; 2012. On the concentration of foreign cults in

the region, see Camp 2001: 296–297; Demetriou 2012: 190, 217–227; Garland 1987: 101–103, 105, 109, 112, 114, 117–122, 126–131, 132–135, and appendix 3. Scholars disagree about how many can be considered foreign, with Garland producing the largest list, and those that are actually introduced by metics. See Demetriou 2012: 217–218; von Reden 1995: 31. The inscriptional evidence for the foundation of such cults dates to the late fourth and early third centuries BCE, but the earliest example is 429/428 BCE (*IG* II² 1283), suggesting their establishment was an accepted and common practice by the fourth century BCE (Demetriou 2012: 222–223).

31. Finley 1951: 65; Garland 1987: 142–143.

32. Various elites were suspicious of the harbors, like Peiraieus: see Plato, *Laws*, 705a–b; Plut. *Them.* 19; cf. Ar. *Frogs* 112–115. See also von Reden 1995: 27–29.

33. Von Reden (1995: 32–33). On otherness, see Cartledge 1993, Hall 1989.

34. A *sunoikia* is a multiple-occupancy building housing tenants and all types of businesses (cf. Aischin. 1.124). On the conflation of residences and businesses, see Tsakirgis 2005. On the lack of zoning for the sex trade, see Glazebrook 2011a, 2011b. On the difficulties of identifying such urban spaces in the archaeological record, see Glazebrook and Tsakirgis 2016.

35. See Wyse (1904: 504–505), who notes further that *nauklēros* (skipper) is used in the case of other tenement houses. On freedwomen managing rental properties and brothels for Athenians, see E. Cohen 2015: 138–144; Glazebrook 2011b, 2014b, 2016b.

36. See Glazebrook 2011a, 2016; also Davidson 1997, but note that he presents *oikēmata* as the Greek equivalent to *cellae meretriciae* (rooms opening directly onto the street) and more typical of male sex laborers than female. He further suggests (1997: 332 n. 55) that this arrangement and her later relationship with Euktemon proves Alke was never a *pornē* in a *porneion*, but the mistake is our assumption that brothels were unsanitary and for customers of low status. See Glazebrook 2011b.

37. See Wyse 1904: 505. The speaker might be repressing this information on account of the stigma associated with freeing such a slave. On manumission of enslaved sex laborers, see Glazebrook 2014b, Kamen 2014. We commonly find freedwomen managing *sunoikiai* and sex laborers. See further Glazebrook 2011a: 50–51.

38. Knigge 1988: 11.

39. See Camp 2001: 261–264; Knigge 1988: 8–13, 39–42.

40. See Knigge 2005 on this structure.

41. On Building Z3 as a brothel, see Ault 2016, Davidson 1997. Knigge (2005), the original excavator, identifies sexual labor as a possible activity at the structure, but does not consider the building a brothel. Whereas Knigge identifies the earlier phases (1 and 2) as an *oikos*, Ault instead associates the earlier phases with a hostelry or tavern, or both, as well as Z3. See Ault 2005, 2016. On the association of the area with sexual labor, see Hesych. s.v. *Dēmiaisi pulais*; also Ar. *Knights* 1243–1246.

42. J. Stroszeck, per. comm., 2006. Also see Knigge 1993.

43. Lind 1988.

44. See Purves 2010: 206–216.

NOTES TO PAGES 53-57

45. Note that there is some speculation among scholars about the actual relationship with the wife at this point, with the suggestion that Euktemon was perhaps divorced or at least separated from her. See the comments on *pantelōs diēitato ekei* (6.21) and *enguatai gunaika* (6.22) in Wyse 1904: 508–509.

46. On Perikles' citizenship law, which restricted marriage to *astoi*, see [Arist.] *Ath. Pol.* 26.4. For details of the law, see C. Patterson 1981.

47. This speech has been used to support bigamy or concubinage as legitimate practices in Classical Athens, since Euktemon supposedly threatened to marry the daughter of Demokrates of Aphidna while possibly still being married to the daughter of Meixiades (6.22). Harrison (1968: 15–17) argues convincingly against bigamy. Other scholars (see n. 45 above and Edwards 2007: 98) suggest he had divorced this first wife. Brenda Griffith-Williams (2017: 52) suggests, in contrast, that we should not take the mention of this marriage too seriously: it may be meant to stress Euktemon's senility further. It is only included to provide the reason why his son Philoktemon eventually agreed to allow Alke's son to go before the phratry and obtain recognition as legitimate.

48. Wyse (1904: 541) notes the inconsistency that in 6.55 the involvement of Androkles and associates began prior to Philoktemon's death, whereas elsewhere (6.29, 38) they joined in with Alke only after his death. On the possible date of Philoktemon's death, see Wyse (1904: 484), who puts it between 378 and 373 BCE.

49. See Wyse 1904: 515. For its common usage to describe the behavior and position of parasites, underlings, subject peoples, and even slaves, refer to Dem. 45.63, 65; [Dem.] 59.43; Aischin. 3.116; Ar. *Knights* 47.

50. See Finley 1951: 54–55; Harrison 1968: 230–232.

51. On the vulnerability of old men, see Griffith-Williams 2019: 61–64.

52. See Eidinow 2016: 37, 326–327; also R. Kennedy 2014: 143–149. The *pallakē*, Theoris, and Ninon were executed for their activities. See further chapter 3 below.

53. See Wyse (1904: 523) on the negative connotations of *kataskeuazein* in particular: "it is not easy to find passages in the orators in which it is used without any suggestion of fraud."

54. Edwards (2007: 99) comments on the tragic manner of this part of the speech (6.18–24); see also Usher 1999: 151.

55. On the possible age of Chairestratos at the death of Philoktemon, see Wyse (1904: 492), who argues that he may have been either a young child or as old as eighteen or nineteen.

56. On the orators' treatment of wealth see Ober 1989: 206–208. A careful study of the tensions between the city and its wealthy citizens in regard to performing liturgies and paying the war tax is Christ 2006: 143–204. Spending wealth on oneself and hoarding wealth were seen as unmanly (Roisman 2005: 90–92) and a sign of one's lack of self-control (Davidson 1997: 207–208). On the war tax in particular, see Wyse 1904: 545.

57. The name of the household is no longer extant in the surviving fragment. See Whitehead (2001: 285) on this account.

58. Wyse (1904: 537), noting Lys. 13.18, 30.27, comments that it was pardonable li-

NOTES TO PAGES 57–59

cense to refer to a freedwoman as a slave, but the practice was clearly intended to undermine the credibility and social standing of such individuals.

59. On the festival, see Burkert 1985: 242–246; Clinton 1996; Demand 1994: 110–120; Dillon 2002: 110–120; Goff 2004: 125–138, 205–211; O'Higgins 2003: 20–30. Stehle (2007: 167–174) offers a unique reading focusing on the personal experience of the participants and how they connect with the goddesses.

60. The Thesmophoria commonly lacked a temple (Paus. 7.27.9, 8.36.6, 9.8.1), and no archaeological remains identifying a Thesmophorion, like an altar or pits for piglets, have yet been found. Homer Thompson (1936: 156–192) suggested a Thesmophorion on the upper terrace of the Pnyx; *contra*, Broneer 1942; note Romano (1985: 441–454), who suggested a racetrack here instead. For summary of discussion, see Henderson 1996: 92–94. On the archaeology of the Pnyx more generally, see Forsén and Stanton 1996.

61. On debate concerning the importance of the Assembly versus the lawcourts in the fourth century, see Hansen 2010.

62. See Isai. 3.80, 8.19–20.

63. On the role of the *Boulē* in monitoring festivals, see Wyse 1904: 538.

64. Some distinguish the two as definite categories, whereas others suggest slippage between them, especially in certain contexts: e.g., [Dem.] 59. For discussion of such terms with examples, see Corner 2011: 75–78; Kurke 1997; McClure 2003: 11–13.

65. See the discussion in Davidson 1997: 78–97; Kurke 1997. Also McClure (2003: 15–16), who stresses "the lack of spatial stability" and considers such instability as analogous to "the unstable social identity of both the hetaera and porne." Although the wife is also mobile in that she moves between *oikoi*, she becomes fixed to her husband's *oikos* with Xenophon's *Oikonomikos* (see Purves 2010: 211–212) and in the orators more generally.

66. On dangerous women (e.g., Ninon in Dem. 19.281 with scholia 495A [Dilts]; Theoris in [Dem.] 25.79–80; Phryne in Ath. 13.590e; Sinope in [Dem.] 59.116–117; Neaira in [Dem.] 59), see Jameson 1997: 102–103 with n. 11; Rebecca Futo Kennedy (2014: 143–149) looks at the actual profession and vulnerability of women so labeled; see also Eidinow 2016: 312–325 (with discussion of Alke, 313–315). Note, however, that Eidinow ignores the prostitute status of many of these women, including Alke.

67. Cox (1998: 170–189) discusses in detail how such women impinged on households despite legislation against their infringements.

68. Note that the law is read out in the current speech, is not transcribed in full, but is quoted only in part (focusing on the mental-illness provision) in Isaios 6.8–9 in connection with Philoktemon's own will and his adoption of Chairestratos. Wyse (1904: 495) adds that the speaker wants to avoid any suggestion that Philoktemon's sister influenced Philoktemon in his decision and so purposefully left out the clause on women (6.9). The emphasis is on Philoktemon's sound mental capacity (*eu phronōn*, 6.10), and thus his actions contrast with Euktemon's, shown to be consequences of senility and mental weakness (*anoia*, 6.29) and under the influence of a woman. For further on the law see chapter 1 above.

NOTES TO PAGES 60–68

69. See also Cox 1998: 170–189.

70. See Roisman (2005: 38–41) on the risks of such relationships: he interprets the danger as stemming from male weakness, which he identifies as the main concern of the speeches, and he reduces the threat posed by the sexual companion herself.

71. See Cox 1998: 178–179, 189; Osborne 1985: 137–138. Cf. Dem. 22.61; Isai. 4.10; Din. 1.71.

72. On an ideal of family along with the role of wife in fourth-century Athens, see Eidinow 2016: 323–325; Younger 2002.

73. Eidinow 2016: 323.

74. Griffith-Williams 2017: 46–47. She also suggests that a supporting speaker was chosen for the speech for his superior skill at delivery.

CHAPTER 3: PART OF THE FAMILY

1. Kapparis 1999: 28.

2. On the authenticity of the documents at sections 16 and 52 and their interpretation, see Kapparis 1999: 198–206.

3. Phillips 2013: 30, with 42 and 176 on *xenias* specifically.

4. On this court see the introduction.

5. For women in the courts see Foxhall 1996, Gagarin 1998, S. Johnstone 1998. Note further discussion in my introduction.

6. See further Kapparis 1999: 45; Trevett 1992. On Theomnestos' family, see *APF* 11672 X.

7. See Lys. 3.9. On the obligations of citizenship in relation to good versus bad citizens, see Christ 2006.

8. C. Patterson 1994: 203–204.

9. Davies doubts the accuracy of this net worth, claiming that three talents is a gross underestimate (*APF* 11672 XI–XII).

10. See Kapparis 1999: 180.

11. See *APF* 11672 XII: "The residue presumably went to his daughters' husbands upon Apollodoros' death, sometime after he wrote and delivered [Dem.] lix in the late 340s." On *epiklēroi*, see Harrison 1968: 132–138; Phillips 2013: 216–221, 232–243.

12. C. Patterson 1994: 205–207.

13. R. Kennedy 2014: 137–140.

14. See Glazebrook 2005: 162, 182–183. For questioning of the status of other *hetairai* in oratory, see Foxhall 1996: 151; Hunter 1994: 113. Cf. Hamel (2003), who accepts Neaira's identity as a working *hetaira*, and Kapparis (2018b: 243–244), who argues that she admitted to being a prostitute, but such conclusions are not clear from the extant text.

15. C. Patterson 1994: 208.

16. Kapparis 1999: 34–39, 282–284; 2018b: 246. Although Carey (1997: 211–212),

NOTES TO PAGES 68-72

Hamel (2003: 77–113), and C. Patterson (1994: 207–209) are more cautious on her status, they agree that Apollodoros has not proven beyond doubt that she was in fact Neaira's daughter.

17. Kapparis 1999: 34; 2018b: 245. See also Hamel 2003: 47–61; C. Patterson 1998: 108.

18. Cole 1984, Scafuro 1994. Also C. Patterson 1998: 108–114.

19. This price appears to be in line with the purchase of untrained slaves. Xenophon (*Mem.* 2.5.2) gives a range of 50 to 1,000 drachmas. See further Whitehead 2001: 282.

20. C. Patterson 1994: 207.

21. Her catalog of clients includes the Athenian poet Xenokleides, the Athenian actor Hipparchos, Simos of Larisa, Timanoridas of Corinth, Eukrates of Leukas, Phrynion of Athens, Epainetos of Andros, Eurydamas son of Medeios (of Larisa), Sotados of Crete. (See Fig. 3.2.).

22. On prices for sex laborers, see Kapparis 1999: 207; Loomis 1998: 166–185.

23. On this procedure, see discussions in Glazebrook 2014b, Kamen 2014. Cf. Zelnick-Abramovitz 2005. Note that Apollodoros uses *erastēs* (lover) to refer to Neaira's clients ([Dem.] 59.26, 29, 30, 31, 41, 64).

24. Glazebrook 2014b: 65–67.

25. For interpretation see Glazebrook 2014b: 66. Aristagora, once a *hetaira* of Hypereides, seems to have found herself in a similar situation (Hyp. Fr. 25 Jensen). See further Kapparis 2018b: 256–257.

26. See C. Patterson 1994: 205–207.

27. Also see [Dem.] 59.28, 48.

28. Calame 1999: 111–112.

29. On the ubiquity of the symposium by the Classical period, see Lynch 2007 and 2011. On the symposium as primarily an elite institution, see (e.g.) Kurke 1997, O. Murray 2009, Węcowski 2014.

30. Davidson 1997: 112, 120–126; 2006. See also Goldhill 1998.

31. Gilhuly 2009: 40–41.

32. Finley 1985: 19; Hansen 1987: 216.

33. For other examples, see [Dem.] 59.19, 20, 23, 30, 33, 41, 114. On access to sex laborers as democratic, see Halperin 1990, Henry 2011.

34. See Cantarella 2005, Ogden 1997, C. Patterson 1998: 157–179. Also see Phillips 2013: 102–115 with further bibliography and sources. Cf. D. Cohen (1991a: 100–109), who argues *moicheia* applied only to illegal sex with the wives of citizens.

35. Bers 2003: 161; Carey 2012: 207; Kapparis 1999: 97; A. Murray 1939: 367.

36. Montanari s.v. *hēlikia* lists "age of marriage or fertility of women" and includes this passage as an example.

37. For age of girls at marriage, see Xen. *Oec.* 7.5, Dem. 27.4–5 with 29.43, and [Arist.] *Ath. Pol.* 56.7. For further discussion, see Kapparis 2018b: 195–196; Pomeroy 1995: 268–269; Sourvinou-Inwood 1988: 26–28.

38. Did the appropriate age for marriage differ from that for sex slavery? Quite possibly, since sex laborers were for pleasure, whereas the primary role of wives in marriage was the production of children. Sexual labor, in contrast, was not in any way connected

178

with childbearing and thus was not dependent upon puberty and menarche. Kapparis (1999: 215) puts Neaira at twelve or thirteen years old and comments: "We should understand that *hēlikia* here has a specific meaning, implying the prime age for a courtesan, the years when a woman was at the peak of her career. The orator says that she had started working as a prostitute from a very young age, before she reached her prime." But Kapparis has a more sympathetic reading than I believe the jurors would have had when listening to the speech delivered.

39. Kapparis (1999: 46–47) comments, "Apollodoros has misplaced the emphasis on her misfortunes because these can raise sympathy and pity." See also Fisher 2001: 189–190.

40. Omitowoju 1997: 11.

41. Apollodoros stresses this accessibility throughout his speech ([Dem.] 59.19, 20, 22, 23, 41, and especially 114); see Glazebrook 2005.

42. For a general discussion of violence (including threatened) against Neaira in this speech see Kapparis 2018b: 222–223, but he does not include this particular episode. Cf. Dem. 19.196–198 with discussion in Glazebrook 2021.

43. Hamel (2003: 41) and Kapparis (1999: 45–46) argue that this episode evokes sympathy, but I agree with Carey (1992: 103) that the account would more likely evoke hostility and highlights Neaira as sexually insatiable. Omitowoju (1997: 11–12, 14) suggests that the episode emphasizes her noncitizen status, since there is no *kurios* to suffer insult at Neaira's treatment and bring a charge of *hubris*. See Glazebrook 2006: 170 on how the episode adds to Apollodoros' negative portrayal of Neaira.

44. Roisman (2005: 170–171) comments, "They reasoned that since women could not control their appetites and were incapable of coping with the power of wine to loosen inhibitions, they would disgrace themselves and the males associated with them." He notes (170 n. 20) that this bias is behind jokes about women's fondness for wine: e.g., Ar. *Lys.* 113–114, 195–205; *Thesm.* 630–633.

45. Omitowoju (2016: 124) comments, "The violence in this speech constantly comes on stage only to perform its own disappearing act." See her full discussion, pp. 124–130.

46. Carey 1992: 103. See also Glazebrook 2005, 2006.

47. On etiquette in naming women in Classical Athens, see Schaps 1977.

48. Cox 1998: 176–177. Christopher Carey (1992: 112) points to the name as appropriate to such a profession. On names of courtesans in general, see McClure 2003: 59–78.

49. Robertson (1998: 99–100) argues that the name Phano was an attempt to hide her past status. Gilhuly (2009: 45) comments on the connection with Stephanos' name. Noy (2009) argues based on inscriptional evidence that there were citizen women named Phano and that the name change was not an indication of the daughter's past status as a *hetaira* but an attempt to provide a "legitimate Athenian identity" to the daughter of a *hetaira*. His argument suggests unconvincingly that Strybele and Phano were originally two different people: Strybele took on Phano's identity when Phano died. Other scholars consider Phano to be one person and likely not the daughter of Neaira and an alien but a woman of citizen status. See Hamel 2003: 77–113; Kapparis 1999: 31–39; C. Patterson 1994: 207–209. Cf. Isai. 3.30.

NOTES TO PAGES 74–79

50. For *ex hetairas*, see Isai. 3.6, 45, 48, 52, 55, 70, 71. See also C. Patterson (1990: 72) on Phile and the commentary by Hatzilambrou (2018).

51. See A. Strong (2012) and E. Cohen (2015: 145–153) on the significance of the mother-daughter relationship in sexual labor.

52. Further Kapparis 2018b: 246.

53. Kapparis 1999: 117.

54. See also the discussion of Lys. 3.6 in chapter 4 below.

55. On this law, see Kapparis 1999: 311–313. S. Johnstone (2002) has argued that the law was not about sexual labor; but regardless, Apollodoros manipulates the law to suggest that it is.

56. Note the inconsistency: Apollodoros narrates here that Epainetos got out of the charge of adultery by claiming that Phano acted as his prostitute ([Dem.] 59.67), but later Apollodoros treats the adultery charge as if it were a conviction (59.85).

57. Where exactly in Athens "near the whisperer Hermes" was remains unknown today, but it appears to have been a well-known, wealthy area of Athens, based on the names of the owners of the neighboring houses. See Kapparis 1999: 246–247.

58. [Arist.] *Ath. Pol.* 26.4; Plut. *Per.* 37.3. For a discussion of this law, see C. Patterson 1981.

59. See Konstantinou (2018: 150–155) on the limits of female mobility.

60. Carey 1992: 141; Kapparis 1999: 400.

61. On the social death of slaves at the time of enslavement, see O. Patterson 1982.

62. On the orators' use of space in the production of *ēthopoiia*, see de Bakker 2012b.

63. Witness testimonies throughout the section on Corinth are probably forgeries (see Kapparis 1999: 215–216, 221–222, 225–226, 235–236), and so it is difficult to know what the witnesses are testifying to. On the function of witness testimony, see Humphreys 1985, Todd 1990b.

64. Carey 1992: 39.

65. In support of sacred prostitution at Corinth, see MacLachlan 1992: 146; R. Strong 1997. Beard and Henderson (1998: 56–79) argue that references to such practices at Corinth are myths. Budin (2008) outright denies any historicity to such stories at Corinth and elsewhere. Spivey (1996: 176) also rejects sacred prostitution but argues instead for secular prostitution at Corinth.

66. On these controversial fragments and their interpretation, see Budin 2008: 112–152; Kurke 1996.

67. Gilhuly 2018: 12 (orig. 2014: 172).

68. Beard and Henderson 1998: 79 n. 72. Gilhuly 2018: 11 (orig. 2014: 172).

69. Kapparis 1999: 241. Aristophanes mentions Simaitha (*Ach.* 524–525).

70. Henderson 1975: 132.

71. Kapparis 1999: 241. For *sphinx* as *pornē*, see Henderson (1975: 132 n. 127), who references Anaxil. 22.22 and Alexis 167.6.

72. See Henderson 1998: 147 n. 94 and 1975: 60, 131.110, 111.

73. Henderson 1998: 157 n. 99 and 1975: 119.42, but note 118.34, where he concludes *ischas* is not phallic. Henderson (1998) appears to have revised this view.

180

NOTES TO PAGES 80–84

74. Cf. Lycurg. 1.141. On the interest of women in the Assembly and lawcourts, see Kapparis (1999: 405) on this passage. Goff (2004: 173–174) argues that the sudden change to plural invokes the collective voice of women at ritual events and evokes the ritual authority of women in a group (specifically the Thesmophoria) to facilitate the voicing of their concerns on legal and political matters. Compare this passage with the discussion of Aischin. 1.187 in chapter 5 below.

75. On female citizenship, see further C. Patterson 1987.

76. Goff 2004: 173; C. Patterson 1994: 208. Also Kapparis 2018b: 246.

77. Goff 2004: 172–174.

78. See the discussion of *metechein* in Blok 2017: 33, 53–63.

79. On [Dem.] 59.111 in particular, see Blok 2017: 33 n. 94, 186–187, 216–217.

80. Gilhuly 2009: 33–34.

81. North (1977) notes that *sōphrosunē* has different meanings depending on whether it is applied to a man or a woman. For example, *sōphrosunē* is often translated "chastity" when referring to women, but the "word does not have a comparable application to the moral or sexual conduct of men until about two centuries later, and it never ranks very high, in this sense, in the table of masculine virtues." (1977: 37). For the exact significance of *sōphrosunē* to male virtue see North's (1966) comprehensive study.

82. For discussions of epitaphs, see Lattimore 1942: 293–300. For Athens in particular, see Tsagalis 2008: 186–187; Younger 2002: 170–178.

83. On the portraits as stereotypes, see Glazebrook 2005, 2006; Kapparis 2021: 164–169.

84. For examples of the use of *plēsiazein, chrēsthai,* or *suneinai,* see [Dem.] 40.8, 27; 59.9, 20, 30, 33, 37, 41, 47, 67, 70, 71; Isai. 3.10, 15; 6.20. Cheryl Cox (1998: 182–183) argues that such verbs are directly opposed to *echein* and *sunoikein,* reserved for legally married women.

85. On the law, see Harrison 1968: 32–38; C. Patterson 1998: 114–132; Phillips 2013: 102–115. See Aischin. 1.183, which adds restrictions on their adornment.

86. Kapparis 1999: 353. Omitowoju (1997: 15–17) argues that the digression on *moicheia* establishes the extent of Phano's illegitimate integration into the polis and thus further highlights Stephanos' crime, since only marriageable women had the status for a charge of *moicheia.* In other words, if Stephanos catches a *moichos,* he is claiming citizen status for Phano. The incident substantiates the main accusation against Stephanos, that "by meddling in the apportionment of respectability afforded to these women in respect of their sexual encounters, he is adulterating the polis in the grossest way." On sex laborers in cult, see Goff 2004: 153–158.

87. See Goff (2004: 23–76) on the importance of ritual to women's agency and autonomy both in the household and in the public realm.

88. Other uses of *pornē* are not in direct reference to Neaira (§§112, 113) or are in a derivative form, such as *peporneumenēn* (§107).

89. Aischin. 1.124; Dem. 19.229; 22.56, 58, 61; Lys. 4.9, 19.

90. A later rhetorician, Hermogenes, suggested that the phrase *apo triōn trupēmatōn tēn ergasian pepoiēsthai* (that she made her living from her three holes) was removed from the original text because of its vulgarity. It does not appear in modern editions,

NOTES TO PAGES 84-87

and its authenticity remains controversial, but [Dem.] 59.114 suggests it would not be out of place in this text. For full discussion with bibliography, see Kapparis (1999: 402–404), who supports its authenticity and Blass's suggestion that it originally appeared in section 108.

91. See Goff 2004: 38–39; Kapparis 1999: 324–331. On sources on the festival, see Hamilton 1992. This speech is one of our best sources for the official events of the festival.

92. See Goff 2004: 38–39, 171–172, on the account in [Dem.] 59 in particular; Larson 2007: 130–132.

93. See Cole 2004: 134; Kapparis 1999: 340–341.

94. Scholars debate whether this marriage included actual intercourse with a priest standing in for the god or some sort of ritual activity with a herm of the god. See Kapparis 1999: 330.

95. See Goff 2004: 172.

96. For a definition of *asebeia* and *asebein*, see Filonik 2013: 14.

97. See further Eidinow 2016: 317–320; Kapparis 1999: 331.

98. Eidinow 2016: 319–320. For a recent discussion of impiety trials in general, see Filonik 2013.

99. On this festival, see Goff 2004: 144–146; Larson 2007: 72.

100. Filonik (2013: 66), following Parker (2004: 60), suggests the penalty was not severe, since Apollodoros does not mention what it was. Penalties in impiety cases included execution, exile, fines, confiscation of property, and disenfranchisement. The most common punishment was death, with the most famous examples being Socrates' in 399 BCE and individuals (incl. Alcibiades *in absentia*) involved in the Mutilation of the Herms in 415 BCE. On methods of execution, see Todd 2000a.

101. Eidinow 2016: 319–320; Goff 2004: 154–155.

102. The trial of Aspasia is known only from later sources, and so its historicity may be suspect. The original charge may have been a comic joke (Filonik 2013: 28–33).

103. For details on these trials, see Eidinow 2016: 11–30; Filonik 2013: 63–70. On Phryne in particular, see Cooper 1995; Kapparis 2018b: 258–261; 2020: 69–72 and 2021: 76–82. Although it was not in an impiety case, Kapparis (2020: 72–74) argues that a speech of Hypereides against Aristagora also focuses on her reputation as a *hetaira* and a *pharmakis* (dispenser of *pharmaka*).

104. On Aspasia's controversial status in the sex trade, see Henry 1995. What is clear is that a number of Athenian authors, especially of Old Comedy, parodied her in such terms. Although not clear in the passages of Demosthenes, the scholion mentions the love potions of Ninon (Eidinow 2016: 18; Filonik 2013: 68).

105. Eidinow (2016: 20, 23) dates the trial of Ninon between 363 and 358 BCE; Phryne's, between 350 and 340 BCE.

106. See Filonik (2013: 78–79) on *asebeia* as rhetorical invective.

107. Eidinow (2016) develops the idea of a discourse of risk as opposed to a discourse of blame. I am directly alluding to this idea with the heading of this section.

108. In other uses of *hubrizein*, Phrastor believes he has been insulted and mistreated (*hubristhai*) by his marriage to Phano ([Dem.] 59.51); an adulterous woman who enters

182

the temenos of a temple is subject to all types of mistreatment (*hubristheisa*), including being physically beaten by anyone who encounters her (59.86); the Spartan king Pausanias insultingly mistreated the rest of the Greeks (59.96). Ironically, Apollodoros reports that Neaira related to Stephanos that the *hubris* of her lover Phrynion was why she left him and was afraid to return to Athens (59.37).

109. See [Dem.] 59.77. Cf. §§44, 72, for *kataphronein* in relation to Stephanos and the laws. Possibly also in §77.

110. See also the discussion of Aischin. 1.192 in chapter 5 below.

111. Roisman 2005: 40.

112. See also chapter 1 above on women and *boulontai*.

113. [Dem.] 59.16, 17, 51, 58, 60, 63, 64, 72, 75, 92, 106, 107, 109, 118, 119 (twice), 121 (twice), 122, 124.

114. C. Patterson 1994.

115. On the sources for Apollodoros' version, see Trevett 1990.

116. For this same strategy used against Timarchos, see chapter 5 below and Lape 2006.

117. Women were not present as litigants or jurors or even in the crowds around the court, but they may have been required to appear as defendants, or they could be brought in to evoke pity for a litigant. See the introduction above. Cf. the use of Timarchos' physical appearance, including Aischin. 1.26, in chapter 5 below.

118. It is also worth noting that the only known examples of conferring citizenship involve men. It is not at all clear that non-Athenian women ever obtained citizenship. This fact makes Neaira's situation even more offensive.

119. On slave torture, see Gagarin 1996; Mirhady 1993–1994, 1996, 2000.

120. Cf. Isai. 3.78–80, where the proofs of female status are a dowry, a marriage feast, introduction of children to the phratry, and the performance of public service (such as the Thesmophoria) on her behalf; Isai. 6.64–65 includes public service on her behalf and the performance of rites at her tomb. Isai. 8.9, 18–20, also include a dowry, marriage feast, introduction of children to the phratry, and financing of the Thesmophoria.

121. For discussion, see Kapparis (1999: iv–vi, 422–424), but note that he argues *hetairai* could also mean brothel workers here. Miner 2003: 31–33. Cf. Gilhuly (2009: 54–55), who reads the passage as a "code of exchange."

122. For some examples, see Davidson 1997: 73; Gilhuly 2009: 55; Lacey 1968: 113.

123. See Xen. *Oec.* 7.25, 36, 42. On this text, see Pomeroy 1995.

124. Lysias, for example, associates *endon* with the inside of the *gunaikōnitis* (Lys. 3.6) and the location of the *moichos* (Lys. 1.11, 23). The inside of the *oikos* is also associated with female plotting about sex: "But as things are, the wicked ones (*hai d'endon*) plot evil within doors, and their servants carry their plans abroad." (Eur. *Hipp.* 649–650, trans. David Kovacs). It is also associated with the marital bed: "Whenever . . . a husband wrongs the inside [*tandon*] by rejecting his marriage bed [*lektra*], a wife wants to imitate her husband and acquire another lover" (Eur. *Elec.* 1036–1038). Euripides also uses *ta endon* metaphorically to evoke the inner versus the external persona of a person: "It is from without that those with the reputation for wisdom are splendid, while

from within [*ta d' endon*] they are no more than the rest of humanity except in wealth: yet wealth has great power" (*Andr.* 331, trans. David Kovacs). In straight reference to wealth (*ta polla endon*), see Lys. 55.47.

125. For *hetairai* being kept *endon*, see [Dem.] 48.53; for *pallakai*, see [Dem.] 59.118.

126. See Xen. *Mem.* 2.1.32, where *Aretē* describes herself as a "faithful guardian of the *oikos*."

127. Eidinow (2016: 318) suggests that the use of *psuchagōgoumenos* to describe the ill Phrastor ([Dem.] 59.55) implies Phano and Neaira have access to special powers.

128. On the different obligations of citizenship based on gender, see Blok 2017.

CHAPTER 4: SAME-SEX DESIRE

1. Cf. Xen. *An.* 5.8.4, which references fights *peri paidikōn*.

2. Lys. 3.8, 17–18, 27. For other examples, see Aischin. 1.58–61; Lys. 4.7. Lys. 3.43 mentions drunken brawls as a result of either *paidia* (games) or *paidika* (male sex object). Carey (1989: 111) and Todd (2007: 339) favor *paidiōn* here. Manuscript X has *paidikōn*, referring to young male sexual companions, but the preposition *ek*, governing it, is unusual and led the scribe of Manuscript C to suggest *paidiōn* (games) instead. (See Carey 1989: 111). It appears odd that Lysias does not reference male companions here, given that the purpose is to list disputes not worthy of the judges' attention, unworthy of a severe penalty, and regretted once sober, but he has just made a similar comment concerning disputes over boys in 3.40, and so such disputes would still be fresh in the judges' minds.

3. See chapter 1. Todd (2007: 281–284), who argues for the existence of both a *graphē* and a *dikē* in such cases, suggests Lys. 3 is in fact a private suit. Carey (1989: 109) considers it a *graphē*.

4. On characterization in Lysias, see Usher 1965. Also Carey 1989: 10, 89–90, in relation to Lysias 3 specifically.

5. Todd 2007: 276. Carey (1989: 86), in contrast, concludes it is impossible to know how soon after 394 BCE the trial occurred. The speech is dated based on the reference to the battles at Corinth and Koroneia (3.45).

6. See further Phillips 2007: 85–88.

7. Phillips (2007: 86) argues that the speaker likely injured Simon with a rock or potsherd and that Simon had witnesses to prove it.

8. For a similar sense, see Dem. 20.7; Lys. 14.31.

9. Todd 2007: 278, 314.

10. On the wealth and status of the opponent, see Carey 1989: 87; Todd 2007: 278–279. The fact that he does not appear to be of elite status supports Fisher's (2001: 27, 34, 59–62) view that same-sex relations were not restricted to a particular class. For the point in relation to this speech, see Herman 2006: 165.

11. See Carey 1989: 87, Todd 2007: 328, on the likelihood that the property valuation is inaccurate.

12. See Todd (2007: 279 n. 18 and 340) on his status and net worth as a hoplite, with bibliography.

13. On a supposed Plataian claiming citizenship but exposed as a slave, see Lys. 23 on Pankleon.

14. For explanations for the use of *to paidion he*re, see Carey 1989: 107; Todd 2007: 332–333. See further Bushala 1968: 66–68. D. Cairns (2002) argues that it is not Theodotos who is offered up for torture but an *akolouthos* (accompanying slave) of the speaker. His argument, contrary to the majority of scholars, rejects *to paidion* as a reference to Theodotos.

15. Free citizens and metics, in contrast, were not normally subjected to torture except in cases of treason. On slave torture see Gagarin 1996; Hunter 1994: 91–94; Mirhady 1993–1994, 1996, 2000.

16. Enslaved: Carey 1988: 242–243; 1989: 87; 1997: 83; Davidson 2007: 448; Lamb 1930: 70; Scodel 1986: 18. Free but not citizen: Bushala 1968: 64–66; Dover 1978: 32–33; Todd 2007: 281. Citizen: E. Cohen 2000a: 168–170; 2000b: 128; Kapparis 2018b: 214, 217.

17. Fisher 1976: 54. See further Todd 2007: 279–281.

18. Cf. Aischin. 1.41, 160, 165. On sexual contracts in general see E. Cohen 2000a: 177–192; 2000b; 2006: 109–112; 2015: 97–114. On the price of sex laborers, see Halperin 1990: 107–112; Loomis 1998: 166–185, 309–312, 334–335.

19. See Carey 1989: 102–103; Todd 2007: 326.

20. Carey 1989: 105. Also E. Cohen 2000b. Todd (2007: 327), in contrast, suggests the speaker may be exaggerating "a much less explicit claim on Simon's part along the lines that his expensive gifts to Theodotos surely created reciprocal obligations," but he seems to be parroting actual claims that Simon made at the trial.

21. Carey 1989: 103. See also Todd 2007: 326–327.

22. Carey (1988: 243) suggests such status, but Todd (2007: 280 n. 24) is skeptical that owners made such arrangements with sex laborers. See Kamen 2011 on the *chōris oikountes*. E. Cohen (2015: 170), in contrast, presents Theodotos as free, based on the fact that he can negotiate contracts.

23. For a discussion of violent abuse of sex laborers, including in Lys. 3 and 4, see Kapparis (2018b: 209–214); more generally, see Glazebrook 2015a.

24. See further Gagarin 2005.

25. For a discussion of the reliability of the speaker's narrative, see Kremmydas 2019.

26. Davidson 2007: 448. Carey (1989: 107) suggests that the boy was sitting in court during the trial.

27. The speaker, curiously, does not offer any explanation why the youth was staying with a friend and not in Peiraieus with him. Was he being provocative or respectful of any female members of his household? (See [Dem.] 59.22.) See Todd 2007: 318. It would have been much more prudent for Theodotos to be kept far from Simon.

28. See further Carey 1989: 90–91, 99; Todd 2007: 284–285, 318, 331, 332.

29. There is discussion about *paidōn* or *paidikōn* here. Todd (2007: 336 n. 42) notes *paides* as sex objects in Lys. 4.7 and so prefers to keep *paidōn* here. Carey (1989: 109) comments that *paidika* (normally in the plural) specifically refers to the *erōmenos* and

NOTES TO PAGES 100-102

so favored its use here. Cf. Xen. *An.* 5.8.4, with *paidika*. But in his Oxford commentary, Carey (2007) keeps *paidōn* because "the trouble with *paidika* (it now seems to me) is its explicitness in a text which strives to be circumspect" (quoted in Todd 2007: 336 n. 42).

30. See Carey 1989: 89.

31. Carey 1989: 100–101.

32. Carey 1989: 89, 100–101. On comedy and rhetoric in Lysias, see Harding 1994: 202–206.

33. See Carey 1989: 89, 109; Todd 2007: 285. Also Davidson 2007: 447, 449.

34. On characterization in Lysias, see Usher 1965.

35. On *ēthos*, see Carey 1994.

36. Close association with female sex laborers is a negative trope in Isai. 3.16–17; Dem. 35.45; [Dem.] 48.53–54; Isoc. 15.287–288. Also see Hdt. 2.135; Ar. *Wasps* 1351–1359; and Men. *Epi.* 136. For a similar bias against male sex slaves, see Aischin. 1.41 (also discussed below).

37. See Roisman 2005: 176–178.

38. On *epithumia* and its cognates, see Carey 1989: 94–95; Todd 2007: 311. Note that Todd interprets all instances in a sexual sense (3.4, 5, 29, 30, 31, 39).

39. Carey 1989: 88, 94. Some scholars interpret his embarrassment as about being a lover at his age, but this depends on scholarly views on the age differential of lovers in a pederastic relationship. Aischines admits to such relationships in Aischin. 1.135–136 without experiencing any shame. The speaker's embarrassment may also stem from being attached to a sex laborer. See further Todd 2007: 278, 310. On stereotypes of young men in oratory, see Roisman 2005: 12–15.

40. Dem. 54.12, 22, exploits such a bias: "But when a man over fifty years of age in the company of younger men, and these his own sons, not only did not discourage or prevent their wantonness, but has proved himself the leader and the foremost and the vilest of all, what punishment could he suffer that would be commensurate with his deeds? For my part, I think that even death would be too mild." (Trans. A. Murray 1939.)

41. Carey 1989: 94–95.

42. Carey (1989: 94) translates *kosmiōtata* "with the greatest propriety / in the most orderly manner"; Todd (2007: 311), "most discreetly."

43. See, for example, Xen. *Oec.* 6.12–17.

44. On women, see chapter 3 above.

45. On the opposition, see MacDowell 1976: 21. On the connection between *hubris* and tyranny, see MacDowell 1976: 18, 20; Hdt. 3.80–82.

46. Todd 2007: 311. See also Lys. 1.38.

47. On this speech, see Roisman 2005: 168–170. On the date of the speech, see Whitehead 2001: 266–267 and chapter 1 above.

48. The name of the speaker is not certain but is accepted by the majority of scholars based on section 24 of the text. See Whitehead 2001: 327.

49. The text does not specify the legal procedure, but the *dikē blabēs* was common in a variety of cases in the fourth century BCE. On the likelihood of this procedure for the trial, see Whitehead 2001: 268.

186

NOTES TO PAGES 102–106

50. For more on Antigona, see chapter 1 above. On the effectiveness of this strategy, see Davidson 2007: 450.

51. Roisman 2005: 168. Whitehead (2001: 271, also 281): "[Desire] was the heart of H's case, and like Lysias in his defence of a similarly-motivated client, ... he hoped that it was a persuasive one." Davidson's (2007: 449–491) suggestion that the speaker "denies *erōs*" is unconvincing.

52. Roisman 2005: 166–167. See Pomeroy (1994: 318) on this passage: "When Xenophon refers to desperate sexual craving, he usually alludes to a relationship between two males."

53. Cf. with Lys. 4 and [Dem.] 48, discussed in chapter 1 above.

54. See Carey 1989: 97.

55. See note 45 above; MacDowell 1976: 21.

56. Sophocles' *Oedipus Tyrannus* (872) credits overwhelming pride and personal ambition—that is, *hubris*—with producing tyrants. See also Hdt. 3.80–82. For an overview of *hubris* in Greek society, see Fisher 1990, MacDowell 1976.

57. On the complex view of *erōs* in oratory, see Roisman 2005: 166–170.

58. On other ways in which their characters are contrasted, see Carey 1989: 92; Todd 2007: 284–285.

59. See Xen. *Hiero* 1.33, which also distinguishes willing consent from compulsion in relations with the beloved. The text is dated to the mid-fourth century BCE. For more specific dating see Aalders 1953.

60. For the law of *hubris* as relevant to sexual violation, see Aischin. 1.15–17. Further, notes 81 and 82 below.

61. Carey 1989: 112.

62. Todd 2007: 332.

63. On the use of drunkenness in oratory, see Carey and Reid 1985 on Dem. 54.3. Also Roisman 2005: 171–175.

64. Also Dem. 37.45.

65. De Bakker (2012b: 390–391) argues that Lysias uses space as an extension of *ēthopoiia*.

66. Carey 1989: 97; Millett 1998: 207.

67. Jameson 1990: 183; Nevett 1995.

68. Although the sources frequently mention a *gunaikōnitis*, such spaces have not been found in the material record. Scholars now talk about a flexibility of domestic space to describe how female family members might avoid non-kin visitors to their home, such as when male kin hosted a *sumposion*. See Jameson 1990; Nevett 1999, 2011.

69. Davidson 2011: 599–601. While *gunaikōnitis* and its opposite, *andrōnitis*, appear in a wide variety of texts, they are not particularly common. As a result, Davidson (601) concludes that such terms "appear not in neutral indications of recognisable and fixed spaces, but as pointed allusions to gendered divisions where these divisions are breached or where gender roles are put in question." The employment of *gunaikōnitis* is thus a rhetorical device that signifies when gender divisions are violated or when gender roles are at risk.

187

NOTES TO PAGES 106–110

70. On the sexualization of the *oikos* and affinity between the house and female body, see Davidson 2011: 603, 607–608.

71. Omitowoju 2016: 122–123.

72. Todd 2007: 332.

73. Todd (2007: 213) suggests the possibility that they are dining in another part of the speaker's home, but concludes that "the more obvious reading . . . is that the speaker (accompanied presumably by Theodotos) was dining elsewhere on the night in question."

74. [Dem.] 59.22 states that Lysias kept the *hetaira* Metaneira at the house of a friend out of respect for his female relatives.

75. Most commentators assume the speaker is not being totally honest here in the narration of events and may have in fact been out to provoke Simon, since he installed the boy near Simon's house. But understandably the speaker suppresses any such provocation given his portrayal of himself as always avoiding trouble. See further Carey 1989: 90–91, 99; Todd 2007: 284–285, 318, 331, 332.

76. Todd 2007: 276–277. De Bakker (2012b: 389) suggests that the speaker is purposefully vague in order to suppress spatial details that would weaken his argument.

77. MacDowell 1976: 15; Roisman 2005: 13–15. On masculine violence and what was and was not accepted, see Fisher 1998b. See Lys. 24.17; Dem. 54.14, 22.

78. See further Carey 1989: 70 and Todd 2007: 103, both with examples, as well as Henderson 1975: 156 n. 25. In Ar. *Eccl.*, what makes the situation comical is the fact that old women are attempting to carry out the assault (1066–1111).

79. On the significance of *hubris* as rape, see Carey 1995, Omitowoju 2002. In the case of Timarchos (Aischin. 1), Fisher (2005: 83–84) argues that *hubrizein* suggests painful sexual activity. See also Xen. *Hiero* 1.31–38 on the use of force and causing a beloved pain. Xenophon's text assumes such abuse is the expected behavior of a tyrant.

80. Dem. 21.47 includes the law, which combines *hubris* with *paranomon*, any unlawful act, against a child, woman, or man, whether free or enslaved. The *graphē* went before the *Hēliaia*. See Phillips 2013: 91–92. For the potential of this procedure in cases of rape, see Carey 1995: 410; Fisher 1990; Harris 1990; Omitowoju 2002: 39–49; Phillips 2013: 104–106. In relation to slaves, see E. Cohen 2014. Lysias 10.18–19 is possibly a case of the rape of an enslaved person, but here the procedure referred to is the *dikē biaiōn*. Omitowoju (2002: 47–48) argues that it is not clear that a *graphē hubreōs* could be used in the case of a sex laborer, especially a female sex laborer. Cf. Kapparis (2018b: 159–160), who argues that such a *graphē* was not a specific procedure for any sexual offenses.

81. Cf. Dem. 21.2–7; See Fisher 1990, 1992, on *hubris* and dishonor. Also MacDowell 1976.

82. See also 3.20. Note Dem. 54.1, 8–9, in which the speaker suggests the *graphē hubreōs*, but actually goes with a lesser charge, the *dikē aikeias*. Dem. 21.31–33 is a charge of *hubris* in a *graphē hubreōs*. The speaker does not suggest a specific charge at 44 and (surprisingly, according to Todd [2007: 340]) does not use any cognate of *hubris* in the anecdote he relates, instead referring to his behavior as *thrasutētos* (most brazen) and *tolma* (daring: 3.45). *Tolma* is a characteristic of Simon throughout the speech and ap-

188

pears associated with his manner more generally (3.1, 20, 22, 25, 26, 29, 39), whereas *hubris* seems reserved for the current dispute and primarily Simon's actual treatment of Theodotos, thus reflecting his relationship to desire.

83. On death as the possible penalty for this *graphē*, see Phillips (2013: 86–87), who cites Dem. 54.1 and Lysias Fr. 178 Carey 2007. To judge from Dem. 21.47, there seem to have been no restrictions on the penalty assessed under this procedure.

84. See Fisher 1990, MacDowell 1976: 25–29, on why. Most of the crimes covered by the *graphē hubreōs* also receive coverage under other laws in a *dikē*. The prosecutor assumed greater risk and did not receive any compensation in a conviction under a *graphē*.

85. See Carey 1989: 111.

86. Todd 2007: 312.

87. See the discussion of Lys. 4 and [Dem.] 48 in chapter 1 above. Also Apollodoros in Dem. 36.45.

88. Davidson 2007: 451. Misgolas' predilection was also lampooned in comedy: Alexis Fr. 3 *PCG*; Antiphanes Fr. 27 *PCG*; and Timokles Fr. 32 *PCG*. See further Fisher 2001: 171–172.

89. Davidson (2007: 465) calls the reference to *epithumia* in 3.5 "that declaration of a sheer, unadulterated, squalid, and 'embarrassing' homosexual desire."

90. Davidson 2007: 465. Note also his comment (67): "*Porneia* then is whorishness in every possible sense of the term: doing it for money, doing it readily, doing it to further your career." Kapparis (2018b: 208) argues that the Athenians were not morally outraged by the practices of sexual labor but objected to the idea of payment. On concern with payment, see E. Cohen 2015: 81–88.

91. On *agrios* as a sexual term, see Fisher 2001: 184. Harpokration s.v. *Agrious* defines it as an excessive desire for boys based on this passage of Aischines.

92. *Erastēs* and *erōmenos* do not appear in this speech, but are used in this section for convenience in referring to the practice of Greek pederasty. As Todd (2007: 312) notes, these two terms are rare in oratory. Other terminology specific to the pederastic relationship in other contexts (e.g., *meirakion, philos*) does appear in this speech. See below.

93. Cf. Lys. 4 in chapter 1 above, [Dem.] 59 in chapter 3 above, as well as Aischin. 1 discussed in chapter 5 below.

94. On age and age categories, see Cantarella 1992: 36–44; Lear 2014: 120–121; Lear and Cantarella 2008: 2–4. On *meirakion*, see Ferrari 2002: 134–137, 140–141, but note that Lear and Cantarella (2008: 41–42, 239 n. 7) disagree with her on facial hair. Todd (2007: 277–278 and n. 12) argues for its use in the case of those in their late teens. Also see Davidson 2006: 45–47, 49–50, and 2007: 68–98, but note he argues against an age difference as characteristic of pederasty. *Meirakion* is also common in Aischin. 1, where it appears 14 times. See chapter 5 below.

95. Note Dover (1978: 33), who in contrast interprets the phrase as a polite reference to *hetairēsis*.

96. Carey 1989: 96. Todd (2007: 311) interprets the phrase as "euphemism presumably for gifts, and possibly also for money."

97. Fisher (1976: 5) comments that *philos* includes kin and non-kin alike, distinguishing personal relationships built on "mutual aid and benevolence." On pederasty and *philia*, see Calame 1996: 35–42; 1999: 95–100. Also Dover 1978: 49.

98. Todd 2007: 281. See also Davidson 2007: 490–491. Also chapter 5 below.

99. Carey 1989: 87.

100. See E. Cohen 2015: 87.

101. The verses of Theognis (1363–1364, 1029–1036) outline the appropriate behavior of the lover toward the *erōmenos*.

102. Attitudes toward pederasty vary between authors. The Archaic poetry of Theognis presents the idealized view, as does Aischines through the example of Harmodios and Aristogeiton (Aischin. 1; see discussion in chapter 5 below). Other authors, like Plato (e.g., *Symposium*) and Aristophanes (e.g., *Clouds*), present multiple perspectives on pederasty. For a summary, see Lear 2014: 122–123; Lear and Cantarella 2008: 15–23.

103. See Padilla's (2000: 200) comments on *anankē* versus *charis* in Euripides' *Alcestis*.

104. Davidson (2007: 490–491) argues that Simon also appropriated the traditional language of pederasty in discussing his relations with the boy, but we have only the speech of his opponent to go on, and it is clear that Simon argues he had a monetary contract with the boy (3.22).

105. Todd 2007: 312.

106. Todd 2007: 326.

107. Todd 2007: 281.

108. Fisher 2005: 83–84.

109. Davidson 1997: 109–112.

110. Lear and Cantarella 2008: 38–52.

111. For discussion of *Wealth* 149–159, see chapter 5 below.

112. Halperin 1990.

113. Fisher (2001: 41) notes a debate regarding whether payment or acts performed is the concern in Aischin. 1.

114. On the appropriation/evolution of *agathos* as denoting a democratic value and not simply one focused on status and social position, see Adkins 1960: 195–219. Fisher (1976: 43) comments on the "development in the use of this sort of language, both in the direction of greater complexity and of relativity of standards, and more particularly in the use of criteria of service to the community and co-operation with other citizens as well as those of wealth, birth and military success and bravery." Lape (2006: 145) notes that values of moderation and self-control "were long associated with the discourse of democratic citizenship."

115. Arist. *Eth. Nic.* 1132b35–1133a4. For discussion, see Millett 1991: 123–126; 1998: 220–222.

116. Todd 2007: 316.

CHAPTER 5: CITIZEN SEX SLAVES

1. For details on his career, see Fisher 2001: 20–23. Also *LGPN* II 36 and *PA* 13636. On his father, see *PAA* 160270, 162075. Since citizens were regularly scrutinized before taking up such roles and upon completing their terms, Timarchos' record of participation indicates his success in past reviews. Blok (2017: 241) stresses that "valuing others was a structural ingredient of the Athenian *politeia*."

2. For a discussion of the grouping and reasoning behind the offenses, see Fisher 2001: 52–53.

3. See Fisher 2001: 118–119 on the structure of the speech and its main strategies. Scholars differ on the extent to which the published speech was revised after delivery. Compare Todd 1990c: 166–167 and Worthington 1991 with S. Johnstone 1999: 12 n. 63 and Ober 1989: 49 n. 113.

4. On the presentation of the laws, see Carey 2017: 268–270; Fisher 2001: 127–128, 138–142; Gagarin 2019: 15–16. For a discussion of the laws, see Kapparis 2018b: 156–171. Wohl (2010) has interesting observations on this use of law and a speaker's authority in this speech. See also Ford 1999: 241–249.

5. I follow roughly the overview offered by Fisher (2001: 118).

6. On this procedure, see Kapparis 2018a: 198–201; Phillips 2013: 118; Fisher 2001: 5–6, 157–162; Harrison 1971: 204–205. Another such charge is possibly Lys. 10.1. But see Todd 2010: 77.

7. On the composition of jurors in the popular courts, see the introduction, pp. 9–11.

8. On the risks for the prosecutor in invoking such a challenge, see Harris 1999. Harrison (1971: 205) assumes that the usual penalty for withdrawing a prosecution or for not achieving one-fifth of the votes in a public suit (*graphē*) applied in this case too. In such cases, an accuser paid 1,000 drachmas and was likely also barred from bringing any prosecutions forward in future (e.g., Dem. 26.9; [Dem.] 53.1). Cf. Hansen 1974: 63–65 and Todd 1993: 143 for the argument that such *atimia* applied only to launching similar lawsuits. The fact that this trial is a type of *dokimasia* may suggest otherwise (see other exemptions in Harris 1999: 128 nn. 19 and 20, 131–132) and explain why Aischines chose this procedure over the *graphē hetairēseōs*. See also Kapparis 2018b: 168–169 n. 46.

9. Fisher 2001: 157–159. On the ban in relation to sex laborers in particular, see Kapparis 2018b: 161–171.

10. Hansen 1975: 119 n. 43. Fisher (2001: 248–249), in contrast, argues *hetairēsis* and embezzlement may have been no more than gossip and thus not part of the formal charge.

11. Another such trial may be referenced by Aristophanes (Ar. *Knights* 876–879), but the identity of the individual named, Grypos, is otherwise unknown.

12. Ford 1999: 245–246.

13. Fisher 2001: 62–67.

14. Fisher 2001: 62–63, 341–342. Aischines employs a similar tactic in Aischin. 3.245–

NOTES TO PAGES 120-124

246. Wolpert and Kapparis (2007: 276 n. 80) also make note of the similarities. See the discussions of [Dem.] 59.110-113 in chapter 3 above.

15. On the subordinate status of boys in Athenian society, see Golden (1984: 309-311), who argues that they were grouped with those of enslaved status in a variety of ways.

16. On pederasty, see the introduction in Lear and Cantarella 2008: 1-37. The seminal work is Dover 1978, but note Davidson (2007), who suggests a model without an age differential, which is not generally accepted by other scholars. See also chapter 4 above.

17. Todd 2010: 77 n. 23. Todd (77 n. 22) argues that the *dokimasia* was before the *Boulē* only, whereas other scholars use *dokimasia* to refer to the whole process (in the deme and before the *Boulē*).

18. See Whitehead 1986: 100-103.

19. Scholars, counting up to six types of scrutiny, argue whether Athenians would have classed all *dokimasiai* together as subdivisions of a single group and thus at core connected, or as completely unrelated (Todd 2010: 79).

20. On this speech and this procedure, see Scafuro 1994: 165-167, 168. Also Blok 2017: 5-13.

21. Lape 2006: 142.

22. On the use of *epitēdeuma* in the speech, see Fisher 2001: 166.

23. Lape 2006: 141. See also Carey 2017: 267 and Fisher 2005: 73-79. An extensive discussion of Timarchos' appetite is Davidson 1997: 255-259.

24. See Goldhill (1999: 5-8), who argues that being in an audience was "a fundamental political act" given the emphasis on evaluating and judging under the democracy. He labels democratic Athens a "performance culture."

25. See Demosthenes' response (Dem. 19.251). He comments that the statue is less than fifty years old and that the sculptor had no idea of Solon's public persona. On Aischines' mimicry here, see Carey 2017: 279-281.

26. I am grateful to Matthew Christ for this observation. Cf. [Arist.] *Ath. Pol.* 28.3 on Kleon's equally offensive habits of speaking. See further Carey 2017: 273-274 on his performance. On the significance of *schēma*, see Goldhill 1999: 4-5. On delivery and rhetoric, see Hawhee 2004: 153-161; C. Johnstone 2001.

27. See further Sissa 1999: 160.

28. On these terms in oratory see Roisman 2005: 163-185. For Aischines 1, see Carey 2017: 276-281.

29. Carey (2017: 272-275, 281) connects the focus on performance in this passage with Timarchos' upcoming speech since it alerts the jurors to an interpretation of his style.

30. See Carey 2017: 274-275.

31. E.g., Lape 2006: 144; Roisman 2005: 165-166.

32. Roisman 2005: 165.

33. Hatzilambrou 2020: 50.

34. Lape 2006: 143.

35. On servile terminology as a form of invective in the orators, see Kamen 2020:

70–73, 81 (on this passage). She argues that Demosthenes and Aischines each hint at and directly allude to the servile origins of the other (e.g., Aischin. 2.78, 180, 3.169; Dem. 19. 209, 210, 18.129–131, 258) in attempt "to trigger certain stereotypes and associations and thereby color [the jurors'] views of the two parties."

36. On this trope, see Dover 1974: 179–180, 208–209; Golden 1984: 314–316.

37. On the importance of this polarization to Greek culture, see Cartledge 1993: 133–166.

38. See further Lape 2006: 150; Fisher 2001: 283–284.

39. Cf. Sissa 1999: 160, "[Timarchos'] biography is a history of his body; it tells how he treated his *soma*, himself." Also Davidson 1997: 219, "Timarchus' very flesh contained a record of his morals."

40. See Carey (2017: 267 n. 8) on how this compares with Aischines' other speeches.

41. Fisher 2005: 73.

42. Davidson 2007: 455.

43. See, for example, Davidson 1997, Dover 1978, and Sissa 1999, respectively. Halperin (1990: 104) also identifies a "symbolic opposition between citizenship and prostitution," but again his opposition centers on penetration.

44. Hatzilambrou 2020.

45. Hatzilambrou (2020: 56) suggests *pornos* was likely an established nickname for Timarchos, but Gottesman (2014: 70) questions the ubiquity of the nickname before the trial.

46. On *pornous megalous Timarchōdeis* as a quotation from a comic play, see Fisher 2001: 57–58, 300–301; Wankel 1988: 385. The date of the play is uncertain. It may have been staged while the trial was pending (Fisher 2001: 7–8). For full discussion, see Wankel 1988. Harris (1985), in contrast, argues for a performance in the previous year.

47. Fisher 2001: 301.

48. For example, see Davidson 1997: 219–221; Fisher 2001: 54–58; or Lape 2006: 141.

49. On the question of a legal definition of sexual labor at Athens, see Lanni 2010. Nowak (2010) argues against a consistent definition of such labor in law. For a general discussion of the laws at Athens, see Phillips 2013: 116–122; Kapparis 2018a: 192–206.

50. See further Millett 1998: 220–221. On problems of payment, see E. Cohen 2015: 85–88; Davidson 2007: 459–463. On *charis* in general, see Millett 1991: 123–126; MacLachlan 1993; and chapter 4 above.

51. Ford (1999: 245–246) argues that Aischines uses the laws to stress a code of conduct for all orators in terms of how they live their lives.

52. Aischin. 1.23–24 is our only source for this practice.

53. On veiling practices, see D. Cairns 2002.

54. Tuan (1991: 694) argues that "taking language seriously shows, moreover, that the quality of place is more than just aesthetic or affectional, that it also has a *moral* dimension."

55. Fisher (2001: 242) questions the accuracy of such statements, claiming that if not land he must have had some liquid assets.

NOTES TO PAGES 129–134

56. On the assumed value of the estate, see Fisher 2001: 231. On wealth classes and liturgies, see Davies, *APF* xxv–xxx and 1981: 21–34.

57. For details on the property, with further bibliography, see Fisher 2001: 231–239.

58. Fisher 2001: 242. On selling property as a way to hide wealth, see Christ 1998.

59. By the mid-fifth century BCE citizenship law required both parents be *astoi*, tying citizenship to a household (Dem. 57.21; [Arist.] *Ath. Pol.* 42.1). Aristotle made the *oikos* the smallest component of the polis (*Pol.* 1252b13–15). On the property classes at Athens, see Plut. *Sol.* 18.

60. On the exaggeration of the age differences in 1.42 (but their importance to Aischines' argument), see Fisher 2001: 10–12, 175; Harris 1988. Timarchos was likely the same age as or slightly older than Misgolas. Davidson (2007: 454) suggests a scribal error at 1.49, where Misgolas is said to be only forty-five at the time of the trial.

61. Other sources (Timokles Fr. 32 *PCG*; Antiphanes Fr. 27 *PCG*; Alexis Fr. 3 *PCG*) corroborate such a reputation. See discussion in Fisher 2001: 171–172; Kapparis 2018b: 248–250. Also Davidson 2007: 451.

62. Adams (1919: 47), for example, chooses "decent" here, whereas I follow Fisher (2001: 83) in preferring "moderation."

63. On the significance of *metrios*, see Roisman 2005: 176–183. Lape (2006: 158 n. 20) argues that prior to Aischines it was not normally associated with control of the appetites.

64. Kapparis (2018b: 250) argues Pittalakos was likely of metic status, freed prior to his relationship with Timarchos. For other interpretations, see Kamen 2013: 25–26. The ambiguity of his enslaved status allows Aischines to both denigrate Timarchos on account of his sexual association with Pittalakos and to evoke sympathy for Pittalakos for his treatment at the hands of Timarchos and Hegesandros. On the problem of Pittalakos' status, see Fisher 2001: 190–191 and further 2005.

65. On gambling dens, see Bell, Davies, and Fisher 2004.

66. See further Fisher 2001: 217–220.

67. Davidson (1997: 306–308) refers to it as a "picture of an anti-Athens."

68. On the homoerotic humor of the passage, see Kamen 2018. For a general discussion, see Fisher 2001: 220–222. On humor targeting others for more than simply laughter, see Halliwell 1991.

69. On the tactics Aischines used to dispel the need for witnesses, see Rydberg-Cox 2000.

70. See Purves (2010: 212–213) on the *oikos*.

71. Carey 2017: 268. Some scholars suggest anal intercourse as central to Timarchos' deviancy, citing 1.84 and 131. See Dover 1978, Foucault 1985, Halperin 1990, and Winkler 1990. More recently Fisher 2001: 45–48 with summary of the arguments, including the contrary view of Davidson 1997.

72. See Davidson (2011: 598) on the gendering of space in the polis. Purves (2014) discusses intimate spaces in Herodotus, where the inside spaces belong to tyrants and connect with desire and power.

73. This is the first instance of *erastēs* in the text. Although Aischines also employs

194

it in other contexts in the speech, he avoids it in referring to Timarchos' partners. See also 1.155, 156, 171.

74. See Fisher 2014 as well as Scanlon 2002.

75. See Foxhall 2013: 125–128; Hawhee 2004: 114; Kyle 1987: 56. On the architectural features of gymnasia generally and at Athens, see Delorme 1960: 51–59; Hawhee 2004: 117–118.

76. For the diverse activities of gymnasia, see Hawhee 2004: 116–128.

77. See Delorme 1960: 316; Hawhee 2004: 114–116.

78. On the association of pederasty and the gymnasium and of the *erōmenos* and athletics in black-figure and red-figure vase painting, see Lear and Cantarella 2008: 90–97.

79. Fisher 2001: 20, 239–240.

80. Nevett 1995: 375–377, 378. On houses generally, see Jameson 1990; Nevett 1999; Tsakirgis 2016; Wycherley 1962: 185–208.

81. See Aischin. 1.41, 75; Alexis Fr. 98 *PCG*; Lys. 3.32; Isai. 6.21. Note that *analambanein* appears commonly in later authors like Plutarch and Diogenes Laertius to refer to *hetairai* and *pornai*. *Lambanein* is common in the Classical period in the case of wives: Dem. 36.8; 43.44, 45; [Dem.] 59.9, 58, 59, 81.

82. Halperin (1990: 34–35) on *gunē* and *gunaikeia hamartēmata* (1.185). Also Sissa 1999.

83. Davidson 1997: 167–182, 210, 256–257, 271–274. See Fisher 2001: 339–340 on the ambiguous meaning of "womanish offenses."

84. See also Davidson 1997: 272–273.

85. For discussion of the feminizing of Demosthenes in this speech, see Carey 2017: 275–276.

86. Davidson 1997: 113–114; 2011: 608.

87. Sissa 1999: 155. See also Davidson 1997: 256–258.

88. See further Fisher 2001: 62–67. The *diapsēphisis* of 346 BCE has already been mentioned. In addition, shortly after the trial, around 340 BCE, the lawcourts underwent some changes in their physical layout and in the process for selecting jurors.

89. Lape 2006: 146–148, 152–156. Also Davidson 1997: 308. On the philosophic echoes in this speech, see Lape 2006: 145.

90. Sissa 1999: 159.

91. On the importance of *sōphrosunē* to citizenship (and the difficulties in assessing the depth of this quality), see Roisman 2005: 176–185.

92. On *anthrōpos*, see Dickey 1996: 150–153. See also chapters 1 and 2 above.

93. Davidson 1997: 252–257.

94. Adams 1919: 151; Fisher 2001: 115; Lape 2006: 143–144.

95. Fisher (2001: 347) notes the "ordinary" and philosophical use of *hexis* to denote "settled dispositions of characters, usually conceived as either good or bad" and suggests it may indicate a widespread view that acts and habits shaped a person's character— a view found in philosophical texts of this period. Lape (2006: 144–146) explores further the connection between this text and philosophers like Plato, Isocrates, Xenophon, and Aristotle, observing that Aischines' view is unique among the orators.

96. McClure 2003: 15. See also Kapparis 2011: 227. Cf. Dem. 22.73.

97. Fisher 2001: 95. The list also includes sycophancy (*sukophantia*), brazenness (*thrasos*), extravagance (*truphē*), cowardice (*deilia*), and a lack of shame (*anaideia*).

98. Aischines describes Pittalakos as committing *toiautas hubreis . . . eis to sōma to Timarchou* (such abuses . . . against the body of Timarchos: 1.55). His other sexual partners, in contrast, are *akolastos* (without restraint: 1.42), and *agrioi* (savage: 1.52) but not *hubristai*. See also on Hegesandros at 1.70.

99. On *hubris*, see MacDowell 1976. Also Fisher 1990, 1992, and more specifically his commentary on this speech (2001: 138-141). MacDowell emphasizes the mental state of the perpetrator, whereas Fisher focuses on the dishonor inflicted on the victim. See Cantarella 1992: 43-44; D. Cohen 1991b; Dover 1978: 34-39; and Omitowoju 2002: 29-50 specifically on its use in the case of sexual offenses.

100. Davidson 1997: 115-117; Fisher 2005: 83-84; Halperin 1990. See also the discussion of *hubris* in chapter 4 above.

101. Dem. 21.47 is generally accepted as an accurate citation of the law.

102. For discussion, see Fisher 2001: 39-53; Phillips 2013: 116-121. Scholars debate the intention and effect of such laws. Many conclude they only affected the elite who dominated in public life and thus reflect a reluctance to regulate private behavior unless it infringed on the honor of other citizens or the interests of the city (D. Cohen 1991a: 229; Fisher 2001: 39-40). Halperin (1990) argues the law was symbolic in that it united the Athenians by granting autonomy to the male citizen body regardless of a citizen's social and economic standing. Lanni (2010) concludes the laws had a measurable impact on the practices of pederasty and gave rise to what Plato's Socrates refers to as a chaste love.

103. See Fisher 2001: 144. Also Ford 1999: 244-250. Those convicted suffered the greatest penalties (*ta megista epitimia*), regularly interpreted to mean death (Harrison 1971: 172). Fisher (2001: 40, 136) suggests that the penalty included death but that that may have been only one of a number of penalties for the jurors to choose from. Kapparis (2018b: 167), however, remains skeptical that the penalty was ever this severe.

104. Fisher 2001: 40-44; Todd 2007: 328-329.

105. Arnaoutoglou 1998: 66; Lanni 2010: 56. Kapparis (2018a: 157, 169-170, 191) suggests a date after the fifth century for the *graphē hetairēseōs* and suggests that the laws on procurement were obsolete by the time of Aischines' speech. See also Kapparis 2018a: 198-199. Cf. Fisher 2001: 37-38.

106. Sissa 1999: 158-159.

107. For the classic discussion, see Dover 1978. See further Hubbard 2003. An alternative view is Davidson 2007. See also note 16 above and the discussion in chapter 4 above.

108. On its association with the gymnasium, see Davidson 2007: 484-485. On pederasty as an elite practice, see Dover 1978: 149-150; Hubbard 1998; Thornton 1997: 193-212; Winkler 1990: 60-62.

109. Hubbard 1998: 67-68.

110. Sissa 2002: 156-157.

111. Lape 2006: 148-151.

NOTES TO PAGES 142–147

112. Fisher 2001: 26–27; also 1998a. Wohl (2002: 6) comments, this "text shows just how important this brand of eros was to the demos as well as to the elite."

113. Davidson 2007: 459–463. E. Cohen (2015: 85–86) highlights the increasingly monetized economy of fourth-century BCE Athens as behind the clash.

114. Fisher 2001: 59–62.

115. For the comparison with female sex laborers, see Glazebrook 2015b. On concern with pederasty, see Hubbard 1998; Lear and Cantarella 2008: 17–22. Davidson (2007: 461) argues that concern gave way to a *"charis* crisis" by the fourth century BCE.

116. See the young man's response to the old women in Ar. *Eccl.* 1098–1111.

117. The term appears eight other times in Aristophanes (*Ach.* 288–289; *Knights* 134, 193, 302–304; *Clouds* 446; *Wasps* 914; *Frogs* 465; *Wealth* 1069) and is normally an insult for any lowlife. See more on the term in Aischines 1 above in "*Sōma* and Polis."

118. The first is my version of Gulick's (1937: 90; following 262K) text in the Loeb edition of Athenaios Book 13. In the second, Fisher (2001: 212) follows the text of Kassel and Austin (Fr. 20 *PCG*), with one change: he substitutes "going out" for "going in."

119. Fisher 2001: 213, with discussion on the social significance of the similarities.

120. See also Fisher 2001: 50–51, 212–213, and discussion in chapter 4 above.

121. See Roisman 2005: 183–184. Also Fisher 2001: 34–36, 49–51. See also chapter 4 above. Note that Lys. 3 expresses some embarrassment around commitment to an enslaved sex laborer, whereas Hyp. *Ath.* expresses no embarrassment at all in pursuing a sex slave.

122. Wohl 2002: 4.

123. A detailed discussion of the tyrannicides and their tradition is Taylor 1981.

124. On the importance of the myth to Athenian values in general, including an erotic ideal, see Stewart 1997: 73 as well as Wohl 2002: 4–10.

125. Taylor (1981: 22–23) argues that the skolia, based on references to them in Aristophanes (*Ach.* 980, 1093; *Wasps* 1224–1227; *Lys.* 632), represent the popular attitude. On the cult, see Fornara 1970; Taylor 1981: 5–9. For the statue, see Taylor 1981: 13–21; Stewart 1997: 70–74.

126. *IG* I³ 131.5–7; *IG* I² 77; Isai. 5.46–47; Dem. 19.280, 20.127, 21.170; Andoc. 1.98. See further Taylor 1981: 1–12.

127. On the democratic connotations of *isonomia* (equality before the law) in the skolia, see Taylor 1981: 22–35, esp. 26.

128. For an analysis of competing traditions and the reason for the popularity of the tyrannicides among partisan groups, see Taylor 1981: 7; Thomas 1989: 238–282.

129. Aischines (1.142) describes Homer as hiding the erotic nature of their relationship, but claims it was obvious to an educated audience. Scholars debate why Homer does not reference pederasty directly in his texts (and the meaning of the omission). Clarke 1978; Dover 1978: 196–199; 1988: 131; Halperin 1990: 75–87; Skinner 2005: 42–44, 69. The nature of their relationship was a topic among Classical writers; see Fisher (2001: 289), who comments further (2001: 291–293) that Aischines adapted Homer to emphasize his own points. Further, Ford 1999: 249–256.

130. See Ford on Aischines' use of Homer. He claims (1999: 254–255) that Aischines'

retelling of Achilles' and Patroklos' deaths is intended to echo the heroic early deaths of Harmodios and Aristogeiton just described. Fisher (2001: 290) notes that Achilles' treatment of Hector's corpse is purposefully left out here and that recounting of Achilles' actions is "heavily idealizing to make the hero another model of noble self-sacrifice."

131. Fisher 2001: 293–294; cf. Wilson 1996: 314–315.

132. It is not simply one's private life and habits, as Ford (1999: 25) argues, but specifically one's erotic life that determines fitness for public life. Sissa (1999: 159) specifically focuses on Timarchos' body and sexuality.

133. On gift exchange versus commodity exchange see Davidson 1997: 109–112 and the discussion in chapter 4 above.

134. On *charis* and the pederastic relationship, see Davidson 2007: 38–50; 2001: 20–28; Glazebrook 2015b: 162–163; Hewitt 1927: esp. 149–151; MacLachlan 1993: 5–8, 56–72; Mitchell 2002: 18–21; Shapiro 1981: 133–143; Vetta 1980: 67.

135. See further Lape 2006 and n. 34 above.

136. Further on pederasty and the *erōmenos* in both literary texts and vase painting, see Dover 1978, Lear and Cantarella 2008. Also Glazebrook 2015b.

137. Davidson 2007: 464.

138. Davidson 1997: 274.

139. Fisher (2001: 244, 246) questions the accuracy of these allegations.

140. Once again on the problem of evidence for these charges, see Fisher 2001: 250–254.

141. On the posts and their chronology, see Fisher 2001: 243–246.

142. Cf. 1.191. On Timarchos' resemblance to a tyrant, see Davidson 1997: 282; Meulder 1998: 318. See also Carey 2017: 271.

143. See, for example, discussions in Davidson 1997; Halperin 1990; Winkler 1990: 45–70; Dover 1978. Dover (1978) and Halperin (1990) associate Timarchos with anal intercourse. Winkler and Davidson both discuss Timarchos as a *kinaidos*. For Winkler (1990: 45–46), the *kinaidos* is a "socially and sexually deviant male" and "socially deviant in his entire being, principally observable in behavior that flagrantly violated or contravened the dominant definition of masculinity." Davidson (1997: 167–182) defines the *kinaidos* as a person who is unable to control the appetites.

144. See discussion in Fisher 2001: 48–49; 2002: 83. Sapsford (2017: 62) identifies it as the paradox of Aischines 1.

BIBLIOGRAPHY

Aalders, G. J. D. 1953. "Date and Intention of Xenophon's 'Hiero.'" *Mnemosyne* 6(3): 208–215.

Adams, Charles Darwin, ed. 1919. *The Speeches of Aeschines*. London, England: William Heinemann.

Adey, P. 2006. "If Mobility Is Everything, Then It Is Nothing: Towards a Relational Politics of (Im)mobilities." *Mobilities* 1: 75–94.

Adkins, A. W. H. 1960. *Merit and Responsibility: A Study in Greek Values*. Oxford, England: Clarendon Press.

Alcock, Susan E. 2002. *Archaeologies of the Greek Past: Landscape, Monuments, and Memories*. The W.B. Stanford Memorial Lectures. Cambridge, England: Cambridge University Press.

Alcock, Susan E., and Robin Osborne. 1994. *Placing the Gods: Sanctuaries and Sacred Space in Ancient Greece*. Oxford, England: Clarendon Press.

Arnaoutoglou, Ilias. 1998. *Ancient Greek Laws: A Sourcebook*. London, England: Routledge.

Ault, Bradley A. 2005. "Housing the Poor and Homeless in Ancient Greece." In *Ancient Greek Houses and Households: Chronological, Regional, and Social Diversity*, edited by Bradly A. Ault and Lisa C. Nevett, 140–159. Philadelphia: University of Pennsylvania Press.

———. 2016. "Building Z in the Athenian Kerameikos: House, Tavern, Inn, Brothel?" In *Houses of Ill Repute: The Archaeology of Brothels, Houses and Taverns*, edited by Allison Glazebrook and Barbara Tsakirgis, 75–102. Philadelphia: University of Pennsylvania Press.

Bastian, M., S. Heymann, and M. Jacomy. 2009. "Gephi: An Open Source Software for Exploring and Manipulating Networks." *AAAI Publications: Proceedings of the Third International ICWSM Conference*: www.aaai.org/ocs/index.php/ICWSM/09/paper/view/154.

Beard, Mary, and John Henderson. 1998. "With This Body I Thee Worship: Sacred Prostitution in Antiquity." In *Gender and the Body in the Ancient Mediterranean*, edited by Maria Wyke, 56–79. Oxford, England: Blackwell.

BIBLIOGRAPHY

Bell, Shannon. 1994. *Reading, Writing, and Rewriting the Prostitute Body*. Bloomington: Indiana University Press.

Bell, Sinclair, Glenys Davies, and N. R. E. Fisher. 2004. "The Perils of Pittalakos: Settings of Cock Fighting and Dicing in Classical Athens." In *Games and Festivals in Classical Antiquity: Proceedings of the Conference Held in Edinburgh, 10–12 July 2000*, BAR International Series 1220, 65–78. Oxford, England: Archaeopress.

Bers, Victor. 1985. "Dikastic Thorubos." In *Crux: Essays in Greek History Presented to G. E. M. de Ste. Croix*, edited by F. David Harvey and Paul Cartledge, 1–15. London, England: Duckworth.

———. 1997. *Speech in Speech: Studies in Incorporated Oratio Recta in Attic Drama and Oratory*. Lanham: Rowman & Littlefield.

———. 2003. *Demosthenes, Speeches 50–59*. Austin: University of Texas Press.

Blanshard, Alastair. 2014. "The Permeable Space of the Athenian Law-Court." In *Space, Place, and Landscape in Ancient Greek Literature and Culture*, edited by Kate Gilhuly and Nancy Worman, 240–275. Cambridge, England: Cambridge University Press.

Blok, Josine. 2017. *Citizenship in Classical Athens*. Cambridge, England: Cambridge University Press.

Boegehold, Alan L. 1995. *The Lawcourts at Athens: Sites, Buildings, Equipment, Procedure, and Testimonia*. The Athenian Agora, vol. 28. Princeton, NJ: American School of Classical Studies at Athens.

Boegehold, Alan L., and Adele C. Scafuro, eds. 1994. *Athenian Identity and Civic Ideology*. Baltimore, MD: Johns Hopkins University Press.

Broneer, Oscar. 1942. "The Thesmophorion in Athens." *Hesperia : The Journal of the American School of Classical Studies at Athens* 11(3): 250–274.

Budin, Stephanie L. 2008. *The Myth of Sacred Prostitution in Antiquity*. Cambridge, England: Cambridge University Press.

Burkert, Walter. 1985. *Greek Religion: Archaic and Classical*. Oxford, England: Blackwell.

Bushala, E. W. 1968. "Torture of Non-Citizens in Homicide Investigations." *Greek, Roman, and Byzantine Studies* 9: 61–68.

Cairns, Douglas L. 1993. *Aidos: The Psychology and Ethics of Honour and Shame in Ancient Greek Literature*. Oxford, England: Clarendon Press.

———. 2002. "The Meaning of the Veil in Ancient Greek Culture." In *Women's Dress in the Ancient Greek World*, edited by Lloyd Llewellyn-Jones, 73–93. London, England: Duckworth.

Cairns, F. 2002. "The Civic Status of Theodotos in Lysias III." *Emerita* 70: 197–204.

Calame, Claude. 1996. *L'éros dans la Grèce antique*. Paris, France: Belin.

———. 1999. *The Poetics of Eros in Ancient Greece*. Translated by Janet Lloyd. Princeton, NJ: Princeton University Press.

Camp, John M. 2001. *The Archaeology of Athens*. New Haven, CT: Yale University Press.

Campa, Naomi T. 2019. "*Kurios, Kuria*, and the Status of Athenian Women." *The Classical Journal* 114(3): 257–279.

Cantarella, Eva. 1992. *Bisexuality in the Ancient World*. Translated by Cormac Ó Cuilleanáin. New Haven, CT: Yale University Press.

———. 2005. "Gender, Sexuality and Law." In *The Cambridge Companion to Ancient Greek Law*, edited by Michael Gagarin and David Cohen, 236–253. Cambridge, England: Cambridge University Press.

Carawan, Edwin. 1998. *Rhetoric and the Law of Draco*. Oxford, England: Clarendon Press.

Carey, Christopher. 1988. "A Note on Torture in Athenian Homicide Cases." *Historia: Zeitschrift für Alte Geschichte* 37(2): 241–245.

———, ed. 1989. *Lysias: Selected Speeches*. Cambridge, England: Cambridge University Press.

———, ed. 1992. *Apollodoros against Neaira: Demosthenes 59*. Translated by Christopher Carey. Warminster, England: Aris & Phillips.

———. 1994. "Rhetorical Means of Persuasion." In *Persuasion: Greek Rhetoric in Action*, edited by Ian Worthington, 26–45. London, England: Routledge.

———. 1995. "Rape and Adultery in Athenian Law." *Classical Quarterly* 45(2): 407–417.

———, ed. 1997. *Trials from Classical Athens*. London, England: Routledge.

———, ed. 2007. *Lysiae orationes cum fragmentis*. Oxford, England: Oxford University Press.

———, ed. 2012. *Trials from Classical Athens*. 2nd ed. London, England: Routledge.

———. 2017. "Style, Persona and Performance in Aeschines' Prosecution of Timarchus." In *The Theatre of Justice: Aspects of Performance in Greco-Roman Oratory and Rhetoric*, edited by Sophia Papaioannou, Andreas Serafim, and Beatrice da Vela, 265–282. Leiden, The Netherlands: Brill.

Carey, Christopher, and R. A. Reid, eds. 1985. *Demosthenes: Selected Private Speeches*. Cambridge, England: Cambridge University Press.

Cartledge, Paul. 1993. *The Greeks: A Portrait of Self and Others*. Oxford, England: Oxford University Press.

Christ, Matthew R. 1998. *The Litigious Athenian*. Baltimore, MD: Johns Hopkins University Press.

———. 2006. *The Bad Citizen in Classical Athens*. Cambridge, England: Cambridge University Press.

Clarke, W. M. 1978. "Achilles and Patroclus in Love." *Hermes* 106(3): 381–396.

Clinton, K. 1996. "The Thesmophorion in Central Athens and the Celebration of the Thesmophoria in Attica." In *The Role of Religion in the Early Greek Polis: Proceedings of the Third International Seminar on Ancient Greek Cult, Organized by the Swedish Institute at Athens, 16–18 October 1992*, edited by Robin Hägg, 111–125. Stockholm, Sweden: Svenska Institutet i Athen.

Cohen, David. 1991a. *Law, Sexuality, and Society: The Enforcement of Morals in Classical Athens*. New York, NY: Cambridge University Press.

———. 1991b. "Sexuality, Violence, and the Law of Hubris." *Greece and Rome* 38: 171–188.

Cohen, Edward E. 1973. *Ancient Athenian Maritime Law*. Princeton, NJ: Princeton University Press.

———. 2000a. *The Athenian Nation*. Princeton, NJ: Princeton University Press.

BIBLIOGRAPHY

———. 2000b. "Whoring under Contract: The Legal Context of Prostitution in Fourth-Century Athens." In *Law and Social Status in Classical Athens*, edited by Virginia J. Hunter and Jonathon C. Edmondson, 113–148. New York, NY: Oxford University Press.

———. 2006. "Free and Unfree Sexual Work: An Economic Analysis of Athenian Prostitution." In *Prostitutes and Courtesans in the Ancient World*, edited by Christopher A. Faraone and Laura McClure, 95–124. Madison: University of Wisconsin Press.

———. 2014. "Sexual Abuse and Sexual Rights: Slaves' Erotic Experience at Athens and Rome." In *A Companion to Greek and Roman Sexualities*, edited by Thomas K. Hubbard, 184–198. Malden, MA: Wiley-Blackwell.

———. 2015. *Athenian Prostitution: The Business of Sex*. New York, NY: Oxford University Press.

Cole, Susan Guettel. 1984. "Greek Sanctions against Sexual Assault." *Classical Philology* 79(2): 97–113.

———. 2004. *Landscapes, Gender, and Ritual Space: The Ancient Greek Experience*. Berkeley: University of California Press.

Connelly, Joan Breton. 2007. *Portrait of a Priestess: Women and Ritual in Ancient Greece*. Princeton, NJ: Princeton University Press.

Conwell, D. H. 2008. *Connecting a City to the Sea: The History of the Athenian Long Walls*. Leiden, The Netherlands: Brill.

Cooper, Craig. 1995. "Hyperides and the Trial of Phryne." *Phoenix* 49(4): 303–318.

Corner, Sean. 2011. "Bringing the Outside In: The Andron as Brothel and the Symposium's Civic Sexuality." In *Greek Prostitutes in the Ancient Mediterranean, 800 BCE–200 CE*, edited by Allison Glazebrook and Madeleine M. Henry, 60–85. Madison: University of Wisconsin Press.

———. 2012. "Did 'Respectable' Women Attend Symposia?" *Greece and Rome* 59(1): 34–45.

Cox, Cheryl Anne. 1998. *Household Interests: Property, Marriage Strategies, and Family Dynamics in Ancient Athens*. Princeton, NJ: Princeton University Press.

Cresswell, Tim. 1996. *In Place/Out of Place: Geography, Ideology, and Transgression*. Minneapolis: University of Minnesota Press.

———. 2004. *Place: A Short Introduction*. Malden, MA: Wiley-Blackwell.

———. 2010. "Towards a Politics of Mobility." *Society and Space* 28: 17–31.

———. 2011. "Mobilities, I: Catching Up." *Progress in Human Geography* 35: 550–558.

———. 2012. "Mobilities, II: Still." *Progress in Human Geography* 36: 645–653.

Cusset, Christophe. 2014. "Melancholic Lovers in Menander." In *Menander in Contexts*, edited by Alan H. Sommerstein, 167–179. Routledge Monographs in Classical Studies 16. New York, NY: Routledge.

Davidson, James. 1997. *Courtesans and Fishcakes: The Consuming Passions of Classical Athens*. London, England: HarperCollins.

———. 2001. "Dover, Foucault and Greek Homosexuality: Penetration and the Truth of Sex." *Past & Present* 170: 3–51.

BIBLIOGRAPHY

————. 2006. "Making a Spectacle of Her(Self): The Greek Courtesan and the Art of the Present." In *The Courtesan's Arts: Cross-Cultural Perspectives*, edited by Martha Feldman and Bonnie Gordon, 29–51. New York, NY: Oxford University Press.

————. 2007. *The Greeks and Greek Love: A Radical Reappraisal of Homosexuality in Ancient Greece*. London, England: Weidenfeld & Nicholson.

————. 2011. "Bodymaps: Sexing Space and Zoning Gender in Ancient Athens." *Gender & History* 23(3): 597–614.

Davies, John K. 1971. *Athenian Propertied Families, 600–300 B.C.* Oxford, England: Clarendon Press.

————. 1981. *Wealth and the Power of Wealth in Classical Athens*. New York, NY: Arno Press.

de Bakker, M. P. 2012a. "Demosthenes." In *Space in Ancient Greek Literature: Studies in Ancient Greek Narrative*, edited by Irene J. F. de Jong, 393–412. Mnemosyne Supplements, vol. 339. Leiden, The Netherlands: Brill.

————. 2012b. "Lysias." In *Space in Ancient Greek Literature: Studies in Ancient Greek Narrative*, edited by Irene J. F. de Jong, 377–392. Mnemosyne Supplements, vol. 339. Leiden, The Netherlands: Brill.

de Jong, Irene J. F. 2012. *Space in Ancient Greek Literature: Studies in Ancient Greek Narrative*. Mnemosyne Supplements, vol. 339. Leiden, The Netherlands: Brill.

Delorme, Jean. 1960. *Gymnasion: Étude sur les monuments consacrés à l'education en Gréce (des origines à l'empire romain)*. Paris, France: Boccard.

Demand, Nancy H. 1994. *Birth, Death, and Motherhood in Classical Greece*. Baltimore, MD: Johns Hopkins University Press.

Demetriou, Denise. 2011. "What Is an Emporion? A Reassessment." *Historia: Zeitschrift für Alte Geschichte* 60(3): 255–272.

————. 2012. *Negotiating Identity in the Ancient Mediterranean: The Archaic and Classical Greek Multiethnic Emporia*. Cambridge, England: Cambridge University Press.

Dickey, Eleanor. 1996. *Greek Forms of Address: From Herodotus to Lucian*. Oxford, England: Clarendon Press.

Dillon, Matthew. 2002. *Girls and Women in Classical Greek Religion*. London, England: Routledge.

Dover, Kenneth James. 1974. *Greek Popular Morality in the Time of Plato and Aristotle*. Berkeley: University of California Press.

————. 1978. *Greek Homosexuality*. Cambridge, MA: Harvard University Press.

Eckerman, Chris. 2014. "Pindar's Delphi." In *Space, Place, and Landscape in Ancient Greek Literature and Culture*, edited by Kate Gilhuly and Nancy Worman, 21–62. Cambridge, England: Cambridge University Press.

Edwards, Mike. 2007. *Isaeus*. The Oratory of Classical Greece, vol. 11. Austin: University of Texas Press.

Eidinow, Esther. 2016. *Envy, Poison, and Death: Women on Trial in Classical Athens*. Oxford, England: Oxford University Press.

Ferrari, Gloria. 2002. *Figures of Speech: Men and Maidens in Ancient Greece*. Chicago, IL: University of Chicago Press.

Filonik, Jakub. 2013. "Athenian Impiety Trials: A Reappraisal." *Dike: Rivista di Storia del Diritto Greco ed Ellenistico* 16: 11–96.

Finley, Moses I. 1951. *Studies in Land and Credit in Ancient Athens, 500–200 B.C.: The Horos Inscriptions*. New Brunswick, NJ: Rutgers University Press.

———. 1985. *Democracy: Ancient and Modern*. New Brunswick, NJ: Rutgers University Press.

Fisher, N. R. E. 1976. *Social Values in Classical Athens*. London, England: J. M. Dent and Sons.

———. 1990. "The Law of Hubris in Athens." In *Nomos: Essays in Athenian Law, Politics, and Society*, edited by Paul Cartledge, Paul Millett, and Stephen Todd, 123–138. Cambridge, England: Cambridge University Press.

———. 1992. *Hybris: A Study in the Values of Honour and Shame in Ancient Greece*. Warminster, England: Aris & Phillips.

———. 1998a. "Gymnasia and the Democratic Values of Leisure." In *Kosmos: Essays in Order, Conflict and Community in Classical Athens*, edited by Paul Cartledge, Paul Millett, and Sitta von Reden, 84–101. Cambridge, England: Cambridge University Press.

———. 1998b. "Violence, Masculinity, and the Law in Classical Athens." In *When Men Were Men: Masculinity, Power and Identity in Classical Antiquity*, edited by Lin Foxhall and J. B. Salmon, 68–97. Leicester-Nottingham Studies in Ancient Society, vol. 8. London, England: Routledge.

———, ed. 2001. *Aeschines: Against Timarchos*. Oxford, England: Oxford University Press.

———. 2005. "Body-Abuse: The Rhetoric of *Hybris* in Aeschines' *Against Timarchos*." In *La violence dans les mondes grec et romain : Actes du Colloque International (Paris, 2–4 mai 2002)*, edited by Jean-Marie Bertrand, 67–89. Paris, France: Publications de la Sorbonne.

———. 2014. "Athletics and Sexuality." In *A Companion to Greek and Roman Sexualities*, edited by Thomas K. Hubbard, 244–264. Malden, MA: Wiley-Blackwell.

Ford, A. 1999. "Reading Homer from the Rostrum: Poems and Laws in Aeschines' *Against Timarchus*." In *Performance Culture and Athenian Democracy*, 231–256. New York, NY: Cambridge University Press.

Fornara, Charles W. 1970. "The Cult of Harmodius and Aristogeiton." *Philologus* 114 (1–2): 155–180.

Forsén, Björn, and G. R. Stanton. 1996. *The Pnyx in the History of Athens: Proceedings of an International Colloquium Organized by the Finnish Institute at Athens, 7–9 October 1994*. Papers and Monographs of the Finnish Institute at Athens, vol. 2. Helsinki, Finland: Foundations of the Finnish Institute at Athens.

Foucault, Michel. 1985. *The History of Sexuality*. Vol. 2, *The Use of Pleasure*. Translated by Robert Hurley. New York, NY: Vintage Books.

Foxhall, Lin. 1989. "Household, Gender and Property in Classical Athens." *Classical Quarterly* 39(1): 22–44.

———. 1994. "Pandora Unbound: A Feminist Critique of Foucault's History of Sexuality." In *Dislocating Masculinities: Comparative Ethnographies*, edited by A. Cornwall and N. Lindesfarne, 133–146. London, England: Routledge. [Reprinted in *Rethinking Sexuality: Foucault and Classical Antiquity*, edited by David H. J. Larmour, Paul A. Miller, and Charles Platter, 122–137. Princeton, NJ: Princeton University Press, 1998.]

———. 1996. "The Law and the Lady: Women and Legal Proceedings in Classical Athens." In *Greek Law in Its Political Setting: Justifications Not Justice*, edited by Lin Foxhall and A. D. E. Lewis, 133–152. New York, NY: Oxford University Press.

Foxhall, Lin, and J. B. Salmon. 1998a. *Thinking Men: Masculinity and Its Self-Representation in the Classical Tradition*. Leicester-Nottingham Studies in Ancient Society, vol. 7. London, England: Routledge.

———. 1998b. *When Men Were Men: Masculinity, Power and Identity in Classical Antiquity*. Leicester-Nottingham Studies in Ancient Society, vol. 8. London, England: Routledge.

———. 2013. *Studying Gender in Classical Antiquity*. Cambridge, England: Cambridge University Press.

Gagarin, Michael. 1996. "The Torture of Slaves in Athenian Law." *Classical Philology* 91(1): 1–18.

———, ed. 1997. *Antiphon. The Speeches*. Cambridge, England: Cambridge University Press.

———. 1998. "Women in Athenian Courts." *Dike: Rivista di Storia del Diritto Greco ed Ellenistico* 1: 39–51.

———. 2001. "Women's Voices in Attic Oratory." In *Making Silence Speak: Women's Voices in Greek Literature and Society*, edited by Laura McClure and A. P. M. H. Lardinois, 161–176. Princeton, NJ: Princeton University Press.

———. 2003. "Telling Stories in Athenian Law." *Transactions of the American Philological Association* 133(2): 197–207.

———. 2005. "The Unity of Greek Law." In *The Cambridge Companion to Ancient Greek Law*, edited by David Cohen and Michael Gagarin, 29–40. New York, NY: Cambridge University Press.

———. 2019. "Storytelling in Athenian Law." In *Forensic Narratives in Athenian Courts*, edited by Mike Edwards and Dimos Spatharas, 11–21. London, England: Routledge.

Garland, Robert. 1987. *The Piraeus: From the Fifth to the First Century B.C.* Ithaca, NY: Cornell University Press.

Garner, Richard. 1987. *Law and Society in Classical Athens*. London, England: Croom Helm.

Gilhuly, Kate. 2009. *The Feminine Matrix of Sex and Gender in Classical Athens*. Cambridge, England: Cambridge University Press.

———. 2014. "Corinth, Courtesans, and the Politics of Place." In *Space, Place, and Landscape in Ancient Greek Literature and Culture*, edited by Nancy Worman and Kate Gilhuly, 171–199. Cambridge, England: Cambridge University Press.

———. 2018. *Erotic Geographies in Ancient Greek Literature and Culture*. London, England: Routledge.

BIBLIOGRAPHY

Gilhuly, Kate, and Nancy Worman. 2014. *Space, Place, and Landscape in Ancient Greek Literature and Culture*. Cambridge, England: Cambridge University Press.

Glazebrook, Allison. 2005. "The Making of a Prostitute: Apollodoros's Portrait of Neaira." *Arethusa* 38(2): 161–187.

———. 2006. "The Bad Girls of Athens: The Image and Function of *Hetairai* in Judicial Oratory." In *Prostitutes and Courtesans in the Ancient World*, edited by Christopher A. Faraone and Laura K. McClure, 125–138. Madison: University of Wisconsin Press.

———. 2011a. "*Porneion*: Prostitution in Athenian Civic Space." In *Greek Prostitutes in the Ancient Mediterranean, 800 BCE–200 CE*, edited by Allison Glazebrook and Madeleine M. Henry, 34–59. Madison: University of Wisconsin Press.

———. 2011b. "Prostitution." In *A Cultural History of Sexuality*, vol. 1, *In the Classical World (800 BCE–350 CE)*, edited by Mark Golden and Peter Toohey, 145–168. Oxford, England: Berg.

———. 2012. "Prostitutes, Plonk and Play: Female Banqueters on a Red-Figure Psykter from the Hermitage." *Classical World* 105(4): 497–524.

———. 2014a. "Sexual Rhetoric: From Athens to Rome." In *A Companion to Greek and Roman Sexualities*, edited by Thomas K. Hubbard, 431–445. Malden, MA: Wiley-Blackwell.

———. 2014b. "The Erotics of Manumussion: Prostitutes and the πρᾶσις ἐπ' ἐλευθερία." *EuGeStA (Journal of Gender Studies in Antiquity)* 4: 53–80.

———. 2015a. "A Hierarchy of Violence? Sex Slaves, *Parthenoi* and Rape in Menander's *Epitrepontes*." In *Beyond Courtesans and Whores: Sex and Labor in the Graeco-Roman World*, edited by Allison Glazebrook, A Special Issue of *Helios*, 42(1): 81–101.

———. 2015b. "'Sex-Ed' at the Archaic Symposium: Prostitutes, Boys, and Paideia." In *Sex in Antiquity: Exploring Gender and Sexuality in the Ancient World*, edited by Nancy Rabinowitz, James Robson, and Mark Masterson, 157–178. London, England: Routledge.

———. 2016a. "Is There an Archaeology of Prostitution?" In *Houses of Ill Repute: The Archaeology of Brothels, Houses and Taverns in the Greek World*, edited by Allison Glazebrook and Barbara Tsakirgis, 169–196. Philadelphia: University of Pennsylvania Press.

———. 2016b. "Prostitutes, Women, and Gender in Ancient Greece." In *Women in Antiquity: Real Women across the Ancient World*, edited by Stephanie Lynn Budin and Jean Macintosh Turfa, 703–713. London, England: Routledge.

———. 2021. "Female Sexual Agency and an Enslaved 'Olynthian': Demosthenes 19.196–8." In *Slavery and Sexuality in Classical Antiquity*, edited by Deborah Kamen and C. W. Marshall, 141–158. Madison: University of Wisconsin Press.

Glazebrook, Allison, and Madeleine M. Henry, eds. 2011. *Greek Prostitutes in the Ancient Mediterranean, 800 BCE–200 CE*. Madison: University of Wisconsin Press.

Glazebrook, Allison, and Barbara Tsakirgis, eds. 2016. *Houses of Ill Repute: The Archaeology of Brothels, Houses and Taverns*. Philadelphia: University of Pennsylvania Press.

BIBLIOGRAPHY

Goff, Barbara E. 2004. *Citizen Bacchae: Women's Ritual Practice in Ancient Greece.* Berkeley: University of California Press.

Golden, Mark. 1984. "Slavery and Homosexuality at Athens." *Phoenix* 38: 308–324.

Goldhill, Simon. 1998. "The Seductions of the Gaze: Socrates and His Girlfriends." In *Kosmos: Essays in Order, Conflict and Community in Classical Athens*, edited by Paul Cartledge, Paul Millett, and Sitta von Reden, 105–124. Cambridge, England: Cambridge University Press.

———. 1999. "Programme Notes." In *Performance-Culture and Athenian Democracy*, edited by Robin Osborne and Simon Goldhill, 1–29. Cambridge, England: Cambridge University Press.

———. 2015. "Is There a History of Prostitution?" In *Sex in Antiquity: Exploring Gender and Sexuality in the Ancient World*, edited by Nancy Rabinowitz, James Robson, and Mark Masterson, 179–197. London, England: Routledge.

Goldhill, Simon, and Robin Osborne. 1999. *Performance-Culture and Athenian Democracy.* Cambridge, England: Cambridge University Press.

Gottesman, Alex. 2014. *Politics and the Street in Democratic Athens.* Cambridge, England: Cambridge University Press.

Green, J. R. 1994. *Theatre in Ancient Greek Society.* London, England: Routledge.

———. 2001. "Comic Cuts: Snippets of Action on the Greek Comic Stage." *Bulletin of the Institute of Classical Studies* 45: 37–64.

Griffith-Williams, Brenda. 2013. *A Commentary on Selected Speeches of Isaios.* Mnemosyne Supplements, vol. 364. Leiden, The Netherlands: Brill.

———. 2017. "Would I Lie to You? Narrative and Performance in Isaios 6." In *The Theatre of Justice: Aspects of Performance in Greco-Roman Oratory and Rhetoric*, edited by Sophia Papaioannou, Andreas Serafim, and Beatrice da Vela, 42–56. Leiden, The Netherlands: Brill.

———. 2019. "Social Norms and the Legal Framework of Forensic Narratives in Disputed Inheritance Claims." In *Forensic Narratives in Athenian Courts*, edited by Mike Edwards and Dimos Spatharas, 55–69. London, England: Routledge.

Hall, Edith. 1989. "Inventing the Barbarian: Greek Self-Definition through Tragedy." Oxford, England: Clarendon Press.

———. 1995. "Lawcourt Dramas: The Power of Performance in Greek Forensic Oratory." *Bulletin of the Institute of Classical Studies* 40: 39–58.

———. 2006. *The Theatrical Cast of Athens: Interactions between Ancient Greek Drama and Society.* Oxford, England: Oxford University Press.

Halliwell, Stephen. 1991. "Comic Satire and Freedom of Speech in Classical Athens." *Journal of Hellenic Studies* 111: 48–70.

Halperin, David M. 1990. "The Democratic Body: Prostitution and Citizenship in Classical Athens." In *One Hundred Years of Homosexuality and Other Essays on Greek Love*, 88–112. New York, NY: Routledge.

Halperin, David M., John J. Winkler, and Froma I. Zeitlin, eds. 1990. *Before Sexuality: The Construction of Erotic Experience in the Ancient Greek World.* Princeton, NJ: Princeton University Press.

Hamel, Debra. 2003. *Trying Neaira: The True Story of a Courtesan's Scandalous Life in Ancient Greece*. New Haven, CT: Yale University Press.

Hamilton, Richard, 1992. *Choes and Anthesteria: Athenian Iconography and Ritual*. Ann Arbor: University of Michigan Press.

Hansen, Mogens Herman. 1974. *The Sovereignty of the People's Court in Athens in the Fourth Century B.C. and the Public Action against Unconstitutional Proposals*. Odense University Classical Studies, vol. 4. Odense, Denmark: Odense Universitetsforlag.

———. 1975. *Eisangelia: The Sovereignty of the People's Court in Athens in the Fourth Century B.C. and the Public Action against Unconstitutional Proposals*. Odense, Denmark: Odense Universitetsforlag.

———. 1976. "The Theoric Fund and the *Graphē Paranomōn* against Apollodorus." *Greek, Roman and Byzantine Studies* 17: 235–246.

———. 1981. "The Prosecution of Homicide in Athens: A Reply." *Greek, Roman and Byzantine Studies* 22(1): 11–30.

———. 1987. *The Athenian Assembly in the Age of Demosthenes*. Oxford, England: Blackwell.

———. 2010. "The Concepts of *Dēmos, Ekklēsia*, and *Dikastērion* in Classical Athens." *Greek, Roman, and Byzantine Studies* 50(1): 499–536.

Hanson, S. 2010. "Gender and Mobility: New Approaches for Informing Sustainability." *Gender, Place and Culture* 17: 5–23.

Harding, Phillip. 1994. "Comedy and Rhetoric." In *Persuasion: Greek Rhetoric in Action*, edited by Ian Worthington, 196–221. London, England: Routledge.

Harris, Edward M. 1985. "The Date of the Trial of Timarchus." *Hermes* 113(3): 376–380.

———. 1988. "When Was Aeschines Born?" *Classical Philology* 83(3): 211–214.

———. 1990. "Did the Athenians Regard Seduction as a Worse Crime than Rape?" *The Classical Quarterly* 40(2): 370–377.

———. 1999. "The Penalty for Frivolous Prosecutions in Athenian Law." *Dike: Rivista di Storia del Diritto Greco ed Ellenistico* 2: 123–142.

Harrison, Alick Robin Walsham. 1968. *The Law of Athens*. Vol. 1. Oxford, England: Clarendon Press.

———. 1971. *The Law of Athens*. Vol. 2. Oxford, England: Clarendon Press.

Harvey, D. 1996. *Justice, Nature, and the Geography of Difference*. Malden, MA: Wiley-Blackwell.

Hatzilambrou, Rosalia. 2018. *Isaeus' On the Estate of Pyrrhus (Oration 3)*. Newcastle upon Tyne, England: Cambridge Scholars Publishing.

———. 2020. "Constructing the Identity of Timarchus in Aeschines 1." In *The Making of Identities in Athenian Oratory*, 47–62. New York, NY: Routledge.

Hawhee, Debra. 2004. *Bodily Arts: Rhetoric and Athletics in Ancient Greece*. Austin: University of Texas Press.

Henderson, Jeffrey. 1975. *The Maculate Muse: Obscene Language in Attic Comedy*. New Haven, CT: Yale University Press.

———. 1996. *Three Plays by Aristophanes: Staging Women*. New York, NY: Routledge.

BIBLIOGRAPHY

———. 1998. *Aristophanes: Acharnians, Knights*. Cambridge, MA: Harvard University Press.

———. 2000. "Pherekrates and the Women of Old Comedy." In *The Rivals of Aristophanes: Studies in Athenian Old Comedy*, edited by David Harvey and John Wilkins, 135–150. Cambridge, England: Cambridge University Press.

Henry, Madeleine M. 1985. *Menander's Courtesans and the Greek Comic Tradition*. Studien zur Klassischen Philologie, Bd. 20. Frankfurt am Main: Lang.

———. 1995. *Prisoner of History: Aspasia of Miletus and her Biographical Tradition*. Oxford, England: Oxford University Press.

———. 2011. "The Traffic in Women: From Homer to Hipponax, from War to Commerce." In *Greek Prostitutes in the Ancient Mediterranean, 800 BCE–200 CE*, edited by Allison Glazebrook and Madeleine M. Henry, 3–13. Madison: University of Wisconsin Press.

Herman, Gabriel. 2006. *Morality and Behaviour in Democratic Athens: A Social History*. Cambridge, England: Cambridge University Press.

Hewitt, Joseph William. 1927. "The Terminology of 'Gratitude' in Greek." *Classical Philology* 22(2): 142–161.

Hubbard, Thomas K. 1998. "Popular Perceptions of Elite Homosexuality in Classical Athens." *Arion* 6: 48–78.

———, ed. 2003. *Homosexuality in Greece and Rome: A Sourcebook of Basic Documents*. Berkeley: University of California Press.

———. 2014. "Peer Homosexuality." In *A Companion to Greek and Roman Sexualities*, edited by Thomas K. Hubbard, 128–149. Malden, MA: Wiley-Blackwell.

Hughes, Alan. 2012. *Performing Greek Comedy*. Cambridge, England: Cambridge University Press.

Humphreys, Sally. 1985. "Social Relations on Stage: Witnesses in Classical Athens." *History and Anthropology* 1(2): 313–369.

———. 1986. "Kinship Patterns in the Athenian Courts." *Greek, Roman and Byzantine Studies* 27: 57–91.

Hunter, Virginia J. 1994. *Policing Athens: Social Control in the Attic Lawsuits, 420–320 B.C.* Princeton, NJ: Princeton University Press.

Jameson, Michael. 1990. "Private Space and the Greek City." In *The Greek City from Homer to Alexander*, edited by Oswyn Murray and S. R. F. Price, 171–195. Oxford, England: Clarendon Press.

———. 1997. "Women and Democracy in Fourth-Century Athens." In *Esclavage, guerre, économie en Grèce ancienne*, edited by Jacques Oulhen and Pierre Brulé, 95–107. Rennes, France: Presses Universitaires de Rennes.

Johnstone, Christopher Lyle. 2001. "Communicating in Classical Contexts: The Centrality of Delivery." *Quarterly Journal of Speech* 87(2): 121–143.

Johnstone, Steven. 1998. "Cracking the Code of Silence: Athenian Legal Oratory and the History of Slaves and Women." In *Women and Slaves in Greco-Roman Culture: Differential Equations*, edited by Sandra R. Joshel and Sheila Murnaghan, 221–235. London, England: Routledge.

———. 1999. *Disputes and Democracy: The Consequences of Litigation in Ancient Athens*. Austin: University of Texas Press.

———. 2002. "Apology for the Manuscript of Demosthenes 59.67." *American Journal of Philology* 123(2): 229–256.

Kamen, Deborah. 2000. *Isaeus' Orations 2 and 6*. Indianapolis: Hackett Publishing.

———. 2011. "Reconsidering the Status of *Khôris Oikountes*." *Dike: Rivista di Storia del Diritto Greco ed Ellenistico* 14: 45–53.

———. 2013. *Status in Classical Athens*. Princeton, NJ: Princeton University Press.

———. 2014. "Sale for the Purpose of Freedom: Slave Manumission in Ancient Greece." *The Classical Journal* 109(3): 281–307.

———. 2018. "The Consequences of Laughter in Aeschines' *Against Timarchos*." *Archimède* 5: 49–56.

———. 2020. *Insults in Classical Athens*. Madison: University of Wisconsin Press.

Kapparis, Konstantinos A. 1999. *Apollodoros "Against Neaira" [D. 59]*. Berlin, Germany: de Gruyter.

———. 2011. "The Terminology of Prostitution in the Ancient Greek World." In *Greek Prostitutes in the Ancient Mediterranean, 800 BCE–200 CE*, edited by Allison Glazebrook and Madeleine M. Henry, 222–255. Madison: University of Wisconsin Press.

———. 2018a. *Athenian Law and Society*. London, England: Routedge.

———. 2018b. *Prostitution in the Ancient Greek World*. Berlin, Germany: de Gruyter.

———. 2020. "Constructing Gender Identity: Women in Athenian Trials." In *The Making of Identities in Athenian Oratory*, edited by Jakub Filonik, Brenda Griffith-Williams, and Janek Kucharski, 63–80. New York, NY: Routledge.

———. 2021. *Women in the Law Courts of Classical Athens*. Edinburgh, Scotland: University of Edinburgh Press.

Kennedy, George A. 1964. *The Art of Persuasion in Greece*. Princeton, NJ: Princeton University Press.

———. 1994. *A New History of Classical Rhetoric*. Princeton, NJ: Princeton University Press.

Kennedy, Rebecca Futo. 2014. *Immigrant Women in Athens: Gender, Ethnicity, and Citizenship in the Classical City*. Routledge Studies in Ancient History, vol. 6. New York, NY: Routledge.

Knigge, Ursula. 1988. *Der Kerameikos von Athen*. Athens, Greece: Krene.

———. 1993. "Die Ausgrabung im Kerameikos 1990/91." *Archäologischer Anzeiger*, 125–140.

———. 2005. *Kerameikos*, vol. XVII, *Der Bau Z*. 2 vols. Munich, Germany: Hirmer.

Konstantinou, Ariadne. 2018. *Female Mobility and Gendered Space in Ancient Greek Myth*. London, England: Bloomsbury.

Kovacs, David, ed. 1995. *Euripides: Children of Heracles, Hippolytus, Andromache, Hecuba*. Cambridge, MA: Harvard University Press.

Kremmydas, Christos. 2019. "Truth and Deception in Athenian Forensic Narratives: An Assessment of Demosthenes 54 and Lysias 3." In *Forensic Narratives in Athenian*

Courts, edited by Mike Edwards and Dimos Spatharas, 211–227. London, England: Routledge.

Kurke, Leslie. 1996. "Pindar and the Prostitutes; or, Reading Ancient 'Pornography.'" *Arion* 4(2): 49–75.

———. 1997. "Inventing the 'Hetaira': Sex, Politics, and Discursive Conflict in Archaic Greece." *Classical Antiquity* 16(1): 106–150.

Kyle, Donald G. 1987. *Athletics in Ancient Athens*. Mnemosyne, Bibliotheca Classica Batava, Supplement 95. Leiden, The Netherlands: Brill.

Lacey, W. K. 1968. *The Family in Classical Greece*. Ithaca, NY: Cornell University Press.

Lamb, W. R. M. 1930. *Lysias*. Cambridge, MA: Harvard University Press.

Lang, M. 2004. *The Athenian Citizen: Democracy in the Athenian Agora*. Rev. ed. Edited by John Camp. Princeton, NJ: American School of Classical Studies at Athens.

Lanni, Adriaan. 2006. *Law and Justice in the Courts of Classical Athens*. New York, NY: Cambridge University Press.

———. 2010. "The Expressive Effect of the Athenian Prostitution Laws." *Classical Antiquity* 29(1): 45–67.

Lape, Susan. 2006. "The Psychology of Prostitution in Aeschines' Speech *Against Timarchus*." In *Prostitutes and Courtesans in the Ancient World*, edited by Christopher A. Faraone and Laura K. McClure, 139–160. Madison: University of Wisconsin Press.

Larmour, David H. J., Paul A. Miller, and Charles Platter, eds. 1998. *Rethinking Sexuality: Foucault and Classical Antiquity*. Princeton, NJ: Princeton University Press.

Larson, Jennifer. 2007. *Ancient Greek Cults: A Guide*. New York, NY: Routledge.

Lattimore, Richmond. 1942. *Themes in Greek and Latin Epitaphs*. Illinois Studies in Language and Literature, vol. 28, nos. 1–2. Urbana, IL: University of Illinois Press.

Law, R. 1999. "Beyond 'Women and Transport': Towards New Geographies of Gender and Daily Mobility." *Progress in Human Geography* 23: 567–588.

Lear, Andrew. 2014. "Ancient Pederasty: An Introduction." In *A Companion to Greek and Roman Sexualities*, edited by Thomas K. Hubbard, 102–127. Malden, MA: Wiley-Blackwell.

Lear, Andrew, and Eva Cantarella. 2008. *Images of Ancient Greek Pederasty: Boys Were Their Gods*. New York, NY: Routledge.

Lefebvre, Henri. 1991. *The Production of Space*. Translated by Donald Nicholson-Smith. Malden, MA: Wiley-Blackwell.

Leigh, Carol. 1997. "Inventing Sex Work." In *Whores and Other Feminists*, edited by Jill Nagle, 223–231. New York, NY: Routledge.

Levin-Richardson, Sarah. 2019. *The Brothel of Pompeii: Sex, Class, and Gender at the Margins of Roman Society*. Cambridge, England: Cambridge University Press.

Lind, Hermann. 1988. "Ein Hetärenhaus Am Heiligen Tor? Der Athener Bau Z und die bei Isaios (6, 20f) erwähnete Synoikia Euktemons." *Museum Helveticum* 45: 158–169.

Loomis, W. T. 1972. "The Nature of Premeditation in Athenian Homicide Law." *Journal of Hellenic Studies* 92: 86–95.

———. 1998. *Wages, Welfare Costs, and Inflation in Classical Athens*. Ann Arbor: University of Michigan Press.

BIBLIOGRAPHY

Lynch, Kathleen M. 2007. "More Thoughts on the Space of the Symposium." In *Building Communities: House, Settlement, and Society in the Aegean and Beyond*, edited by R. Westgate, N. Fisher and J. Whitley, 243–249. London, England: British School at Athens.

———. 2011. *The Symposium in Context: Pottery from a Late Archaic House near the Athenian Agora. Hesperia*, suppl. 46. Princeton, NJ: American School of Classical Studies at Athens.

MacDowell, Douglas M. 1966. *Athenian Homicide Law in the Age of the Orators.* Publications of the Faculty of Arts of the University of Manchester, no. 15. Manchester, England: Manchester University Press.

———. 1976. "'Hybris' in Athens." *Greece and Rome* 23(1): 14–31.

———. 1978. *The Law in Classical Athens*. Ithaca, NY: Cornell University Press.

MacLachlan, Bonnie. 1992. "Sacred Prostitution and Aphrodite." *Studies in Religion* 21(2): 145–162.

———. 1993. *The Age of Grace: Charis in Early Greek Poetry*. Princeton, NJ: Princeton University Press.

Marshall, C. W. 2021. "Love-Sick in a Different Way: Sex and Desire in Lysias 4." In *Slavery and Sexuality in Classical Antiquity*, edited by Deborah Kamen and C. W. Marshall, 121–140. Madison: University of Wisconsin Press.

McClure, Laura. 2003. *Courtesans at Table: Gender and Greek Literary Culture in Athenaeus*. New York, NY: Routledge.

Meulder, M. 1989. "Timarque, un être tyrannique dépeint par Éschine." *Les Études Classiques* 18: 317–322.

Millett, Paul. 1991. *Lending and Borrowing in Ancient Athens*. Cambridge, England: Cambridge University Press.

———. 1998. "Encounters in the Agora." In *Kosmos: Essays in Order, Conflict and Community in Classical Athens*, edited by Paul Cartledge, Paul Millett, and Sitta von Reden, 203–228. Cambridge, England: Cambridge University Press.

Miner, Jess. 2003. "Courtesan, Concubine, Whore: Apollodorus' Deliberate Use of Terms for Prostitutes." *American Journal of Philology* 124(1): 19–37.

Mirhady, David C. 1993–1994. "Torture in Athenian Litigation." *Proceedings of the Canadian Society for the Study of Rhetoric* 5 (April): 1–10.

———. 1996. "Torture and Rhetoric in Athens." *Journal of Hellenic Studies* 116: 119–131.

———. 2000. "The Athenian Rationale for Torture." In *Law and Social Status in Classical Athens*, edited by Virginia J. Hunter and Jonathon C. Edmondson, 53–74. New York, NY: Oxford University Press.

———. 2007a. "The Dikasts' Oath and the Question of Fact." In *Horkos: The Oath in Greek Society*, edited by Alan H. Sommerstein and J. Fletcher, 48–59. Liverpool, England: Liverpool University Press.

———. 2007b. "Torture and Rhetoric in Athens." In *Oxford Readings in the Attic Orators*, edited by Edward Carawan, 247–268. Oxford, England: Clarendon Press.

Mitchell, Lynette G. 2002. *Greeks Bearing Gifts: The Public Use of Private Relationships in the Greek World, 435–323 B.C.* Cambridge, England: Cambridge University Press.

Murray, A. T. 1939. *Demosthenes VI: Private Orations L–LVIII; In Neaeram, LIX*. Cambridge, MA: Harvard University Press.

Murray, Oswyn. 2009. "The Culture of the Symposium." In *A Companion to Archaic Greece*, edited by Kurt A. Raaflaub and Hans van Wees, 508–523. Chichester, England: Wiley-Blackwell.

Naber, S. A. 1905. "Adnotationes Criticae ad Antiphontis Aeschinis Hyperidis Dinarchi Orationes." *Mnemosyne* 33(2): 157–185.

Nevett, Lisa C. 1995. "Gender Relations in the Classical Greek Household: The Archaeological Evidence." *Annual of the British School at Athens* 90: 363–381.

———. 1999. *House and Society in the Ancient Greek World*. Cambridge, England: Cambridge University Press.

———. 2011. "Towards a Female Topography of the Ancient Greek City: Cases-Studies from Late Archaic and Early Classical Athens." *Gender and History* 23: 577–597.

North, Helen. 1966. *Sophrosyne: Self-Knowledge and Self-Restraint in Greek Literature*. Cornell Studies in Classical Philology, vol. 35. Ithaca, NY: Cornell University Press.

———. 1977. "The Mare, the Vixen and the Bee: *Sophrosyne* as the Virtue of Women in Antiquity." *Illinois Classical Studies* 2: 35–48.

Nowak, Maria. 2010. "Defining Prostitution in Athenian Legal Rhetoric." *Legal History Review* 78(1/2): 183–197.

Noy, David. 2009. "Neaera's Daughter: A Case of Athenian Identity Theft?" *Classical Quarterly* 59(2): 398–410.

Ober, Josiah. 1989. *Mass and Elite in Democratic Athens: Rhetoric, Ideology, and the Power of the People*. Princeton, NJ: Princeton University Press.

O'Connell, Peter A. 2017. *The Rhetoric of Seeing in Attic Oratory*. Austin: University of Texas Press.

Ogden, Daniel. 1996. *Greek Bastardy in the Classical and Hellenistic Periods*. Oxford, England: Clarendon Press.

———. 1997. "Rape, Adultery, and Protection of Bloodlines in Classical Athens." In *Rape in Antiquity*, edited by Susan Deacy and Karen F. Pierce, 25–42. London, England: Duckworth.

O'Higgins, Laurie. 2003. *Women and Humor in Classical Greece*. Cambridge, England: Cambridge University Press.

Omitowoju, Rosanna. 1997. "Regulating Rape: Soap Operas and Self-Interest in the Athenian Courts." In *Rape in Antiquity*, edited by Susan Deacy and Karen F. Pierce, 1–24. London, England: Duckworth.

———. 2002. *Rape and the Politics of Consent in Classical Athens*. Cambridge, England: Cambridge University Press.

———. 2016. "The Crime That Dare Not Speak Its Name: Violence against Women in the Athenian Courts." In *The Topography of Violence in the Greco-Roman World*, edited by Werner Riess and Garrett G. Fagan, 113–135. Ann Arbor: University of Michigan Press.

Ormand, Kirk. 2014. "Foucault's *History of Sexuality* and the Discipline of Classics."

In *A Companion to Greek and Roman Sexualities*, edited by Thomas K. Hubbard, 54–68. Malden, MA: Wiley-Blackwell.

Osborne, Robin. 1985. *Dēmos: The Discovery of Classical Attika*. Cambridge, England: Cambridge University Press.

———. 2011. *The History Written on the Classical Greek Body*. Cambridge, England: Cambridge University Press.

Padilla, Mark. 2000. "Gifts of Humiliation: *Charis* and Tragic Experience in *Alcestis*." *American Journal of Philology* 121(2): 179–211.

Parker, Robert. 2004. "What Are Sacred Laws?" In *The Law and the Courts in Ancient Greece*, edited by Edward Monroe Harris and Lene Rubinstein, 57–70. London, England: Duckworth.

Patterson, Cynthia. 1981. *Pericles' Citizenship Law of 451/50 B.C.* New York: Arno Press.

———. 1987. "*Hai Attikai*: The Other Athenians." In *Rescuing Creusa: New Methodological Approaches to Women in Antiquity*, edited by Marilyn B. Skinner, 49–67. Lubbock: Texas Tech University Press.

———. 1990. "Those Athenian Bastards." *Classical Antiquity* 9: 40–72.

———. 1994. "The Case against Neaira and the Public Ideology of the Athenian Family." In *Athenian Identity and Civic Ideology*, edited by Alan L. Boegehold and Adele C. Scafuro, 199–216. Baltimore, MD: Johns Hopkins University Press.

———. 1998. *The Family in Greek History*. Cambridge, MA: Harvard University Press.

Patterson, Orlando. 1982. *Slavery and Social Death: A Comparative Study*. Cambridge, MA: Harvard University Press.

Phillips, David D. 2007. "*Trauma ek Pronoias* in Athenian Law." *Journal of Hellenic Studies* 127: 74–105.

———. 2013. *The Law of Ancient Athens*. Ann Arbor: University of Michigan Press.

Pomeroy, Sarah B. 1994. *Xenophon, Oeconomicus: A Social and Historical Commentary*. Oxford, England: Clarendon Press.

Purves, Alex C. 2010. *Space and Time in Ancient Greek Narrative*. Cambridge, England: Cambridge University Press.

———. 2014. "In the Bedroom: Interior Space in Herodotus' Histories." In *Space, Place, and Landscape in Ancient Greek Literature and Culture*, edited by Nancy Worman and Kate Gilhuly, 94–129. Cambridge, England: Cambridge University Press.

Richlin, Amy. 1991. "Zeus and Metis: Foucault, Feminism, Classics." *Helios* 18(2): 1–21.

———. 1992a. *The Garden of Priapus: Sexuality and Aggression in Roman Humor*. New York, NY: Oxford University Press.

———, ed. 1992b. *Pornography and Representation in Greece and Rome*. New York, NY: Oxford University Press.

Robertson, Bruce G. 1998. "Personal Names as Evidence for Athenian Social and Political History, ca. 507–300 B.C." Doctoral thesis, University of Toronto.

Robson, James. 2009. *Aristophanes: An Introduction*. London, England: Duckworth.

———. 2013. *Sex and Sexuality in Classical Athens*. Edinburgh, Scotland: Edinburgh University Press.

BIBLIOGRAPHY

Roisman, Joseph. 2005. *The Rhetoric of Manhood: Masculinity in the Attic Orators.* Berkeley: University of California Press.

Romano, David Gilman. 1985. "The Panathenaic Stadium and Theater of Lykourgos: A Re-examination of the Facilities on the Pnyx Hill." *American Journal of Archaeology* 89(3): 441–454.

Rosivach, Vincent J. 1998. *When a Young Man Falls in Love: The Sexual Exploitation of Women in New Comedy.* New York, NY: Routledge.

Ruffell, Ian. 2014. "Character Types." In *The Cambridge Companion to Greek Comedy,* edited by Martin Revermann, 147–167. Cambridge, England: Cambridge University Press.

Russell, D. A. 1990. "Ethos in Oratory and Rhetoric." In *Characterization and Individuality in Greek Literature,* edited by C. B. R. Pelling, 197–212. New York, NY: Oxford University Press.

Rydberg-Cox, J. A. 2000. "An Unusual Exclamation in Aeschines' 'Against Timarchus' (1.73)." *Mnemosyne* 53(4): 419–430.

Sanders, Teela. 2005. "'It's Just Acting': Sex Workers' Strategies for Capitalizing on Sexuality." *Gender, Work and Organization* 12: 319–342.

Sapsford, Thomas. 2017. "The Life of the *Kinaidoi*." PhD dissertation, University of Southern California.

Sato, Noboru. 2019. "Inciting *Thorubos* and Narrative Strategies in Attic Forensic Speeches." In *Forensic Narratives in Athenian Courts,* edited by Mike Edwards and Dimos Spatharas, 102–116. London, England: Routledge.

Scafuro, Adele C. 1994. "Witnessing and False Witnessing: Proving Citizenship and Kin Identity in Fourth-Century Athens." In *Athenian Identity and Civic Ideology,* edited by Alan L. Boegehold and Adele C. Scafuro, 156–198. Baltimore, MD: Johns Hopkins University Press.

———. 1997. *The Forensic Stage: Settling Disputes in Graeco-Roman New Comedy.* Cambridge, England: Cambridge University Press.

Scanlon, Thomas F. 2002. *Eros and Greek Athletics.* Oxford, England: Oxford University Press.

Schaps, David M. 1977. "The Woman Least Mentioned: Etiquette and Women's Names." *Classical Quarterly* 27(2): 323–330.

Scodel, Ruth, ed. 1986. *Lysias, Orations I, III.* Bryn Mawr, PA: Thomas Library, Bryn Mawr College.

Scott, Joan W. 1986. "Gender: A Useful Category of Historical Analysis." *American Historical Review* 91(5): 1053–1075.

Shapiro, H. A. 1981. "Courtship Scenes in Attic Vase-Painting." *American Journal of Archaeology* 85(2): 133–143.

Sidwell, Keith. 2000. "From Old to Middle to New? Aristotle's *Poetics* and the History of Athenian Comedy." In *The Rivals of Aristophanes: Studies in Athenian Old Comedy,* edited by David Harvey, John Wilkins, and K. J. Dover, 247–258. London, England: Duckworth.

———. 2014. "Fourth-Century Comedy before Menander." In *The Cambridge Companion to Greek Comedy*, edited by Martin Revermann, 60–78. Cambridge, England: Cambridge University Press.

Sissa, Giulia. 1999. "Sexual Body Building: Aeschines, *Against Timarchus*." In *Constructions of the Classical Body*, edited by James I. Porter, 147–168. Ann Arbor: University of Michigan Press.

Skinner, Marilyn B. 2005. *Sexuality in Greek and Roman Culture*. Malden, MA: Wiley-Blackwell.

Sosin, Joshua D. 1997. "A Word for 'Woman'?" *Greece, Rome, and Byzantine Studies* 38: 75–83.

Sourvinou-Inwood, Christiane. 1988. *Studies in Girls' Transitions: Aspects of the Arkteia and Age Representation in Attic Iconography*. Athens, Greece: Kardamitsa.

Spatharas, Dimos. 2006. "Wounding, Rhetoric and the Law in Lysias IV." *Revue Internationale de droits de l'Antiquité* 53: 87–106.

Spivey, Nigel Jonathan. 1996. *Understanding Greek Sculpture: Ancient Meanings, Modern Readings*. London, England: Thames & Hudson.

Ste. Croix, G. E. M. de. 2004. *Athenian Democratic Origins and Other Essays*. Oxford, England: Oxford University Press.

Stehle, Eva. 2007. "Thesmophoria and Eleusinian Mysteries: The Fascination of Women's Secret Rituals." In *Finding Persephone: Women's Rituals in the Ancient Mediterranean*, edited by Maryline G. Parca and Angeliki Tzanetou, 165–185. Bloomington: Indiana University Press.

Stewart, Andrew F. 1997. *Art, Desire, and the Body in Ancient Greece*. Cambridge, England: Cambridge University Press.

Strong, Anise K. 2012. "Daughter and Employee: Mother-Daughter Bonds among Prostitutes." In *Mothering and Motherhood in Ancient Greece and Rome*, edited by Lauren Hackworth Petersen and Patricia B. Salzman-Mitchell, 121–139. Austin: University of Texas Press.

Strong, R. A. 1997. *The Most Shameful Practice: Temple Prostitution in the Ancient Greek World*. Los Angeles: University of California Press.

Taaffe, Lauren K. 1993. *Aristophanes and Women*. London, England: Routledge.

Taylor, Michael W. 1981. *The Tyrant Slayers: The Heroic Image in Fifth-Century B.C. Athenian Art and Politics*. New York, NY: Arno Press.

Tempest, K. 2007. "Saints and Sinners: Some Thoughts on the Presentation of Character in Greek Oratory and Cicero's Verrines." In *Sicilia Nutrix Plebis Romanae: Rhetoric, Law, and Taxation in Cicero's Verrines*, edited by J. R. W. Prag, 19–36. Bulletin of the Institute of Classical Studies, Supplement 97. London, England: Institute of Classical Studies.

Thomas, Rosalind. 1989. *Oral Tradition and Written Record in Classical Athens*. Cambridge Studies in Oral and Literate Culture, vol. 18. Cambridge, England: Cambridge University Press.

Thompson, Homer A. 1936. "Pnyx and Thesmophorion." *Hesperia: The Journal of the American School of Classical Studies at Athens* 5(2): 151–200.

BIBLIOGRAPHY

Thompson, Wesley E. 1970. "Isaeus 6: The Historical Circumstances." *Classical Review* 20: 1–4.

Thornton, Bruce S. 1997. *Eros: The Myth of Ancient Greek Sexuality*. Boulder, CO: Westview Press.

Todd, Stephen C. 1990a. "Lady Chatterley's Lover and the Attic Orators: The Social Composition of the Athenian Jury." *Journal of Hellenic Studies* 110: 146–173.

———. 1990b. "The Purpose of Evidence in Athenian Courts." In *Nomos: Essays in Athenian Law, Politics, and Society*, edited by Paul Cartledge, Paul Millett, and Stephen Todd, 19–39. Cambridge, England: Cambridge University Press.

———. 1990c. "The Use and Abuse of the Attic Orators." *Greece & Rome* 37(2): 159–178.

———. 1993. *The Shape of Athenian Law*. Oxford, England: Clarendon Press.

———. 2000a. "How to Execute People in Fourth Century Athens." In *Law and Social Status in Classical Athens*, edited by Virginia J. Hunter and Jonathon C. Edmondson, 31–51. Oxford, England: Oxford University Press.

———. 2000b. *Lysias*. The Oratory of Classical Greece, vol. 2. Austin: University of Texas Press.

———. 2007. *A Commentary on Lysias, Speeches 1–11*. Oxford, England: Oxford University Press.

———. 2010. "The Athenian Procedure(s) of *Dokimasia*." In *Symposion 2009: Vorträge zur griechischen und hellenistischen Rechtsgeschichte*, edited by Gerhard Thür, 73–99. Vienna, Austria: Verlag der Österreichischen Akademie der Wissenschaften.

Townsend, Rhys F. 1995. "The Square Peristyle and Its Predecessors." In *The Lawcourts at Athens: Sites, Buildings, Equipment, Procedure, and Testimonia*, edited by Alan L. Boegehold, 104–116. The Athenian Agora, vol. 28. Princeton, NJ: American School of Classical Studies at Athens.

Traill, Ariana. 2008. *Women and the Comic Plot in Menander*. Cambridge, England: Cambridge University Press.

Trendall, A. D. 1967. *Phlyax Vases*. 2nd ed. University of London, Institute of Classical Studies, Bulletin, Supplement 19. London, England: Institute of Classical Studies.

Trevett, Jeremy. 1990. "History in [Demosthenes] 59." *Classical Quarterly* 40(2): 407–420.

———. 1992. *Apollodoros the Son of Pasion*. Oxford, England: Clarendon Press.

Tsagalis, Christos. 2008. *Inscribing Sorrow: Fourth-Century Attic Funerary Epigrams*. Trends in Classics, Supplementary Volumes, vol. 1. Berlin, Germany: de Gruyter.

Tsakirgis, Barbara. 2005. "Living and Working Around the Athenian Agora: A Preliminary Case Study of Three Houses." In *Ancient Greek Houses and Households: Chronological, Regional, and Social Diversity*, edited by Bradly A. Ault and Lisa C. Nevett, 67–82. Philadelphia: University of Pennsylvania Press.

———. 2016. "What Is a House? Conceptualizing the Greek House." In *Houses of Ill Repute: The Archaeology of Brothels, Houses and Taverns in the Greek World*, edited by Allison Glazebrook and Barbara Tsakirgis, 13–35. Philadelphia: University of Pennsylvania Press.

Tuan, Yi-Fu. 1977. *Space and Place: The Perspective of Experience*. London, England: E. Arnold.

———. 1991. "Language and the Making of Place: A Narrative-Descriptive Approach." *Annals of the Association of American Geographers* 81: 684–696.

Usher, Stephen. 1965. "Individual Characterization in Lysias." *Eranos* 63: 99–119.

———. 1999. *Greek Oratory: Tradition and Originality*. New York, NY: Oxford University Press.

Uteng, T. P., and T. Cresswell. 2008. *Gendered Mobilities*. Aldershot, England: Ashgate.

Vetta, M. 1980. *Teognide, libro secondo: Introduzione, testo critico, traduzione e commento*. Rome, Italy: Edizioni dell'Ateneo.

von Reden, Sitta. 1995. *Exchange in Ancient Greece*. London, England: Duckworth.

Wankel, Hermann. 1975. "Aischines 1, 18–20 und der neue kölner Papyrus." *Zeitschrift für Papyrologie und Epigraphik* 16: 69–75.

———. 1988. "Die Datierung des Prozesses gegen Timarchos (346/5)." *Hermes* 116(3): 383–386.

Webster, T. B. L, and J. R. Green. 1978. *Monuments Illustrating Old and Middle Comedy*. 3rd ed. London, England: University of London, Institute of Classical Studies.

Węcowski, Marek. 2014. *The Rise of the Greek Aristocratic Banquet*. Oxford, England: Oxford University Press.

Wharton, Amy. 2009. "The Sociology of Emotional Labor." *Annual Review of Sociology* 35: 147–165.

Whitehead, David. 1977. *The Ideology of the Athenian Metic*. Proceedings of the Cambridge Philological Society, Supplementary volume no. 4. Cambridge, England: Cambridge Philological Society.

———. 1986. *The Demes of Attica, 508/7–ca. 250 B.C.: A Political and Social Study*. Princeton, NJ: Princeton University Press.

———. 2001. *Hypereides: The Forensic Speeches*. Oxford, England: Oxford University Press.

Wilson, P. J. 1996. "Tragic Rhetoric: The Use of Tragedy and the Tragic in the Fourth Century." In *Tragedy and the Tragic: Greek Theatre and Beyond*, edited by M. S. Silk, 310–331. Oxford, England: Clarendon Press.

Winkler, John J. 1990. *The Constraints of Desire: The Anthropology of Sex and Gender in Ancient Greece*. New York, NY: Routledge.

Witzke, Serena. 2015. "Harlots, Tarts, and Hussies? A Problem of Terminology for Sex Labor in Roman Comedy." In *Beyond Courtesans and Whores: Sex and Labor in the Graeco-Roman World*, edited by Allison Glazebrook, A Special Issue of *Helios*, 42(1): 7–27.

Wohl, Victoria. 2002. *Love among the Ruins: The Erotics of Democracy in Classical Athens*. Princeton, NJ: Princeton University Press.

———. 2010. *Law's Cosmos: Juridical Discourse in Athenian Forensic Oratory*. Cambridge, England: Cambridge University Press.

Wolpert, Andrew, and Konstantinos Kapparis, eds. 2007. *Legal Speeches of Democratic Athens: Sources for Athenian History*. Indianapolis: Hackett Publishing.

Worthington, Ian. 1991. "Greek Oratory, Revision of Speeches and the Problem of Historical Reliability." *Classica et Mediaevalia* 42: 55–74.

BIBLIOGRAPHY

———, ed. 1994. *Persuasion: Greek Rhetoric in Action*. London, England: Routledge.

Wycherley, R. E. 1962. *How the Greeks Built Cities*. 2nd ed. New York, NY: Norton.

Wyke, Maria, ed. 1998. *Gender and the Body in the Ancient Mediterranean*. Oxford: Blackwell.

Wyse, William. 1904. *The Speeches of Isaeus*. Hildesheim, Germany: Georg Olms.

Younger, John G. 2002. "Women in Relief: 'Double Consciousness' in Classical Attic Tombstones." In *Among Women: From the Homosocial to the Homoerotic in the Ancient World*, edited by Nancy S. Rabinowitz and Lisa Auanger, 167–210. Austin: University of Texas Press.

Zeitlin, Froma I. 1996. *Playing the Other: Gender and Society in Classical Greek Literature*. Chicago: University of Chicago Press.

Zelnick-Abramovitz, Rachel. 2005. *Not Wholly Free: The Concept of Manumission and the Status of Manumitted Slaves in the Ancient Greek World*. Mnemosyne, Bibliotheca Classica Batava, Supplementum 266. Leiden, The Netherlands: Brill.

Zweig, Bella. 1992. "The Mute Nude Female Characters in Aristophanes' Plays." In *Pornography and Representation in Greece and Rome*, edited by Amy Richlin, 73–89. Oxford, England: Oxford University Press.

GENERAL INDEX

abandonment, 53

Acharnians (Aristophanes), 14, 79

Achilles, 146–147, 198n130

adornment, 14

adultery, 71, 75–76, 82, 85, 91, 147, 180n56

Against Athenogenes (Hypereides), 19, 36, 37, 102

agathos, 101, 115, 137–138, 149, 190n114

agency of women, 30–35, 41. *See also* gender roles and norms

age standards: and accusations against Simon, 108, 109, 113; citizenship and civic participation, 121, 127, 141; and defendant in Lysias 3, 100–101, 115, 186nn39–40; and marriage, 72, 178n38; and pederastic relationships, 101, 112, 145, 186n39, 189n94, 192n16; and sex slaves, 170n47

the Agora, *xviii*, 11–12, 50, 84

Aischines: and accusations against Timarchos, 117, 118–119, 154; on age and desire, 100–101, 186n39; and authorship of speech, 11; and choice of suit type, 191n8; and comedic elements of speech, 13–14, 15; on composition of juries, 12; focus on citizenship standards, 156–157; focus on physical body in case against Timarchos, 122–126; *hexis tēs psuchēs* phrase, 139, 195n95; and *hubris* charge against Ti-

marchos, 140–142, 149–150, 196n98; legal issue in trial, 18; and "love-craze" in Lysias 4, 28; and pederasty in Athenian culture, 142–149, 190n102, 197nn129–130; and political significance of charges against Timarchos, 119–122; on purchased sex as *hubris*, 111–112; on threat posed by Timarchos' behavior, 137–140, 158–159; and Timarchos' violations of civic space, 127–137; use of slave stereotypes, 193n35, 194n64. *See also* Aischines 1, *Against Timarchos*

Aischines 1, *Against Timarchos*: characterizations of Timarchos, 149–150; charges and suit type, 118–119; focus on citizenship ideals, 137–140; focus on civic space, 127–137; focus on the physical body, 122–126; and *hubris* charges, 140–142; implications for social stability, 119–122; overview of, 18–19, 117–118; and pederasty in Athenian culture, 18, 142–149; recent commentaries on, 15; spatial networks of, *130*

aischrōs, 57, 122, 123, 138, 148, 150

Aischylos, 59

akolasia, 75

Akropolis, 9, 11, *50*

Alexis, 39, 78, 144–145

GENERAL INDEX

alien residents of Athens. *See* metics

Alke: and accounts of sexual labor in Attic oratory, 1; and characterizations of sex laborers, 68–69, 154, 174n36, 176n66; and context of pseudo-Demosthenes 59, 64; and context of study, 16–17; and date of Philokte-mon's death, 175n48; and dispute in Isaios 6, 43, 44, 151; and fear of do-mestic instability, 52–56, 56–58, 152, 153, 159; and fear of female influence, 58–61, 61–62; and fear of women's mobility, 16–17, 49–52, 78, 92, 153; and genealogies in Isaios 6, 47, 47–49; and longevity of sexual labor relation-ships, 152; scarcity of information on, 173n26; and sex and gender norms, 156–157; and stereotypes in Lysias 4, 37, 42; and women's role in the polis, 81, 155

Alkmaionids, 146

anachorism, 8

anandria, 149

Andokides, 119

Androkles, 44, 46, 48–49

andrōn-andrōnitis, 69, 187n69

Andros, 149

Androtion, 119, 140

aneleuthera, 168n13

annulment of wills, 35, 54, 59

Anteia (Eunikos), 38

Anthesteria, 68, 84–85, 155

anthrōpos: and Alke's background, 58–59; and characterizations of sex laborers, 154; and characterizations of Timar-chos, 126, 138–139; and fear of civic instability, 57; and fear of domes-tic instability, 53–54, 56; and fear of female influence, 37, 61; and fear of sex laborers' influence, 152; and gen-der norms in Athenian society, 156; and genealogies in Isaios 6, 48; and

place associations in Isaios 6, 49; and sexual desire in Lysias 4, 29; and stereotypes of sex laborers, 38, 39, 41, 42; and testimony in Lysias 4, 26–27; and woman's status in Lysias 4, 30–35

antidósis, 22–23, 25, 31–32

Antigona, 36, 37, 56, 68–69, 102

Antikles, 126, 132

Antiphanes, 39

antisocial behavior, 102–103, 140

Apatouria, 45

Aphrodite, 14, 78

apodutērion, 134

Apollodoros: and appeals to civic order, 120; and characterizations of Neaira as sex laborer, 2–3, 158–159, 178n23, 179n43; and civic risk posed by Neaira, 87–89; and context of pseudo-Demosthenes 59, 63–64; and context of study, 13, 17–18; and dis-pute in Lysias 4, 25; and dispute in pseudo-Demosthenes 59, 64–65; family integrity in narrative of, 65–68; and fear of female influence, 60; and fear of women's mobility, 153; focus on citizenship standards, 156; on *hubris* of Phrynion, 183n108; and longevity of sexual labor relation-ships, 152; manipulation of law, 76, 180n55, 180n56; and marriage's role in citizenship, 89–91; and Neaira's travels, 76–78; and Neaira's *xenē* identity, 68–73, 179n39; *oikos* of, 67, 177n11; and penalties in impiety cases, 86, 182n100; and Phano's identity, 67–68, 74–76, 178n16; on privileges and obligations of female citizens, 155; and status claims, 31; and women's role in the polis, 79–84, 84–87, 92–93

appeals of legal judgments, 10, 121

arbitration, 25

Archaic Greece, 6, 190n102

GENERAL INDEX

Archias, 85–86

Archōn Basileus, 84–85

Areios Pagos, 11

Areopagus (place), 11, *50*, 132. *See also* Council of the Areopagus

Aristeides, 123, 127

Aristogeiton, 145–146, 147, 149, 190n102, 198n130

Aristokritos, 100

Aristophanes, 12–14, 37–38, 78–79, 109, 121, 143, 190n102

Aristophon, 119

Aristotle, 4, 13, 81, 126

Arizelos, 129

Arkhippos, 34

aselgeia, 105, 150, 154–155

Aspasia, 86, 182n102, 182n104

Assembly (*Ekklēsia*): and accusations against Timarchos, 117, 118, 151; and composition of juries, 9–10; and feminization of Timarchos, 135–136, 137, 149; focus on physical body in Timarchos' case, 122; and *hubris* charge against Timarchos, 141; and role of women in the polis, 155, 181n74; and status of male sex laborers, 156; and threat posed by Timarchos' behavior, 137, 138, 159; and Timarchos' violations of civic space, 127–128, 132

astē-astai: and charges against Alke, 58, 60; and charges against Neaira, 76–77; and charges against Stephanos, 17; laws and standards regulating, 82, 85, 89–91, 93, 156; and Phano's status, 82–83; and ritual obligations, 85

astoi, 46, 47

astu, 49, 51–52

Astu Gate, *50*

Athenaios, 38, 144

Athenian identity, 50–51. *See also* citizenship

Athenian law: and female influence, 35–37; gender and legal liability, 64–65; inheritance disputes and laws, 9, 11, 29, 43, 54, 81, 88, 151, 155; and participation in legal system, 10–11; and pederasty, 196n102; protecting paternal *oikos*, 44; and women's interests, 30–35

Athenogenes, 36, 98, 102

athletics, 134, 195n78

atimia, 83, 117, 129, 150, 191n8

Autokleides, 126

Azenia deme, 119

barudaimonia, 26, 28–30, 34, 41

basanos, 22–23, 32, 91, 97, 168n21

Basilinna, 68, 84–85

Battle of Marathon, 89–90

bdeluros-bdeluria: and characterizations of Timarchos, 123, 126, 134, 137–140, 150, 154; and Lape's work, 18; and pederastic relationships, 143

Bers, Victor, 170n51

bigamy, 175n47

blackmail, 148

Blok, Josine, 18, 80–81

body: = building metaphor, 136; "physiognomic strategy," 122. *See also* *sōma*

Boukoleion, 84

Boulē (Council), 10, 58, 121, 148, 192n17

bribery, 118, 137, 148

brothels: and Alke's background, 43, 58; and attitudes on sexual labor in Classical Athens, 5; and Building Z_3, 51–52, 174n41; and characterizations of Alke, 174n36; and characterizations of sexual labor, 159; and civic threat posed by sex laborers, 153; and domestic threat posed by sex laborers, 152; and fear of female influence, 60–61; and fear of women's mobility, 9, 17, 49–51; and feminization of Timarchos, 136–137; and Neaira's

GENERAL INDEX

background, 67, 69; and Phano's background, 76; and portrayals of sex laborers in Attic oratory, 1; and stereotypes of sex laborers, 39–40; and Timarchos' violations of civic space, 133
Building A, 165n46
Building B, 165n46
Building C, 165n46
Building D, 165n46
Building Y, 51
Building Z, 50, 51
Building Z$_3$, 51–52, 174n41

Calame, Claude, 70
Carey, Christopher: on age and desire, 100; on dispute in Lysias 4, 23; on nature of desire in Aischines 1, 101, 103; and Neaira's background, 72, 73; on Neaira's travels, 77–78; on personal habits of Timarchos, 123; on Simon's wealth, 97; on status of Theodotos, 98; on transgression of domestic space, 105
Chabrias, 70, 73
Chaireas, 46
Chairestratos, 11, 43, 44, 45, 176n68
charis, 7, 38, 112, 115, 126, 147
child sex laborers, 2, 3, 140–141. See also paidiskai
choiroi, 13
Chremylos, 143
chrēsthai, 35
Chrysis (Antiphanes), 38
cithara players, 111
citizenship: age standards, 121; Alke's threat to social stability, 56–58; and appeals to civic order, 120–122; and attitudes on sexual labor in Classical Athens, 5; and behaviors of sex laborers, 156–157; and characterizations of Timarchos' behavior, 124–125,

126; and charges against Timarchos, 151; and civic risk posed by Neaira, 87–89; and disenfranchisement penalty, 66, 118, 137, 182n100; and dispute in pseudo-Demosthenes 59, 63–64, 64–65, 65–68; and domestic threat posed by sex laborers, 152; exile as punishment, 10, 24, 182n100; and fear of domestic instability, 53; and fear of female influence, 60; and fear of women's mobility, 77, 153–154; and female roles in religious ritual, 17; granted to non-Athenian men, 183n118; and hubris charge against Timarchos, 140–142; and impiety charges against Phano, 86; legal significance of Theodotos' status, 111–113; and male sexual labor, 7; marriage's role in, 89–91; and metechein concept, 81, 83–84, 89, 155; and Neaira's background, 3, 69, 71–72, 73; and outcomes of legal cases, 11; and pederasty in Athenian culture, 146, 148–149, 158, 196n102; and Phano's identity, 74–76, 179n49, 181n86; and "physiognomic strategy," 122–123; and Plataians, 97; privileges and obligations of female citizens, 154–155, 155–156; and religious rituals, 45–46; and self-control, 190n114; self-control as civic virtue, 115–116; sex labor associated with enslavement, 117–118; and speaking privilege, 118–119; and standing to bring suits, 110, 165n39; status of Theodotos, 97; and threat posed by Timarchos' behavior, 137–138, 139–140, 149–150; tied to the oikos, 194n59; and Timarchos' violations of civic space, 127, 129, 131, 132–134; and torture of witnesses, 97, 185n15; and value of self-control, 101–102, 103; witnesses to, 173n18;

224

and women's role in the polis, 80–84, 84–85, 92–93. See also *astē-astai*

Cohen, Edward, 5, 7

collective suffering, 65

comedy: and characterizations of Timarchos, 125; comedic elements of Aischines' speech, 13–14, 15; comic mask types, 38–39; influence on court oratory, 13; Middle Comedy, 15, 38, 143; New Comedy, 1, 5, 69; Old Comedy, 5, 15, 37, 39, 182n104; sex laborers in, 14, 37–40, 42, 145; and speaker's tactics in Lysias 3, 100; women's influence as theme in, 60

concubinage, 175n47

contracts, 97–98, 113, 114–115, 125

Corinth, 78–79

corruption, 118, 137, 148

cosmetics, 14

Council (*Boulē*), 10, 117, 121

Council of the Areopagus: and dispute in Lysias 3, 95; and dispute in Lysias 4, 22, 23, 43; and focus on physical injuries in Aischines 1, 111; and impiety charges against Phano, 85; judges vs. jurors, 10, 168n4, 172n9, 173n26; structure of Athenian courts, 9, 11, 12

Cresswell, Tim, 8

cross-examinations, 10

Cynosarges, 134

daimoniōs espoudakōs, 28

Davidson, James: on Aischines' characterizations of Timarchos, 124, 139, 148; on body = building metaphor, 136; on cithara players, 111; on definition of *hetaira*, 71; on dispute in Lysias 3, 99; on feminization of Timarchos, 135; on forms of transactional sex, 114; on *gunaikōnitis*, 187n69; on homosexual lust, 111; on *hubris* charge against Timarchos, 140; on *kinaidos*,

198n143; on pederasty in Athenian culture, 142; and penetration model of sexual relations, 19, 135; and prior research on sex laborers, 6, 7; on use of *gunaikōnitis* term, 106

death penalty, 82, 87, 110, 182n100

de Bakker, M. P., 8, 187n65, 188n76

deception, 2, 15, 38, 92

Delphinion, 9, 11

Demeter, 57

democracy and democratic values: and acceptance of sexual labor, 14; and accusations against Timarchos, 117, 123; and failures of self-control, 115–116; and fear of female influence, 61; and fear of women's mobility, 153–154; importance of legitimate marriages, 89–90; and Neaira's background, 71; and pederasty in Athenian culture, 142, 145–149, 158; and "performance culture," 192n24; and personal virtue, 101–102, 115–116, 122–123, 149, 190n114; and prior research on sex laborers, 6–7; privileges and obligations of female citizens, 156; and public speaking, 119; and Solon's reforms, 154; and threat posed by sexual laborers, 149–150; and threat posed by Timarchos' behavior, 137, 140; and Timarchos' service to the polis, 157; and Timarchos' violations of civic space, 127–128, 132, 135; and value of self-control, 101–102, 103; and women's role in the polis, 80–84, 84–85, 92–93

Demophilos, 121

dēmos, 17

Demosthenes: and authorship of Demosthenes 59, 17; characterizations of, 149–150; and characterizations of Apollodoros, 60; and characterizations of Timarchos, 129, 149; on home invasion cases, 105; misconduct case

GENERAL INDEX

against Aischines, 120; and outcomes of cases, 11, 87; and references to Socrates, 120; and speech against Androtion, 119

Demosthenes 48, *Against Olympiodoros*, 19, 29–30, 36, 60

Demosthenes 57, 81

Demosthenes 59. *See* pseudo-Demosthenes 59, *Against Neaira*

diamarturia, 44

diapsēphisis, 121–122

dia toutous, 35

Didymai/Aulētris (Antiphanes), 39

di' ekeinēn, 32

Dikaiopolis, 14, 79

dikastai, 10

dikē, 10, 21, 110

dikē aikeias, 24, 188n82

dikē biaiōn, 188n80

dikē phonou, 23

dikē pseudomarturiōn, 10, 44

dikē traumatos ek pronoias, 22–24, 95

Diodoros, 119

Diokles, 38

diōmosia, 9, 22

Dion, 43, 47–48, 53

Dionysia, 29

Dionysos, 84

Dipylon Gate, 50

disenfranchisement, 66, 118, 137, 182n100

divorce, 45, 55, 75, 85, 175n45

dokimasia tōn rhētorōn, 18, 118–119, 121, 122, 141, 191n8

domestic privacy, 104–107

Double-Lais (Kephisodoros), 38

doulē: and characterizations of Timarchos, 123; and fear of civic instability, 57; and fear of female influence, 37, 41; and Neaira's background, 71; and terminology associated with sex laborers, 154; and testimony in Lysias 4, 26; and woman's status in Lysias 4, 31, 34

Dover, Kenneth, 19, 198n143

dowries, 68, 75, 183n120

Drosis, 91

drugs, 35. *See also pharmaka*

drunkenness, 26–27, 28, 104–105, 115, 169n36, 179n44

duserōs, 16, 27–29, 41

educational system of Athens, 119–120

Eidinow, Esther, 54, 86, 92, 182n107

Eleusinian Mysteries, 72, 76

eleuthera, 23, 25, 168n13

Emporion, 50

"enchantress" stereotype, 14

Endon, 91

entrapment, 15

Epainetos, 75–76, 85, 180n56

Ephippos, 143–144

Epidemics, 30

epiklēros, 44

Epikrates, 36, 102, 120

epithumia, 18, 101–103, 111, 113, 115–116, 189n89

Epitrepontes (Menander), 39

Eponymous Heroes of Athens, 10

erastai: Aischinese use of term, 134, 194n73; and characterization of Neaira as sex laborer, 178n23; and pederasty in Athenian culture, 112–113, 142, 145, 147–148, 189n92; and Timarchos' violations of civic space, 134

erēmiai, 132–133

Ergamenes, 43, 45

Eroiadai, 68

erōmenoi, 112, 134, 142–149, 185n29, 189n92

erōs, 27–28, 30, 102, 142, 145–147

ēthos, 4, 100

ethrepsen, 47–48

Eukrates, 75

Euktemon: and bigamy speculation, 175n47; and characterizations of Alke, 174n36; deme of, 172n11; and dispute

226

in Isaios 6, 17, 43; family tree, *45*; and fear of civic instability, 58; and fear of domestic instability, 52–56, 56–57; and fear of female influence, 59–61, 61–62, 176n68; and fear of women's mobility, 153; and genealogies in Isaios 6, 44–49; and longevity of sexual labor relationships, 152; marital status of, 43, 45–48, 53, 175n45, 175n47; Philoktemon contrasted with, 176n68; and place associations in Isaios 6, 51–52; speculation on marital status, 175n45
Eunikos, 38
Euripides, 59, 147, 183n124
Eurydamnos, 3
Euthydikos, 131
Euxitheos, 121
examartousa, 32–33
exile, 10, 24, 182n100

false witnessing, 10, 44
fertility rites, 57–58
fines, 10, 63, 64, 66, 121, 182n100
Fisher, Nick: on accusations against Timarchos, 119; on Aischines' characterizations of Timarchos, 124, 147; on democratic values, 190n114; on Ephippos' *Sappho*, 144; on *hetairēsis*, 141; on *hexis*, 195n95; on *hubris* in Aischines 1, 113; on pederasty in Athenian culture, 142; on political significance of charges against Timarchos, 120; and prior research on sex laborers, 6–7; recent commentaries on featured works, 15; on sexual acts of Timarchos, 140–141; on status of Theodotos, 97; on Timarchos' mismanagement of paternal estate, 129; on use of *graphē hubreōs*, 110
flute girls, 15, 26, 37–38
Flute Lover (Theophilos), 39
Ford, Andrew, 119

forensic oratory, 3–4, 5, 13, 15, 38, 100, 170n51
Forgetful One/Thalatta (Pherekrates), 38
Foucault, Michel, 163–164n18, 164n21
freed slaves, 25, 32, 47, 60, 67, 69

Gagarin, Michael, 170n51
gambling, 118, 132, 139
gender roles and norms: and accusations against Timarchos, 118; and attitudes on sexual labor in Classical Athens, 5; and characterizations of sex laborers, 7–8; and conferred citizenship, 183n118; and court proceedings, 183n117; and female mobility in Greek culture, 8–9; and lack of self-control, 28–30; and legal liability, 64–65; and marriage's role in citizenship, 89–91; and masculinity, 18; and name use conventions, 74; and participation in legal system, 10–11; previous scholarship on, 15; and women's interests in legal cases, 30–35; and women's role in the polis, 79–84, 84–85, 92–93
genealogies, 17, 44–45
genos, 16–17, 44–46, 53, 58–59, 62, 173n18
gift exchange, 6, 114, 143
Gilhuly, Kate, 6, 17, 71, 78, 81
Goff, Barbara, 80–81
Goldhill, Simon, 5
graphē, 10, 21, 63, 118, 191n8
graphē asebeias, 86–87
graphē hetairēseōs, 140–141, 191n8, 196n105
graphē hubreōs, 110–111, 140, 141, 188n80, 188n82, 189n84
graphē paranomōn, 66
graphē xenias, 63, 65, 86, 153
Greater Panathenaia, 70, 76
Griffith-Williams, Brenda, 16, 17, 40, 61
gunaikōnitis, 104–106, 183n124, 187n68, 187n69
gunē: and fear of female influence, 36;

and feminization of Timarchos, 135; and genealogies in Isaios 6, 48; and impiety charges against Phano, 85; and Neaira's travels, 76; and privileges and obligations of female citizens, 81, 84, 89, 91, 156

gymnasia and *gumnasion*, 9, 124, 127, 134–135, 139, 142, 156, 159

Habrotonon, 39–40

Hall, Edith, 12

Haloa, 86

Halperin, David, 7, 19, 114, 135, 140, 196n102

Hamel, Debra, 17

Harmodios, 145–146, 147, 149, 190n102, 198n130

Harpokration, 127

Harrison, Alick Robin Walsham, 191n8

Hatzilambrou, Rosalia, 123, 125

Hector, 147, 198n130

Hegemon, 43, *45*

Hegesandros, 98, 119, 125, 126, 133, 135, 148–149

Helen, 13, 52

Hēliaia, 9, 165n46, 188n80

hēlikia, 72, 100, 121, 179n38

helkein, 109

Henderson, Jeffery, 38, 79

Hephaisteion, *xviii*

Herman, Gabriel, 165n43

Hermogenes, 181n90

Herodotus, 146

hetairai: and Alke's background, 58; and *analambanein* term, 195n81; and the Archaic symposium, 6; as brothel workers, 183n121; and civic risk posed by Neaira, 86–87, 88–89; and dispute in Lysias 4, 21; and family integrity in suit against Stephanos, 66–67; and fear of domestic instability, 56; and fear of female influence, 15, 36–37, 60; and feminization of Timarchos,

135; and functions of women in Athenian society, 90–91; and *hubris* charge against Timarchos, 141; and legal standing of children, 173n20; and Neaira's background, 3, 68–71, 177n14; and Neaira's travels, 76, 78–79; and pederasty in Athenian culture, 143, 144; and Phano's identity, 74, 179n49; and portrayals of sex laborers in Attic oratory, 1, 4; and sexual desire in Lysias 4, 29; and stereotypes of sex laborers, 38–40; terminology issues, 19–20; and varied settings of sexual labor, 152; well-known cases against, 86–87, 182n103; and woman's status in Lysias 4, 31

hexis, 139, 195n95

hierodouloi, 78

Hipparchos, 145

Hippias, 145–146

Hippiskos (Alexis), 39

Hippocratic medicine, 30

Hippodamian Agora, *50*

Histoire de la sexualité (Foucault), 164n21

ho boulomenos, 10, 71, 151

home invasion, 104–107

Homer, 59, 146, 197n129

homicide cases, 9, 11

hoplites, 97

household. See *oikos*

Hubbard, Thomas, 142

hubris: and characterizations of Timarchos, 140–142, 149, 150, 196n98; and *dikē biaiōn*, 188n80; and failures of self-control, 115–116; and *graphē hubreōs* prosecutions, 110–111, 140, 141, 188n80, 188n82, 189n84; Lape's scholarship on, 18; and legal significance of Theodotos' status, 113–114; on nature of desire in Aischines 1, 101–104; and penalties for adultery, 182n108; and sexual violence, 108–111, 188n79; and spatial element of dis-

228

pute in Asichines 1, 104–106; and status of sex laborers, 157–158, 179n43; and terminology associated with sex laborers, 154

humorism, 30

humors (in Hippocratic medicine), 30

Hypereides, 36, 37, 56, 68–69, 87, 102

impiety, 13, 14, 66, 82, 84–87, 182n100

inheritance disputes and laws, 9, 11, 29, 43, 54, 81, 88, 151, 155

Inner Kerameikos, *50*

insanity, 26, 28–30, 34, 35, 41

invisible property, 54

Iobakcheia, 84

Isaios 3, *On the Estate of Pyrrhos*, 18

Isaios 6, *On the Estate of Philoktemon*: and fear of civic instability, 56–58; and fear of domestic instability, 52–56; and fear of female influence, 58–61; and fear of women's mobility, 49–52; and household comparisons, 44–49; nature of dispute, 44; overview of, 16–17, 43–44; possible outcome of case, 11; prior commentaries on, 15

Ischomachos, 52, 103

Isthmias, 79

itinerant populations of Athens, 50, 76

Johnstone, Steven, 30, 37

joint ownership of slaves (*koinē*), 1, 21–26, 31–33, 168n13, 168n20

judges, 13, 24, 29, 40, 100, 168n4, 172n9. *See also* juries and jurors

juries and jurors: and Apollodoros' tactics, 79–80, 82–84, 85–87, 88, 89–91; appeals to sympathy and revenge, 66; and case against Timarchos, 118, 119–121, 123, 125; and characterizations of Neaira, 71–72, 173n26; and civil penalties, 63, 64; and dispute in Lysias 3, 96; and fear of domestic instability,

59; "judges" contrasted with, 168n4, 172n9; and protocols for speakers, 127; and rights of citizens, 71; size and composition of, 9–10, 164n34; typical pay, 165n36; use of sex laborers to sway judgment, 61

kakōs, 123, 138

Kallias, 79

Kallippe, 43, *46*, 47

Kallistratos, 29–30

Kantharos Harbor, *50*

Kapparis, Konstantinos: on *akolasia*, 75; on characterizations of Neaira, 179n39, 179n43; on laws governing *moicheia*, 82–83, 181n86; on metic status of Pittalakos, 194n64; on Neaira's age, 72, 179n38; on Neaira's travels, 78; on Phano's background, 75; and prior research on sex laborers, 5–6, 7; recent commentaries on featured works, 15

katharos, 137, 157

Kedonides, 126

Kennedy, Rebecca, 67

Kephisia deme, 11, 44–46

Kephisodoros, 38

Kerameikos, 49, 51–52, 60

kinaidos-kinaideia, 149–150, 198n143

Kitchen (Pherekrates), 38

Kleon, 14

klērouchos, 46–47

Klytaimnestra, 59

Knights (Aristophanes), 14

Kokkaline, 91

kōmos, 26

Konstantinou, Ariadne, 9

Korianno (Athenaios), 38, 424

Korinthiastēs (Philetairos), 78–79

Korinthiastēs (Poliochos), 78–79

koureion, 45

Ktesippos of Kydantidal, 70, 76

kulikes, 69–70, *70*

GENERAL INDEX

Kunagis (Philetairos), 13
kurioi: and civic risk posed by Neaira, 88; and domestic threat posed by sex laborers, 152; and fear of female influence, 61; and fear of women's mobility, 92; and genealogies in Isaios 6, 48; and legal standing of women, 64–65, 179n43; and participation in legal system, 10; and privileges/obligations of female citizens, 156; and threat posed by sexual desire, 103; and transgression of domestic space, 105
Kurke, Leslie, 6

Laches, 97
Laïs, 78
Lamb, W. R. M., 33, 35
Lampon, 107
Lanni, Adriaan, 196n102
Lape, Susan, 19, 122, 123–124, 138, 139, 142, 190n114
lawlessness, 57, 108–111
legitimacy of children, 43, 45–48, 59, 63
Leigh, Carol, 19
Leodamas, 119, 135
Lind, Hermann, 51
liturgical duties, 23, 57–58, 96–97, 129, 175n56
logographers, 11, 159
logos, 4
lovesickness, 27. See also *duserōs*
lumainesthai, 56, 60
Lyceum, 134
Lysias, 76, 183n124
Lysias 3, *Against Simon*: characterization of relationship in, 100–104, 111–115; charge and defense, 95–96; compared with Lysias 4, 22; issues in dispute, 96–100; overview of, 17–18; physical injuries, 108–111; recent commentaries on, 15; self-control as key theme, 115–116; and transgression of the household, 104–107

Lysias 4, *Concerning a Case of Intentional Wounding*: account of trial, 25–27; authenticity of, 21–23; central issue of dispute, 23–24, 24–25; and fear of female influence, 35–37; fragmentary nature of, 41; and "love-craze" issue, 27–30, 41; overview of, 16; recent commentaries on, 15; and stereotypes of sex laborers, 37–41, 41–42; woman's involvement and interests in case, 30–35
Lysimachos, 107

Macedon, 120, 137
magistrates, 10, 34
mainesthai, 29–30
Malthrake (Antiphanes), 38
mania, 102–103, 115. See also *duserōs*
manumission, 1, 38
marriage: age of, in Athenian society, 72, 178n38; and context of pseudo-Demosthenes 59, 63–64; dispute in pseudo-Demosthenes 59, 64–70, 82–83, 85–86, 88–89, 92–93; and Phano's background, 74–76; and ritual practices, 84; role in citizenship, 89–91; and women's role in the polis, 80
Marshall, C. W., 17
masculinity: and athletics in Athenian culture, 134; and characterization of Timarchos' behavior, 149; and comic portrayals of sex laborers, 42; and desire for sex laborers, 21, 27, 35, 118; and *kinaidos* term, 149–150, 198n143; and love-crazed, 28–30; and previous work on Attic oratory, 7–8; and sexual labor vs. pederasty, 18; and Simon's behavior, 116; and *sōphrosunē*, 181n81; and threat posed by sexual desire, 103. *See also* gender roles and norms
matrilineage, 74

GENERAL INDEX

McClure, Laura, 139–140
Medea, 59
Megarian piglets tale, 14, 79
Meidias, 105
Meixiades, 45, 48
melancholos, 30
Melitta (Antiphanes), 38
Memorabilia (Xenophon), 1–2
Menander, 15, 39
mental illness/incapacity, 35–36
Metaneira, 72, 76
metechein, 81, 83–84, 89, 155
metics (alien residents): and Alke's background, 59, 61, 159; and Athenian household ideal, 44–45, 55–56; and characterizations of sex laborers, 118, 126, 156; and charges against Stephanos, 17, 66, 92–93; and *graphē xenias*, 63, 65, 86, 153; and homicide cases, 9; legal standing to initiate trials, 165n39; and Neaira's background, 69, 76, 77, 79–80, 87, 159; and Peiraieus, 50, 174n30; and Phano's identity, 79–80, 85, 179n49; and Pittalakos' status, 194n64; and public nature of trials, 11; and status of Theodotos, 97; and torture of witnesses, 97, 185n15
metrios, 123, 131–132, 137
Middle Comedy, 15, 38, 143
Millet, Paul, 8, 105
Miner, Jess, 17
Misgolas, 111, 125–126, 129, 131–132, 194n60
mobility: and case against Akle, 49–52; and fear of female influence, 60; fear of female mobility, 9, 49–52, 62, 76–79, 92, 153–154, 156–157, 176n65; and Neaira's background, 3, 25, 76–79
modesty, 123
moicheia, 82, 181n86
Mounychia Harbor, *50*
murder trials, 23–24
Mutilation of the Herms, 182n100

name-use conventions, 74
Nannion (Euboulos), 38
Nannion (Timokles), 38
Neaira: and accounts of sexual labor in Attic oratory, 1–3; characterization as sex laborer, 158–159, 177n14, 179n43; characterization as *xenē*, 68–73; and citizenship claims, 90, 183n118; context of charges against, 151; and context of pseudo-Demosthenes 59, 63–64; and context of study, 13, 16, 17; and dispute at center of case, 64–65; dispute compared with Lysias 4, 24–25; and family integrity in suit against Stephanos, 67–68; and fear of women's mobility, 76–79, *77*, 153, 156–157; and *hubris* of Phrynion, 183n108; and longevity of sexual labor relationships, 152; and marriage's role in citizenship, 90–91; and Phano's identity, 67–68, 74–76, 178n16, 179n49; speculation on age, 72, 179n38; and status claims, 31; and stereotypes of sex laborers, 37, 42; and terminology associated with sex laborers, 154–155; and threat of boundary-crossing, 92, 184n127; and women's role in the polis, 79–84, 84–87, 87–89, 92–93
Neaira (Philemon), 13
Neaira (Timokles), 13, 38
neōtera, 72
New Comedy, 1, 5, 69
Nikarete, 3, 67–72, 74–76, 78
Nikias, 28
Ninon, 54
North, Helen, 81–82, 181n81

oaths, 9, 10, 11, 22, 23
Odeion of Perikles, 11, *50*
Odysseus, 59
oikeioi, 47, 65
oikēmata, 127, 136, 174n36
oiketai, 47

GENERAL INDEX

Oikonomikos (Xenophon), 52
oikos: and Building Z₃, 174n41; and civic threat posed by Neaira, 87; and context of pseudo-Demosthenes 59, 63–64; and context of study, 15–17, 151; and dispute in Isaios 6, 44; and family integrity in suit against Stephanos, 66–68; and fear of domestic instability, 52–56; and fear of female influence, 58–61, 62, 183n124; and fear of women's mobility, 76, 78, 159, 176n65; and genealogies in Isaios 6, 44–49; and male sex laborers, 9; members and boundaries of, 172n10; and Neaira's background, 69, 70; and pederasty in Athenian culture, 144; and place associations in Isaios 6, 50, 52; and previous scholarship, 15; and structure of the polis, 129, 194n59; and Timarchos' violations of civic space, 128–131, 134; and varied settings of sexual labor, 152; and women's role in the polis, 80, 81, 83, 89, 91, 92, 153–154
Old Comedy, 5, 15, 37, 39, 182n104
Olympiodoros, 29–30, 36
Omitowoju, Rosanna, 73, 106, 181n86, 188n80
On the Mysteries (Andokides), 119
ostrakon, 22, 24, 25
Outer Kerameikos, 50
oxucheir, 28

paideia, 120, 160
paidiskai, 43, 51, 67, 68–69, 74, 76, 170n47
Palladion, 9, 11
Pamphilos, 135
Panathenaic Way, 11–12
pankration, 122–123
Parabyston, 165n46
paranomia, 49, 102–103, 104, 110, 114, 116
paroinos, 27, 28, 169n36. *See also* drunkenness

parōxummenos, 29, 41
parthenos, 85
Pasion, 65
passion, 41
paternity, 11, 48, 132. *See also* legitimacy of children
pathos, 4
patrimony, 119
patrōios, 129
Patroklos, 146–147, 198n130
patronymics, 74
Patterson, Cynthia, 17, 67, 69, 80–81, 89
pederasty: and accusations against Timarchos, 117; and age differentials, 101, 186n39, 189n94, 192n16; and Homer's writing, 146, 197n129; implications for civic order, 120, 158; language associated with, 189n92, 190n104; laws regulating, 196n102; and legal significance of Theodotos' status, 112; role in Athenian culture, 142–149; and Timarchos' violations of civic space, 134–135; varied attitudes toward, 190n102
Peiraieus, 49, 50, 51, 60, 107, 131, 173n30
peithein, 37, 54
peithomenos, 30, 35, 36
Peloponnesian War, 28, 90, 97
Penelope, 59
penetration model of sexual relations, 19, 135, 140, 149
Perikles, 77, 86–87, 123, 127
perjury, 44
pernanai, 3, 20
Persephone, 57
Persian Wars, 78
Petalē (Pherekrates), 38
phallos, 7
Phano: characterizations as sex laborer, 74–76, 156, 180n56; and context of pseudo-Demosthenes 59, 63; and context of study, 17; and dispute in pseudo-Demosthenes 59, 64–65; and family integrity issue, 67–68; and *hu-*

232

bris claims, 182n108; and *moicheia* charge, 181n86; secret identity theory, 179n49; and threat of boundary-crossing, 92, 184n127; and women's role in the polis, 79–81, 82–84, 84–86, 92, 155

Phanostratos, 44, 46

pharmaka, 54. *See also* drugs

Pherekrates, 38

Phile, 74

Philemon, 13

Philetairos, 13, 78

philia, 112–113, 143, 146

Philip II of Macedon, 18, 118

Phillips, David, 23

philoi, 2

Philokleon, 13, 37–38

Philoktemon, 11, 43–45, 48, 53–55, 172n11, 175n47, 176n68

Philostratos of Kolonai, 76

Philullios, 38

Phoinix (Euripides), 147

Phrastor of Aiglia, 68, 75, 85, 182n108, 183n108

Phryne, 13, 86–87, 182n105

Phrynion, 2–3, 25, 69, 72–73, 76, 156, 158, 183n108

pimps, 76, 78–79

Pindar, 78

Pistoxenos, 43, 46, 47

Pittalakos, 98, 126, 132–133, 140

Plangon (Euboulos), 38

Plataians, 81, 89–90, 97

Plato, 146

Pnyx, 11, 50, 57–58, 127, 132, 133, 176n60

Poliochos, 78

polis: and fear of women's mobility, 16–17, 44, 49–52, 62, 153–154; and gendered conception of space, 8; role of sexual labor in, 5; and threat posed by Alke's actions, 56–58; women's role in, 6, 18, 79–84, 84–87, 87–89, 92–93, 153–154, 156. *See also* citizenship

political trials, 18

Pollux, Julius, 38–39

pornē: and age of sex slaves, 170n47; and Alke's background, 58; and characterizations of Alke, 174n36; and characterizations used in Lysias 4, 22; and fear of female influence, 36–37, 41; and fear of women's mobility, 176n65; and Neaira's background, 3; and pederasty in Athenian culture, 143–145; and prior research on sex laborers, 6; and sexual desire in Lysias 4, 30; and status of woman in Lysias 4, 31, 34; and stereotypes of sex laborers, 38, 40; terminology issues, 19–20; and testimony in Lysias 4, 26; and women's role in the polis, 83

porneia, 125–127, 136–137, 139, 148, 189n90. *See also* brothels

porneuein, 125–126, 139, 141, 145

pornikon telos, 125

pornos: and accusations against Timarchos, 117, 124–126, 141, 150–151, 157, 193n45; and pederasty in Athenian culture, 144–145; and terminology associated with sex laborers, 154; terminology issues, 19–20; and threat posed by Timarchos' behavior, 139–140; and Timarchos' violations of civic space, 137

prasis ep' eleutheriai, 25

premeditation, 22, 24

prosēkontes, 47

prostatēs, 64, 69. See also *kurioi*

prostitution. See *pornē*; *pornos*

Prytaneion, 84

pseudo-Demosthenes 59, *Against Neaira*: characterizations of Neaira, 2–3; and civic risk posed by Neaira, 84–87, 87–89; context of, 63–64; legitimacy and citizenship issues, 65–68; and mobility of Neaira and Phano, 76–79; and Neaira's background, 68–73;

overview of, 17; and Phano's background, 74–76; recent commentaries on, 15; rivalry at center of dispute, 64–65; and women's role in the polis, 79–84

public notice of trials, 10

purification ceremonies, 127

Pythian Games, 70, 73

reciprocity, 126

Reden, Sitta von, 51

religious rituals and festivals: and *Basilinna* role, 68, 84–85; and Euktemon's household, 45, 48; and fear of civic instability, 57–58; and fear of female influence, 59; and Neaira's travels, 76; Phano's role in, 68, 84–85; ritual obligations, 52, 55, 80–81, 183n120; sacrifices, 57; and women's role in the polis, 17, 79–84, 84–87

Rhetoric (Aristotle), 12

Roisman, Joseph, 7, 28, 88, 102, 103, 123

Royal Stoa, *xviii*

Sacred Gate, *50*

sacrifices, 57

sacrilege, 3, 85–86

same-sex relations, 18

Sappho (Ephippos), 143–144

scapegoating of sex laborers, 14

Scott, Joan Wallach, 7

Seisactheia, 154

self-control. See *sōphrosunē*

self-defense, 26

Semonides, 59

senility, 35, 54, 175n47, 176n68

sexual slavery and trafficking, 1, 19. See also *doulē*; slavery and enslavement

sexual violence, 108–111

"sex work" term, 19

shared and common property, 24–25

Sicilian Expedition, 28

Simon: and details of dispute, 17–18, 22, 31, 95–96, 96–100, 184n7, 185n20, 188n75; and failures of self-control, 115–116; and focus on physical injuries, 108–111; and *hubris* accusations, 22, 102–104, 108–111, 112–115, 149, 157–158, 188–189n82; nature of relationship with Theodotos, 100–104, 112–115, 149, 185n20, 190n104; and spatial element of dispute, 104–107

Simos of Larisa, 3

Simos of Thessaly, 76

Sinope, 86

Sissa, Giulia, 19, 137, 138, 141, 142

slavery and enslavement: and *anthrōpos* status, 58–59; and characterizations of Timarchos, 124; evidentiary torture of enslaved persons, 22–23, 32, 91, 97, 168n21; and fear of women's mobility, 62; joint ownership of sex slaves, 1, 21–26, 31–33, 168n13, 168n20; *paidiskai*, 43, 51, 67, 68–69, 74, 76, 170n47; and participation in legal system, 10; and Peiraieus, 50; and purchases for the purpose of freedom, 25; role in Athenian households, 44; and sexual violence, 109; and terminology issues, 19–20; and testimony in Lysias 4, 26–27. See also *doulē*

Socrates, 1–2, 120, 182n100

Solon, 36, 138, 146, 154

sōma, 19, 122–126, 127–137, 137–140. *See also* body

sōphrosunē: and characterization of Neaira as sex laborer, 88, 155; and characterizations of Timarchos, 123, 149–150; as civic virtue, 115–116; and focus on physical injuries in Aischines 1, 110; and gender norms, 181n81; and nature of desire in Aischines 1, 100–104; and pederasty in Athenian culture, 112–113, 145–148; and threat posed by Timarchos' behavior, 137–139; and Timarchos' violations of civic space, 127–128, 134; and women's role in the polis, 81–84, 91, 93, 156

Sotados, 3

Spatharas, Dimos, 16

speaking privilege, 118–119

speechwriters (logographers), 11, 159

stage performance, 13

Stephanos: and accusations against Neaira, 3, 151, 155; and civic threat posed by Neaira, 87; and context of pseudo-Demosthenes 59, 63; and context of study, 17; and dispute in Lysias 4, 25; and dispute in pseudo-Demosthenes 59, 2–3, 64–65; and family integrity issue, 65–68; and impiety charges against Phano, 85; and longevity of sexual labor relationships, 152; and marriage's role in citizenship, 90–91; and *moicheia* charge, 181n86; and Neaira's background, 69–70, 76–77; and Phano's background, 74–76, 179n49; and women's role in the polis, 80, 92

Stheneboia (Euripides), 147

Stoa of Attalos, 11

Stoa of Zeus, *xviii*

Stoa Poikilē, *xviii*, 11, 12

Strabo, 78

Strybele, 74

sumphora, 55–56, 101, 115

sumposion: and Alke's background, 58; and attitudes on sexual labor in Classical Athens, 5; and dispute in Lysias 4, 21; and flexibility of domestic space, 106, 187n68; and male sex laborers, 9; and Neaira's background, 69–70, 74; and Neaira's travels, 76, 78; and pederasty in Athenian culture, 142; and prior research on sex laborers, 5–6; and scope of "sexual labor," 19; and status of male sex laborers, 156; and stereotypes of sex

laborers, 37–40; and testimony in Lysias 4, 26; and varied settings of sexual labor, 152

suneinai, 1

sunēn, 47, 73

sungeneis, 47

sunoikia-sunoikiai, 47–48, 49–51, 52–53, 127, 129, 132, 136, 174n34, 174n37

symposium. *See* sumposion

Teisis, 34

Thalatta (Diokles), 38

thanatos, 110

Theater of Dionysos, 11, *50*

Themistokles, 123, 127

Themosphoria, 81, 176n60

Theodote, 1–3, 71

Theodotos: and context of study, 17; and details of dispute, 22, 31, 96–100, 185n27, 188n73; enslaved vs. free status, 97–99, 109–110, 112, 185n22; and fear of women's mobility, 153; and focus on physical injuries, 108–111; and *hubris* accusations against Simon, 22, 102–104, 108–111, 112–115, 149, 157–158, 188–189n82; and nature of desire in Aischines 1, 100–104; nature of relationship with Simon, 100–104, 112–115, 149, 185n20, 190n104; as object of desire and dispute, 100–104; significance of juridical status, 112–115; and spatial element of dispute in Asichines 1, 105–107; and torture of slave witnesses, 97, 185n14

Theogenes, 80, 85

Theognis, 190n102

Theoinia, 84

Theomnestos, 63, 64, 65–68, 71, 74, 85, 87, 89

Theophilos, 39

Theoris of Lemnos, 54, 87

Thersandros, 125–126

Thesmophoria, 57–58, 183n120

GENERAL INDEX

Thompson, Homer, 176n60
Thratta, 91
Thucydides, 28, 146
thugatēr, 48
Timanoridas, 75
Timarchos: and associations with sex laborers, 15; behavior as civic threat, 137–140; charges and accusations against, 117–119, 124–126, 140–142, 149–151, 157, 193n45, 196n98; comedic elements of Aischines' speech, 13, 15; compared to Misgolas, 111–112; context of charges against, 151; and dispute in Lysias 3, 98; focus on physical body in case against, 122–126, 149–150; legal issue in trial, 18; and outcome of lawsuits, 11; and pederasty in Athenian culture, 142–149; and Pittalakos' metics status, 194n64; political significance of charges against, 119–122; and violations of civic space, 127–137
Timokles, 13, 38
Todd, Stephen: on dispute in Lysias 3, 99; on dispute in Lysias 4, 23–24, 32; on *hetairēsis* term, 141; on jury pay, 165n36; on legal significance of Theodotos' status, 113; on lovesickness in Lysias 4, 27; on nature of desire in Aischines 1, 102; on physical injuries in Aischines 1, 108; recent commentaries on featured works, 16; on Simon's wealth, 97; on spatial element of dispute in Asichines 1, 107; on testimony in Lysias 4, 26; and woman's status in Lysias 4, 33
Tomb of Themistokles, 50
topography, 107
torture, 11, 22–23, 91, 97, 168n21

traders, 50
transactional sex, 20, 144–145, 151–152
transgressive behaviors, 49
tropoi, 88, 93
Tyranny (Pherekrates), 38

Ulpian, 78
urban space, 5, 21, 107, 127, 135, 149, 174n34

visible property, 54

Wasps (Aristophanes), 13, 37–38, 121, 165n36
wealth, 55. *See also* inheritance disputes and laws
Wealth (Aristophanes), 78
weapons, 25–26
Whitehead, David, 102
wine district of Athens, 51
Winkler, John J., 198n143
Wohl, Victoria, 28
women's quarters. See *gunaikōnitis*
wounding trials, 11
Wyse, William, 16, 54, 176n68

xenē, 68
Xennis, 91
Xenophon: and accounts of sexual labor in Attic oratory, 1–2; and fear of women's mobility, 176n65; on Ischomachos' household, 52; and Neaira's background as sex slave, 178n19; sexual abuse associated with tyrants, 113–114, 188n79; on threat posed by sexual desire, 103; and women's role in the polis, 91

Zakynthios (Antiphanes), 39
Zea Harbor, 50

INDEX LOCORUM

Aischines
1.1–5, **118**
1.5, **124–125**, **140**, **149**
1.6–11, **137**
1.6–36, **118**
1.7–17, **121**
1.8, **119**, **139**
1.11, **100**
1.13, **113**
1.13–14, **140**
1.13–15, **72**
1.15, **111**, **140**
1.15–17, **187n60**
1.17, **141**
1.19, **12**
1.19–21, **140**
1.22, **119**, **127**, **141**
1.23, **71**, **119**, **127**
1.23–24, **193n52**
1.25, **123**, **127**, **137**
1.26, **122**, **127**, **128**, **183n117**
1.28–32, **118**
1.29, **140**
1.31, **137**, **138**
1.34, **119**, **139**
1.37–76, **138–139**
1.37–116, **118**
1.39, **139**
1.40, **51**, **124**, **126**, **131**, **132**, **136**, **137**
1.41, **28**, **111**, **115**, **124**, **126**, **131**, **135**, **185n18**, **186n36**, **195n81**

1.41–42, **139**, **158**
1.42, **15**, **29**, **123**, **129–130**, **131**, **135**, **137**, **147**
1.43, **132**, **135**
1.45, **124**
1.47, **129**, **131**, **135**
1.48, **157**
1.50, **131**, **135**
1.51, **124**, **126**, **131**, **132**
1.51–52, **141**
1.52, **112**, **124**, **125–126**, **132**, **135**, **196n98**
1.53, **124**, **132**, **135**
1.54, **124**, **126**, **132**, **135**, **137**
1.55, **115**, **124**, **133**, **158**, **196n98**
1.56–57, **126**
1.56–58, **132**
1.57, **135**, **139**
1.57–76, **119**
1.58, **124**, **135**
1.58–59, **98**, **169n37**
1.58–61, **184n2**
1.59, **124**
1.64, **119**, **132**, **135**
1.65, **123**, **137**
1.69–70, **119**
1.70, **115**, **124**, **125**, **133**, **134**, **158**, **196n98**
1.71, **149**
1.73, **124**
1.74, **51**
1.74–75, **133**
1.75, **15**, **129**, **132**, **195n81**

INDEX LOCORUM

1.75–76, **144**
1.76, **124**
1.77, **121–122, 125**
1.77–78, **122**
1.79, **122, 125**
1.81, **137**
1.81–84, **132**
1.86, **121**
1.86–87, **137**
1.87, **140**
1.90, **132, 157**
1.95, **135**
1.95–96, **123, 147**
1.96, **129**
1.97, **129**
1.97–105, **138–139**
1.99, **129**
1.102, **129**
1.103–104, **129**
1.105, **123, 129, 140**
1.106, **148**
1.107, **148**
1.108, **140, 142, 158**
1.110, **148**
1.110–111, **135**
1.111, **119**
1.113–114, **148**
1.115, **15, 123**
1.116, **140, 158**
1.117–176, **118**
1.118, **157**
1.119, **125**
1.123, **124, 125, 140**
1.123–124, **136**
1.126, **145**
1.127, **137, 157**
1.129, **157**
1.130, **124, 125, 140**
1.131, **149**
1.132, **145, 149**
1.133–134, **145**
1.135, **134**
1.135–136, **186n39**

1.136, **134**
1.136–137, **142**
1.137, **111, 140, 147–148**
1.138–139, **124, 146**
1.139, **147**
1.140, **134, 145**
1.141, **140, 146**
1.142, **197n129**
1.145, **146, 147**
1.146, **146**
1.147, **146**
1.150, **146**
1.151, **147**
1.152–153, **147**
1.154, **125**
1.155, **125**
1.155–157, **145**
1.157, **13, 124, 125**
1.158–159, **145**
1.159, **125, 145, 166n51**
1.160, **125, 185n18**
1.163, **140**
1.165, **185n18**
1.173, **120**
1.177–196, **118**
1.179, **157**
1.181, **149, 150**
1.183, **119, 139, 181n85**
1.185, **135, 140**
1.186–187, **120**
1.187, **119**
1.188, **124, 125, 137, 140, 158**
1.189, **119, 125**
1.189–190, **139**
1.190–191, **120**
1.191–192, **119**
1.192, **119, 139**
1.195, **157**
2.5, **166n51**
2.23, **150**
2.78, **193n35**
2.88, **150**
2.93, **169n29**

238

INDEX LOCORUM

2.99, **150**

2.151, **150**

2.177, **173n20**

2.180, **193n35**

3.51, **169n29**

3.55–56, **166n48**

3.56, **166n51**

3.116, **175n49**

3.169, **193n35**

3.207, **166n51**

3.212, **169n29**

3.220, **71**

3.245–246, **191n14**

Alexis

Agonis/Hippiskos

1–3K, **15**

389K, **78**

Fragment 3 *PCG*, **189n88, 194n61**

Fragment 98 *PCG*, **195n81**

Anaxilas

Kalypso, 11K, **15**

Kirke, 12–13K, **15**

Andokides

1.100, **15, 119**

1.98, **197n126**

4.13–14, **152**

Antiphanes

Hydria, 103K, **39**

Fragment 27 *PCG*, **194n61**

Antiphon

1.14–15, **152, 171n62**

1.14–19, **54**

5.13, **12**

6.14, **166n51**

6.21–24, **166n48**

Aristophanes

Acharnians

288–289, **197n117**

524–525, **180n69**

529–537, **14**

729–817, **79**

729–835, **14**

739, **14**

782, **79**

789, **79**

791–796, **14**

796, **79**

801, **79**

802, **79**

818, **79**

880–896, **14**

915, **166n48**

960–961, **14**

980, **197n125**

989–999, **38**

1093, **197n125**

1198–1201, **14**

1198–1231, **38**

1198–1234, **14**

Clouds

53–55, **14**

446, **197n117**

1005–1008, **134**

Ecclesiazusae

689–709, **14**

718–724, **14**

1066, **109**

1066–1111, **188n78**

1087, **109**

1093, **109**

1098–1111, **197n116**

1159–1162, **14**

Frogs

112–115, **174n32**

465, **197n117**

1325–1328, **14, 167n65**

Knights

47, **175n49**

134, **197n117**

193, **197n117**

302–304, **197n117**

347–349, **166n55**

763–766, **167n66**

765, **14**

805, **167n66**

876–879, **191n11**

239

INDEX LOCORUM

1242, **15**

1243–1246, **174n41**

1284–1286, **167n65**

1316–1318, **166n51**

1389–1408, **14**

1399–1405, **167n65**

Lysistrata

113–114, **179n44**

195–205, **179n44**

632, **197n125**

Peace

164–165, **51**

337–345, **14**

439–440, **14**

648–660, **14**

894–904, **38**

Thesmophoriazusae

339–346, **14**

630–633, **179n44**

655–658, **57**

1160–1231, **38**

Wasps

34–36, **14**

550–551, **166n52**

562–570, **166n52, 166n55**

566–567, **12**

578, **121**

579–586, **166n52, 166n55**

623–627, **166n50**

912, **166n50**

914, **197n117**

1015–1035, **14**

1224–1227, **197n125**

1326–1449, **38**

1347, **37–38**

1349–1350, **38**

1351–1353, **38**

1351–1359, **186n36**

1352–1359, **60**

1354–1359, **29**

Wealth

149–152, **78**

149–156, **14**

149–159, **114, 143, 190n111**

153–159, **15**

244, **14**

975, **143**

981–986, **143**

992–1002, **143**

993, **143**

1006–1024, **143**

1069, **197n117**

Fragment 354K, **79**

Aristotle and Pseudo-Aristotle

Athēnaiōn Politeia

2.10, **134**

18–19, **146**

26.4, **175n46, 180n58**

28.3, **192n26**

35.2, **171n60**

42, **172n13, 173n18**

42.1, **81, 155, 194n59**

42.1–2, **121**

56.7, **178n37**

Nicomachean Ethics, 1132b35–1133a4, **126, 190n115**

Politics, 1252b13–15, **194n59**

Rhetoric

1356a1–4, **163n7**

1356a4–8, **163n7**

1356a20–25, **163n7**

1366a23–28, **163n7**

1377a20–28, **163n7**

1403b24–30, **166n55**

1404a1–8, **166n55**

1417a3–8, **163n7**

1417a36–b2, **163n7**

1417b27–28, **163n7**

1428a36–38, **163n7**

Athenaios

Deipnosophists

13.567c, **38**

13.569d, **51**

13.572c, **145**

13.572c–d, **144**

13.573c–574a, **78**

INDEX LOCORUM

13.577b, **173n20**
13.589c, **173n20**
13.590d–e, **87**
13.590e, **176n66**
13.591e, **87**
13.592a, **173n20**
13.592d, **173n20**
13.592e, **173n20**
13.594b–c, **78**
15.695a, **146**

Demosthenes and pseudo-Demosthenes
18.52, **166n51**
18.129–131, **193n35**
18.171, **55**
18.258, **193n35**
18.294–296, **157**
18.318–319, **13**
19.196, **166n51**
19.198, **169n36**
19.209, **193n35**
19.210, **193n35**
19.229, **181n89**
19.233, **117, 145**
19.251, **192n25**
19.257, **11, 150**
19.280, **197n126**
19.281, **54, 87, 176n66**
19.283, **129**
19.284–286, **11, 150**
20.7, **184n8**
20.127, **197n126**
21.31–33, **188n82**
21.36, **169n27**
21.44, **188n82**
21.47, **188n80, 188n81, 189n83,**
　　196n101
21.78–80, **105**
21.103, **10**
21.170, **197n126**
22.21–24, **15, 119**
22.56, **181n89**
22.58, **140, 181n89**

22.61, **173n20, 177n71, 181n89**
23.18–19, **166n51**
23.69, **13**
24.9, **164n34**
24.114, **134**
24.149–151, **10**
24.197, **170n58**
25.56–57, **171n62**
25.79–80, **54, 87, 176n66**
25.80, **173n20**
25.98, **166n48**
27.4–5, **178n37**
27.24–25, **50**
29.26, **173n24**
29.33, **173n24**
29.43, **178n37**
29.56, **173n24**
36.8, **195n81**
36.44–45, **60**
36.45, **189n87**
39.3, **11**
39.3–4, **173n24**
40.8, **181n84**
40.10–11, **11, 173n24**
40.27, **181n84**
40.32–33, **169n29**
43.9, **10**
43.44, **195n81**
43.45, **195n81**
45.6, **166n51**
45.8, **10**
45.63, **175n49**
45.65, **175n49**
47.38, **105**
47.40, **24**
47.41, **169n29**
47.52–61, **105**
47.57, **170n51**
47.60, **105**
48.53–54, **29, 186n36**
48.53–55, **29, 60, 184n125**
48.53–56, **153**
48.55, **30**

241

INDEX LOCORUM

48.56, 30, 170n47
54.1, 188n82
54.8–9, 188n82
54.12, 186n40
54.14, 169n27, 170n56, 188n77
54.22, 186n40, 188n77
54.41, 166n51
57.8, 10
57.17, 81, 155
57.21, 194n59
57.26, 81, 155
57.46, 81, 155
57.49, 121
57.54, 81, 155
57.66–70, 121
57.68–70, 172n12
59.1, 64, 65, 66
59.2, 65
59.4, 71
59.4–5, 64
59.6, 64
59.6–7, 66
59.7–8, 64
59.8, 66
59.9, 66, 181n84, 195n81
59.9–10, 64
59.11, 66
59.11–12, 64
59.12, 66, 71, 85, 87
59.13, 64, 65, 66, 71, 74, 85, 87
59.16, 71, 183n113
59.16–17, 63, 89
59.17, 183n113
59.18, 67, 68, 71, 170n47
59.18–19, 74
59.18–49, 69
59.19, 67, 79, 178n33, 179n41
59.20, 71, 178n33, 179n41, 181n84
59.21–22, 76
59.22, 71, 72, 152, 179n41, 185n27,
  188n74
59.23, 71, 178n33, 179n41
59.24, 70, 76, 152

59.25, 70
59.26, 71, 78, 178n23
59.28, 70, 81
59.29, 68, 71, 75, 170n58, 178n23
59.29–30, 24, 152
59.30, 69, 72, 78, 178n23, 178n33,
  181n84
59.31, 178n23
59.31–32, 25
59.32, 78
59.33, 70, 76, 178n33, 181n84
59.33–34, 73
59.35, 3
59.35–36, 76
59.35–37, 25
59.35–38, 79
59.36, 71, 72, 78
59.37, 70, 181n84, 183n108
59.38–39, 76
59.40, 25, 31
59.41, 178n23, 178n33, 179n41,
  181n84
59.43, 175n49
59.44, 85, 183n109
59.45–47, 21, 25
59.46, 69
59.47, 181n84
59.48, 70, 152
59.49, 70, 71
59.50, 68, 74
59.50–51, 74
59.51, 182n108, 183n113
59.51–52, 68
59.52, 63
59.55, 184n127
59.58, 89, 183n113, 195n81
59.59–60, 68
59.60, 183n113
59.63, 89, 183n113
59.64, 178n23, 183n113
59.65, 75
59.66, 71, 75
59.67, 75, 76, 180n56, 181n84

INDEX LOCORUM

59.68, **76**
59.70, **181n84**
59.71, **181n84**
59.72, **68, 85, 156, 183n109, 183n113**
59.73, **57**
59.74, **85**
59.74–78, **68**
59.75, **85, 183n113**
59.77, **85, 88, 183n109**
59.78, **84, 85**
59.80, **71**
59.80–83, **85**
59.81, **195n81**
59.85, **71, 180n56**
59.86, **71, 82, 183n108**
59.88, **71**
59.90, **71**
59.92, **81, 183n113**
59.94–95, **89**
59.94–106, **89**
59.96, **183n108**
59.102, **90**
59.103–106, **90**
59.104–106, **97**
59.106, **183n113**
59.107, **85, 87, 90, 183n113**
59.107–108, **3**
59.108, **71, 77, 158**
59.109, **85, 183n113**
59.110, **77, 120**
59.110–111, **170n51, 173n24**
59.110–113, **192n14**
59.111, **89, 153, 155, 181n79**
59.111–112, **88**
59.112–113, **153**
59.113, **88–89**
59.113–115, **120**
59.114, **72, 83, 170n47, 178n33, 179n41, 182n90**
59.115, **86, 90, 123**
59.116, **86**
59.116–117, **86, 176n66**
59.117, **85, 86**

59.118, **71, 183n113, 184n125**
59.118–119, **90, 91**
59.118–120, **65**
59.119, **183n113**
59.120–121, **90**
59.121, **183n113**
59.122, **90, 183n113**
59.124, **183n113**
59.126, **86**
Dinarchus
   1.13, **51**
   1.30, **166n48**
   1.66, **166n51**
   1.71, **173n20, 177n71**
   2.19, **166n48, 166n51**

Ephippos, *Sappho*, Fragment 20 *PCG*,
   143–144
Euboulos, *Kampylion*, 43K, **15**
Eupolis, *Philoi*, 274K, **167n66**
Euripides
   Andromache, 331, **184n124**
   Electra, 1036–1038, **183n124**
   Hippolytus
      193, **28**
      649–650, 183, **183n124**

Herodotus
   2.121, **51**
   2.135, **186n36**
   3.80–82, **186n45, 187n56**
   4.79, **30**
   5.55, **146**
   6.123, **146**
Hipparchos, *Thais*, 3K, **15**
Hippocratics
   Diseases, 4.1, **30**
   Epidemics, 5.1.2, **30**
Homer
   Iliad, 6.132, **30**
   Odyssey
      18.406, **30**
      21.298, **30**

INDEX LOCORUM

Hypereides
  Against Athenogenes
    1–4, 170n51
    2, 51, 68, 102
    3, 56, 69
    4, 102
    8, 102
    9–10, 102
    13, 102
    17–18, 36
    23, 102
    23–25, 51, 98
  Against Demosthenes, 22, 166n51
  Fragment 25 Jensen, 178n25

Isaios
  3.2–3, 10
  3.6, 180n50
  3.6–17, 173n20
  3.10, 181n84
  3.11–14, 74
  3.14, 70, 152
  3.15, 181n84
  3.17, 15, 60
  3.30, 179n49
  3.45, 180n50
  3.48, 180n50
  3.52, 180n50
  3.55, 180n50
  3.70, 180n50
  3.71, 180n50
  3.78–80, 183n120
  3.79–80, 172n12, 173n19
  4.10, 177n71
  5.20, 166n48
  5.46–47, 197n126
  6.1–2, 44
  6.5, 55
  6.6, 46
  6.8, 44
  6.8–9, 176n68
  6.9, 55, 176n68
  6.10, 43, 44, 45, 46, 176n68

6.11, 46
6.12, 44
6.12–13, 47
6.13, 43
6.15, 47
6.16, 47
6.17, 43, 56
6.18, 43, 55, 56
6.18–19, 55
6.19, 43, 49, 51, 68, 170n47
6.20, 43, 47, 49, 181n84
6.21, 37, 48, 52, 54, 175n45, 195n81
6.21–24, 48
6.22, 53, 175n45, 175n47
6.23, 53, 54
6.27, 54
6.29, 48, 54, 55, 175n48, 176n68
6.30, 46, 54
6.33–34, 43, 54
6.35, 54
6.36, 46
6.38, 54, 55, 56, 175n48
6.38–42, 52
6.39, 49
6.39–40, 52
6.41, 48
6.43–44, 44
6.45, 44
6.47, 46
6.47–48, 56
6.48, 37, 49
6.49, 156
6.49–50, 57
6.50, 58
6.51, 43
6.55, 54, 55, 175n48
6.57, 44
6.58, 44
6.60, 43
6.60–61, 55
6.61, 54
6.64, 47, 48
6.64–65, 183n120

244

6.65, 47
8.9, **183n120**
8.18–20, **183n120**
8.19–20, **81**
Isocrates, 15.287–288, **186n36**

Kallias, *Pedetai*, 15K, **167n66**
Kratinos, *Cheirons*, 241K, **167n66**

Lysias
1.11, **183n124**
1.12, **109**
1.12–13, **170n51**
1.16, **170n51**
1.19–20, **170n51**
1.23, **169n24, 183n124**
1.38, **186n46**
1.47, **120**
3.1, **23, 96, 108, 189n82**
3.3, **100, 101**
3.4, **100, 101, 102, 104, 112, 115**
3.5, **97, 103, 108, 110, 111, 112, 113, 114–115, 116**
3.6, **75, 97, 103, 112, 115**
3.6–7, **98, 104–105, 169n24**
3.7, **106, 110, 115**
3.8, **100, 106, 184n2**
3.8–9, **98**
3.9, **96, 100, 101, 108, 115, 177n7**
3.10, **98, 99, 100, 109, 112**
3.11, **104, 152**
3.11–12, **99**
3.11–18, **107**
3.12, **100, 104, 112, 115, 116, 157**
3.13, **101**
3.15, **101, 104, 108, 112, 113**
3.15–16, **99**
3.16, **108, 113, 116**
3.17, **104, 108, 109, 110, 113, 140**
3.17–18, **99, 184n2**
3.18, **100, 101, 108, 112, 115**
3.20, **96, 101, 188n82, 189n82**
3.22, **97, 98, 112, 189n82, 190n104**

3.23, **106, 108**
3.24, **97, 111, 114**
3.25, **189n82**
3.26, **98, 108, 110, 112, 113, 114, 116, 189n82**
3.27, **104, 107, 184n2**
3.27–28, **99**
3.28, **111, 169n26**
3.28–31, **99**
3.29, **106, 112, 169n26, 189n82**
3.30, **101**
3.31, **31, 98, 99, 101, 102, 111, 112, 115**
3.32, **101, 112, 195n81**
3.33, **96, 99**
3.34, **108, 110, 169n26**
3.35, **111, 112**
3.36, **101**
3.37, **101, 108, 112, 113, 169n26**
3.38, **24, 111**
3.39, **96, 189n82**
3.40, **100, 101, 108, 110, 111, 184n2**
3.41, **24, 169n26**
3.42, **169n26**
3.43, **100, 169n26, 169n27, 170n56, 184n2**
3.44, **110, 111**
3.44–45, **111**
3.45, **97, 104, 188n82**
3.46, **111**
3.47, **96, 101, 115**
3.48, **100, 101**
4.1, **23, 24, 25, 26, 31, 35**
4.1–4, **27**
4.2, **31, 41, 152**
4.3–4, **29**
4.5, **22, 25, 31, 37**
4.5–7, **27**
4.6, **26**
4.7, **26, 184n2, 185n29**
4.8, **26, 27, 31, 33, 34, 38, 41**
4.9, **26, 28, 31, 37, 41, 169n38, 181n89**
4.10, **23, 24, 25, 26, 31**
4.11, **26**

4.12, **23, 24, 25, 26, 30, 31**
4.13, **35**
4.14, **23, 24, 25, 26, 30**
4.15, **26**
4.16, **23, 26, 31**
4.16–17, **32**
4.17, **31, 41**
4.18, **26**
4.19, **26, 31, 34, 37, 41, 181n89**
10.11, **23**
10.18–19, **188n80, 191n6**
13.18, **175n58**
14.31, **184n8**
21.19, **116, 157**
24.17, **188n77**
30.27, **175n58**
32.11, **170n51**
32.11–17, **173n24**
32.11–18, **11**
32.12–17, **170n51**
54.1, **189n83**
55.47, **184n124**
Fragment 178 Carey, **189n83**
Fragment 279.6 Carey, **170n55**

Menander
Epitrepontes
136, **186n36**
511–515, **40**
535, **40, 171n72**
538–540, **40, 171n72**
555–560, **40**

Pausanias
2.7.5, **30**
7.27.9, **176n60**
8.36.6, **176n60**
9.8.1, **176n60**
Pherekrates
Korianno
67K, **14**
69K, **14**
70K, **14**

Plato
Laws, 705a–b, **174n32**
Republic, 3.404d, **79**
Symposium, **190n102**
176a, **70**
182c, **146**
Plato Comicus, *Sophistai*, 134K, **167n65**
Plutarch
Moralia, 849e, **87**
Parallel Lives
Pericles
32, **86**
37.3, **180n58**
Solon
15.3, **20**
18, **194n59**
21.3–4, **171n60**
Themistocles, 19, **174n32**

Thucydides, 1.54–59, **146**
Timokles, Fragment 32 *PCG*, **189n88,**
194n61

Xenophon
Anabasis, 5.8.4, **184n1, 186n29**
Cyropaedia, 6.1.31–37, **101**
Hiero
1.31–38, **113–114, 188n79**
1.33, **187n59**
Memorabilia
1.1.16, **103**
2.1.32, **184n126**
3.11.4, **1–2**
Oikonomikos
6.12–17, **186n43**
7.25, **183n123**
7.36, **183n123**
7.42, **183n123**
7.5, **178n37**
8.1–10, **52**
12.13, **28**
12.13–14, **103**
Symposium, 2.1, **70**

246